D1213434

March of America Facsimile Series

Number 27

Journal of a Voyage to New York

Jaspar Dankers and Peter Sluyter

Journal of a Voyage to New York

by Jaspar Dankers and Peter Sluyter

ANN ARBOR
UNIVERSITY MICROFILMS, INC.
A Subsidiary of Xerox Corporation

LIBRARY OF CONGRESS CATALOG CARD NO. 66-23059

MANUFACTURED IN THE UNITED STATES OF AMERICA

Foreword

Journal of a voyage to New York and a tour in several of the American colonies in 1679-80, by Jaspar Dankers and Peter Sluyter, printed in Brooklyn in 1867, is valuable to anyone interested in the social, economic, institutional, or geographical conditions in the early period of the settlements along the Atlantic seaboard. In addition the diary serves not only to shed light on the characters and personalities of some of the leading colonial figures of the day, but also to illustrate the holier-than-thou attitude of the author, Jasper Danckaerts, a representative of the Labadist sect. He came, along with his companion, Peter Sluyter, as a secret agent for the Labadists in order to find a place for the group to settle in the New World, since they were no longer welcome in Europe. Viewed with suspicion in both New York and Massachusetts, Danckaert's selection of a site in Maryland on the property of Augustine Hermans was partially due to the spirit of religious toleration there, and it resulted in the establishment of the first communal experiment in America in 1683.

Throughout the *Journal,* from his visit in New York to his last day in Boston, Danckaerts gives his impressions of the weather, soil conditions, crops, game, fish, and local customs. While the natural aspects of this new land may have potentialities, the author's opinion of the people, most of whom were hospitable to him, may be summed up by the following description: "We spoke seriously to Robert Sanders about his pride, arrogance, temper and passion, although according to the world's reputation he was not a bad man. His wife is more simple and a better person; we spoke to her also, as well as to their children.... He and all of them promised to reform, and we saw with consolation that they in some things commenced to do so."

Danckaert's manuscript was discovered by Henry C. Murphy, the translator and editor of the 1867 edition reprinted here. Preceding the work itself is an introduction tracing the history of Labadism. Accompanying the text are footnotes which further identify persons, places, and things mentioned by the author. Found with the manuscript were six pen and ink drawings which are reproduced in facsimile along with some later sketches correcting portions of the original views. For a later edition of the *Journal* see *Journal of Jasper Danckaerts, 1679-1680*, ed. Bartlett B. James and J. Franklin Jameson, Original Narratives of Early American History (New York, 1913), reprinted in 1952.

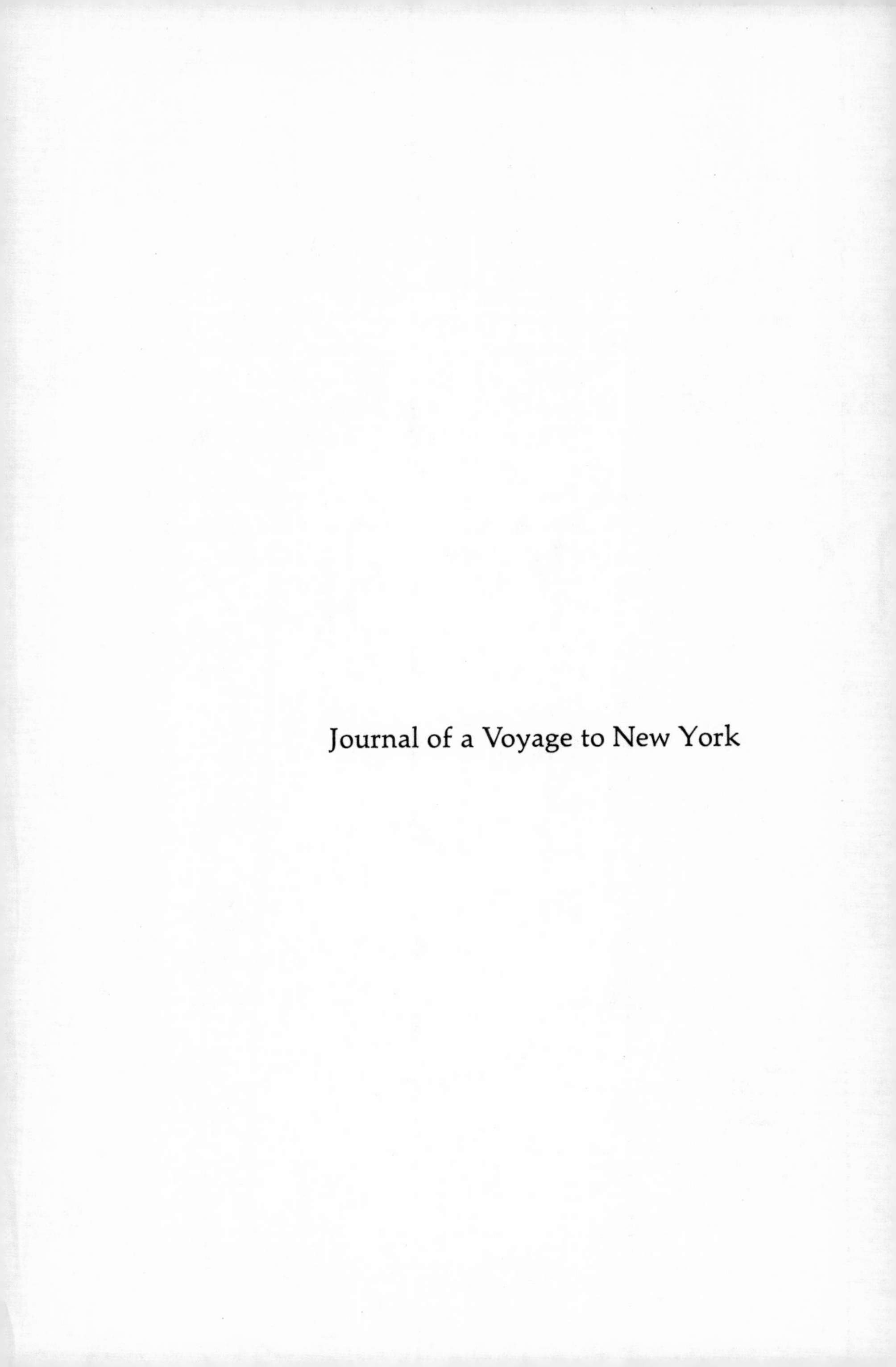

Journal of a Voyage to New York

JOURNAL

OF A

VOYAGE TO NEW YORK

AND A

Tour in Several of the American Colonies

IN

1679-80,

BY

JASPAR DANKERS AND PETER SLUYTER

OF WIEWERD IN FRIESLAND.

TRANSLATED FROM THE ORIGINAL MANUSCRIPT IN DUTCH FOR THE LONG ISLAND HISTORICAL SOCIETY, AND EDITED BY

HENRY C. MURPHY,

Foreign Corresponding Secretary of the Society.

BROOKLYN

1867

CONTENTS.

PREFACE.

The manuscript from which the following translation has been made, came into my hands a few years since in Holland. In what manner it had been preserved up to that time, could not be ascertained. It was in the possession of Mr. Frederick Müller, bookseller at Amsterdam, when I procured it; but, the probability is, it was taken in charge by some member of the community, at the time of the dispersion of the Labadists from Wiewerd, and had been handed down, from one person to another, afterwards, until its character and value failing to be appreciated, it became at last the mere waif he found it. The text appears to be a carefully transcribed copy, plainly written in a different handwriting from that upon the drawings or views which accompany it, and which, as the marks upon them show, are the original sketches made upon the spot.

The journal thus fortuitously recovered is a plain story, told in simple language, of a voyage across the Atlantic nearly two hundred years ago, and of journeys to many of the American settlements at that time. It was written under the influence of peculiar religious views and national attachments, which are sought to be explained in the introduction, and for which the reader will know how to make the proper allowances. My task has been to render it into English as faithfully as possible, without suppressing any remark however personal or trivial it might seem. The names of persons and places have been retained in the orthography of the writer, although it is very often different in regard to the same word. The *italic* letter has been used by the printer in order to denote when it is the same as in the original. The French phrases are also the same as in the journal.

It is proper to remark that a portion of the manuscript still remains untranslated. It is a fragment of a general account of the Indians, and occurs after the hiatus mentioned on page 361. It has been omitted because it does not purport to give the observations of the journalist himself, but is a mere compilation for the most part from printed sources, of descriptions of the manners and customs of the race, presenting little or nothing new. What the writer saw and experienced in regard to them is given in the journal; and is all that is of any value or interest, from its showing the actual condition and notions of the Indians, as modified by their contact and intercourse with the Europeans for little more than half a century. With the exception of this imperfect summary of Indian customs and two of the views elsewhere mentioned the manuscript is given entire.

In preparing the notes and introduction, I have received much aid in regard to the documentary evidence at Albany and Annapolis from Dr. E. B. O'Callaghan, of the former city, and Mr. George L. Davis, of Baltimore, and also valuable suggestions from the former in other respects. The rectified drawings of the views of New York, are by Mr. J. Carson Brevoort, who has also kindly furnished notes to the original illustrations.

H. C. M.

BROOKLYN, *February* 1, 1867.

INTRODUCTION.

Upon the liberation of the ecclesiastical interests of Holland from the hierarchy of Rome, there commenced a series of controversies in the reformed church in regard to its government, doctrines and discipline, which continued for many generations, and some of which are hardly settled at this day, giving rise, whatever may have been the effect upon the cause of religion itself, at least to great dissension and strife. At first the questions were confined to the authority of the magistracy in the church. Most of the ministers adopted the views of Calvin, attributing to the state the right only to protect the church and its external interests, and considering the church an entirely distinct and independent body, with a law-making power within itself; while others favored a system of subordination to the civil power, objecting to the maintenance of an independent spiritual authority as a restoration of the papal system which had been overthrown. Arminius advocated the latter plan, and thence arose, in the first part of the seventeenth century, the great controversy in regard to it between the Gomarists and Armenians, which came to involve finally and almost exclusively the doctrines concerning fore-ordination, the atonement of Christ and other points of faith, which were finally determined by the decrees of the famous Synod of Dort. The Armenians were there overthrown, and the doctrines authoritatively declared by that synod, and definitively established as fundamental dogmas of the Dutch reformed church, that election is the unchangeable purpose of God, whereby he has, before the foundation of the world, chosen from the whole human race a certain number of persons to redemption in Christ, and that others are passed by in the eternal decree whom God has decreed to leave in the common misery into which they have plunged themselves; and that it was the will of God, that Christ should effectually redeem *those only* who were from eternity chosen to salvation. These points being settled, contentions of a different character soon arose, relating primarily to the application of the systems of scholastic philosophy to biblical science and the method of scriptural interpretation, and afterwards to the interpretation itself. Johannes Kok, professor of divinity in the University of Leyden, whose name, latinized, according to the fashion of the learned at that time, into Cocceius, gave the name of Cocceians to his partisans, sought to separate theology from the old philosophy, and to confine the expositions of the Bible to biblical terms. In this particular he seems to have had the vantage ground; but he maintained other opinions which were considered dangerous to religion. He maintained that the events of the church in all future time are prefigured in the Old Testament, and its words and phrases are to be used in any sense of which they are susceptible; and thus the ten commandments were promulgated by Moses not as a rule of obedience, but as a representation of the covenant of grace. The commandment in regard to the observance of the Sabbath, he held, was abrogated by the sepulture of Christ. These views were combated by Gysbert Voet, called Voetius, professor of theology at Utrecht, who had been a member of the synod of Dort. He held that the theology of the reformed church must stand or fall with the philosophy of Aristotle. He insisted upon a strict observance of the Sabbath according to the Jewish law. This controversy became general, and all the ministers of the church were ranged under the Cocceian or Voetian banner. As a consequence, disorders existed in the church; with one, the least domestic employment on the Sabbath was a sin; with another, the day was no more holy than other days; "the one village on Sunday was a dead house; the other a house of feasting."

The Cocceians were accused of adopting the philosophy of Des Cartes which had then come into vogue, and which had, however, only this in common with the notions of Cocceius, that it discarded the philosophy of the schools. The fundamental principles of the Cartesian system, that in beginning to philosophize, every thing was to be doubted, and the only axiom to be received was: "I think, therefore, I am," were deemed atheistical; and so also the proposition that the inspired writers, when they spoke of the facts of nature, spoke according to men's understandings at the time, which were uninformed, as when they spoke of the earth standing still, the contrary being the fact; besides other deductions of his, really more liable to the charge. These views were falsely attributed to the Cocceians, however, and served to embitter the controversy.

Such was the condition of the reformed church in Holland at the time of the rise of the remarkable sect whose history it becomes necessary briefly to present to the reader in order that he may understand the circumstances under which the following Journal was written and the spirit which actuated its authors, and be able more correctly to estimate its character and value. This narrative is the production of two persons who visited this country in 1679, during the infancy of European settlements here, with the view of ascertaining the nature of the country and government, and selecting a suitable place for the establishment of a colony of the religious community to which they belonged. This sect, which, originating ten years before in the islands of Zeeland and, leaving there, was debarred full religious privileges in Holland, had now, after wandering in a body first to Westphalia and afterwards to Denmark, for the sake of those liberties which the magistrates of Middleburgh and Amsterdam had denied it, become permanently established with the consent of the states of Friesland, at Wiewerd, a small village in that province. Its members were known as Labadists, professing a kind of mysticism, regulating their lives by the divine light of the inner man, and seeking to bring together all the elect of God, separate from the world into one visible church, which, as they said, like a city, set upon a hill, could not be hid. In doctrine they held the tenets of the Dutch reformed church; but they also maintained other opinions and adopted practices not recognized by the authority of that church. Its founder, Jean de Labadie, born near Bordeaux in 1610, of a good family, was an enthusiast, believing himself, from the first, inspired by God, and chosen by him to build up his church on earth. Educated in the college of the Jesuits at Bordeaux, he became while there a member of that famous order and in due time was ordained a priest. During his novitiate he had applied himself with great assiduity to the reading of the Bible, to prayer and other acts of piety, and at the same time had prosecuted his studies of rhetoric and the scholastic philosophy, with remarkable success. With his priestly office he claimed to become possessed of the spirit of John the Baptist, and like him, in the wilderness, lived on herbs; which, however, so enfeebled his health as to compel him to ask his dismission from the order, which was honorably given. He then assumed the habit of a secular priest, and preached at Bordeaux and neighboring places with great fervor and eloquence, moving his audience to tears and sighs. His fame spread to Paris whither he was invited by the General of the Oratory. He was now thirty years of age, with a mind matured and stored with scriptural and profane learning. He was not less successful in the French capital than he had been in the province. His rare powers attracted great crowds of all descriptions of persons; men of state and ecclesiastics, bishops and priests all thronged to listen to his discourses. The bishop of Amiens tendered him the position of prebendary of the Collegiate church of St. Nicholas in that city, which he accepted. Here he distinguished himself by his holiness and zeal, especially insisting upon the necessity of reading the Holy Scriptures; and, in order to facilitate that object, caused a large number of copies of the New Testament in French to be sold. His views in regard to the Jesuits underwent a change, and after several years' service at Amiens he retired to Port Royal des Champs and entered into full communion with the Jansenists. From thence he went to Bazas near Bordeaux, and to Toulouse, and finally to Graville among the Carmelite friars, at which places he taught the doctrine that a contemplative life in which the soul enjoyed the divine grace was perfection on earth, and that it was necessary to practice mental prayer, and a condition so abstracted from the world as to be entirely insensible even to the touch of another. As he had charge of a nunnery at Toulouse he was accused of teaching this doctrine for base purposes, with being a mammillarian and guilty of other abominable practices. These charges seem to have been the inventions of his enemies; at all events they are discredited generally by the Dutch writers. He now made public pretensions to divine inspiration, declaring openly in a sermon that he was directed by the Savior himself to assume his name, and he did accordingly call himself Jean de Jesus Christ; claiming also the spirit of prophecy, and wearing the white habit of the Carmelites, because it was, he said, the garb of Elias. He prophesied that the beginning of the reign of the kingdom of grace would take place in the year 1666. These vagaries subjected him to ecclesiastical censure, which he avoided by flight to Montauban, the citadel of Calvinism in France; where, on the 19th of October, 1650, he totally abjured the Catholic religion. He made a declaration of faith at that time, in which he alleged that the spirit of God was leading him to be a reformer; that when he was ordained a priest in the Roman church he felt on the occasion that Jesus Christ laid his hands upon him, before the bishop did, and he was much more sensible of the inward ointment the Holy Trinity poured upon his heart than the oil with which the bishop anointed his hands; that he was sanctified from his mother's body to the purpose of reforming the Christian religion; that in his infancy he had felt the inspiration of the Holy Ghost which, like Samuel, he was not able to understand in consequence of his youth; and while living with the Jesuits he had learned from the Holy Spirit how to pray and meditate, and through heavenly influences was able to write and speak appropriately of the greatest mysteries of the gospel according to the rule of the true faith. This was the language of the blindest enthusiasm; but it furnishes the key to his subsequent life. After two years of preparation at Montauban, he was ordained a minister in the Protestant church; where, and at Orange and Geneva, he passed sixteen years of his life; discharging the duties of a pastor faithfully, and with great acceptance. "He has not only," wrote the consistory at Montauban on his leaving that place, "exceeded others by the eloquence of his discourses, but by the uprightness of his example. He has gone before them like a blazing torch placed upon a height whereby the unfruitful works of darkness have been exposed. He has excelled others in expressing in his life what he taught in the chancel. He has not sought after the earthly and worldly, or had any desire therefor, but has pursued with zeal heavenly and divine things. In short he has been to us a joy, comfort and example." At Geneva he revived his views in regard to the approach of Christ's reign upon earth, and his own claim to divine inspiration. He was eloquent in denouncing the manners of the times, and the cold and formal religion which prevailed among professing Christians. He gained converts to his peculiar notions, among whom were two who adhered to him through life, Pierre Yvon and Pierre du Lignon. The former succeeded to his power and position as father of the Labadists, and the latter occupied as long as he lived, a position only second in the community.

While de Labadie was at Geneva he was heard by John Godschalk van Schurman, minister at Basle. This clergyman was originally from Utrecht, whence his zeal in the cause of religion had led him to Germany, and thence to Switzerland. He visited Geneva in 1662, where he heard de Labadie; and wrote enthusiastically to Holland, in relation to his piety, devotional zeal, and his efforts to reform the church. He returned to Utrecht two years afterwards, and repeated the story of the marvellous gifts, spiritual fervor and reformatory labors of de Labadie; and, at his request, a correspondence was opened with the preacher, which led to his call in 1667, to take charge of the Walloon church at Middleburgh, in Zeeland, through the instrumentality of Voetius and other professors at Utrecht. Not less distinguished even than Voetius for piety and learning was the sister of John Godschalk, Anna Maria van Schurman, of Utrecht, a lady also of rare genius and elegant acquirements. She wrote both prose and verse, in Arabic, Hebrew, Latin, Greek, German, Italian and French, as well as in Dutch, her mother tongue; and enjoyed an extensive correspondence with learned men at home and abroad. Captivated from the first with the eloquence and religious devotion of de Labadie, she at once embraced his views, abandoned her home and her associations with the learned, followed him in his persecutions from place to place, sitting, as she declared, "at the feet of her beloved minister, like Paula at the feet of her highly prized Hieronymus in a foreign land," and, after his death, cloistered herself with the rest of his followers at Wiewerd, where she died in full communion with this extraordinary sect, always regarded by them as the greatest triumph of their religion. On his journey to Middelburgh, de Labadie stopped at her house in Utrecht, where he spent ten days in conference with Voetius and other eminent professors. But he did not impress the mind of Voetius favorably; on the contrary, that learned and pious man, who prayed and labored for reform in his beloved church, discovered in de Labadie the schismatic and fanatic, and quickly repudiated all connection with him, notwithstanding his agency in calling him to Holland. De Labadie proceeded to Middelburgh by the way of Amsterdam, preaching everywhere reformation in the church. "If Christianity," he said, "will, it can become what it has been. It is just that the last coming of Messiah should be in the condition in which it was left by the first."

He was now fifty-seven years old, and had reached a period of his life when the purpose of his enthusiasm if not of his ambition, was matured; or, to speak more according to his own language, the year had arrived when the churches of Christ were to be collected together, and the reign of the true church was to commence on earth, under his guidance, as the chosen instrument of God for that purpose. His power over the popular mind had been nowhere exhibited more strongly than it was now in Holland. His intense religious feeling, his fervent eloquence addressed to the Walloons in their own language, and his simplicity, bordering on austerity of manners, touched the hearts and imaginations of all who listened to him, and produced an unexampled excitement wherever he appeared. He preached at Middelburgh to immense crowds, deploring the decay of the church, attacking abuses and exhorting to a more holy life. He seemed now fully to address himself to the great work of reform, and would brook no interference. As he had left Geneva without testimonials of dismission, so he commenced his ministration at Middelburgh in defiance of the requirements of the Walloon church, refusing to sign its confession of faith and discipline, and alleging as a reason that Christ was declared in it to have suffered on the altar of the cross, whereas nowhere in the Bible is the cross of Christ called an altar. He denounced several eminent divines of the Dutch church as unsound, and inveighed particularly against a book written by the minister of the Walloon church at Utrecht, on the interpretation of the scriptures, pronouncing it infamous and heterodox, and demanding from a synod held at Naarden its condemnation for that reason; but the synod declared it to be orthodox, and condemned de Labadie to make reparation to the author, which he refused. The synod then passed a decree suspending him from the ministry until the meeting of the next synod. He disregarded their decree; another synod was held at Dort, called by the states of Zeeland for the purpose of determining the controversy, when, after a session of eight days, which he attended, he was absolutely deposed. This also he set at defiance. Returning to Middelburgh with his friends, they forced open the doors of the church, and he preached in it and administered the Holy Communion. The magistracy had now to interfere, and he was compelled to leave the city.

In this controversy there were on both sides deeper causes which hastened the catastrophe. De Labadie himself was intractable, and with the mission he claimed from God, he could not be otherwise. To admit the supremacy and control of this church over him involved the abandonment of the great purpose of his life. He could acknowledge no higher church than the one which under his instrumentality was to collect all the truly pious together into one membership apart from the world. He seems, from the first moment he put his foot on Dutch soil, to have contemplated there the fulfillment of his prophecy, and the reformation or conversion of the churches of Holland, as the beginning of the end. Therefore it was that Voetius and Essenius, when they heard his sentiments from his own lips, discovered in his purposes an inevitable schism. On the other side there were jealousies and suspicions of him as an innovator. He not only offended the Dutch and Walloon ministers by the freedom and arrogance of his remarks concerning them, but he had emptied their churches. Their congregations, rich and poor, had forsaken their pews and their old pastors, to listen to the pious and persuasive words of this foreigner, and to lament with him the abuses of the church and the absence of spiritual religion. He led them into his views of returning to the model of the primitive church; and to believe that there, in the islands and marshes of the Northern ocean, the truth was to burst forth and, as from a centre, to irradiate the world. The ministers were, therefore, alarmed for their influence over their people. Thus it was, impelled by his own convictions and purposes on the one hand, and opposed by the clergy on the other, de Labadie became an outlaw of the Dutch church. He was, however, sustained by a powerful party in Middelburgh, who regarded his condemnation as illegal, and he still preached to them. They met daily for religious services, morning and evening, and on Sundays three times, sitting without any distinction of rank or position promiscuously on benches, he and the elders like the rest, except that his seat was a little more elevated for the sake of enabling them to hear and see him better when he spoke. "There is so much modesty, union, zeal and piety," he wrote in a private letter, "that we cannot sufficiently admire and praise God for having enabled us to see such a church springing up, composed of such leaders, for we have many doctors and other eminent persons, but all humble, fervent, pious, marvellously edifying; so that all the world agree there are no better or more exemplary members than ours, well informed and enlightened, and prepared for all consequences, be it the loss of goods, houses and conveniences. We do not permit any abuse or excess either in dress or ornaments, or in the business which they follow. We regulate every thing evangelically and apostolically, being determined, as far as we can to restore the living image of the primitive church as well as the pure doctrine which astonished the world. Many persons, moreover, are attracted to us from other places; for God has made everywhere an union with us and with our manner and spirit, so that we hope the Lord will soon display his virtue and power in grace which we call the coming of the king."

Banished from Middelburgh, de Labadie betook himself with many of his adherents to the neighboring city of Veere on the same island about five miles distant. At the present time an utterly insignificant place, Veere was then a city of some importance and trade, and enjoyed independent municipal privileges. Its civic authorities received the outcast with honors. They conceived the idea of founding a church to be under his administration, as an important addition to their city. Meanwhile the Dutch and Scotch churches there opened their doors to him. A new day of prosperity seemed dawning upon the place. Many of the principal Middelburghers, including the ministers of the Walloon consistory, removed thither with their families and property. The new church, under the name of the Evangelical church, now declared itself independent of all human authority, and to be free to follow no other rule than the pure doctrines of the gospel according to the examples of the Apostolic church. De Labadie, they said, had not abandoned one popedom to assume another. Thus the separation of the Labadists from the authority of the reformed church was complete; though they avowed their adhesion to its cardinal doctrines.

Many persons of Middelburgh who adhered to de Labadie, could not change their residence and follow him; but the distance between the two cities was so short they could easily go to Veere and attend his preaching, especially on the Sabbath, which they did in large numbers. It was a melancholy spectacle for the ministers and magistrates of Middelburgh to see their own temples deserted, and the roads on Sunday and week days even, filled with people on foot and in vehicles, leaving their city; and it could not be endured. There arose, in consequence, a contest between the cities, which was the more serious, in consequence of the political rights which attached to the cities of the Low Countries, of independence of each other, and of any common superior in their municipal affairs. The magistrates of Middelburgh demanded of those of Veere, the expulsion of de Labadie; and on the refusal of the Veerians to comply with their demand, applied to the states of Zeeland, which ordered the authorities of Veere to expel him. The Veerians stood firm upon their chartered privileges, and still refused; and bound each other by an oath to maintain and defend their rights. The walls were put in a state of defense; the gates were closed; and the burghers placed under arms, to await the attack which the Middelburghers were preparing to make. Every sign betokened a bloody conflict. At the critical moment de Labadie appeared as the man of peace, appealing to the citizens to abstain from force. The kingdom to which he belonged was not of this world. He would leave the city for the sake of order, and in obedience to the suggestions made to him by the Lord.

Such self-sacrifice won still more on their regard, and extorted admiration even from his opponents. The Veerians finally complied with his request, and he immediately left the city.

He turned his eyes and steps toward Amsterdam. Perhaps that was the original destination he had contemplated. Rich, powerful, tolerant, receiving law from no other city, but giving high example at least to all, it was the pride and glory of the Dutch capital to open her gates to all good citizens of whatever sentiment. She had sheltered and protected the Brownists, and others not in communion in doctrine or practice with the reformed church. Shielded by the enlightened magistracy of that great city he would be safe in building up the new church. He arrived there in August, 1669, accompanied by Yvon, du Lignon, Menuret, and other disciples and adherents, male and female. They hired the upper part of a large house, containing a commodious hall, where they all met, morning and evening, for religious exercises. They also eat their meals there together as one family.

The Labadists were well received at Amsterdam, and enjoyed, at first, every protection from the burgomasters. The eloquence of de Labadie was not forgotten, and the circumstances attending his sojourn in Zeeland had increased his fame. He was permitted to preach publicly, which he did in the large hall before mentioned. The members of the new church increased rapidly. He sent out his disciples to other cities, Utrecht, the Hague and Rotterdam, where proselytes were made and societies formed, as branches of the church at Amsterdam. His particular doctrines were promulgated;[1] that by certain inspirations of the Holy Spirit, Christ could be seen in God, and God enjoyed and glorified; the exoteric or external in religion was distinguished from the refined or elevated, the former only was contained in the scriptures, the latter was inspired in the elect by God. It behooved men to stand every moment of the day, according to the special influence of God's spirit, which is bound to no time or place, and, therefore, Sunday was no holier than other days of the week, nor was the reading of the Bible actually necessary; but, at all events, they should give less attention to its literal meaning, than to the suggestion of God's spirit. The members of the true church were to be discovered by their zeal and fervor in glorifying God and Jesus Christ, by the purity of their lives, their humility and patience, their union in spirit, their communion in every thing, even in temporal goods. His converts were, therefore, to join their fortunes with his, or abandon his church. Many persons accordingly prepared to go and live in his community, by selling their property, and even abandoning their families, for one of the true faith could not, with propriety, live even with a husband or wife, who was not of the elect, as such marriages were not Christian, and, in fact, were null and void by the law of God. In some respects his views assimilated to those of the quakers; and

[1] Among others who embraced the new faith at this time was Ch. de Rochefort, minister of the Walloon church at Rotterdam. He is known as the author of the work bearing the title of "Histoire Naturelle et Morale des Antilles de l'Amerique," which was first published at Rotterdam, in 1665, and afterwards with additions in 1667 and 1681. He, however, soon abandoned Labadism and became one of its greatest opponents.

Robert Barclay and George Keith, well known preachers of that sect, went over from England to Amsterdam, to confer with him, and offered to take him into their society, which he declined.[1] The success of the new church alarmed the ministers of Amsterdam, and they made frequent applications to the burgomasters to silence him, but in vain, until a change of a portion of these magistrates took place the next year. Then the burgomasters issued an edict, forbidding any one from attending the services of de Labadie, who was not a member of his household-community. This order was, seemingly, a compromise, by which the purposes of the clergy might be attained, and the members of the society not interfered with in the enjoyment of their religious convictions. But it deprived de Labadie of the opportunity of preaching to the public at large. Shut up within the walls of his own house he could make no converts. To remain, therefore, at Amsterdam any longer was incompatible with the progress of the church.

In this extremity the Labadists were not without friends elsewhere, able and willing to afford them full religious liberty. Among others who favored them was Elizabeth, daughter of the Elector Palatine, and abbess of the free

---

[1] "Either on that account," says Gerard Croes, "or in derision by their opponents, the name of quakers was applied to the Labadists at that time, and followed them from Amsterdam to Herford, where they were often saluted with the name, and stones thrown at them."—*Historia Quakeriana*, 516. William Penn, who afterwards visited them, both at Herford and Wiewerd, declared that "they were a plain, serious people, and came near to Friends, as to silence in meeting, women speaking, preaching by the spirit, plainness in garb and furniture in their houses."—*Penn's Travels*, 4 ed., 98.

abbey of Herford in Westphalia. This princess, eminent for her piety, was a friend of Anna Maria Van Schurman, who had joined her fortunes with the community at Amsterdam, and through whom she tendered them the freedom of Herford, which was accepted. They prepared to leave; some sold their property; such as could not now go, supplied the others with money, and amid tears and sorrowing of a large crowd who witnessed their departure, de Labadie and his little band left Amsterdam.

At Herford every thing promised well. The Princess Elizabeth was charmed with de Labadie; he taught her the vanity of the world; he consoled her in sickness. Having entire freedom to preach he gained converts rapidly. A printing press was established. Religious excitement prevailed so in the town that the inhabitants neglected their affairs, rejoicing in the inward light. Most reprehensible practices, however, were indulged in. On one occasion, after having partaken of the Holy Communion, some of them, men and women, drank and danced together for spiritual joy. Some of the most intelligent of the society, disgusted at the circumstance, abandoned the society altogether. Marriages were formed in private without conforming to the law of the country; being regarded as spiritual unions, emblems of the highest degree of communion with Christ, that is between the truly pious, the elect. In consequence of these proceedings the intervention of the Imperial Diet was asked, and orders were given to the Princess Elizabeth to cause the Labadists to leave Herford.

They accordingly removed in 1672 to Altona, in Denmark, where entire freedom of religion existed by royal decree. In 1674 de Labadie died there, satisfied his mission on earth was accomplished and the church established. "Nothing," said he, "remains for me to do except to go to my God." "Death is merely ascending from a lower and narrower chamber to one higher and loftier." Yvon succeeded to his position and title of Father; but the society did not remain at Altona much longer after that event. Disputes arose with the authorities of the place in regard to a tax for the benefit of the Lutheran church. Besides a war was impending between Denmark and Sweden and they wished to avoid the scene, perhaps the levies. They therefore in the spring of 1675 made another migration and their final one, to Wiewerd in Friesland.

Among those who, like Anna Maria Van Schurman, had followed the fortunes of de Labadie from Amsterdam, were three ladies of gentle birth, sisters, who had resided at the Hague, and had abandoned ease and affluence as well as rank and position in society, in order "to be of those who should sit down with him in a separation from the vain and dead worships of this world." "We are a family," said one of them to William Penn, on his visit to Wiewerd, "that live together in love — of one soul and one spirit, entirely given up to serve the Lord." They were the daughters of Cornelis van Aarssens, Lord of Sommelsdyk, who was considered the richest man in all Holland; and sisters of Cornelis van Aarssens, his son, also Lord of Sommelsdyk, who was governor of Surinam, and was killed in a mutiny of the soldiers there in 1688. Their mother was Lucia van Walta, through whom they inherited from their grandfather the castle called Thetinga-State, or

Walta House, at Wiewerd. This property was appropriated by these ladies to the use of the Labadists, who there, amid its groves, were more completely separated from the world than they had ever been before.[1] The synod of Friesland, not forgetful of their past history, applied to the estates of that province for an investigation into their doctrines. That body committed the inquiry to Witsius, a learned professor in the University at Franeker, who made report that their creed was in conformity with the tenets of the reformed church. They were, therefore, permitted to exercise the privileges of that church in the performance of the marriage ceremony, the ringing of bells for public service, and other acts of ecclesiastical authority. They now, at last, enjoyed repose from persecution; and, though frequently threatened, they were never afterwards disturbed by the civil power. It happened, too, that their return to the Netherlands was signalized by a great accession to the community. Persons flocked from all the provinces and from Germany, seeking membership among them; many ministers left their positions in the reformed church, Peter Dittelbach, who afterwards wrote the account of the decline and fall of the Labadists, being of the number. They were a great household, of which Yvon was the father, Anna Maria van Schurman was the mother, and the others were brothers and sisters, subdivided into teachers or speaking brothers, choristers, overseers, waiters on the table, and the like. Some attended to the sick,

---

[1] Thetinga-State was, at that time, surrounded by trees; and the place was afterwards familiarly called the Labadists' woods, and the Labadists were styled the people of the woods — *bosch-lieden.*

others superintended the clothing, or the provisions, or the education of the children, or labored on the farm. But, after all, the means of sustaining so large a body of persons were not certain. The addition of poor ministers and poor men brought no capital to the common stock; and their labor was not sufficient to supply all their physical wants, simple as they were. To provide for the deficiency, as well as to secure a safe retreat for the society and extend the boundaries of the church, the community, shortly after their removal to Wiewerd, resolved upon colonization in America. They set their eyes upon Surinam, which had just been surrendered by the English to the Dutch, by the treaty of Breda, in 1667, as a compensation for the surrender of New York to the English. The new West India company had become the proprietors of the recently ceded territory, and after reserving one-third to themselves, disposed of the other two-thirds, one to the city of Amsterdam, and the other to Cornelis Van Aarssens van Sommelsdyk, brother of the three sisters before mentioned, who had been appointed governor, and was residing here. The country being the only place in America under Dutch jurisdiction, it was deemed the most eligible for a colony, and measures were accordingly taken to establish one there. The colonists left Wiewerd in high hopes and with high encomiums. They were designated as the founders of the great work of God in America. Lucia van Aarssens, the youngest of the Sommelsdyks, seizing hold of the hand of Dittelbach in rapture, exclaimed, "The Lord calls us to great things, and gives us, also, great hearts for their accomplishment." The colonists reached

Surinam in safety. The deep green foliage and exuberant fertility of the soil induced them to pronounce it at once another Eden. They sent most favorable reports accordingly back to Wiewerd. They had laid the foundations of a town called Providence, and now required more settlers. A second company followed, under the direction of Jaspar Dankers, the writer of the following journal. They were, however, unfortunate; the ship in which they embarked was taken by the pirates; who, after robbing them of all their stock, permitted them to proceed. They arrived at Surinam, only to cause sore disappointment to the colonists, who had expected to receive, and not to give succor. The truth now came out; the selection of Surinam was really most unfortunate. The country was subject to deadly malarias, which clearing the land only would mitigate. It was covered with heavy timber of the hardest wood; which, once cut down, the growth was so rank that in four or five years it was all covered again. It produced sugar abundantly, by means of slave labor, and that was all. The necessaries of life had to be imported, save the roots of which, after the Indian mode, they made their bread. The first settlers soon sickened, and many of them died, and to those who survived, the residence was intolerable. They were not only harrassed by the mosquitoes and other poisonous insects, but "the snakes crept through the houses as the mice did in Holland." The colony was a complete failure in every respect, and was soon abandoned.

The former Dutch dependency of New Netherland, although surrendered to the English, presented a better promise for carrying out the plan. It would have been preferred in the first instance had it not been for several reasons: first, because vessels sailing thither from Holland were compelled to stop in England on their voyage, for the purpose of paying duties; secondly, the trade in tobacco, which was the principal staple of commerce, was objectionable, as the use of that article was prohibited in the community; a third reason was that Andros, the governor, was a papist. The necessity of the case, however, now overcame these objections. In order that a proper situation might be secured, Jaspar Dankers who had conducted the second company to Surinam, and Peter Sluyter who was one of the ablest members of the community, were sent, as a measure of precaution, on a tour of observation through New York and the adjoining colonies, as detailed in the journal. Sluyter, or more properly Schluter, was from Wesel in Germany, and with his brother Hendrik and sister Elizabeth joined the Labadists at Amsterdam.. The two brothers, theologically educated, occupied prominent positions in the society. Hendrik, however, became disgusted with the practices at Altona and left it. The two travelers after visiting the settlements in the colonies of New York and New Jersey, along the Delaware and as far as the Chesapeake, were most pleased with a tract of land called Bohemia Manor, situated at the junction of the Elk river and Bohemia river at the head of Chesapeake bay and lying mostly in the present state of Maryland, but partly in the state of Delaware. A patent for this land, embracing nominally four thousand acres, but, in fact, upwards of twenty thousand, had been issued in 1660 by the proprietary of Maryland to Augustine Hermans or Heermans, a Bohemian by birth and a surveyor by profession, who had formerly lived among the Dutch at New Amsterdam and obtained some distinction there, as a compensation for his services in preparing for Lord Baltimore a map of the country. The grant also conferred manorial privileges and rights upon Hermans and his heirs and assigns.[1] Sluyter and Dankers returned to Friesland and made a favorable report to the community at Wiewerd on the subject. They were again dispatched to New York for the purpose of establishing the colony. They left Wiewerd accordingly on the 12th of April, 1683, embarking at Amsterdam in the ship New York, Captain Rich, and arriving at the city of New York on the 27th of July following.

In the course of their former visit Sluyter and Dankers had been assiduous in making converts to the faith and had been in some measure successful.[2] Among those who

[1] A confirmatory patent made in 1662, is in the records of the Land Office in Maryland in *Liber C. B.*, No. 3, fol. 15, 16.

[2] Rev. Henricus Selyns, the minister of the Dutch church in New York, writing from that city under date of 28th of October, 1682, to the classis of Amsterdam, mentions the fact that there were some Labadists at that time in New York, who attended his morning and evening preaching on the Sabbath, and in the afternoon assembled by themselves. Domine Selyns arrived in New York in the summer of that year, but Sluyter and Dankers had before his arrival returned to Holland, and were in Fatherland at the time of his letter; which proves that Sluyter and Dankers had succeeded in securing converts in New York, during their first visit to this country, independently of what is shown to that effect by their own journal. When they returned to New York in 1683, they attended Selyns's preaching with the others, but he exposed in a letter to William a Brakel both their purposes and their true names.—*Anthology of New Netherland*, 92–6. As to the existence of the Labadists in New York in 1692 as a

became impressed with their views was Ephraim Hermans, the oldest son of Augustine Hermans, and to whom and his issue Bohemia Manor was by the will of his father to be entailed. He was clerk of the courts on the Delaware and had become acquainted with the two Labadists while he was at New York for the purpose of consummating his marriage. He had promised them before they left New York to return home, that if they would come back again and establish their church in this country they should not fail for want of land, as Bohemia Manor should not with his consent be applied to any other purpose. It was therefore through his son's instrumentality that Augustine Hermans agreed to convey a large portion of his manor to Sluyter, Dankers and others, promising himself by this measure the building up immediately of a large community adjoining his domain. The names of the other parties were John Moll of New Castle, a judge of the courts on the Delaware; Arnoldus de la Grange, a trader to that river, and Peter Bayard, a hatter of New York, son of Annake Bayard, the sister of Governor Stuyvesant. Augustine Hermans, however, repented of his bargain, before executing the deed, apprehending no doubt the names were used as a device to secure his conveyance, and refused to fulfill the contract, until he was compelled to do so by the court.[1]

---

distinct sect, see also extracts from the Memoirs of M. Lamothe-Cadillac, in *N. Y. Documentary History*, II, 559. They are there called *Abadiens*.

[1] The final deed of conveyance was executed by Augustine Hermans on the 11th of August 1684, to Peter Sluyter *alias* Vorsman, Jasper Danckaerts *alias* Schilders, of Friesland, Petrus Bayard of New York,

Secure in the possession of this large tract of land, Sluyter and Dankers took immediate measures to provide shelter for the colonists, and to establish the community. A company of men and women came from Wiewerd, including in it several families. A few persons residing in New York also removed thither. Ephraim Hermans, abandoning his young wife and bright worldly prospects, submitted to this secluded life.[1] Sluyter sent to Friesland for his wife, who came over and was installed a kind of abbess over the female portion of the establishment. Two of his brothers also came. Thus really was formed not only

---

and John Moll and Arnoldus de la Grange of Delaware, in company. The land conveyed embraced four necks, bounded on the west by Long creek, north by the great cart road, leading to Reedy island in the Delaware, east by the Appoquinimink path leading from the great cart road to the head of Bohemia river, and south by Bohemia river. This piece of land was afterwards known as the Labadie tract and contained 3,750 acres. Moll and de la Grange immediately released their interest in the land to Sluyter and Dankers, which indicates that they had allowed their names to be used for the purpose of deceiving Augustine Hermans. Bayard held on till 1688, when he also assigned his interest to the same parties. Finally the whole title was concentrated in Peter Sluyter by a conveyance from Dankers to him in 1693, executed in Holland whither Dankers had then returned. Sluyter and Dankers were naturalized by act of assembly of Maryland, together with Peter Bayard and Arnoldus de la Grange on 26th Sep., 1684.—*Bacon*, *sub anno* 1684. Dankers is called Dauntrees, and Sluyter, Slayter, in the act.

[1] Not only did Ephraim Hermans forsake his family to join the Labadists, but Peter Bayard did the same, leaving his wife in New York. Ephraim Hermans soon repented of his folly and returned to his wife, but in less than two years was taken suddenly sick, became crazy, and died, fulfilling by his untimely end, the malediction of his father who, as it was said, pronounced the curse upon him that he might not live two years after uniting himself with the sect. Augustine Hermans died in 1686, leaving a will in which he speaks in emphatic terms of condemnation of the connection of his son with the Labadists.

a new colony in America, but the daughter church, *dochter gemeente*, as they themselves were pleased to style it, of the Labadists of Walta House, of which Peter Sluyter declared himself the bishop under Yvon, archbishop at Wiewerd. Sluyter was now both sole proprietor of the land and sole director of the church. He seems to have exercised the severest discipline over the members—the *tucht kinderen* or novices. He at the same time carried on a brisk trade in the planting of tobacco and in employing and selling slaves. In fact he was absolute lord and master. The position was desirable for a man of less pretensions to separation from the things of this world, than a Labadist with his penances. When *Strauch*, a leading brother at Wiewerd, died, Yvon sent for Sluyter to come to Walta and take his place. Sluyter refused, reasoning with Yvon according to the logic of their religion. what God has once willed he will not recall, and God having, according to their comprehension, manifested his will that his children should live herè, they could not consistently with his will leave the country.

The members belonging to this community did not at any time exceed an hundred, men, women and children, which appears to have been the number shortly after its commencement, and also fifteen years later. Two contemporaneous accounts of it have come down to us in print, one of which affords an interior view of the establishment, exposing its management and discipline, and the other an external picture, such as it appeared to an outside observer. The first is from no friendly hand. Petrus Dittelbach, before mentioned, was at Wiewerd at the time of the sending out of the colony, and for some time after it was organized. He, however, abjured Labadism afterwards, on account of its baleful doctrines in regard to marriage, and wrote a work exposing the character of the sect in that respect more particularly.[1] As he had been one of their number, and understood their sentiments thoroughly, he could speak more boldly. He says:

"A friend of mine, arriving from Sluyter's community, in New Netherland, has made many revelations to me in regard to their doctrine of marriage; for it appears that there they go to work more boldly when necessity requires it, than in this country, where they proceed more prudently. He went there with a full surrender of himself, family, goods and effects. His penitence, Sluyter wrote, was unusual. The letter was read to us at Wiewerd, and we rejoiced exceedingly over his conversion; but now, since he has left them, they charge and blacken him with sin. He was compelled to submit not only to the mortifications imposed by Sluyter, but also to those imposed by Sluyter's wife, who had shortly previous arrived from Wiewerd, and took a little hand in mortifying. What they thought of at night had to be done some how or other during the day. Indeed, they made it so sharp, that a brother, who had been sent over from Wiewerd, would stay with them no longer, and returned to Wiewerd, where

---

"Verval en Val der Labadisten of derselver leydinge en wyse van doen in haare huys-houdinge, en kerk-formering als ook haren op-en nedergang in hare colonien of volk-plantingen, nader ontdekt, voornamelik derselver leere en leydinge omtrent het Christelyk huwelik uitgehalt en tegengesproken alles in 3 brieven. Door Petrus Dittelbach." Sm. 4to, Amst., 1692.

also he was humiliated. This abasing cannot continue a long time among those people. My friend's wife had five small children, whom she brought with her to this new cloister discipline. Whenever she kissed one of them she was rebuked for showing so naturally her fleshly cleaving. They threatened *to chill* the mother, who had brought some small tubs of butter there, and put syrup on their bread, and to sell their negress slave, whom they had brought with them, because she took a small pot of beer and bread, without the knowledge of the abbess, to her sick master, who, however, did not partake of them. I could tolerate at Wiewerd, in some measure, that there should be no fire made in the cells, although it is cold there in the winter, because turf is dear, and so many families could not be supplied unless at great expense; but this friend told me Sluyter would not allow them to have any fire, in order to harden them and to mortify and subdue the sins of the body, while there was so much wood there that they were obliged to burn it in the fields to get it out of the way; but Sluyter had his own hearth well provided night and day. My friend had never suffered more cold and hardship than among those people, and he frequently made a fire in the woods in order to warm himself. His wife had no mind to remain in this cloister life under such an abbess, who censured her at the time she had a child nursing at her breast, because she drank too much at the table; and when afterward she drank less, because she left off too soon. As they saw these things did not please his wife, they began to talk to him somewhat more plainly and freely concerning marriage, arguing that *hell was full of ordinary marriages*, saying, among others, these abominable words: *It was for God alone to judge whether he cohabited with a harlot or with his wife.* The wife, fearful lest they would take her husband away from her, of which there had been at that place more than one instance, sought every opportunity to speak with her husband privately, and to exhort him to steadfastness, as she had come away with him from Amsterdam, and was there in a strange land with her little children. They had succeeded, however, with him so far, that he began to keep himself away from her. His wife, being very angry about it, the abbess jeeringly asked her if she could not be one night without her husband? The husband finally began to attack their doctrine about marriage out of the Scriptures, showing that the apostles had not taught so. He asked Sluyter what marriage *he* came of? Whether *his* parents were not married in the ordinary way? They began to wonder at this man's opposing them out of the Scriptures, until, finally, he told them roundly that all connection between him and them was severed. They were confounded, and went at him another way, saying, we have several times spoken about marriage, which is a delicate subject, but we must also say to you that when there are any who cannot conduct themselves in that way in their marriage relation, we still tolerate them. But how tolerate, as a brother? No; but only as regards community of goods and living together. This was a new trick to get him in; but they had already blabbed too much, and he had heard too much. They did not look favorably upon his going back to Holland, and attempted to frighten him from it, asking him if he were not afraid to trust himself on the sea, and fall from one pit into another? But he persevered, and the Lord helped him and his, in an especial manner, to reach the Fatherland in safety.

"We learn also from this friend how the colony has run down and is detested by the people of the country, so that Sluyter can do nothing there for the furtherance of the work which they call the Lord's. But as regards himself he has good times there with his wife, and the question which he once proposed to this friend, whether he did not see that these people did not fare badly? shows clearly enough that he has good things there. But in the meanwhile what is done for the Lord? Or is it no great matter that he has taken one Bayard, an innocent man, *whom we have seen here*, away from his wife who is now living in New York. It is wonderful how Sluyter can be easy when he reflects upon the manner in which the Lord has dealt with one of his novices, whom also he had enticed away from his wife, but finally permitted to go back to her, supposing they had him sufficiently confirmed in the marriage discipline. They regarded him as one who listened to them, and he went everywhere in their meetings. He began to cry out to his wife, 'O God, I can live no longer, I can live no longer; wherever I go Satan pursues me!' 'I have told you that all the time,' answered his wife; 'why have you allowed yourself to be so deluded by these men?' He went one day to Sluyter's exercises, and found a horse of one of the neighbors loose in the woods, which he took along with him for the purpose of delivering up to the owner. The horse pleasing Sluyter, he caused it to be tied in order to have it ridden after the worship was over in order to see whether he could exchange one of theirs for it. They put the man on its back, but in galloping along he struck his head against a tree in turning too shortly a corner of the road, and fell dead to the ground. They had good hopes of him, however, they said, because he had remained firm in the way of the Lord; but for Ephraim Hermans, who had obtained the land from his father and secured it to them, they had not much hope."[1]

The doctrine of marriage of the Labadists to which we have before alluded, and out of which these practices grew, was, as expressed by themselves, simply this: that both parties must be born again, because otherwise, the marriage was not holy, and a believer must not put on the yoke with an unbeliever; therefore it was right for them to separate if they were not both endued with grace. They, however might live together if both were not so endued, but the believer must love Christ more than his worldly spouse; for whoever loved father or mother, wife or husband more than Christ, was not worthy of him. It seems also that no person could be admitted into full membership as a brother or sister at Bohemia Manor, unless upon the direction of the father at Wiewerd, and for that purpose the proofs of true conversion were sent to him for such direction. Most of the persons attracted to the community under Sluyter were novices, or probationists, who were undergoing the discipline and mortifications which were necessary to prove their faith.

The other account of the colony before alluded to, gives

---

[1] *Veræl en Val.*, 75-7.

us a glimpse merely of their manner of living. It was written by Samuel Bownas, the quaker preacher, who visited Bohemia Manor in 1702. He thus briefly describes his visit, after leaving Chester in Maryland:

"After we had dined we took our leave, and a friend, my guide, went with me, and brought me to a people called Labadies, where we were civilly entertained in their way. When supper came in, it was placed upon a long table in a large room, where, when all things were ready, came in at a call, twenty men or upwards, but no women. We all sat down, they placing me and my companion near the head of the table, and having passed a short space, one pulled off his hat, but not the rest, till a short space after, and then one after another they pulled all their hats off, and in that uncovered posture sat silent, uttering no words that we could hear, near half a quarter of an hour; and as they did not uncover at once, so neither did they cover themselves again at once; but as they put on their hats, fell to eating, not regarding those who were still uncovered, so that it might be ten minutes' time or more, between the first and last putting on of their hats. I afterwards queried with my companion, concerning the reason of their conduct, and he gave for answer, that they held it unlawful to pray till they felt some inward motion for the same; and that secret prayer was more acceptable than to utter words; and that it was most proper for every one to pray, as moved thereto by the spirit in their own minds.

"I likewise queried if they had no women amongst them? He told me they had, but the women eat by themselves, and the men by themselves, having all things in common respecting their household affairs, so that none could claim any more right than another to any part of their stock, whether in trade or husbandry; and if any had a mind to join with them, whether rich or poor, they must put what they had in the common stock, and afterwards if they had a mind to leave the society, they must likewise leave what they brought, and go out empty handed.

"They frequently expounded the scriptures among themselves, and being a very large family, in all upwards of an hundred men, women and children, carried on something of the manufactory of linen, and had a large plantation of corn, tobacco, flax and hemp, together with cattle of several kinds."[1]

The colonists conformed in most respects to the mode of living adopted at Wiewerd. They slept in the same or adjoining buildings, but in different rooms which were not accessible to each other; but were ever open to the father, or such as he appointed for the purpose of instruction or examination. Their meals were eaten in silence, and it is related that persons often eat together, at the same table, for months, at Wiewerd, without knowing each others' names. They worked at different employments in the house, or on the land, or at trades, and were distributed for that purpose by the head of the establishment. Their dress was plain and simple, eschewing all fashions of the world. Gold and silver ornaments, jewelry, pictures,

[1] "An account of the life, travels and Christian experiences in the work of the ministry of Samuel Bownas." 8vo, London, 1756, p. 58–9.

hangings, carpets, lace and other fancy work were prohibited, and if any of the members had previously worked at such trades, they had to abandon them. They worked for the Lord, and not for themselves. The product of their labor was not to satisfy their lusts and desires, but like the air, simply for their physical existence, and hence all their goods and productions should be as free and common as the air they breathed.

They were to live concealed in Christ. All the desires or aversions of the flesh were, therefore, to be mortified, or conquered. These mortifications were to be undergone willingly. A former minister might be seen standing at the wash-tub, or a young man of good extraction might be drawing stone or tending cattle. If any one had a repugnance to particular food, he must eat it, nevertheless. They must make confession of their sinful thoughts in open meeting. Those who were disobedient were punished by a reduction of clothing, or being placed lower down the table, or final exclusion from the society. There were different classes among the members, which were to be successively attained by probation, in conforming to the rules of the establishment, and the final position of brother obtained by entire severance from the world.

Sluyter departed from the principles of the society, essentially in cultivating tobacco and in dealing in slaves. It was charged against him particularly that he was extremely cruel towards his slaves.

While Sluyter was building up the colony at Bohemia Manor, the seeds of dissolution were developing themselves in the mother church at Wiewerd. The residence of the

Labadists at Walta could, of necessity, be only temporary, that is, during the lives of the sisters Sommelsdyk. When they should die, the estate would devolve upon other members of their family. In the meantime, the number of children in the community was increasing, and nothing was being added to the common fund. In 1688, some of them, particularly Henry van Deventer, an esteemed preacher at Wiewerd, began to agitate the division of the common property, and giving each his own, in order that such of them as chose might go out again into the world for the purpose of providing for their families. Nature thus began again to assume her proper sway, and the artificial bonds in which she had been bound began to give way. Godly reasons were not wanting to justify the proposed change. It was the will of the Lord that they should remain together no longer, but should separate and go abroad into the world, and disseminate their doctrines. The church of Jerusalem had been scattered over the earth, and so must theirs be; and, like its members, they must go everywhere, and build up the house of God. The resolution to divide the property was accordingly taken, and carried into effect. The poor and moneyless of the community left the establishment, while those who were able to do so remained at Wiewerd, using their portion of the property to pension out their lives. Yvon, and Thomas Servaasz, who succeeded him as father on his death, and some others of the leaders, staid behind. On the other hand, there were no additions to the community, and it now became only a question as to the duration of the lives of the sisters Sommelsdyk to determine when the whole congregation would be separated; and so it happened.[1]

The partition of property does not seem to have been immediately followed by the colony at Bohemia Manor. It had not taken place, according to Bownas, fourteen years after it had been made at Wiewerd. Yet in 1698, a kind of division was made of the land, for in July, in that year, Sluyter, who, as we have seen, had become sole proprietor of the entire lands, conveyed three of the necks to Herman van Barkelo, Nicholas de la Montaigne, Peter de Koning, Derick Kolchman, John Moll, Junior, Hendrick Sluyter and Samuel Bayard. It is readily discoverable from these names that they were members of the community. Sluyter retained one of the necks himself, and became a wealthy man in his own right. He died in 1722, after his wife, leaving by will all his estate, the plantation and land belong-

[1] Anna Maria van Schurman died in 1678. Yvon survived her nearly thirty years, till 1707, when he was succeeded by Servaasz. The last of the three sisters Sommelsdyk passed away about 1725, when Thetinga-State reverted to Count Maurice, of Nassau, son of Isabella, their elder sister, not a Labadist, spouse of Hendrick, Count of Nassau. From him, it passed to Baron Ailva, who died in 1733, and whose heirs allowed the building to go to entire decay. We, ourselves, visited Wiewerd in 1861, and found hardly a vestige of the Labadists remaining there. The church in which they worshiped was still standing, but not a stone marked the site of Thetinga-State, although it was pointed out to us as preserved by tradition. In a vault under the church are eleven bodies, which have been for generations marvellously preserved from decay, through some unexplained natural cause, atmospherical or otherwise. The coffins were opened, and the bodies exhibited to us, and stiff and light, lifted out on their feet. One of them thus exhibited, the old schoolmaster who had the *graaf kelder* in charge, said was that of Anna Maria van Schurman. But that could not have been so. Wiewerd now contains less than 200 inhabitants, mostly boors, living in small cottages, and does not afford even a residence for a minister. Its religious interests are attended to by a neighboring clergyman, who preaches in the church at stated intervals.

ing to it, negroes, horses, cattle, household stuff, and what had been belonging to his apothecary shop and chemistry, to his son-in-law, Petrus Bouchell, subject to certain legacies, and bequeathing to his brother, Johannes Sluyter, his papers and books, and to his cousin, Henry Sluyter, his watch. He makes no mention of any son, and he, therefore, probably has no descendant of his name living. We gather from his will that he died in the faith in which he had lived, and, obscurely, that he left some of the believers behind him still living. "And for my body," he says, "I leave it to be buried *after our own humble way*, in the garden of the so-called Great House, where several of my brethren and sisters in Christ Jesus are expecting the general resurrection of the dead and eternal life of the soul and body, in the everlasting communion with God and all his saints, through Jesus Christ, our gracious Lord, Saviour, king-head, and all what can be wished and expected."[1] The Labadists were certainly all scattered and gone, and nothing of them remained as a religious community on Bohemia Manor five years after his death.[2]

And thus both in Friesland and Maryland the mother-church and daughter-church expired about the same time. The sincerity of the founder of Labadism and of his followers may be conceded, the charges made against

[1] This will is signed Peter Sluyter, *alias* Vorsman.

[2] Bownas, 59. Johannes Sluyter and Henry Sluyter, who survived him, were probably the last of the sect who resided there, and with them, therefore, passed away the last disciples of de Labadie in America. They were both dead in 1736, as we learn from the proceedings on the admission of the will of Peter Sluyter, to probate a second time. This will is recorded in the office of the Registrar of Wills, at Annapolis.

their lives may be admitted to be the inventions of malicious minds, conceived from what might have been, rather than from what were the abuses of the system, yet the doctrines which they preached, and the discipline which they practiced, were repugnant to the wise purposes of the Creator in placing man upon earth. They were the refinements of a subtle mind, following the idea that the world had reached the last condition of the church, before the coming of Christ. Maintained with great success by the eloquence and zeal of de Labadie, and the marked ability of Yvon, his successor, they failed when these supports were withdrawn, showing it was their personal influence, rather than its adaptation to the spiritual wants of man, that constituted the strength of Labadism. Like a ship without a pilot, it soon drifted upon the rocks, went to pieces and disappeared [1]

---

[1] The principal authorities which we have consulted are: *Historisch Verhael Nopende der Labadisten Scheuringh.* Door Jacobus Koelman. Amsterdam, 1683. *Verval en val der Labadisten*, &c., Door Petrus Dittelbach. Amsterdam, 1692. *Nouveau Dictionnaire Historique.* Par Jacques George de Chaufepié. Amsterdam, 1753. *Vaderlandsch Woordenboek.* Door Jacobus Kok. Amsterdam 1794. *Geschiedenis der Nederlandsche Hervormde Kerk.* Door A. Ypey and J. J. Dermout. Breda, 1824. *De Labadie en de Labadisten.* Door H. Van Berkum. Sneek, 1851. *Anna Maria van Schurman.* Door G. D. J. Schotel. 's Hertogenbosch, 1853. We have not spoken of the Mennonists, a sect occasionally referred to in the journal, as they owe their origin to a period just anterior to the Dutch reformed. It may, however, be stated that their founder, Menno Simonis, embraced the leading doctrines of the Anabaptists, especially in holding that infants were not the proper subjects of baptism, Christ's second coming on earth, and a rigid habit of living; but he opposed the attempt they made at Munster and other places to abolish civil government by force, though adhering to the doctrine that no magistrate should be admitted into the church. This sect differs little at the present time in their religious views from the Baptists of our own country. The Mennonists attempted a settlement on the Delaware in 1622, (*post* p. 220–1, *note*).

JOURNAL

OF OUR

VOYAGE TO NEW NETHERLAND

BEGUN IN THE

NAME OF THE LORD AND FOR HIS GLORY, THE 8TH OF JUNE, 1679,

AND UNDERTAKEN

In the small Flute-ship, called the Charles, of which Thomas Singleton was Master; but the superior Authority over both Ship and Cargo was in Margaret Filipse, who was the Owner of both, and with whom we agreed for our Passage from Amsterdam to New York, in New Netherland, at seventy-five Guilders for each Person, payable in Holland. Our Names were registered, that of my Friend as P. Vorstman, and my own as J. Shilders.

VOYAGE TO NEW YORK.

On the eighth of June, 1679, we left home [1] at four o'clock in the morning, taking leave of those with whom God had joined us fast in spirit, they committing us, and we them, with tenderness of heart, unto the gracious protection of the Highest. Although, for a time, separated in body, we remained most closely united in soul, which is, always and everywhere, one and the same. We went on foot to Oost[erend], expecting there to take the canal boat, which we did, at six or half past six o'clock, after waiting an hour. We took leave finally of those of our beloved and very worthy friends who had accompanied us, and thus far made it a pleasant journey for us. Our hearts had been strengthened in discoursing, on the road, of God and his will concerning us, and of the disposition and readiness of our hearts, as we then felt, to endure whatever might happen, although we foresaw there would be enough to mortify us. We arrived at B[olsward] about eight o'clock, where we discovered the reason why there were so few people in the boat and tavern. The ringing of the bells announced it was a holiday, namely, Ascension day, which suited us very well, as we thus had an opportunity of being alone in the tavern, and eating out of our knapsack a little breakfast, while waiting for the *treckschuit* to leave. We were pleased, while we were in the tavern, to see some persons come in, on behalf of the schout, who was then on a visit to all

[1] Thetinga-State, at Wiewerd, in Friesland.

the inns in the city, looking after drunkards and other disorderly persons liable to punishment. When the time arrived, we stepped on board the canal boat, where we found few people: but these passed the whole way in tattling, principally about a certain miser who had died and cheated his friends, leaving them to find more than they believed could be found. As our own thoughts were otherwise employed, this talk was very annoying to us. We reached W[orkum][1] before the hour fixed for departure from there. Meanwhile, however, we went to the Amsterdam packet, on board of which there were different kinds of people, but all wicked. Among them was a family consisting of father, mother and children, who even after the manner of the world, were not spoken of much better. They had two daughters of a very easy disposition. We had the good fortune to have the cabin to ourselves, where we were perfectly accommodated. We left Workum at twelve o'clock with a strong head wind, but open sailing, so that it was six o'clock before we passed Enkhuisen. We came to anchor before Amsterdam about eleven o'clock at night.

9th, Friday. We stepped ashore early and went first to look after our ship, the Charles, which we found lying in the stream. There were some passengers already on board. We inquired when they intended to sail. The mate, who like the captain, was a quaker, answered, "to-morrow," that is, Saturday. We went immediately to the house to which our chest had been directed, taking another with us. We lodged there as long as we were at Amsterdam. The proprietor made no objection to deliver us the chest which

---

[1] Workum is the port, on the west shore of Friesland, where they took the packet to cross the Zuider Zee to Amsterdam. The omission of the name of the place of their departure, Wiewerd, and giving only the initials of Oosterend, Bolsward and Workum, indicate some prudential motive for concealment of their movements on the part of the travelers, probably the same as induced them to give themselves fictitious names, to prevent a discovery of the plans of the community, which might happen in case their journal should be lost.

had arrived before us, upon our showing what we brought. This done, we went to Margaret's,[1] to whom we spoke of ourselves, voyage and purpose, and who showed us some attention. All this was accomplished before noon-time, when we went to our lodgings to rest ourselves. The house being full of people the whole time, it was very difficult for us, though we obtained a bed room, to be tolerably alone during the day; but as the people who carried on this business would have been willing to have much money spent, and as it was not for us to do so, we went out a great deal into different parts of the city, and returned there in the evening, where we slept together.

10*th*, *Saturday*. We performed some errands, and also spoke again to Margaret, inquiring of her when the ship would leave. She answered she had given orders to have everything in readiness to sail to-day, but she herself was of opinion it would not be before Monday. We offered her the money to pay for our passage, but she refused to receive it at that time, saying she was tired and could not be troubled with it that day. We had some conversation with her, and she asked us if we were. not such and such persons, who lived at such a place, to which we generally answered, yes.

In the afternoon we took on board our chest and what we deemed necessary for the voyage, by means of an ordinary row-boat. We reached the boom without the least remark, as the officers of the customs were employed with a lighter inspecting some wine of which they needs must taste. We selected our berth, put our bed-clothes in it, and requested the mate to keep the berth for us, which was next to the large hatchway, according to Margaret's orders. We then returned to our lodgings.

11*th*, *Sunday*. Not being able to do anything in the city,

---

[1] Margaret Filipse.

we determined to cross over the Y[1] to Buiksloot, where we went to hear the preaching, which was wretched. It was by an old minister and according to the doctrines of Voetius. His text was of the seed sown among thorns. We had hitherto eaten out of our provision basket without refreshment, and we therefore took the opportunity now to refresh ourselves a little. We went at noon to Nieuwendam and heard a sermon by a person who had recently settled there. He gave a short exposition of his opinions, from which we clearly saw that he was a Cocceian; and he seemed zealous, but not serious or earnest enough. We recrossed the river in the evening and went to our lodgings.

12*th*, *Monday*. This whole day we were in expectation of the ship's leaving, and therefore went out continually to see about it; but it was to no purpose. I went again to inquire at the house of Margaret, but could obtain no assurance. Our lodging house was the while constantly full of drunkards, and we did as well as we could to avoid them.

13*th*, *Tuesday*. The ship still lying in the stream: we expected she would sail; but no word coming from her at the time, we went on board and found there more passengers than before. We inquired again of the new mate when they had determined to leave, but we could obtain no information. The mates advised us to go to the Texel and wait there for the ship, and this, for other reasons, we concluded to do. I saw to-day a certain cooper who had visited us several times at A[ltona] and who conversed very familiarly *chez la famine reformé*, and I believe comes also to the assembly of Mons. B. He looked at me, but made no salutation, and passed along. This is the only one of my acquaintance whom I have seen at Amsterdam.

14*th*, *Wednesday*. Having resolved to go to Texel to-day, whether the ship left or not, we prepared ourselves for the

[1] The river or inlet upon which Amsterdam is situated, is so called.

journey. We took dinner with our host and paid him for our lodging there. About seven o'clock we went in the Texel barge, where we found many passengers, but it was ten o'clock at night before we got off. After leaving the piles we had a strong head wind, which gradually increased to blow so hard that we could scarcely keep before it, fearing otherwise to sail ashore.

15*th*, *Thursday*. We passed Enkuisen early in the morning, and had then to proceed against the wind with hard weather. We kept tacking with great assiduity till about midday, when the tide compelled us to stop, and we came to anchor under the Vlieter.[1] The boat being full of drinking people, there had been no rest the whole night. My good friend [Sluyter, or Vorstman] was sea sick, and particularly suffered from the tooth ache, but felt better after taking a little of his usual medicine. The wind subsiding somewhat, and the tide having fallen, some of our passengers were put on board a ship-of-war, which was riding at anchor under the Vlieter, and then we proceeded on our course to Texel. Tacking until in the evening, as far as the Oude Schild, we came near being run down, which happened in this way. There came a small English ship in from sea, when an English galiot, lying close in shore, weighed anchor and set sail in order to speak to her. Coming down close before the wind, they were just going to speak to the ship, when we lay on their bow in order to wear about. They kept on their course taking no notice of us, when we shouted and screamed out to them; but they did not hear us until we came close to them and redoubled our cries, when they hauled off. It was a narrow escape, as they were within two inches of being right upon us; but as there was a ship-of-war's boat on our vessel, we were probably in no great danger of losing our lives, since by means of that we could have saved ourselves. We landed

[1] A shoal in the Zuider Zee, opposite the island of Wieringen.

at the Oude Schild about half past nine in the evening, and took lodgings at the *Hof van Vrieslant*,[1] one of the principal inns, although we had been recommended to the *Moriaens Hooft*[2] but that did not suit us, because it was most frequented by tipplers. Having taken something to eat, we retired together to rest in a quiet little chamber which they prepared for us.

16*th*, *Friday*. My companion still suffering from the tooth ache and also a pain in the stomach, remained in bed till noon, when he found himself better. We dined with our landlord and then wrote a letter home, which we posted. We were in momentary expectation of the arrival of our ship, for which we were constantly on the look out; but as it continued blowing hard with a contrary wind, we did not discover any thing of her, and by force, took this time to recruit ourselves a little.

17*th*, *Saturday*. Waited for our ship the whole day, but saw nothing of her.

18*th*, *Sunday*. Went to hear preaching this morning at Oude Schild by a very poor man, both in body and mind. He was crooked in face and feet, up and down, in and out; but displeasing as he was to look at, he endeavored to please everybody. His text was, "humble yourselves under the mighty hand of God." We went in the afternoon to the Burgh, the principal village on the island, walking along the dunes and sea shore, where we were amused by the running about of an incalculable number of rabbits. We went along the outside of the strand, and had a view of the breakers of the North sea, which were driven against the shore by the northwest wind. In going around the Burgh we came to a brewer, the only one, not only in that place, but on the island. We drank of his beer, which in our opinion was better than any we had found on

---

[1] Court of Friesland.

[2] Moor's Head.

our journey. Being a Mennonist he would gladly have entertained us with pleasant conversation, but admonished of the time, we returned to our lodgings at Oude Schild.

19*th*, *Monday*. We looked out again for our ship, going along the dyke to Oostereind, a considerable village, but we saw no signs of her. We therefore left the shore and returned home inland, passing through another small village, called Seelt.

20*th*, *Tuesday*. Perceiving nothing of our ship we began to feel very anxious, for besides being at much expense for our lodgings, we were sometimes compelled to eat with very godless men. Our lodging house was the one most frequented by the superior officers of the ships-of-war, of which there were seven or eight lying there ready to convoy different fleets to various parts.

We went in the afternoon to the Hoorn, quite a large village west of the Oude Schild. When we had passed through it, we found ourselves near the dunes, over which we crossed to the beacon, walking upon the shore to the extreme point of the island, from whence we saw the Helder before us on the other side, and between, the two mouths of Texel's deep, observing how the lines agreed with the beacons. Time running on, we returned to the Hoorn, where we were compelled to drink once. The landlord of the house was a papist, who quickly took us to be Roman ecclesiastics, at which we laughed between us for his so deceiving himself. He began to open his heart very freely, and would have told us all his secrets if we had asked him; but we cut off the conversation, and answered his questions with civility. When we reached home in the evening, we saw some ships had arrived, and supposed certainly one of them was ours; but, as it was dark, we were compelled to wait till next morning.

21*st*, *Wednesday*. As soon as we had taken a little breakfast we went along the dyke to Oostereind, near which the ships had come to anchor. As we approached the place, we could no longer doubt ours was there, which we were the first to discover. We therefore hired a boat immediately and went on board, when we not only found it was our ship, but that she was full and overladen. She was so full of passengers of all kinds, and so stowed, that we saw no chance of finding a place in which to sleep, and there were scarcely any of our goods to be found. The berth, which we had selected, had been taken by others, which there was no use of resisting; but it caused us no regret, as we thereby secured another near the cables, almost entirely out of the way, and always removed from the greatest noise. We determined to go ashore and come back the next day; but after taking our dinner there and paying our landlord, we returned on board. When we came on the ship, they began immediately to inquire of us about everything, and we answered them discreetly and civilly. Among others who thus made themselves conspicuous, was Jan, whom we did not know, and whose deportment did not accord with what we had imagined of him; but we supposed he was one of the passengers, and one of the best, and most slovenly. He asked my comrade if we were not of such a people, expressly naming them, who answered him according to his and our condition. After we had been on board some time, seeing we obtained no place, I went myself to look after one and observed where we could make a berth. I spoke to the captain, who had the chests removed and a berth arranged for us on the larboard side near the fore-hatch; but as the cable was lying there so that it could not be stretched out as long as it ought, and as there was room enough, I took a little old rope and set to work to lengthen it out, which I accomplished before evening, so that we could sleep there that night. Certainly we had reason to thank the Lord that he had given us a berth in a more quiet place than we ourselves had chosen, which he had of his will allowed to be taken from us. His providence truly extends over all things and his foolishness is wiser than the wisdom of men, and sometimes even of his children.

22*d*, *Thursday*. We slept little during the night in consequence of the clatter of so many godless and detestable men, and the noise of children and others. We had, however, to content ourselves. I went in search of our chest, which was stowed away in the bow, but to no purpose, as it was necessary to creep on hands and knees to get in there. We remained in the hope it would come to light at Falmouth. The ship was so low between decks, that sitting on the chest we could not sit upright even between the beams, for it was only about three feet high. But we were here in the forecastle well content.

23*d*, *Friday*. My comrade wrote a letter home. Our captain having caused the boat to be made ready in order to go with his wife to another English ship, we requested permission to accompany him ashore. He roundly refused us; and we had to wait for a boat to pass and hail it, which we did. Having posted the letter on shore, and refreshed ourselves somewhat, we started to go on board again. We found our boat, when our captain and the captain of the English ship came up. Our skipper asked us if we would accompany them, to whom we civilly replied, and so went on board with them in the evening. The sailors had caught some plaice which were for the guests in the cabin. I assisted in cleaning them.

24*th*, *Saturday*. The wind was southeast, the same as yesterday, which made us all very anxious for Margaret to arrive, so that we might not miss a good wind. Jan and some others of the passengers were much dissatisfied, and said: "We know very well where she is. She is in Friesland." Upon this Jan declared, "if this wind blows over our heads, I will write her a letter which will make her ears tingle," and used many other rude expressions. He was one of the greatest of grumblers, and even against her. He revealed himself more freely in a conversation with my companion, from which we could clearly discover that he was of the feelings of Boheem,[1] though he denied he had ever read his books. He also expressed himself profanely and in very foul language, worse than the foulest sailor or dock-loper would have done. The wind changed towards evening, and thus this day passed with murmuring, and we doubted no longer that this was Master John.[2]

25th, Sunday. It blew very hard from the west so that we had to lower the topmasts and let drop the sheet anchor. We saw at daylight a yacht coming down to us before the wind and were rejoiced to find that Margaret was on board, with some other females. The yacht not coming well up, our captain sent a boat to her, but they could not reach her on account of the current. However, the yacht succeeded in coming along side of us, and Margaret came on board with her little daughter, and a Westphalian woman, who was a widow, and a girl, both of whom were in her service, and to go as passengers. They were welcomed by all, and all of them came and shook us by the hand. Some said they thought she had been to Friesland. Whereupon she answered: "How do you know where I have been?" We had nothing to detain us now, except the wind.

26th, Monday. The wind began to blow a little from the south, but calmly. It veered round more and more to the southeast so that we determined to get under sail. We therefore took a pilot, weighed anchor, and set sail about ten or eleven o'clock. We sailed smoothly onward to the Helder. The pilot had a brother who was older, and had been a pilot longer than he had, and who sailed ahead of

---

[1] Jacob Boehme, the German theosophist.

[2] The reference to Friesland alludes, no doubt, to the community at Wiewerd; but the connection of both Margaret Filipse and Jan with that society, so distinctly hinted in this day's journal, and more obscurely before, are left without any further explanation.

us in the pilot boat, continually sounding the depth of water with the deep lead. When we were going by the Oude Schild there came a barge off with two more women who desired to go with us; but as they could not reach the ship, the pilot boat went after them and took them on board of her, where they had to remain until the ship arrived outside. It was about two o'clock when we came in the channel of the Land's-diep or Nieuwe diep. You run from Oude Schild strait to the Helder, and so close to the shore that you can throw a stone upon it, until you have the capes on this point opposite each other, namely, the two small ones; for to the westward of these there is a large one which is not to be regarded. Having the capes thus opposite each other, you are in the middle of the channel and by the first buoy. The current runs outside along the shore, east and west, to wit: the ebb tide westerly, and the flood easterly, and also very strong. The ebb runs until it is half flood. There are still two other channels, the old one which is the middle one, and the Spanish channel stretching to the east. We had reached the middlemost buoy when it became entirely calm, for which reason we could hardly steer the ship, and, in the meanwhile, the current was steadily setting us over to the west bank. Hereupon a dispute arose between the pilot in our ship and those in the pilot boat going ahead of us. The one in the ship on throwing the lead and finding it begin to be shallow, and seeing, moreover, that the current was driving us more upon the shoal, was of opinion that we should wear ship, which his brother was not willing to do, saying that she should stand over further. This continued so long that at last it became entirely dry, when he wished to tack about; but it could not then be done in consequence of the current running with so much force upon shallow ground, and carrying the ship violently against the shoal, where the current ran obliquely. They got out the boat at the bow of the ship to row, which would not yield in consequence of the strong current which also drove the boat as well as the ship; so that, in a word, we were aground on the west bank of the channel, and although the water was nearly at its lowest there was still a strong ebb tide. Immediately there was great clamor and running to and fro both of seamen and those not acquainted with navigation. Every one was alarmed, and every one did his best in that respect, the more so, because there was not far from us the wreck of a ship with her masts sticking out of water, though it was on the east side of the channel. Nevertheless, we remained fast, and the ship began to thump hard and fall entirely on one side. They ran straitway to the pumps, but found no leak. The pilot remained in good spirits, though put out and angry with his brother, who had misled us, and who, in consequence of the strength of the current, and the lightness of the wind, could not come on board of us. They said we were in no danger, although it looked very strange, as the current had washed the sand very much from under the lee of the ship whereby she had fallen much on her side. But we hoped with the flood tide she would come off again.

There were several passengers, not only women, but men, and some of the bravest, who began to secure the best they had, and were ready and looking out how they might safely reach the land. But the Lord possessed us with his grace. Though seeing all this and knowing the danger, I was disturbed by it. Margaret proposed throwing some of the cargo overboard, but the pilot and I dissuaded her from it. The captain wished to start the tanks of fresh water, but we hindered him. Of all the men in the ship I saw no one who was so frightened as Jan. He ran backwards and forwards and hardly knew what he said or did. This happened about half past three o'clock in the afternoon, and as we had not yet taken any dinner, and could effect nothing as long as the ship was fast, the victuals were brought out to be eaten. We sat before the hut and eat; but we had not finished when I perceived the ship dragging, as had been predicted. I sprang up quickly and cried out: "We are afloat; the ship's afloat." Immediately thereupon the whole ship was in commotion. The victuals were removed, the boat put to the bow, and every one did his best, rowing as well as he could. The ship, floating more and more, gave some good pushes and was brought into four fathoms of water, in the middle of the channel, and there anchored. My companion and myself thanked God in our hearts, and all were very much rejoiced. But no sooner was the danger over, which had somewhat bridled the godlessness of these bad men, than they returned to their old courses, with cursing and foul language. They were not affected in the least by what had happened, nor by God's gracious preservation of us. Truly was his hand visible, for it remained perfectly calm, so the ship labored very little. It would otherwise have been all over with us, for our ship not being the strongest, and being moreover very heavily laden, if the wind had changed to the east and forced us on a lee shore, she would have soon gone to pieces; or if we had grounded on the opposite side, which might easily have happened, there would have been little probability of her getting off, because the flood tide would have driven us higher up, especially if it had blown somewhat hard. The flood having run in and a light breeze springing out of the S. E. and S. S. E., the anchor was raised and in a short time we came outside, having been there about six hours. The pilot was paid, and he left the ship; the women whom he had taken in his boat were put on board and we bid him adieu, and set our course.

Before we proceed further we will say a word concerning the island of Texel, where we were about eight days, although the island is well known. It is said to be twenty-eight miles[1] in circumference, and is nearly oval in form. The shore, inside along the Texel deep, is dyked; on the outside, along the North sea, it is beset with dunes. There are six villages,[2] namely Oostereind, Seelt, the Hoogh, the Burgh, which is the principal one, and has privileges like a city, such as that of inflicting capital punishment and others; the Oude Schild, which is mostly resorted to by ships, the Hoorn, and also the West End, which has now fallen into decay. We saw four of them but not the Hoogh which lay out of the way, and the West End which had fallen into decay. Inland the country is rough, and some of it high, so that there are few ditches, except in the low lands for the most part on the side of Texel's deep. Otherwise they protect their land with small dykes of earth. The soil is sandy, which affords very good water in the high places. The meadow lands are somewhat dry, but yield a fine grass. The inhabitants gain their livelihood, for the most part, by raising sheep and making Texel cheese. The sheep are smaller, but fatter and more hardy than they are in Friesland. They seldom bring forth two young at a birth, and when they do, one usually is killed in order that the other may be better nourished. The inhabitants have cows for their own use. The dyke is not high or thick, but is lined with *wier*, a kind of sea grass, which they put together and lay against the dyke somewhat higher than the earth work. Piles are driven outside to hold this wier against it, and prevent the sea from washing it away. This dyke is repaired every year by contract. Many fishermen and pilots live along it, both qualifications generally being in the same person, as well as the other pursuits pertaining to navigation. There are about five hundred pilots in all

---

[1] The distances and measurements will continue to be rendered, as in this instance, according to the English scales.

[2] There were according to this enumeration, seven villages; five instead of four of which were visited by them.

living on the island of Texel, as can be seen by the numbers which they carry on their sails or wings.

The law is that no ship can go in or out without a pilot; and in case any captain will not take a pilot, he is nevertheless bound to pay the fees of one, and in case the captain will not pay them, the pilots can go to Amsterdam and there obtain it at the expense of the captain. And if the captain take no pilot and an accident happen, the consequences fall upon him; but I believe this first rule only applies to ships belonging to Amsterdam or other ports in Holland; and that foreign ships are more free in that respect, but cannot relieve themselves from the second. The pilots who bring in ships from the outside bring them to the Texel roadstead or the Helder, and others take them to Amsterdam or elsewhere; and those who take them from Amsterdam, go no further than the Texel road or the Vlie, and other pilots carry them out to sea. The fees of the pilots is a guilder a foot for every foot the ship draws, though any sum may be fixed by agreement.

During the whole time we were there we saw few or no fish, though we supposed this was the place for fish. We remarked further that the inhabitants of Texel were more polite than the boors of Friesland. A large portion of them are inclined to Rome. There was no home brewed beer tapped in the taverns, but it was all foreign beer, and this I suppose was for the purpose of saving the excise. They are under the jurisdiction of West Friesland and the particular government of the city of Alckmaer, whose weights and measures they use. West of the Oude Schild there is a small fortification with four points and two redoubts on the dyke, and some small batteries; but they afford little protection to the place, and still less to the harbor. It was closed and without men, when we were there. When we first came there, the people, unaccustomed to see such persons, regarded us as some individuals in particular. The innkeepers took us to be farmers of the revenue, especially of brandies, and supposed our presence there was to prevent their smuggling, as they themselves told us. The Roman Catholics, as they declared, looked upon us as priests; the Mennonists, as a class of their exhorters; and the ordinary Reformed, as preachers; whereby they all showed they did not know us in truth, according to the word in Christ Jesus.

Leaving Texel and the land we came outside the coast, laying our course S. W. with a S. E. wind, with which we sailed some distance from the shore. Towards evening the wind began to blow from the S. and S. S. W. quite hard, and so we stood off through the whole night. I do not know that I ever had in my life so severe a pain in the breast as I had this evening, whether it was from hard work or change of our condition.

27th, Tuesday. The wind from the same quarter as before, but blowing harder, for which reason we reefed our topsails. We had twenty-six and twenty-eight fathoms of water. By evening it was somewhat calmer; but as the wind was not steady we stood off from the shore.

28th, Wednesday. Finding ourselves in twenty-five and twenty-six fathoms of water and the wind still south and southwest we sailed over by the wind. It continued to blow hard, and we sailed for the most part N. by E. and N. N. E. It annoyed me that I could not get at our chest, in order to obtain my charts and books of navigation. Our mate and others observed the latitude, and found it to be 52° 16′; and we tacked about. The wind continued in the same quarter, sometimes a little lighter, sometimes sharper. We kept mostly a S. S. E. course, with hard weather the first part of the night.

29th, Thursday. Having twenty-six and twenty-seven fathoms of water we lay over again. Every day there were many mackerel caught, which for several days were for the cabin only, whatever number were caught, because they were taken with the captain's hooks; but the passengers and sailors began to get their hooks ready also and thus every one began to catch and eat. The weather was delightful. I had obtained my things out of the chest, and found the latitude 37° 18′. We stood over to the Flemish or Zeelandish coast, calculating we were not far from Sluis and Bruges. I therefore went aloft frequently to look out for land. We saw several fishing boats, one of which we hailed toward evening. He was from Zierick zee, and told us Walcheren was about twenty-eight miles E. S. E. of us, and we could see it from the mast head, as was the fact. We laid over again immediately. It now began to blow more from the S. W. and S. W. by W. We had sailed the last night west by north, according to reckoning, twenty-eight miles. This result agreed with my observation less than four miles, and that of our mate, named Evert. But the captain's and the English mate's calculation brought us before the Maes, as Evert told me.

We sailed now for a day or two among great quantities of chub fish and crabs which had been driven off from the land and drowned, which caused us to reflect upon what God did formerly in Egypt and elsewhere, and still often does, for his power is always the same, although it is not always understood.

30*th*, *Friday*. We tacked over to the Flemish coast this morning in twenty-five fathoms of water; but it was so calm that we made little progress. It was too cloudy to take the latitude. The wind was very variable, and we could not keep on S. W., or even south, and so drifted for the most part with the tide.

JULY 1*st*. *Saturday*. We had drifted the whole night in the calm, and had gone backwards instead of forwards; but in the morning the wind began to blow out of the N. W. and N. N. W. with a stiff breeze. We therefore set all sail, and went ahead tolerably well on a straight course W. by S. and W. S. W. against the current. We saw land many times about two hours distance, both on the starboard and larboard, that on the starboard being the point of Dover, and on the larboard, the point of Calais. There was a free wind and fine weather, though a little haze on the horizon. The land began to loom up more distinctly, and I sketched it twice with crayon. We continued to catch plenty of mackerel, and also peterman and whiting. We arrived before Dover at sunset, when we fired a gun, and a boat came off to us immediately, by which the captain sent some letters ashore. We inquired of them the news, and they answered us all was well; but they told the captain privately that 30,000 Scotch papists had taken up arms for the conspirators.[1]

It is proper I should say something here of the North sea. In case you are driven about by strong contrary winds and cannot obtain the latitude, and, indeed, under any circumstances, you should use the deep lead frequently, for the depth is well shown on the chart, and often you cannot get sight of the land. The Flemish coast is the least dangerous, although the English is the most surveyed, because the water becomes shoal gradually. You may get into thirteen and fourteen fathoms of water. In the true channel it is twenty and twenty-two fathoms, and in the middle it is deeper, namely, twenty-six and twenty-eight and over, but it is somewhat more uneven. In approaching the English coast the shoals are more even as twenty-six, eighteen, seventeen fathoms. To navigate the channel it is best to keep nearest the Flemish coast, because it affords a better course, and the current makes it easy to go north, and the sandbars such as the Galper and others, especially Goyn, are more to be avoided than the

[1] This refers to the conspiracy to murder Charles II, charged by Oates.

Flemish banks; and, moreover, close by the shore it is very deep, yet by the setting of the current to the north you may soon be upon them, that is, with an ebb tide.

2*d*, *Sunday*. Made fair progress during the night. We found ourselves in the morning before the point of Bevesier,[1] which I sketched. The wind was northerly with a cool air. About breakfast time a large English ship came up behind us, which we hailed. She was from London and bound for the Straits. She had much sail on, and after passing us, set all she had; but not long afterwards a small breeze blowing off shore, she was compelled to begin to take in her topgallant-sails and upperstay-sails. This was scarcely half done when her maintop-mast and mizzen-top-mast went by the board, and remained hanging on the side of the ship. The man who was taking in the topgallant-sail fell overboard. When this accident happened she was only a short distance ahead of us; and we, therefore, all ran forward to the forecastle to see whether there were any pieces of wood at our bow to damage us. We sailed by her, close under her lee, and saw somewhat of a crowd running about the ship. Finally they launched their jolly-boat for the purpose of looking after the man who had fallen overboard with the top-mast. Whether there were any more we did not know, and as we sailed ahead of them with considerable speed, we could not see whether they fished any one up or not; but the ship sailed before the wind the best she could, when her top-mast went overboard; we took in very quickly our own topgallant-sail, which we had set, but more from precaution than necessity. Shortly afterwards it was so calm that we merely drifted along; and being nearly midway between Bevesier and the Isle of Wight, and the ebb tide running out, we were compelled by the current to anchor about a mile from the shore.

---

[1] Beachy Head.

About four o'clock in the afternoon Margaret came to me while I was engaged in sketching the Isle of Wight. We talked over various matters which were almost the same as those about which she had conversed with my companion the day before, and I therefore met her with the same objections.[1]

3*d*, *Monday*. We did not advance any during the night, and had drifted along; but a breeze springing up we went ahead a little. It was very foggy, so that we could not see the land. It cleared up in the afternoon, when we found ourselves off against the Isle of Wight; but the wind subsiding, and the tide being spent, we ran for the point of the island, and came to anchor in ten or eleven fathoms near some other ships which were waiting there for a good wind and tide. The jolly-boat was launched and our Dutch mate and two other persons went ashore in order to see if they could obtain some fresh provisions. The tide having passed, and the wind shifting, we signaled to them to come on board again, which they did in the evening, when we were already most under sail. They brought nothing with them, except a little milk which served us as a good refreshment for this evening. Sailing ahead, we steered above the point with the wind W. S. W., and so gained the open sea. There is a very strong current here, and hard beating along the shore and around the point. The current sent us ahead more than the wind. The coast is quite good and it is deep enough close up to the shore.

4*th*, *Tuesday*. We found ourselves in the morning opposite Wight with the wind S. S. E., and quite still. After a while there came up a breeze. We passed Peveril point, however, with the ebb. About noon a flute-ship came near us which we hailed. She was from Amsterdam, bound to Cadiz. It was so calm in the evening that we

---

[1] What these subject-matters were do not appear.

rifted, and turned round several times. We perceivedd fifteen or eighteen large ships on the French coast, which saluted each other with many heavy guns. The ebb being spent, we came to anchor again in twenty-one fathoms of water, about two miles from the shore. The flood having run out by evening, we weighed anchor, and before we were under sail had a fresh wind astern. We therefore set all the sail we could, having a favorable wind and tide, by which means we came before Portland.

5*th*, *Wednesday*. We still had a fair wind and kept our course W. by S. We passed Portland, and came in sight of Goldstart,[1] and arrived off against it about noon. Our mate was of opinion that we had run by the rock of Meeusteen or Jetstone,[2] and should have it on the larboard; but on looking out afterwards we found it right before us, about four miles off. We had therefore to hold up and leave it on the starboard. It is a large rock having its head just above the water. It rises up straight, but is very much hacked, which makes it look like a reef. Whenever the sea is rough it is under water. It is dangerous enough, and lies far out in the channel, farther than it is marked down on my chart. We certainly had reason here again to observe the care of the Lord, and his protection through his good providence, which always watches paternally over his children, shown in our becoming aware of this rock before the evening, and just before the evening, for we had not well gone by it before it was dark. If we had been sailing so at night, or if we had not now discovered it, the mate's calculation being as it was, we certainly would not

[1] Start Point.

[2] The Eddystone is here meant — formerly one of the most dangerous reefs on the south coast of England. There was no light-house upon it at this time. The first one was commenced in 1696; the present famous one in 1759. The Dutch name, Meeusteen, signifies Mewstone — a name derived from the gull or sea mew.

missed sailing upon it; for when we first saw it, it was straight before us, and we were sailing with a fair wind and tide up to it. We were therefore touched, and thankful to the Lord. This passed, we still, while the sun was going down clear, made Deadman's head, a point jutting out from England, so that we reckoned we were still twenty-eight or thirty-two miles from Falmouth bay; but the wind had fallen off some. My calculation was, that we were about twelve or sixteen miles from Falmouth.

6th, Thursday. During the night I heard the ship tack close about, and therefore supposed that the wind had changed, or that the ship had run too far, or, what was more probable, I was afraid, the wind being about S. E., we had fallen more to the shore. Our mate Evert and I thought we should stand off a little till daylight; but the captain tacked about again, so that we then sailed N. E., intending thus to enter the harbor of Falmouth, but we found no opening, and when the day broke, discovered that they had made a mistake, and had taken the point of Deadman's head for the point of Falmouth bay. When the sun rose, they saw they were deep in the bay, on a lee shore, where it all looked strange, and they had a tolerably hard wind. When they saw they were wrong it continued so some time before they became informed. They then wore ship, and sailed with quite easy sheets out of the bay.

This mishap was mainly caused by Master Jan, who wishing to play the part of a wise man, though truly it was from fear, had been on deck several times during the night in order to look out, afraid, as he said himself that we might sail upon the point of the Lizard. Coming up at this time with drowsy eyes, and catching a glimpse of the land, through the mist, he began to call out, that we had passed by Falmouth, and would certainly sail upon the Lizard. It was the English mate's watch, who was not very well acquainted with him, and could not keep him still. The captain was therefore called, who also came up rubbing his eyes, and unable to see the land well in the mist. He coincided with Jan, being apprehensive that the ship had sailed more than they thought, and as I myself considered might well be the case, and so let the ship tack about. I deemed it better, however, to keep off from the shore till daylight, when they could see where they were; but the captain relying more upon Jan's opinion, and wishing to accomplish half a master piece, by going into Falmouth in the dark, and surprising the people there to whom the ship was consigned, and so to pass hereafter as a good and skillful captain, insisted upon sailing in, and so they went in, as has been mentioned. It is no part of the business of a good seaman to run into a place by night, or when it is dark, where he is not well acquainted; but in such case he should work off shore slowly, waiting until day and light, and know where he is, and then see what can be done. Thus the fear of one danger, and the rashness accompanying it, brought us into another, greater than the first.

Sailing then out of this bay, around the west point, we saw at once the neck from which this point of land takes its name of Deadman's head. It is shaped like a coffin or the mound of earth which peasants form over a grave, one end a little higher than the other, and going up sharp on either side; but it is on the top somewhat jagged. It is on the east side of the point, three or four cable lengths from the main land. We had a third mate (Titus), on board the ship who was to go on the other ship at Falmouth, and who was well acquainted here. He said he had passed through the opening between the rock and the main land, and that it was a mile wide and tolerably clear and deep enough. After having passed Deadman's head and this rock, we came to a small pretty sand-bay, but it lies open. From Deadman's head you can see, on the point of Falmouth bay, a church with a small spire, and near it a stone wind-mill, which forms a good land mark, for along the whole coast there are few or no steeples. As you sail along this point the castle[1] comes into view standing upon the west point of the harbor of Falmouth, where also there is a stone wind-mill. The easterly point should be avoided, for it runs out considerably. It is hard bottom, and at low tide there is three fathoms water always; and we sailed in with that depth. As soon as you perceive it is deeper, you have passed the east point. Then keep along this shore if the wind be fair, for there is a rock almost directly in the channel. You can go around it close enough, but this should not be done. As it was low water when we entered, it stuck up out of the water. At high tide it is covered. There is a spar or pole upon it, which cannot be seen far, but the breakers are sufficiently visible. When you sail in, in this manner, you see the other castle[2] also, lying on the east side, on a point inside. After having passed the rock, keep a little again on the inside, and then to the west, so as to avoid the second point, upon which the east castle is situated. As soon as you have passed that, you have deeper water and softer bottom; and you must then look out that you do no damage to the shipping, for the roadstead commences there, and you can see the city or village of Falmouth lying upon the west side of the bay, and appearing somewhat prettier than it is in fact. When we arrived, we found a large number of vessels lying there; but being desirous of sailing high up, several ships received good thumps from us, in passing by them, and our endeavoring to keep off the shoals. It would have resulted much worse, if our sheet anchor, which was lying up forward, had not caught between the rails of a small vessel, whose mizen-

[1] Pendennis.

[2] St. Mawes.

mast we also came foul of, whereby our ship turned round, and at the same time our anchor fell, and we touched bottom in the mud, with fine weather and still water. We thanked our God again, with our whole hearts, for the double mercy shown us this morning, having not only in a fatherly manner preserved us from an apprehended danger, but delivered us from this one into which we had truly fallen, and had then caused us to arrive so well. To him belongs all praise and glory, from all his children, and especially from us, to all eternity. Amen.

Our anchor had not yet touched bottom when the inspectors or tide-waiters all came on board to examine. Our captain and Margaret went immediately ashore; and after the cook had served the breakfast, most all the passengers, both old and young, putting on their best clothes, did the same. My comrade also went to see if any letters had arrived for us, whilst I remained on board to look after things a little; for all our goods were in the berth, and otherwise within reach, and the ship was constantly full of strange people. My comrade soon returned, but brought no letters. This morning while we were launching the boat, I hurt myself in the loins, on my left side; the pain extended through the whole of that side of my body, to my left breast, and across the middle to the right breast. I was all bent up while standing, and had to sit down. I could scarcely draw a breath or move myself; but I felt it was my old complaint, forced upon me anew when I hurt myself. This pain continued for some days, when it gradually passed over. At high water we towed the ship higher up, to the warehouse, where we had to unload. The custom house officers, and Mr. Rogers, came on board with some other persons, and when they left, they promised us the ship should be unladen by Tuesday, for which we were glad.

7*th*, *Friday*. They began early to break open the hatches

and discharge the ship. My comrade and I went ashore to a place called Penryn, a little further up the bay, and as far as they can go with any vessels. We walked thence into the country, over and among the hills, for the purpose of recreating and recruiting ourselves, which refreshed us very much, after having been so long in an overburdened ship and with such wicked men.

We returned to Penryn at noon in order to see if we could obtain some place or other to lodge and rest ourselves for a time. By chance we came to an inn in that place, called The English Ship, the landlord of which was named Master Jean, who spoke a little Dutch, and, as we afterwards discovered, better French, so well indeed that we could converse with him. We took dinner there, and agreed with him to lodge there for several days, with the privilege of a chamber to ourselves.

8th, Saturday. Having slept on board the ship we went in the morning to our new lodgings, where we breakfasted, and then rambled into the country to divert ourselves, and thence to Falmouth, and so returned by evening to our lodgings.

9th, Sunday. My companion being disposed to write, I went to the Episcopal church where I was surprised to find in the churchyard a great crowd of people sitting together, smoking tobacco and waiting for the last toll of the bell. On entering the church I was still more astonished at the ceremonies which indeed did not differ much from those of popery, and continued quite long enough. Then followed a sermon, if it may be called such, delivered in a white gown, as were the first services and other ceremonies in like vestments. The sermon was read out of a little book, without the addition of a single word. It began about ten o'clock, and was not very edifying. The text was from 2 Cor., xiii, 11. It continued till about half-past eleven, when church was over, and the burgomasters or mayors, with two golden royal sceptres, were carried home. In the afternoon I took a walk to the ship, and thence in a small half-hour to Falmouth. She was lying midway between the two places for the purpose of being unladen.

10*th, Monday.* We remained at our lodgings almost the whole day writing letters. Our ship was nearly discharged, which I went in the evening to ascertain.

11*th, Tuesday.* We continued still at our lodgings, but in the afternoon visited the ship in consequence of their telling us that our chest would be examined, as indeed took place. There were some passengers on shore whose chests were broken open, because they did not attend to them, and the inspectors would not wait. They cut to pieces the cords of their berth under which they found some things; but although there were more berths so arranged, and still better furnished than this one, they did nothing to them, as they well knew beforehand whose they were, and why they did what was done. When they examined our chest, they took almost all our goods out of it. However, they did not see our little box, or perhaps they thought it contained medicines, as they found in the other one. The two small pieces of linen were entered, and my name signed to them. They went to our berth, but did nothing; nor was any thing there.

12*th, Wednesday.* This whole day was a writing day for the post, which would leave to-morrow. They began to reload the ship in the afternoon. I went on board, and also went to see if there were any letters for us, which turned out to be the fact; for, on finding the captain, he gave me a letter for which I paid twenty-two pence postage. This was the first letter we had received from home. It is unnecessary for me to say that I was rejoiced, or that we thanked the Lord that he still thought of us. I went immediately with it to my companion, who was as glad as

I was, for the letter came just in time to be answered, as we did with joy and tenderness of heart.

13*th*, *Thursday*. As the post was soon to leave, we took our letters to the post office at Penryn, next to The White Dolphin. The package was weighed, and was one ounce and a quarter in weight, for which we paid fifteen pence postage to London; and they informed us it would reach London on Monday. Our ship being almost laden again, we paid our landlord and returned on board ship. We could have easily remained a day or two longer at our lodgings, but our landlord had given us reasons for leaving. Coming on board the ship, we began to arrange our place a little for keeping house again. Meanwhile I helped fill the water casks. There was also some beef to be salted in barrels.

14*th*, *Friday*. Our ship was entirely laden, that is, with the goods she had to take, for there was a large quantity of them which had come out of her, remaining for the other ship which Margaret had bought there, and which was to be made ready there to go to the Isle of May, and thence to Barbadoes. She was a large but very weak ship, short and high, small and meagre as regards bulk, not altogether old, but misbuilt. She sailed tolerably well, but was very lank. Two of our crew went with her, namely, Titus, who was to be boatswain, and one of our carpenters, named Herman, who was the best one we had. They went, from the first, to work upon her, for she was lying in winter quarters. Our ship being laden, our captain went on board the large one with an English lad, the cabin boy, and his, the captain's wife. This captain had obtained a quaker for his mate, a young man and a very poor seaman, as I have been able to observe. Hereupon our English mate, named Robert, who also was a quaker, became captain in the place of the other, and our Dutch mate, or rather New Netherland mate, named Evert van Duike — for he was a

New Netherlander born, and his parents and relations were still there, though he had married at Amsterdam and had lived there a long time, but was now taking his wife and children with him to New Netherland — became mate in place of the other. In return for the three persons and the boy who had gone from our crew, we obtained only one in their place, a poor creature, called Jan, the doctor, of Boston, who seemed more a charlatan in his behavior and gestures than a good seaman. Meanwhile we went walking, to see the country, and in the afternoon came to the east castle, where a soldier conducted us from the gate and took us before the governor, who asked us who we were, where we came from, what flag our ship bore, when and with whom we had arrived, and for what purpose we had come to the castle. We answered him politely; but we could not make ourselves well understood by him, for he spoke nothing but English, which we could not do, or very little, though we could understand it pretty well. He finally ordered the soldier to conduct us around the castle, in order that we might look at it. Having satisfied the soldier, we left, and went down the hill. The beer brewed at the castle is very poor; there is little or no fresh water up there, and what there is, does not amount to much. The castle is otherwise strong and well provided, having over an hundred guns in different batteries, which command the harbor and the entire roadstead.[1] When we reached the ship she was laden.

[1] On the restoration of the Stuarts, Richard, Lord Arundell, was made governor of Pendennis castle, which his father had bravely defended to the last extremity against the parliamentary forces in 1646, the garrison having been reduced to the necessity of eating the flesh of dogs and horses before the sturdy old governor surrendered. Richard was succeeded by his son, John, Lord Arundell, and one of these two was, no doubt, governor at the time of the visit of our travelers. The castle was built by Henry VIII, on the site of an old fortification, for the purpose of defense against the French.— *Lyson's Mag. Brit.*, iii, 104-5.

Falmouth at that time contained about 250 houses, and soon after

15*th*, *Saturday*. As our ship was now full, and orders had come to haul the ship at high water from before the warehouse and off from the ground, they did so this morning. We went to Penryn to buy some butter, and when we returned the boat was sent for fresh water, which was brought on board, and the ship then towed to the roadstead below, where she arrived in the evening, somewhat late, and was moored at once.

16*th*, *Sunday*. The weather was misty and rainy. We went ashore with one of the passengers and one of the sailors, a young fellow, a Scotchman, by birth, from the Orkneys, and a presbyterian by profession, named Robert, who took us, at our request, to the presbyterian meeting, which we left quite satisfied with the zeal of the preacher. Their mode of service is not different from that of the Reformed in Holland, but the common people sat there with very little reverence. At noon we went to dine at a very good inn, called The Golden Fleece, and in the afternoon we attended the meeting of the episcopalians, of whose church service we have before spoken, and so in the evening returned on board the ship.

17*th*, *Monday*. We went this morning again with some passengers to Penryn, where the yearly market day was held, with the intention of laying out a little money in some purchases, having rid ourselves of Mr. Jan, who had sought to get it out of our hands, and would by that means have cheated us. He promised us, if we would let

---

became a place of some importance as the port of the post office packets to the West Indies and elsewhere. In 1755 there were two packets employed between Falmouth and New York, and, in 1763, four.

Penryn is a very ancient town, older than Falmouth. It had a court leet before the Norman conquest, and sent two members to parliament. The borough was incorporated by James I, and by its charter it could hold three fairs annually, namely: on May 1st, July 7th and December 21. The town has no trade or commerce, but is said to be beautifully situated on a ridge, which, on the northern side, goes down into a valley watered by a branch of Falmouth harbor. — *Itinerary of Cornwall*, 128 - 9.

him have the money, thirty per cent interest payable in New York, or ducats there at twelve guilders of zeewan each;[1] but the Lord, who has care over the least of his children, saved us from this fox, and excited the attention of another passenger, namely, Jan Theunissen, who lived on Long Island, and who advised us what to do.[2]

We bought several things on which we thought we could make a profit, because the peril of the sea was to be encountered. The Lord, who as I have said, takes care of the least of his children, so ordered it that we not only did not lose any thing by our Dutch money, which commonly brings not more than five shillings for a ducat; but we received for almost all that we used, five shillings and six pence, that is 67 stuivers. The reason of this was, that the man who took our money was about going to Norway, for timber, where he could pay it out at a higher rate than English money. Having made our purchases, we went to Falmouth, but as we could not take our goods on board the ship without first declaring them, we had to take them to Mr. Rogers's, where one Mr. Jacobs lived, who had assisted in inspecting the ship's lading, and who would do the same with these. Thinking over the purchases we had made at Penryn, we discovered there was a mistake in the

[1] A ducat was a small gold coin of Holland, worth about two dollars our currency.

[2] This was Jan Theunissen van Dykhuis, who married Aagje (Agatha) daughter of Elbert Elbertsen, of Amersfoort, now Flatlands, on Long Island. He does not appear to have been any way conspicuous; but his father-in-law was at this time a man of considerable note, having risen from a low condition to be one of the most substantial citizens of the colony. He came to New Netherland as a servant to Wouter Van Twiller, at a very tender age, and was afterwards in the service of Kiliaen Van Rensselaer. He was one of the nine men appointed by the colonists in 1649 to represent their grievances to the States General. He became proprietor of Bergen's island, and other lands, in Flatlands, and died about 1686.—*Genealogy of the Bergen Family*, by Hon. Teunis G. Bergen, p. 99.

payment of a bill, arising from the counting of the money by our Dutch mate and Jan Theunissen. The difference amounted to one pound sterling. We, or our friends on our account, had paid the bill. We discovered the mistake at Falmouth, and immediately went back to Penryn, informed the merchant of the mistake, which he did not have much trouble in comprehending. He gave us back the money, for which we were glad, and returning, arrived by evening on board the ship.

18*th*, *Tuesday*. One Mr. Lucas, the most rigid of the inspectors and custom house officers came on board this morning. We spoke to him, told him what we had bought, and requested him to examine them. We said we might buy something more and he could assess them all together. He replied he did not wish not to examine our chest, or what we might have bought previously; but would go ashore with us and look at what we had there. He told us also that he had a small piece or two of stuffs, which, if we would buy, he would let us have at a bargain. We went to Mr. Jacobs's where he looked over what we had bought. He told us we had paid dear for them, although we thought we had bought them cheap. Mr. Jacobs said he had a remnant of tin which he would sell us for ten stuivers a foot, and we had paid twelve for ours. We were directed to pay Mr. Jacobs three shillings English for duties upon the goods we had there, whenever we should have all our merchandise together. Mr. Lucas went with us to a shop over the door of Mr. Rogers, where he bought several things for us at a low price; he even compelled the merchant almost to give us the goods for what he chose, for the merchant did not dare to refuse or disoblige him. They were always good purchases. He also brought us something of his own which he sold us on favorable terms. I supposed these were confiscated goods, which they wanted to get rid of, and that this was the reason they were so accommodating to us. Our purchases being completed, he took us to an inn where we regaled him for the trouble he had taken with the above-mentioned merchant. We were compelled this evening to eat and sleep ashore, which we did at the inn, The Golden Fleece.

We had heard a great deal said for some days past, and to-day, of great danger from the Turks, who had taken four Dutch ships. This caused no small apprehension in our ship, and especially in Mr. Jan.

19*th*, *Wednesday*. My companion wrote a letter home from on board the ship. We did our best this whole day to get our little merchandise on board, but without success, because it was not yet declared. However, every thing concerning the ship and the lading was finished to-day; and the passengers obtained the bills of their goods, and paid them. Having accomplished nothing the whole day, we returned on board the ship.

20*th*, *Thursday*. My comrade having finished the letters, we went on shore to Mr. Rogers's, in order to post them in time, and paid the postage to London. We bought also some brandy, vinegar and other articles, for we began to see it would go slim with us on the voyage. We were engaged the whole day in declaring our goods and carrying them on board, which was completed early in the evening, and the goods stowed away. We then paid Mr. Lucas a ducaton[1] for the duties on our goods. He told us what the duties on the whole of the ship's cargo amounted to, and gave us various other information, all very willingly, because, after he heard that I was somewhat acquainted with the wine business, he desired some particulars in regard to it from me, which I gave him in writing to his satisfaction. We were now all cleared.

---

[1] A silver coin at that time of Holland, worth about a dollar and a quarter.

21*st*, *Friday*. This morning it was very misty. The wind was well to the N. E., but quite still, and they talked of leaving immediately. The bow anchor was therefore raised, and we got under weigh, and ran to the mouth of the bay, where we came to anchor again under the castle. The captain, Margaret, and many of the passengers went ashore, but my comrade and I remained on board. For some days past we had heard it rumored that our ship's boat was to be taken from us, and we were to have the boat of the large ship in its place, or that we would go to sea without a boat. Whichsoever it might be, it was a matter of importance to all who might be in our ship. As to going to sea without a boat, it could hardly be thought of, for how much depends upon one, experience has fully shown. It was evident we must submit to take that belonging to the other ship, or hold on to our own by force. We had seen the other ship's boat several times, and we knew she was very badly built, and not only not serviceable, but very incommodious. All things considered, it would be causing us a great inconvenience to put this boat upon us, by reason of the little or no service which we could derive from it. We were also afraid of it, as it was much larger than ours, and ours was already too large for the ship; for when it was hauled on board there was scarcely room at the main hatchway or the forehatch to climb out; and if the other boat, which was much larger, were placed there, the hatches would certainly have to be closed entirely. What an inconvenience that would have caused to all the passengers, who, in such a great number lodged between the two decks, can not be fully expressed. It would in all probability have produced sickness. In the next place the boat was so heavy, that with the small number of our crew remaining, namely: ten men with the captain and mate, it could not have been properly managed. But the worst of all was, it was so rotten that you could not keep it above water, and you could tread holes in it with your feet. We could not, therefore, consent to an exchange. It only remained for us to oppose the measure, and point out its injustice: that the boat of the ship in which we had taken passage was a part of the vessel, and in depriving us of it, they would take away from us what was ours by agreement. There was no person in the ship who did not object to it, except Margaret and the captain of the old ship, or rather the captain of the other ship alone, who was master here. He never did any thing except to please these miserable, covetous people, namely: Margaret and her husband, who would not have another boat built in Falmouth, but it must be done in New York, where timber was a little cheaper. Our captain, who had been only made captain for this voyage, durst not set himself against it and thus induce the other captain, and consequently the merchant, to oppose Margaret. Everybody else was opposed to it. Mr. Jan, who did not enquire much after the merchant, having a great fear of him, and whom Margaret could compel, also opposed it. But now, when it came to the point, no one dared to speak; the sailors, who are very tightly bound and severely treated on board of English ships, dared not say any thing; and the passengers grumbled among themselves; but when it was necessary that something should be said, no one was willing to be the first to speak out. They stood like children and let themselves be easily appeased. We, however, considered the matter, and I resolved rather to speak out now, than, at the best, to sit in the dark, to be stifled with the heat and stench, to be sick and not have a breath of air, as must have been the consequence to us in the bow of the ship. Finally, our old captain and our two former sailors, who went with him on board the other ship, brought their old boat in order to take ours away with them. Mr. Rogers, Mr.

Lucas, Mr. Jacobs and others came also on board. I thought I would do nothing until the last moment, and no one else opposed it. It seemed to me to be my duty then, for the general welfare, and especially for my worthy companion and myself, to do all I could. Our boat then coming along side with the captain and passengers in it, I told the passengers to remain in and keep it, and not to come out of it, for nothing was easier in case they came out of it, than for the old captain to take possession and carry it away; yet they all came out, notwithstanding I had requested them to remain. I know not why it was, whether they did not understand me, having drank once, or whether they dared not do so. I therefore jumped into the boat myself, when the captain inquired what I had said, and I answered that we were determined not to let our boat go. He then stood up, laughing derisively, and opposed me in an angry manner. I told him that rather than part with the boat, and subject ourselves to the danger of the other one, we would see him thrown overboard, and my opinion was, he deserved to be shipwrecked, if it should so happen to us as was contemplated. I do not know whether he well understood me, or whether I had expressed myself properly, for I did not speak good English. I was amazed at seeing all the other passengers standing round like children. He came running from the stern of the boat to the front, where I was, with his cane uplifted, and saying: "You will throw me overboard, will you?" Seeing the quaker wished to strike me, I sprang into the middle of the boat and grappling him, held him so tight that he could not do it, when the others separated us. He went on board the ship, and declared he would have me put in prison, because I had threatened to throw him overboard, as he said; but he was better informed by some of the passengers, who heard and understood what I had said better than he did. Otherwise there was not a passenger who ventured to say a word. Some wives only cried and bawled about what was proposed to be done. The mate's wife, who, with two small children, was placed directly opposite our berth, and would there have suffered much also, ran with another woman, screeching into the cabin, and there bemoaned herself. Mr. Jacobs spoke against me, and said the captain was right in his acts and threats; miserable time servers, encouraging any one in what they are convinced in their own hearts is not right, as our captain and Margaret themselves afterwards acknowledged. I came out of the boat myself, not being able to accomplish any thing alone; when, finally, the passengers began here and there to say a word. But, nevertheless, the old captain ordered his sailors to put the gear in our boat, in order to take her away. Mr. Jan, standing nearest by, prevented that being done, and then ran forward to the cabin, where there was a violent wrangling going on. At last the mayor or burgomaster came upon deck, and promised us all that we should retain our boat, and told us henceforth to rest easy. I went up to him and thanked him politely, and offered him an apology for speaking hastily perhaps, which he accepted, and gave me his hand. Afterwards our old captain came to me and said, "Well, I did not think you were such a man;" for he had to say something. I replied, that he must in conscience say if he were in our place he would not have permitted it. He said, "No, I would not have permitted it, and you did right in opposing it, though you could have done so in a little different manner." "Yes," said I, "and we might in the meantime have lost our boat." At which he went away, repeating that he was not surprised that we had opposed it. Finally all became quiet, and were glad we had held on to the boat. Even our own captain said, this same day, that he was as glad as any one on board the ship could be, though he was sorry it happened as it did. The sailors who came from the other ship, raved and swore about the old boat in a way not to be repeated; but said they were glad on our account, and also their own, because it would be the means, perhaps, of their obtaining a new boat; that they had railed out so against the old boat because as we had refused to have it, they would have to use it to lift the large anchors, and even to unload and load the ship, for which it would be still less serviceable. The matter certainly went off well, and we thanked the Lord in our hearts.

We then weighed anchor and got under sail, leaving on the left hand the rock which lies in the mouth of the harbor. It is on account of this rock that this place is called Falmouth, or Foulmouth, that is, *foul mouth.*[1] The wind was about S. E., but when we reached outside, it shifted more and more to the south, and became quite light, so that by evening we were opposite Black point. It then became entirely calm, and we had to keep off and on, and the ship herself afterwards tacked about. After supper the watch was set. Another passenger, named Gerrit, and myself, were added to the mate's watch. While we were in the first watch, and four glasses[2] had not yet run out, black clouds began to rise, accompanied with heavy thunder and lightning. It was frightful. The crew were immediately called on deck, the topsails taken in, the other sails furled, and every thing made fast, when it

---

[1] Falmouth, like other sea ports of England whose names have the same termination, such as Plymouth, Dartmouth and Yarmouth, takes its name from being the mouth of a river, that of Fal, the little stream which here empties itself into the sea. The town is so called from the bay; and, as has already been observed, is of comparatively modern date. The locality was at an early period called Pennycomequick, a popular expression, it is said, composed of three Cornish words *pen*, *coom*, *ick*, signifying, narrow valley by the creek.—*British Gazetteer.*

[2] A glass runs half an hour.

began to rain so exceedingly hard, that I do not recollect ever to have seen it rain harder. We were thoroughly wet through. It continued the whole night. Whenever it lightened we could see a great distance from us, and perceived several ships, two or three large vessels and some small ones, which increased our fear of the Turks. When there was no lightning we could not see our hands before our faces. I remained up the whole night, as there was no opportunity to sleep.

22*d*, *Saturday*. The wind during the day-watch changing from the west to the north, we tacked towards the shore in order to run in again, and about eight o'clock we came to anchor inside the castle. Towards evening our carpenter and his wife having forgotten something, went ashore, and on their return brought the news that a small ship which had run out to sea further than we did, and had come in again after us, had seen in the morning a ketch, which went to sea with us, taken by the Turks; for which reason they had now come inside. This news produced not a little consternation in our ship. Whether it were true or not, we did not know; but we were overwhelmed with a sense of the careful providence of God, who perhaps for the preservation of his children, had directed this storm and caused the wind to change, whereby we were compelled to come inside again; for otherwise, if we had seen any opportunity of proceeding, we would have remained outside.

23*d*, *Sunday*. The weather was calm. At noon my companion went ashore, while I remained on board. In the afternoon several ships came in, all bringing bad news of there being such and so many Turks on the coast. One said five and another two large ships, and that they had fourteen captured vessels with them; that twenty-three had sailed from Algiers, and would blockade the entire channel to the Flemish islands. This news was brought by a small ship from the straits, and had reported it to one of those vessels which had run in here. But in the afternoon a ketch came in and sent a boat up to Falmouth to land some persons, and ran out again immediately, without coming to anchor. The boat came along side of us. Mr. Lucas, who came out to our ship with this boat, said that the ketch was cruising for English East Indiamen, some of which had arrived, and had been cruising several days without seeing any suspicious ships; but had met some French vessels from the straits, which had fired a shot for him to come off to them, because they wanted to speak to him, which he did. He spent an hour with them, for which reason other English ships, which had observed this at a distance, supposed these French ships were Turks and this ketch had been captured by them; and therefore they had saved themselves by flight. The boat went to the other ships, and on her return brought still more news than we had yet heard, so that we were still in doubt. In the meantime my comrade came on board, and related how he had been to the quakers' meeting, and gave me an account of their devotions, preaching, and meals.

24*th*, *Monday*. The wind being northeasterly this morning, we raised the bow anchor early; and the other was also wound up. The boat went once more ashore, to fill the remaining empty water casks, in order that we might get immediately under sail; but before the casks were filled, the wind shifted round, and we had to remain where we were. In the afternoon I went with some others to assist in hauling off Margaret's other ship which was aground, and take her to the shipyard.

Before we leave England and the channel, a word in regard to them may be useful. As to the channel, it is well to observe, that those who have to sail through it should keep nearest the English coast, because it is safer than the French; but to keep as close as we did I do not consider best, because there is much calm wind made from the shore, whereby there is slow progress; and, in the second place, storms or tornadoes sometimes come over the high land during these calms, and as there is then usually much sail set, they fall upon the ship, and cause much inconvenience, as we experienced. Thirdly, because when the wind comes from the sea, you are on a lee shore, and in some danger; and sometimes if the wind continues, you are compelled to make a harbor where you would hardly otherwise be willing to do, and from whence you can not always readily come out again. It is well to throw the lead in dark and foggy weather, in order to ascertain the bottom, and whether there be any current; also to calculate the tides at the place where you may be, so as to make good reckoning; and when the tide stops, to make sail. In case it happen you are compelled to run in anywhere, you should know well where it is, or if you do not, and it is so that you cannot by reason of the night or other obscurity, obtain sight of the land, it is better to lie with light sail off from the shore until it clear up, so that you may not be at a loss when you approach the land, as we were. It is always the practice of a good seaman, and it is proper, to keep well away from the shore, because there are several rocks which lie further out than they are laid down upon the charts, as we have observed, and you are therefore in danger of sailing upon them.

As to this part of England, and the places of Falmouth and Penryn, where we have been for about three weeks, we have to observe, that from the straits (of Dover) to Land's End the land is high, but higher in some places than others, and is diversified with many hills and dales. The coast is broken and rocky. From Dover to the Isle of Wight it is chalky white; from thence it is red and harder; and towards Land's End, it is black as if it were burnt. Extending inland, the country is beautified with green fields and cultivated farms, among and out of which rise the spires of churches, presenting, as you sail along them, as we did, in the summer time, a pleasant and agreeable prospect. And as the children of God can see the hand of their Father everywhere, they clearly and lovingly see it in this glorious exhibition; beholding here his power, wisdom, goodness, majesty and purity, and being drawn by it to him; a sight which for six days long we had now enjoyed. Happy the souls which find God in his works! What do not they enjoy, wherever they may be, when God lifts, only a little, the curtain, and lets his creatures see him? Or when he, even before we know it, looks from behind the wall or through the lattice, how soon they know him and how soon they are with him; how quickly they adore and glorify him; and how soon they unite themselves with him and are lost in him! But what shall I say? This is for those who truly experience it, and not for every one. Heaven is for man to behold, who goes with head erect; the earth, with what is below upon it, is for the beast, which carries its head down. The country around Falmouth and to the west of it is called Cornwall because it is so fruitful in corn.[1] Its hills are tolerably high, and it has deep valleys supplied with running streams of fresh water. Although at some depth below the surface, and in some places deeper than others,

[1] This derivation is not more fanciful than that given in the *Illustrated Itinerary of the County of Cornwall*, referring it to the figure of the county, "which is that of a cornucopia, or horn of plenty." "The truth seems to be that the country was called," says a good authority, 3 *Mag. Brit.*, III, "by its ancient inhabitants Kernou, or as the Welsh write it Kerniw or the Horn, from its projecting promontories; that it was Latinized to Cornubia; that when the Saxons gave the name of Wealas to the Britons, they distinguished those who had retired into Kernou or Cornubia by the name of Cornwealas and their country, Cornwall, that is Cornish Wales."

there is much rock, and indeed almost nothing else, there is nevertheless much produced from the soil. We saw growing on the highest hills fine wheat, rye, buckwheat and oats, besides good grass, on which cattle were pastured, and from which long hay was mown. There were few fruits or garden productions. The fields are not set off by ditches or wooden fences, but by small dikes formed either partly with stones collected from the fields and placed upon a little earth, or entirely of earth, on the top of which they plant small trees and shrubbery, so that their roots may hold them firm. This is not only suitable for inclosing the land, but it affords a pleasant sight like a neat seam on a green or other colored garment.[1] The land also yields very good tin, of which there is a fine mine near Penryn, where we saw the workshop and mills. The town of Penryn, that is, *eyelid*, as well as Falmouth, are open towns (not fortified), quite long, having one or two streets laid out on the side of the hill. Penryn is larger than Falmouth, and has a surface stream of fresh water running through its whole length, from one end to the other, affording great convenience to the inhabitants. The town appears very neat and pretty outside, but inside it does not signify much. The houses are built for the most part of stone in their rough state, laid in loam, and plastered on the outside, entirely white, with lime; upon this plastering they throw small pebbles for the sake of ornament, and then draw lines in squares, so as to make it look as if the houses were constructed of large blocks of

---

[1] This fertility of some parts of Cornwall and almost up to Land's End is fully confirmed by modern statements. "From the Tamar to the Fowey," says the *Itinerary*, "on the southern side of the county, there is a very fertile district producing immense crops of corn: for here climate, soil, and convenience of lime carriage, all contribute to the fertility. By Mount's bay sixty bushels of wheat have been raised on an acre, and it is said that 1,000 acres around Penzance now let for £10,000 per annum." Mount's bay and Penzance are between the Lizard and Land's End.

stone. The best houses are floored with plank or stones; in the others there is nothing but earth. The people are quite civil, but very ignorant in religious and godly things; though very shrewd in worldly affairs, especially in entrapping strangers. Fish is good and cheap. There was once a fisherman along side of us, who asked only ten stuivers[1] for a codfish, which is esteemed there, as in many other places, the choicest of fish. We offered him eight stuivers, but did not obtain it. You cannot procure much merchandise in these towns, as it has to be brought from other places. English goods even, can be bought cheaper in Amsterdam than here, as they have to be carried upon poor small horses, for wagons cannot be used for the purpose in consequence of the steepness of the hills. As to the commerce carried on in their own ships, it is not large, and is with small vessels. The bay or river is navigable to Penryn and no further, where it stops. Falmouth lies in front. It has many inns and taverns, but few churches. The beer brewed here is not heavy, but light and sour, and not very good-tasted. Fuel is extremely dear; so that bakers, brewers and others who use much fire, burn for the most part, a certain kind of weed or thorn, which grows along the roads and fences, and give out a great heat. From all this you may, in some degree, gather the condition of these places, of which I myself had previously the impression they were large and capital towns.

25*th*, *Tuesday*. The wind being N. and N. N. W., we did not conclude to leave. Mr. Jan alone opposed leaving, so much afraid was he; but the wind blowing fresh, the captain ordered them about noon to weigh anchor, and we got under sail. We were scarcely outside, when we perceived two large ships and several others around the

---

[1] Ten cents.

point of the Lizard, at which Mr. Jan was filled with fear. Seeing a ketch coming from there, we bore up to her, and inquired what ships they were. They answered they were English ships-of-war, which was confirmed by a fisherman engaged in fishing there, whom we spoke. Whereupon our ship was as full of joy as it had before been of fear. On approaching these ships we found it to be as reported, although we did not speak to them, which was an oversight in the captain, it seems to me, on several accounts. What reasons he had for not doing so I do not know, although they might be easily guessed. They both sailed to the west. When we came off the Lizard, we laid our course for the Scilly islands, although it was near the wind. We sailed thus the whole night W. and W. by S. During the first watch the two ships came close along side of us, and passed us without our speaking to them. They were beating up the channel.

26*th*, *Wednesday*. The wind same as before, and we sailed on our former course. In the morning we could still see the Scilly islands behind us. The sun shining, we observed the latitude at 49° 4′. We then set our course west by south, reckoning our longitude to be 10° 10′. We had a very light breeze. We still saw several ships, but one ship-of-war was still to the larboard of us, which at evening beat before the wind to look, as it seemed, after her companion which had fallen behind. We had a light breeze all night, and kept on the same course.

27*th*, *Thursday*. Early this morning we saw a ship on the larboard about eight miles off under full sail, which circumstance revived the fears on board of our ship, for she did not appear to be, as she was, the before mentioned ship-of-war. She was sailing on the same course as ourselves; a practice which privateers or pirates adopt in order to see whether they can sail faster than those they have their eyes upon. But as regards us in particular, the Lord caused us to put our trust in him, and held our hearts quiet in him. This fear gradually subsided when it was observed that the ship came no nearer to us. At noon there was a fog, so that the sun could not shine through it, and we could not take the latitude well; but according to what we did obtain, the latitude did not differ much from that of the day before, only some minutes further south. We continued on our course a distance computed to be sixty-four miles, in longitude 8° 6′. By evening the before mentioned ship was almost out of sight. We had no longer any doubt that she was the ship-of-war.

28*th*, *Friday*. The wind still N. and N. N. W., with a light breeze, and we proceeded W. and W. by N., in order to keep due west. The before mentioned ship had come up during the night, and was now almost in front of us, and continued thus sailing with us. At noon it was entirely calm; the latitude observed was 49° 24′; the distance now was computed to be sixty-eight miles, and found to be sixty miles; our course was a little more southerly than west; and the longitude calculated to be 7° 6′. In the afternoon the ship-of-war ran south on the other bow, and by evening was so far to the leeward that we could hardly see her. It was very calm, and in the evening and first part of the night, the wind became more and more westerly, so that when the watch was set we could only sail W. S. W. The ship was tacked about in order not to fall too far off to the south; and we could then sail N. and N. by E., but the wind changed again more to the north, so that we were compelled to keep more easterly.

29*th*, *Saturday*. The wind as we have said, drawing to the north, the ship was tacked about at eight o'clock, sailing with a fine topsail breeze W. by N. At noon we found the latitude was 50° 8′, so that our reckoning was twenty or twenty-four miles further west than the westerly point of Ireland, that is, in longitude about 4° 40′. The before mentioned ship had left us the past night; but before we leave her in our thoughts, we cannot omit to observe how we were touched by the good and fatherly care of God, the Lord, over his children, sending her to this same place, where the danger of the enemy, the Turks, was always to be feared; sending her there, I say, through his mysterious providence, as a good convoy to meet their weakness; for otherwise he alone, and his faithful care are sufficient, albeit he was pleased to work it out by such means as pleased him. Thus we have not only discovered no enemy, but were conveyed by this ship-of-war, or ships, through the most dangerous part where the enemy was most to be feared; although these ships intended nothing else than to execute their commission, which was to cruise after the East India ships. Certainly if we did not see the hand of God in this, we were truly blind; if we were not touched by it, we were indeed insensible; and if we did not tenderly acknowledge it, we had been the most unthankful men in the world. No, no, his spirit inclines and works in us to other things. What reason his children have to rely upon him; to lose themselves and their ways in him! Praise the Lord, all ye who have so often experienced this, for his faithfulness endures for eternity. Yea, praise the Lord, for he shows himself to be what he is. But this is sufficient, and leaving you to him and in these thoughts, we will, in the same trust, resume our voyage. By evening it was very calm, and the wind westerly, so that we could sail only W. by S., and did so half the night, except when we tacked, and then we sailed, N. by W., and N. N. W.

30*th*, *Sunday*. It remained quite calm until in the morning, with the wind N. N. E., and our course set west by north. About eight o'clock, however, the wind shot out of the south with such a stiff topsail breeze that we turned the helm again, and in the afternoon were able to sail freely W. by N. The weather being overcast we could not ascertain the latitude, but calculated it to be 50°, and the distance run ninety-six miles. The course was west, a little southerly, and the longitude 3°. At evening it began to blow hard; our topsails were first reefed, and afterwards taken in entirely. We were in the first watch, during which it began to rain so hard, and we shipped so much water from the sea, that there was not a dry place anywhere to sit down; for walk or stand we could not, and so let the water run under us. The man at the helm had the tiller knocked out of his hands two or three times. Our sails, though small, had as much as they could bear, and I wondered why either the sails did not burst, or the masts break; for our mate let them stand so that every thing that was on them shook and shivered. Before our watch was out the weather appeared to moderate gradually; and when it was out I crept, all wet as I was, into the berth, for there was no other course. I had lain there hardly half an hour, when we shipped a heavy sea, whereby many articles were thrown over to the lee side. My comrade requested me to feel whether any of our goods and clothing which were lying upon our chest, before the berth, were thrown off which I did; but I could not find either goods or chest. I arose, and went groping about for them; I found the chest below the middle of the forehatch, and lifted it as well as I could, again to the windward. The other articles I found mostly under the berth of the persons opposite to us; when the boatswain coming along with a light, to see whether any of the ship's property was injured, we brought every thing in order again, and found that no damage had happened to the medicines, as we had apprehended.

31*st, Monday.* The wind having become more calm we sailed W. by N., but it veering gradually round to the west, we tacked about again, sailing then about W. S. W., with a rolling sea, and making little progress. We calculated our latitude was the same as yesterday. The distance run was seventy-two miles, and the longitude about 1° 18′. By evening took the wind again gradually till we had to furl in our topsails. Course N. N. W.; in the first watch N. W.; in the second N. W. by W.; and in the third W. N. W.; and so the wind by degrees changed to the south.

August 1*st*, *Tuesday*. It still blew hard from the S. W. We saw a ship ahead of us to the leeward, coming towards us under full sail, and steering for us in order, apparently, to speak us; but in consequence of the rolling of the sea, she could not come close to us. She flew the flag of the Prince (of Orange), and we the English flag. She then sailed by us, so that we could distinguish the vessel. She was the Eendracht (Union) of Flissingen (Flushing), the same one which the East India ship took from the English, and carried to Hamburg in the year 1673. We found the longitude at noon 49° 4′. The wind increased more and more till it blew a storm. We not only took in the topsails, but had to reef in the lower sails, and so lay over the whole night, N. N. W., making little progress. There was a great noise, moaning, and lamentation among the women between decks in the dark, for they could not lie down, or sit or stand, in consequence of the tossing of the ship. But we kept up our spirits and courage. We had several hard showers of rain, accompanied with wind; but after midnight the weather began to moderate, and the sea to fall. It was very cold the whole night, and although it was in the middle of summer, and we were further south than Holland, we had to clothe ourselves well.

2*d*, *Wednesday*. The wind subsided a little in the day watch, and we made sail again, being able to sail W. by N., with fair speed. The latitude at noon was 50° 39′; the distance was computed to be eighty-eight miles; the course W. N. N., and N. W. by W., and the longitude 358°. During the night the wind blew sharper again.

3d, Thursday. This morning, the wind being very fresh, we tacked about and sailed S.; but about noon, observing two ships to the leeward of us, we tacked back again. These ships observing us, immediately tacked about with us, causing again no little fear in our ship. One of them was a large ship, the other a ketch; but in about an half an hour they both left us. They were without doubt ships on their homeward voyage, and would have spoken us, for they laid their course towards the channel. We sailed N. W., and gradually more westerly. We were in 51° 21′ of latitude, and 357° 10′ longitude; our course was N. W. by W., and distance seventy-two miles. In the afternoon the wind increasing and blowing in gusts, we reefed the topsails and let them stand so for the night.

4th, Friday. The topsails were taken in during the day watch, for though the wind was in the same direction as before, it blew harder and we had to lie to a little in a good rain, thus making but little progress. We found the latitude 51° 49′; the distance we calculated at eighty miles, the longitude 355° 30′, and the course N. W. by W. At noon the wind was due west, so that we could only keep to the north. At evening we tacked over on the other bow, and could then sail S. W. and S. W. by S. But the wind crept back again to the west, with heavy squalls, during the whole night, and finally was W. S. W.

5th, Saturday. In the day-watch the wind fell off, and the topsails were again set. The wind was more and more southerly. Our latitude was 51° 9′; the course S., so that we had kept the same longitude and progressed as much as the difference in latitude. The reefs of the topsails were let out and the cross-sails made. The wind then was S. E. and E. S. E., and we held our course with a stiff backstay breeze, carrying all sail, and making fine headway.

6th, Sunday. The wind favorable with a thick mist, which cleared up about nine o'clock, when it was quite calm. A girl attempting to rinse out the ship's mop let it fall overboard, whereupon the captain put the ship immediately to the wind and launched the jolly-boat, into which two sailors placed themselves at the risk of their lives in order to recover a swab, which was not worth six cents. As the waves were running high, there was no chance of getting it, for we could not see it from the ship. Yet the whole voyage must be delayed; these seamen be sent roving at the risk of their lives; we, with all the rest, must work fruitlessly for an hour or an hour and a half, and all that merely to satisfy and please the miserable covetousness of Margaret. Such wretched man-servers were these quakers. The jolly-boat came back, and we could not, without great difficulty and damage, get the sailors out of it, and haul the boat on board again. They looked as pale as if they were dead; one of them was poor Robin. Every thing being secured we again got under sail. It was so foggy at noon, we could not take the latitude. The calculation was, it was four miles less than yesterday. Our course had been W. S. W. and W. by S.; the distance run was about eighty miles; the longitude 353° 20′. In the afternoon the wind being ahead we had to lay over on the other bow, and then we could only sail W. N. W.; but by evening it began to blow and rain so hard that the topsails had to be taken in, and the mainsails struck. We were sailing on a cross sea, by reason of which our ship pitched so much that we could not stand or sit; but about midnight the weather moderated, the sky became clear; though the ship tossed still more than before.

7th, Monday. At day-break it was entirely calm, with the wind to the west, so that we drifted, with muzzled sails, in fine weather and sunshine. The latitude observed to-day was, 50° 58′; the distance run was calculated to be thirty-two miles; the entire course held about west. It remained calm the whole day and the following night.

8th, Tuesday. We had drifted in this way all night; but in the morning, there sprung up a light breeze from the east, which shifted a little to the north, and increased so, that we soon set sail, and for some hours made good progress. About nine o'clock we saw a large fish, some said it was a *pots-kop*,[1] others that it was a North-caper whale.[2] He had remained long enough with his back above water to be seen, spouting the sea-water high up in the air, like smoke. He swam close by the ship, before and behind; so that we all looked at him, his tumbling affording us a sweet and innocent amusement. In the meanwhile it continued misty and rainy. The wind was N. E., and the course S. W. by W. We calculated the latitude to be 50° 30′; the distance forty miles; and the longitude 351° 50′. The wind fell off towards evening; though while the sails remained wet, we went ahead tolerably fast, which encouraged the passengers as well as the others.

9th, Wednesday. The wind and course the same as before; the weather misty and rainy; and the progress good. Although we were now midway between the Land's End and Newfoundland, we saw to day a small bird, a sort of snipe. It was a little smaller than a *virvitan*. I think I have seen the like in Friesland; but we had noticed every day so many other water fowl, that I did not observe this one particularly. In consequence of the fog, we took no latitude, but computed it 49° 30′; the distance sailed one hundred and twenty miles; the longitude 349° 25′;

---

[1] The spermaceti whale.

[2] The ordinary whale from the North cape.

and the course S. W. by W. In the afternoon it was still; in the evening more so; and at night we drifted along becalmed.

10*th*, *Thursday*. In the day-watch the wind was from the west. We had for some days perceived fish, and did again to day, but we could not catch any. There was also a large whale or fin-fish near the ship, which we could see fully. About eleven o'clock, we observed a large ship ahead of us on the larboard. Every one immediately was alarmed again. The wind being at the same time from the east, we sailed S. and S. by E., in order to remain to the windward of the ship, which continued sailing in company with us thus the whole day. We found the latitude at noon, 49° 6′; the progress made was calculated at seventy-two miles; the longitude 347° 20′, and the main course W. by S. Towards evening, the ship hoisted her sails, which still more excited suspicion. Night coming on, and she being yet to the leeward, almost out of sight, the wind too being south, we ran straight before the wind, due north, without any light in the binnacle, in order that no flickering might be produced which would enable it to be seen from a distance. It was calm, with occasional breezes, and we sailed so the whole night.

11*th*, *Friday*. The wind during the day-watch again S. E., and more easterly, and we accordingly lay upon our old course, S. S. W. We looked after ships, but could see none, which allayed the fears of the passengers, and especially of Mr. Jan, who, however, imagined he had seen the other ship yet this morning. We obtained the latitude, which was 49° 16′; the course about W. by N.; the distance according to the log-board of yesterday till now, was about thirty-two miles. At times we had a light wind, at others it was calm, and so it continued the whole night. The longitude was 346° 20′.

12*th*, *Saturday*. We were somewhat aroused at night, by

two large whales, which swam in the dog-watch[1] close up to the ship, and drove sleep from our eyes by their hard blowing. It was pleasant and diverting in the clear atmosphere to see them. In the day-watch the sky began to be overcast, and a good wind to blow, which kept increasing till noon. During the morning there were many tunny fish around the ship or sea-hogs, for their heads and snouts are just like those of swine, and when they are cut open, so are their entrails.[2] They amused us with their quick swimming and tumbling. The harpoons and pikes were made ready, but none of them were struck. We found the latitude at noon 48° 58′; the course, W. S. W., the calculated distance forty-four or forty-eight miles; and the longitude 345° 25′. In the afternoon the breeze increased still more, and put all in good spirits; but our hearts ascended higher, and adored the giver of the wind, who brings it forth from his treasury when it pleases him. The breeze was fresh out of the northeast, and our course, W. N. W.; and so we advanced.

13*th*, *Sunday*. This morning the wind and course were the same as before, with misty and rainy weather, which made the sails tight, and aided our progress. There were many tunnies this morning around the ship, which again diverted us by their exhibitions and celerity; but none of them were harpooned. It was so foggy we could not obtain an observation of the sun, which we preferred to miss rather than lose the headway we were making, We computed it to be 48° 20′; the distance run one hundred and twenty miles; the course W. S. W., a little more west; the longitude 342° 30′. We had now for several days had an entirely different air, which felt sweet and agreeable, especially when the weather was clear and

---

[1] The two short watches between 4 and 6 o'clock, and 6 and 8 o'clock P. M. are called dog-watches.

[2] Porpoises.

fine; and even when it was cloudy and misty it was not so cold or sharp, but very pleasant and desirable. I knew I breathed differently from what I did before. There was no moon, and we made rapid progress; and it seemed the whole night, as if we were sailing through fire, in consequence of the sparkling of the water.

14*th*, *Monday*. From noon yesterday, and so on the night through, we had made very good progress, though not so great as the day before, the wind being somewhat lighter and more northerly, and during the night N. N. W. Last evening we had a great many porpoises around the ship, which, after supper, again amused us. At night the sea sparkled, and other fish appeared near the ship, bennets, dolphins and others, but we could not catch any of them. Our course was still W. S. W., with a light breeze. As it was cloudy we could not obtain the latitude, but calculated we were in 47° 30′; our progress one hundred and four miles; longitude 340° 30′; the course W. S. W. The sea had been for several days so smooth that the ship went ahead almost as gently as if we had been sailing on a river; but to-night we feared this would not last long, for we began to have some great threatenings out of the N. N. W. The wind also pulled so we could not sail sharp by the wind. So we ran S. W. by W., with fair progress. It began to blow a little more, and we took in the top gallant sails.

15*th*, *Tuesday*. The wind W. N. W., so we kept on our old course, and made rapid headway. About ten o'clock in the morning, we saw a ship ahead of us to the leeward, doing her best to come up to us; but not seeking or caring for that, we sailed a point higher, that is W. S. W., our old course; and continuing on this course, we saw that we outsailed her, and she fell off directly behind us. The sun broke out occasionally, and we endeavored to obtain an observation, but we could not hit it exactly, in consequence of the clouds and rolling sea; and I dared not, therefore, trust my own altogether. It was 46° 6′; the computed distance one hundred and thirty-six miles; the main course S. W. by W., a little westerly. We reckoned we had at noon to-day completed half our voyage, and we raised our hearts to God in thankfulness that he had hitherto preserved us by his fatherly care. Being now out of danger from the Turks our enemies, and as we thought, for the most part, from storms, we supplicated him to continue his blessings towards our persons, and towards the purpose to which he has called us, in order that we may perform it with gladness and sincerity of heart, to his glory, unto the going down of the sun. The sea began to be smooth again, and the wind to abate.

16*th*, *Wednesday*. In the day-watch it was perfectly calm. At day-light, we found ourselves between two ships, one lying close by us to the windward, with mizzen sail hoisted, and the other lay astern of us to the leeward, they being in company, as it appeared afterwards. We perceived still another vessel as far as we could see, behind us. We did not know what to think of all this; sometimes we kept up good courage; at other times we were fearful, the more so because when we showed our colors none of them did the like. The one astern of us, being the largest, did her best to pass us, or rather to get up to her companion. As we hauled off a point or two of the wind, our course being thus S. S. W., and a little breeze springing up at the same time, each one went her way; and as they sailed off by the wind, we gradually separated from them. We had no doubt they were French ships bound for Newfoundland or Canada. In looking at the water we saw the color was changed as if we were on soundings, which we did not doubt, because our reckoning or calculation made us against the false bank of Newfoundland. About ten o'clock we saw another ship ahead of us, sailing on the same course as the others, so that we ran across her. As it was sunshine and calm, it was a good opportunity to take the latitude. I found it 44° 35′. The course was S. W. by W. and W. S. W., which entirely agreed with our being as we thought this morning, upon the false bank of Terre Neuf. The distance run was one hundred and twelve miles, and the longitude 335° 30′. Although I heard that I differed in my reckoning from all the others, except the mate, which I did not know, I adhered nevertheless to my own. At noon we saw a piece of wood drifting, similar to a hanging ladder with which they climb trees, and some sharks swimming in sport and continually tumbling around it. We threw out a hook baited with a large piece of pork, but could not catch any of them. By evening it was quite calm, and in the night still more so.

17*th*, *Thursday*. In the day-watch the wind was S. E., and S. S. E., but light, though we could keep our course. The water was smooth and the sky clear, with an entirely different atmosphere from that over the sea in Holland. The breeze, however, began to increase gradually, and at noon we went forward finely. We saw another ship ahead of us, on the larboard, sailing west, like ourselves. We were able to take the latitude very exactly, and found it 44° 16′. Our progress we calculated at thirty-two to thirty-six miles, but setting our plan on the chart of increasing degrees upon the obtained latitude, according to the course sailed, we found we must have gone a greater distance. There must either have been some current, or the plan of the foregoing day did not stand southerly enough; for it should have stood at 35′ and did stand at 58′, that is 23′ difference. The longitude was 333°. We expected to see some signs of the bank of Newfoundland, as we had for a day or two sailed through very many *quallen* or galls, besides some little *mizzens* or *galleys*, which are a kind of galls, drifting or sailing upon the water, having membranes like a small sail, in the form of a mizzen or galley sail, from which they are so called.[1] These were all signs of the banks of Newfoundland. However, I dared not trust myself entirely, because others who had so much more experience in those things than I had, did not make us so far west. At noon it blew harder, and we had a rolling sea from the S. S. W., so that our topgallant sails were taken in. The sea did not look entirely blue nor black, as it does where there is no bottom, but a clearer green, almost the same as you see in running out of the channel; but about six o'clock in the evening, we observed the water had perceptibly changed greener, but by dark it was all gone again. We judged from this circumstance, that we had sailed certainly over a point of the great bank, as our calculation showed.

18*th*, *Friday*. The wind continued N. N. E. and N., and we kept our course. We observed some paleness in the water. My good friend having eaten last evening some salted fish, cold, and only with a little vinegar, was seized in the night with a severe pain in his stomach, but having taken about nine o'clock a little warm wine, with Spanish soap, he vomited and felt better, and began to rest and recover, for which we were tenderly sensible of the goodness of our Father. This morning a ship ahead of us to the windward, came straight down upon us, evidently with the design of speaking to us. We braced the foresail to the mast and waited for her. As she approached she let fly the English

---

[1] *Besaenties of galleytics.* Reference is here made to a species of vivified substance, — the *physalis pelagicus*, commonly called, by sailors, the Portuguese man-of-war, which floats like the nautilus upon the surface of the sea, with its body inflated in order to catch the wind, as a sail, and with tentacles extending below to guide it. The common stinging gall of our waters belongs to the same family. Our word *gall* as applied to such fishy matter, seems to be a local word, handed down to us by the Dutch settlers.

flag, and we immediately did the same. She ran astern of us, and we hailed her. She was from the West India islands, bound for England. We told them where we were from and where bound, and how it stood with England and France; with which they were content, and sailed on their course, and we on ours. We found the latitude at noon 43° 34′; the distance eighty miles, and the longitude 334° 20′. In the afternoon it began to blow hard, and we reefed our topsails. The wind kept increasing more and more, and at evening we could sail only W. by S., and in the first watch, only west. It blew so hard that the topsails were taken in; and the wind sharpening up still more, we wore around about midnight and steered S. S. W., making little headway in consequence of the rolling of the sea and the short sail on.

19*th, Saturday.* The wind abating somewhat at day-light, the topsails were set again; but the wind afterwards springing up on the other bow, we could at last only sail southerly. The latitude at noon was 43° 12′; the whole distance run from noon yesterday was sixty miles, and the longitude was 330° 20′. In the afternoon we saw weeds drifting, which grow on the bottom of the sea, and in Holland, on piles which stand in the salt water, by which we were confirmed in our belief that we were on the banks. We had not had for a day or two those heavy swells, but short and pushing ones as they are in the North sea, beating against each other. We could now sail only S. by E. and S. S. E., but the wind afterwards running out we sailed S. by W. and S. S. W.

20*th, Sunday.* The wind being still westerly, we sailed S. by W. and S. S. W., and it blowing a little harder, we reefed our main topsail again. A whale aroused us for a while with his tumbling around the ship. We saw also flying fish, from which we supposed there were dorados or other fish near by, but we neither saw nor caught any.

We found the elevation of the pole above the horizon at noon to be 42° 12′; the course due south; the distance from *bestek* to *bestek*,[1] sixty to sixty-four miles; and of course the same longitude as before, 330° 20′. The wind continued westerly, and we made no great progress.

21*st*, *Monday*. The wind kept the same, and we continued the same course. The latitude was 40° 34′, being that of Sandy Hook in New Netherland, and we only wished now an easterly wind which might carry us about twelve hundred miles westerly. The distance traversed was eighty to eighty-four miles; the longitude 330°; and the course nearly S. by W. Our cooper was a little Friesland boor from Bolswart, whom Margaret had hired for four years, for twenty-eight dollars a year. He had to work hard at his trade on board the ship, although his wages were not to commence until he reached land, It has been frequently a wonder to me that he has not recognized me, for he has at * * * * *.[2] Hendrick, the ship's pump-maker, worked a little at our house, where I have seen him myself, and although he claimed no acquaintance, he complained to me at times how Margaret had cheated him, and all who were now in her service. He began to-day to make some buckets in which he could not succeed very well for want of tools. I had compassionating blood, and helped him make them right. I made him a bucket, at which Mr. Jan and the captain

[1] We adopt this word from the Dutch of the journal for the sake of convenience, as there does not appear to be any corresponding word in English. It is used to indicate a plan or plot marked out on a chart for the purpose of designating the course of a ship during the preceding day, or any other given time, and the point attained in sailing, during that period. It is employed in the present instance in the text, metonymically, to signify the time of day of making the plot or plan. From *bestek* to *bestek* therefore means here, from noon of the preceding day to noon of the day under mention. It seems to have been a kind of traverse table.

[2] This blank occurs in the original, in which it is left purposely unfilled.

were highly pleased, and that perhaps was the reason why Mr. Jan was so liberal of Margaret's property, for he gave every one of our mess a glass of Madeira wine, which was quite a wonder, for we had never seen any thing of the kind in him. Towards evening the ship was washed out, and in doing it, they found a sea-cat asleep which was not longer than a finger, but really monstrous. We supposed from this circumstance we were near dorados or dolphins, but we discovered none. The wind was somewhat northerly, so that we could sail S. W. and W. S. W., but it changed back again afterwards. The sea, which was exceedingly smooth, and a very clear and soft sky, made the evening hour extremely fine. The sky, with thin transparent snow-white clouds upon its glittering blue, was adorned by a bright, clear setting sun, which, in proportion as it declined and departed to another world, there to display the splendor which the creator has bestowed upon him, changed these clouds from white to shining brightness, and imparted to them for a while the golden luster of his fire. The sky around was not a pure sky-blue, but was of a mixed blue and green, sparkling like the flame when copper is brought to a glowing heat; that which was nearer the sun being more like the sun, and that further removed from him, gradually fading into bright blue mingled with silver; so that we not only saw all the colors of the rainbow, but all hues and colors, all shining according to their natures, with a brilliancy of their own, displaying them in that perfect splendor, which is so agreeable, and capable of enrapturing man. But one of the greatest beauties to be observed was their wonderful unity or harmony, or blending together; for although these colors and shining splendors were as manifold as the degrees and minutes, yea points of removal from their centre, the sun, which shone the brightest and most, yet one could not discover where they separated or where they united, or even a point where one could be distinguished from the next, so united were they all, and so manifold and distinct was their unity without being divided. And although all this had a great and starry brightness, it was nevertheless so moderated and tempered through all the diversity of colors that we could not only look at each one in particular, but also the whole together, yea even at the sun itself, the centre of this lordly perspective, and distinct from these surrounding splendors, as the extreme point of their concentration. No part lost any thing by viewing the whole, and the whole lost nothing by viewing a part, nor did any one part lose by viewing any other part, nor the most excellent by viewing the least, nor the least, by viewing the most excellent, so exact was their unity in their multiplicity, and their multiplicity in their unity. No sooner had their glorious beauty left us, than turning around we saw not indeed the same, but its expression and projection, in a full moon, coming up in the east, as the sun was setting in the west. And as the one had shown himself like burning gold, the other showed herself as well polished, or burnished silver, upon the same field as the sun had done, but according to her nature and power and color; for as the sky and the clouds which were next the sun participated most in the color of the sun, so those nearest the moon had the greatest resemblance to the moon. These indeed were as white as snow and transparent, so that the light of the moon shining through their white thinness gave them a luster like silver and that upon a heaven's blue field. The outermost clouds were black or dark, while the outermost of the other (the sun) were a pure white, so that the one began with a color and glory with which the other terminated.

The peculiar feelings which the Lord excited in us over these and the like occurrences are not the material for the relation of a voyage. They can be expressed in some other place or perhaps never. He is master, and does as it pleases him.

I have strayed far out of my course, and must look again upon the compass and see how we sailed. It was about S. S. W, and S. W. by S., through the whole night, during which it was very warm. In the day-time we were on deck, under the sails, which threw down upon us much of the wind they received, so that we did not feel the heat; but at night and in our berth it was much greater, because there were so many persons shut up close together, the greater portion of whom were women and children. Right over our berth was the mate's wife with one child sick with the measles, and another one which we expected every moment to die, and to which we rendered our services by giving our medicines, as well as to others; yes, and even to Margaret, after providence had shown they were needful to any one, as well as any thing else we might have which the Lord had given us by his goodness.

22d, Tuesday. The wind having shifted a little, as we have said, we could sail only S. W. and S. W. by S., with a light breeze and a smooth sea. The weather was fine and pleasant, but warm, so that we were dressed in somewhat less than our summer clothing. Many began to go bare-legged; and to sleep out of their berths. We found the latitude at noon 39° 27′, the course S. W., the distance computed at ninety-two to ninety-six miles, and the longitude 328° 24′. When we came from table at noon, we were diverted with a very pleasant exhibition upon the smooth and level surface of the sea. A great fleet of porpoises came from the south, extending as far off as we could see, leaping and tumbling with such swiftness and speed towards our ship, that it seemed as if they would certainly have taken it by storm. It is incredible how far they sprang up into the air; but us they came near to us they checked themselves, and went swimming, leaping and tumbling around us. One of the largest of them sprung full the length of a man high out of the water, and cutting capers in the air, made every one laugh; then fell backwards between two waves and disappeared beneath them, and we saw him no more. This was the final exhibition in the scene, which lasted half an hour, and then they all left. There were flying fish also flying out of the water while the others were swimming in it. Some are of opinion that these do not fly, but only spring out of the water; but I am certain such persons have never well looked at this fish, or observed how it flies. It is about the size of a herring, though we saw none as large as that during the voyage; it is more like the smelt. Close behind the head where other fish usually have two small fins, the flying fish has two long ones, which when stretched out, reach nearly to the tail. The fins have five or six little bones in them, which beginning at the end of the fin run finer and finer to nothing, and constitute the strength of the fin. You never see this fish spring out of the water like other fish, and fall in it again; but it comes from the water not upward, but like an arrow shot from a bow, spreading its two fins like wings which it does not flap as the feathered tribe does, for it is not of that nature; but moves them quickly and gently, the same as a certain insect which I have seen in Europe, and which in Friesland they call *coolwachter* and in the land of Cleves *rontbout.* It is true it does not fly high, although sometimes it flies as high as a ship; nor far, yet as far as a musket shot; but whether it be true that it cannot fly any further, because its wings are dry, or because it has no power to sustain its body longer in the air, which is more probably the truth, or for both reasons, I cannot say, nor do I believe any body can. It flies seldom alone, but in schools sometimes of hundreds together. Fish in the sea swim together much in schools or fleets, and it seldom happens when you see a fish of a certain kind alone that there are not more of the same sort to be seen about. When a school of other fish, whether dorados or others, come among a school of flying fish, which serve as food for them, and the large fish hunt the flying fish for this purpose, the flying fish strive to save themselves by flying. This is *en passant*. The view of these fish was much more agreeable than the sight and smell of a quantity of spoiled salted fish among our provisions, which was so offensive you could not stand near it, and which was being dried so that it might be used in the ship. The wind freshened up in the evening so that we could only sail S. S. W. and S. W. by S., and thus we proceeded the whole night.

23*d*, *Wednesday*. The wind continuing almost the same, our course was nearly the same, sometimes a little less, and sometimes a little more than S. W. by S. There was a light breeze, beautiful and clear weather, and a smooth sea. This was delightful. If one could always have such sailing on the sea, it would be a very agreeable business. The cheerfulness which such fine weather excited in us was disturbed when we saw the captain, looking like a dark cloud, beat our cook severely with a rope, for some trifling reason, as they said; but as he is a quaker, we will take occasion to describe him and his, in another place. The latitude to-day was 37° 51′ the course kept S. S. W., the calculated distance 112 miles, and the longitude 327° 30′. At noon we saw a turtle drifting past the ship, quite large, and lying asleep on the surface of the water. We saw also a school of flying fish. The wind and our course continued the same, not only until evening, but all night.

24*th*, *Thursday*. The wind being still westerly, our course was mostly S. W., with a light breeze, calm sea and clear sky; but the wind began to shift gradually to the north so that we could sail S. W. by W., and finally W. S. W. Towards noon the wind ran N., and N. by E., but we continued to hold our course. Our latitude at noon was 36°

32′, the course S. W., the distance 104 miles, and the longitude 325° 56′. In the afternoon the wind improved still more, so that it was due east, when we sailed W. by S., and this continued all day and night, with a good top-sail breeze.

25*th*, *Friday*. We sailed till eight o'clock in the morning W. by S., when we changed our course to the west, having sailed upon the former course according to calculation 88 miles. The wind was now E. N. E., and thus for the most part we sailed before it, and therefore our bonnet sails were made. We observed dolphins or dorados near the ship, which are agreeable to look at, especially when they are swimming. We did our best to catch or strike some of them, but without success. The latitude at noon we found to be 35° 37′, the distance sailed 124 to 128 miles, and the longitude 323° 48′.

26*th*, *Saturday*. The wind still N. E., and we kept our course W., and W. by N., with a light breeze, fine weather and a smooth sea, making fair headway. Although we had hitherto caught no fish, one caught itself during the night. The fish line had been left trailing out behind the ship, by which means it had been caught, and dragged along. It was not only dead, but the belly was all burst open, by reason of the quantity of water which had been forced in it, for his mouth was wide open with the hook and line in it. It had strained the line so that the line itself was almost parted. It was almost like an eel, or rather a *geep*.[1] It was so hideous and looked so savage, that my companion inquired if it were not a sea-devil. As he had heard of sea-devils, he thought this certainly was one. I had never to my knowledge seen the like, except only the picture of one at Amsterdam, caught under the equinoctial, and

[1] A small fish of a sea-green color, with a long pointed nose like the beak of a snipe. It is caught by means of nets, by thousands along the sea shore of Holland, at certain seasons of the year, and is used to bait hooks to catch other fish.

painted on account of its rarity. I have sketched it here as well as I could.

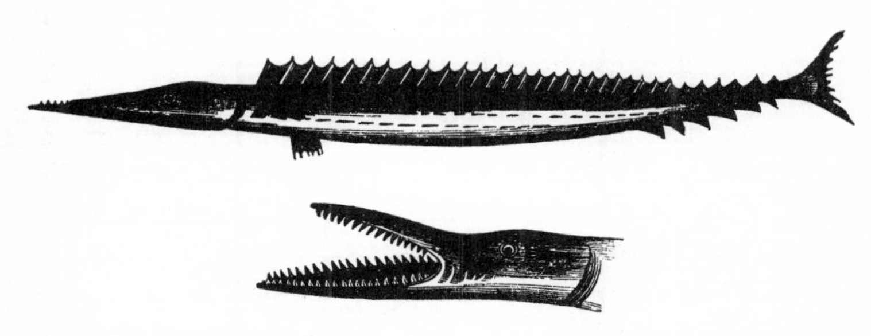

Its flesh, when it was cooked, was quite good, tasting almost like a mackerel's.[1] Our latitude at noon to-day was 36° 14′; the course held W. by N.; the distance sailed 112 miles; and the longitude obtained 321° 40′; and so our progress continued this day and the following night.

27*th*, *Sunday*. Every thing went on sweetly during the night. The sky was beautiful and the sea still. Our course west with a light breeze. For two days, now, we had perceived a motion of the sea from the S. E., which sometimes forbodes such a wind. We found the latitude 36° 6′, having been carried a little south, which sometimes happens from the swaying of the rudder, or it indicates sometimes a current. The distance we had run was seventy-five miles, the course more W. than W. by S. At noon the wind shifted round to the south. The longitude was 320°. The mate came at noon to-day, while I was putting my *bestek* on the chart, and looked at it. He was surprised that I was so far west. He said I differed 320 miles from him, which might well be, as I had never put my knowledge in practice, and could not now use any thing except compasses on the chart; but the result will show how it was, though we recalled afterwards how doubtful he was in his language on the subject.

---

[1] It appears to have been the Spanish mackerel.

28*th*, *Monday*. The wind continued with a light breeze, and our course was due west; as the wind was a little more on the side, we set more sail, which drove the ship more rapidly ahead. The sea rolled a little out of the S. S. E. and S.; its color was changed, as if there were no bottom. The latitude was 35° 52′, so that we had gained a little south. The distance we calculated at 80 miles. The course was S. and W. by S., and so continued during the day and night.

29*th*, *Tuesday*. During the night we had some gusts of wind, accompanied with lightning and rain. For several days it had been very hot. The wind then changed from the S. E. to the S. and S. S. W., with heavy swells of the sea from the S. W. We had for several days past seen some arrowtails, a species of bird like sea gulls, and so named because their tails ran out sharp, like an arrow. They are entirely white, with the exception of a little black on the head and extreme tip of the wings. They are somewhat smaller than those I have seen in the (West India) islands. They kept flying around the ship continually, as if they wanted to alight, but when they saw the people they flew away. We sailed close by the wind, W. by N. and W. N. W. The latitude at noon was 36° 17′, the course W. by N., the distance sailed 64 to 68 miles, and the longitude 318° 20′. It was five weeks to-day since we left Falmouth, and we estimated we were still about 950 miles from our place of destination. Before evening the wind was S. S. W., so that we could not sail higher than N. N. W. and N. W. It shifted at length to W. and W. N. W., so that we had to sail N. and N. by E. About midnight we had a severe gust of wind with much thunder and lightning and heavy rain. We wore ship half round to the south, and were able to sail S. W. and W. S. W., although soon afterwards the wind subsided.

30*th*, *Wednesday*. The wind was W. S. W., and we therefore steered N. N. W. and N. W., with a rolling sea, but not a hard blow, and thus could make little headway. The arrowtails still flew about the vessel, and some of them came nearer. Our latitude was 36° 59′, the course kept N. W., the distance sailed 60 miles, and the longitude 310°. The wind veered more and more to the west, and we could only sail S. S. W. and S. W. by W., with a light breeze, and making slow progress. This continued the whole afternoon, but in the night it became entirely calm.

31*st*, *Thursday*. The wind was very still, and we steered the same as yesterday; but we did nothing except drift. We were in hopes, however, of a good wind, and it seemed with some probability, for the sea swells came strong out of the north, and there were also heavy swells out of the south and S. S. W., which struck very hard against each other, and caused the waves to roll high in the air, and retarded our progress. We observed a large sea pike near the ship, six feet long, but we could not catch it. We could not obtain the latitude in consequence of the rain. We reckoned our course S. S. W. and S. by W.; the distance 32 to 36 miles, and the longitude 315° 20′. We had again a pleasant diversion in a large school of porpoises, which came springing out towards us as if each one wished to be the first near the ship or into it; but after they had sported about half an hour they left us. In the afternoon the wind blew from the south, but not steadily. The billows drove against each other so that they stood like mountains. A little later the wind began to blow faintly from the north, and towards evening more and more from the east, when the swells in the south and the north began to strike against each other, although the wind came between them from the east, as if to separate them. About the third hour of the evening-watch it thundered and lightened so frightfully that we were all stupified and blinded. The sea ran so high that we worked lustily to take in all sail as soon as possible, in order to prevent our being upset. The mainsail was lowered and furled, but we kept up a little sail afore. We sailed then W. by N., and sometimes W. by S., till in the day-watch, when the wind changing from the east to E. by S., with thunder and heavy rain, we made gradually a little more sail, but we were quickly compelled by the squalls to take it in again. This was in the night, when we saw several meteors which sat upon the mizzen-mast and yard arm, which is generally considered a sign that the storm is at its highest and will soon abate; but how this rule may be, we had some experience, and will mention. We also heard a great screaming of sea gulls and other birds, which now in the dark flew around the ship and above the masts, the like of which the mate and others, who had long navigated the sea, said they had never heard before.

September 1st, *Friday*. The wind still E. and E. S. E., with a stiff breeze; but the great swells from the S. and S. S. W., as well as from the north, continued, by which we were tossed about the same as we had been for several days. We were afraid the ship's boat might be thrown out of its place, as it was not too firmly fastened, and cause us great inconvenience, which we already began to experience from some full water casks which stood on deck, and were rolling about loose, and which we had great difficulty to bring right. We could not obtain the latitude this noon, in consequence of the cloudy sky. We calculated it to be 37°; the distance sailed 80 miles, the course W. by N., and the longitude 314° 10′. The before mentioned birds remained with us still. We saw also two flocks of other birds, of fifteen or sixteen each; they were larger than starlings, and of a black color. They flew about the ship. We observed, besides, great numbers of fish continually springing out of the water. At first we supposed they were springers, a species of fish so called because they are continually jumping up out of the water; but these were larger and like haddock. We also saw a turtle. All these signs denoted land, and the weather indicated the Bermudas, that is to say, the Bermuda storms, for I do not know that they ever pass this island without encountering a storm. Long experience has established the fact; and the old mariners call it the sea of devils, not only because it is never passed without a terrific storm and heavy thunder and lightning, but also on account of the apparitions of frightful forms and faces and other spookery, which appear, some really such, and some frivolous. How it was in the first discovery of strange lands and wildernesses, we cannot now say, or determine from present experience, because such things have happened heretofore which no longer occur. As to the storms, they are established facts; as to the sights, they are not without probability, and they were confirmed, to some extent, in my mind, by our mate, who had passed by this island several times, and had never failed of the storms; and as for the sights, he told me that being once close to the island, beset by a severe storm and a dark night on a lee shore, it seemed as if the air was full of strange faces with wonderful eyes standing out of them, and it so continued until daylight. He told this without any leading to such things, or without having ever heard what I myself had read concerning them. It was in my youth that I had read of them, in a little book called *De Silver Poort-Klock* (The Silver Gate-bell). This island lies in 30° 32′ north latitude, and 313° 40′ of longitude; but nearly a degree further west than it is laid down on the charts, as the mate told me he had observed. It is a small, but very fertile and healthy island, about seven hundred and sixty miles from the main land of America, and of all its neighbors bears the best cedar now to be obtained. I have conversed with persons who said they had had, at the same time, the cedar of

Lebanon and the cedar of the Bermudas, and they could not discover any difference between the two, and the Bermuda was as brown and strong as the Lebanon. This is rendered probable, to some extent, because the island, lying in the middle of the sea, has a cooler atmosphere. It produces plenty of oranges, apples and lemons, which the English who live there carry by ship loads to Virginia, New Netherland and New England, where they do not grow, in order to sell them, as I have observed myself in New Netherland; and I think also tobacco, sugar, indigo, ginger, speckled wood, Campeachy wood, &c. It is somewhat rocky around it, and has, on the north and west points, great reefs which extend far out into the sea. This island we were now passing, at a distance of about 260 to 280 miles to the north by east.

2*d*, *Saturday*. The wind had been increasing through the whole night from the S. E. In the morning we saw some flocks of birds flying around us, a kind of small snipes like those of New Netherland, as some passengers said, who recognized them. We could obtain no observation to-day in consequence of the cloudy sky. While going ahead with a strong S. S. E. wind, sailing west, we had heavy rolling from the south. We reckoned the latitude 36° 30′, the distance 160 miles, the course W. by S., and the longitude 314° 20′. In the afternoon the wind blew so by degrees from the S. S. W. and S. W., that we had before evening taken in all our sails, and ran along without any sails at all at the rate of 120 miles in twenty-four hours, but not long. It was such frightful weather that I am unable to describe it.

The heavens were entirely shut off, and not the least opening was to be seen. The wind blew so hard from the S. S. W. and S. W., that it was incredible; for when we stood close by each other and called out as loud as we were able, we could scarcely hear or understand each other.

The billows ran as high as mountains; yes, as mountains. They were extremely large and majestic, and exhibited the great power of their creator, as pleasing as they were fearful to us to behold. They rolled on with an inexpressible order and gravity, moving slowly and loftily. They were dark and grey in color, and bore upon their round backs other small waves, from which the wind drove off into the air so much water incessantly, that it flew like smoke or snow over the sea without the least diminution. This flood of flying sea water had such a direction over the ship, which was lying across the sea, that we could not see during the day from the stern to the bow; and at night we could not see the least thing before our eyes. Although these large billows did not pour, for if they had done so we could not have withstood them a quarter of the time, yet the water of the small waves had such a passage to the ship that it was as if it were constantly thrown from above; and it came with such force and in such quantity that the ship could not discharge it through the scuppers, but was all the time under water. We had taken down our topmast early, and struck the yards and secured them against dangling. The rudder, which was held by two or three persons, and which was sometimes turned to avoid the falling of the sea, was several times wrested out of their hands, and those who had hold of it thrown from one side to the other upon one another, in great danger of being injured by the tiller or otherwise. Several times they came running up because they supposed the tiller was broken, although it was made entirely of iron. The compasses, which were wet continually, could hold no point in consequence of the terrible rolling of the ship, which rolled so awfully that the yard arm seemed every time to touch the great billows on the *windward* side. Every thing bent and cracked so that you could hear nothing else. There were no means of going about, or standing, or sitting, or lying down, but you had to do all these things together, as well as hanging on, in order to keep yourself secure, whether you were in your berth or out of it. It was as if you were in the sea, except that the water came falling on the head, and so over the whole body. Mouth, nose and eyes were so full of water from the spray, that you could not draw a breath or see. All were constantly wiping their eyes and blowing their noses, like boys swimming. Our eyes suffered the most, for they felt as if they were frosted with sand or water. They bound a flag to the back stay or mizzenmast, before their eyes, in order to see how the wind shot, but they had to go close to it before they could see it, and it was not there a long time before it was blown into a thousand tatters. Indeed, I cannot describe how wretched it was. I was on the first watch, although there was not much watch kept. In short, the sea air and water were so mingled together you could scarcely discern where they separated; and so it was day and night. I stood much by the mate, in order to help him watch the pouring of the sea. We imagined several times we saw openings in the sky, which led us to believe there would be a change, but they were merely the falling of the sea, so high did it run and so much did it fill the air. It continued so all night, and even seemed to increase. My watch being out, I went below — not to sleep, for there was no probability of that, but to rest myself somewhere on a chest, wet as I was. Even that was not to be done, for the casks and chests were all loose and being thrown from one side to the other, so there was danger of being injured. As there was no one else there to assist in making them fast, Gerrit, the passenger, and myself, did our best endeavors to do so, and after much scrambling succeeded in putting them in place a little. It was not, however, much better below than above deck, for all the hatches being shut it was so close and confined that one seemed to be stifled with a stinking, burning air, which, if it had continued long, would have produced sickness. The pumps had to be kept going all the time, for, although the ship was tolerably tight below water, she was very leaky above; and so much water came down the hatchways, although they were covered with tarpaulin, that it was the same as if water were poured down on our heads. To put on dry clothes was not to be thought of, as it was equally wet below and above; and even if we did not put our heads out, the first wave which broke over the ship made us as wet as before. As day approached the storm rather increased than diminished. Hearing a clamor, I went on deck again, in order to see what the Lord might will concerning us, and arriving above I beheld a sad prospect indeed. The ship looked as desolate as if she had already suffered shipwreck; the mainmast swinging to and fro, the shrouds and ropes attached to them flying, their chains and chain bolts loose, the pumps choked with sand, gravel and pebbles, and their spouts broken. The carpenter was called, in order to repair the pumps, which kept him constantly at work. He cursed and swore at Margaret, because there was no leather in the pump, which was true, for there had been only a little in it, or the leather was like duck, and also because there were no more spouts, of the necessity of which he had warned her at Amsterdam, but which were not bought by her through parsimony, disregarding what the carpenter told her. I did my best to pacify him. He was a wicked wretch, and unwilling because he could not have a moment's rest. He had afterwards to secure the mast, whereupon he raved and swore anew at the captain, and declared he would not do it unless they first threw overboard the jolly-boat, which was over his tool-chest, for the captain had set the chest in the boat, and had placed the jolly-boat upside down over the boat, so that the chest could not be got at as easily as he wished, and he had, on that account, grumbled and scolded throughout the whole voyage. The captain attempted to strike him. The sailors cursed and swore at each other. I had told the mate during the night that this drifting across seas could not continue long without sail, and that the course was to take below all that was on deck, or we would be turned upside down, or stove in, by a single wave. Now I heard that the captain and mate were disagreed on this point, the mate proposing and wishing to make some sail, the captain interposing objections, either because he did not understand it, or because he was afraid of the sails. Observing this, and knowing our danger, my heart rose to God that he would look upon us in our condition, and be merciful to us in whatever manner he might be pleased to treat us, committing ourselves into his strong and gracious keeping. This was while the captain and mate were standing together, and having their conversation. I made bold and went up to them. I told the captain that sail should be made aft, if it were not more than a hand's breadth, or else, to all appearances, it would not continue long with us; that this would turn the ship against the sea. He made difficulty. I said they could try it with a bonnet, stretching it from the main shrouds to the mizzen shrouds, when they would see it would help them. Meanwhile, feeling my heart touched and tender, I went below to tell my comrade our condition. I embraced him and committed him, and he me, to our beloved Father, in case there might be no opportunity afterwards to do so, if he were pleased further to dispose of us. He dressed himself as well as he could, and we clambered on deck, one behind the other. He was astonished at seeing us in such a state, and was able to tell how it was, although ignorant of many particulars. He posted himself aft, before the hut, on the larboard side, to the windward, under the tent; but he had not stood there long before a sea came over the gunwale, breaking everywhere, and streaming over him. He turned his back to it, and said he never felt such a weight. In such cases one must hold himself fast where he is, or he will be washed overboard. In the meanwhile they were busy in doing what I had proposed, and succeeded, with great difficulty and danger, in fastening the bonnet from one set of shrouds to the other. As soon as it was done they found relief for the ship, and that she resisted the waves better; and it encouraged them immediately to see if they could not make more sail, and even set the mizzen-sail. The mizzen-yard was below and all hands were called to get it up. They fastened the sail upon the *stoot garen*, which was not very good; and therefore before it was hoisted half way up, the *stoot garen* broke into pieces, and the sail was blown quickly to tatters, which was not to be wondered at, for the sail was very old. This was dangerous work for the poor sailors, who were dispersed here and there, and liable to be struck by the sail, and some of whom were hanging and dangling from the ropes over the sea; but none of them were injured. The yard arm was hauled down again, the old sail taken off, and a new mizzen-sail brought out set upon better *stoot garen*, and hoisted as it had to be. They immediately found it to be a great help. In the mean time, I went to my comrade, who observing me was much affected, and said to me, *le Seigneur s'elevera et nous sauvera.* Indeed, the weather was then at its worst, and continued so till noon. There were no means of eating or drinking any thing, except small pieces of dry bread, when any could be found dry, for it was most all wet which could be got at; and much of that in the bread room, was wet with salt water. The water, which was to be had was brackish. We had great alteration either from working or from the flying salt water which we had taken in through our mouths and noses; and it was necessary for us to take a little strong drink. In the afternoon some said it began to moderate; but so slowly they could hardly work. They therefore let every thing be as it was. As the storm had arisen slowly, so it subsided even more slowly. When the weather began to moderate my comrade inquired of several persons who had been much at sea, and of one who had made three voyages to the East Indies, whether they had ever experienced such weather, and they said they had not. Neither had I. There are, however, always some persons very haughty as to what happens to them, and so now, there were one or two who said they had seen worse storms. What they may have seen I do not know; but this I do know, that this one was something extraordinary, according to all that I had ever heard, or could conclude from other storms of which I had heard or read. It is not to be supposed that those are greater in which many ships are lost, for that happens frequently when the storms are not half so severe; or that those are lighter where there are none lost, as in this case; for that is according as it pleases the Lord, who makes it light or heavy for the accomplishment of his purposes. I remarked this storm, or the force of this storm, was very high up in the air, whereby the sea was driven up so high, and so slowly, and so easily, that is, rolled without breaking by reason, perhaps, of the great depth there.

When I reflect upon what the Lord thus exhibited to me, what power, what majesty, what gravity, order and regularity, what glory, what grandeur and extensiveness, how many of his attributes, did he display, such as when, by his infinite power, he created all things. So much does he manifest these perfections where he works, and after he works, which is only a continuation of his power and attributes in part, as he has shown them in the whole. But especially what a glorious picture did he vouchsafe to represent to us, over a small part of the earth, of what he did over the whole earth, at the time of the deluge, when he swept away all that was upon it. These sentiments I have expressed in a measure before; and perhaps the Lord will cause them to be still better expressed, for he permits such things to come before us in order that we may see as in a glass who he is, and that he always works according to what he is, that is, all his works are worthy of him, especially those which he does extraordinarily, and so that we can apprehend them. It is certainly to his greater glory, and for the purpose of teaching us to know who he is, and who we are, so that we may learn to fear him, and give him what belongs to him. Amen. This doleful Sunday passed, the wind gradually abated; and so we passed the night.

4*th*, *Monday*. The wind having subsided, they were early on hand this morning to repair damages. It looked wretchedly enough. The topmast was raised, the yards hoisted up and sail made. Every one looked as weather beaten as if he had been in the water, as indeed was the fact. The hatches were opened through which an air and dampness issued as from an oven; and clothes and bedding were brought on deck to be dried and aired. The ship was so full of them up to the round top that she looked strange from the outside. They lay all over the ship as thick as if it had been the North Market at Amsterdam. Every thing had become wet. There was not a berth which had been tight or free from water. We let those who were most in a hurry go ahead, and as there was no room for us we took the next day to ourselves. The ship was turned to the south, for the wind has shifted round a little more westerly. We obtained an observation at noon, and found the latitude was 37°. We reckoned the distance we had sailed and drifted at sixty to sixty-four miles; the course west by north; and the longitude 313° 8′. At noon we were drifting in a calm; the fish came shooting up from below, and many dolphins were near the ship. Although we did our best we could not catch any of them. We drifted thus the whole afternoon and night, which happened very well, as it afforded every one on board an opportunity to rest, for all were tired out, and we particularly so. My eyes were so sore that I could hardly open them. Whenever I looked at a candle, many rings, colored like the rainbow, appeared around the flame. All my limbs seemed as if they were broken, and I also suffered much internally.

5th, Tuesday. It still continued calm. We caught a dolphin early in the morning. It is a very pretty fish, a species of round fish, but flat on the sides. Its color is a sky-blue ground with a golden hue over it, and I observed the older it is the more golden it is. On account of this golden appearance, I believe it is called *dorado* by the Portuguese, who doubtless were the first to eat it, when they began to make their long voyages. On the blue skin there are spots of a darker blue, which look pretty, and are set off by the gold color. It has no scales, or very small ones; its fins and tail are very bright, and exhibit great brilliancy when it is swimming. Its flesh is good but rather dry, as is the case generally with all sea fish. The captain had this one prepared and dressed with sauce; it was good and refreshed and strengthened us very much; but when we went to breakfast, we found there had happened a great misfortune to our mess. All our butter had been lost during the storm, through the negligence of the person having it in charge. The latitude at noon to-day was 36° 45′, the distance sailed forty miles; the course W. by N., the longitude 312° 20′. Shortly after midday we caught a shark which had been swimming for an hour alongside of the ship. He was so heavy that it was as much as three of us could do, to haul him on deck. When we got him in the ship, every body had to keep out of his way. He tried hard to bite, for which purpose there were three rows of teeth in his mouth close to each other. They endeavored to thrust a stick of wood down his throat, into his belly, in order to prevent his biting; but he struck around lustily whenever they came near him for that purpose. They cut off his tail with an ax, thus depriving him of his greatest power, and he soon bled to death. They then opened his head and took the brains out, which were as white as snow; these are esteemed a valuable medicine for women in childbirth; for which purpose the English use it a great deal. They also skinned him. The skin when dried is used to smooth and polish woodwork. If the sailors wish to eat the flesh they cook it by the fire as ours did; but this desire generally passes off with their first voyage, for the flesh is not good for much. It is like that of the thorndike or scate, but hard, and of a strong flavor. There is only one bone in the body, the back-bone, which the sailors cut out and preserve as a rarity, and make buttons out of it for their frocks and trowsers. We also caught several small fish of different kinds, like the carp, sole, seableak and others. The calm continued nearly till midnight, when a light breeze sprang up out of the south, and we continued sailing west. It was now six weeks since we left England.

6th, Wednesday. The wind, and our course remained as before. The sailors were still employed in repairing the ship and rigging. We found the latitude to-day to be 36° 56′; the computed distance sailed forty-eight miles; the course mostly west, and the obtained longitude 311° 20′. We caught another dolphin which happened well for us. We kept our course as before; and at night the wind began to freshen up a little.

7th, Thursday. The wind was S. S. W.; the course W. N. W., with a topsail breeze, fine weather and smooth water. The sailors commenced scraping the outside of the ship, in order to dress her up and make her look well by the time we arrived in port. They smeared her over with a mixture of grease and tar, so that she might not look brown; and this pride and man-pleasing did not offend the quaker spirit. Mr. Jan performed a Roman feat this morning, catching a dolphin with his hook, which he had been trying to do for three weeks. Another was stuck with a halberd. The latitude was 37° 47′, the distance sailed we estimated at eighty miles, the course held was mostly N. W., the longitude 309° 56′. In the afternoon the wind shifted to W. S. W. entirely, and we could only sail N. W., and N. W. by N. It was quite calm during the night, but there came up a frightful storm of thunder, lightning and rain; we lay almost all night drifting with muzzled sails.

8*th*, *Friday*. It continued calm. We employed ourselves fishing, as there were daily many fish round the ship, and caught a few small ones. The sailors finished scraping the ship. We could get no observation of the sun to-day; but we set down the latitude at 38° 8′, the distance run thirty-six miles, the course N. W., and the longitude 309° 16′. Shortly after midday the wind veered round during a thunder storm, to the N. E., and gradually increased to blow. We changed our course to W. by N., and by evening were compelled to take in sail. We saw several pieces of stakes drifting along, from which we supposed we were appproaching the land. Towards evening we threw the deep lead, in order to see if we could find bottom, but we did not succeed, although we cast 120 fathoms; the lead was too light and the ship drifted too much. We sailed during the night, W. by N. and west, and made fair progress.

9*th*, *Saturday*. It did not blow so hard during the night, and by daylight the wind fell off still more. We obtained the latitude at noon, namely, 38° 16′; the course was a little more north than west, the distance 100 miles, the longitude 307° 30′. The color of the water was changed to a paler green. I saw a stick of dry wood drifting, like a piece of a bough, which induced all of us to believe we were near land. It was so calm in the night that our ship boxed the compass. We had not seen a finer sky during the whole voyage, so clear and so still.

10*th*, *Sunday*. During the day-watch a breeze sprung out of the northeast. We kept our course W. and W. by N., but the wind fell off before noon, and we drifted in a calm. The sea began to be a little covered with reeds and stubble, which we regarded as more signs of land. Numerous dolphins and other fish, besides small sharks, came near the ship, but we could catch none of them. We cast the deep lead at noon, but found no bottom. We had 38° 39′ of latitude, the progress we had made was over twenty miles, the longitude was 307° 25′, and our course had been N. W. We all longed for a good wind, to take us speedily to the end of our voyage. The calm continued all night.

11*th*, *Monday*. A breeze began to blow with the coming of the day. We caught several dolphins, one of them over five feet in length. About ten o'clock we saw a ship to the windward or larboard, when we luffed up, and she came towards us, and reached us about 12 o'clock. We hauled in our sails to wait for her. She showed English colors, and we did the same. We launched the jolly-boat, and our mate went on board of her, and after a little while returned, bringing her captain with him. She was an English ship from Guinea, and last from Virginia, which she had left three weeks previously. She had encountered many storms and contrary winds. Many of her crew were sick, and Margaret sold the captain a hogshead of ship's beer, for which her little daughter[1] was honored with a good lump of gold. We had expected some refreshment,

[1] This daughter was Annetje, or Anneke Filipse, then aged nearly twelve years; she became the wife of Philip French.

but there was nothing to be had for money, though some good apples were presented to Margaret. We asked him for his reckoning, which he told us was 270 leagues from Cape Henry, in the Virginias, differing considerably from ours, for that would make us 640 miles from New York, whereas my reckoning made it from 392 to 400 miles. However, all the other reckonings were different, one more and another less. The mate was nearest his, and the captain furthest off, as the mate said. This Englishman had made a mistake, as we afterwards discovered. Each one, nevertheless, kept his own chart. Our captain went on board the other vessel to see whether we could not obtain some vinegar, of which we were in want, as we had none, owing to the terrible parsimony of Margaret, of which I will speak hereafter. I never saw so many dolphins as there were around this English ship. They kept leaping up continually against her. The Englishman, in parting from us, about four o'clock, in order to show his civility, came up close along side of us, whereby many of the dolphins playing around his ship came to ours, and we caught some of them. In parting, he discharged several musket shots, but we did not return the salute. We had a small breeze, and with that we laid our course to the west. Every one had been so occupied with this Englishman that no one had taken the altitude except myself. I found the latitude 39° 29′, the distance could not be more than sixteen miles. As the weather was so calm, and we were under no headway, and had been carried almost a whole degree to the north, we concluded there must be a very strong current running in that direction. Towards evening the water changed. We sailed on several courses during the night, and afterwards drifted a little ahead.

12*th*, *Tuesday*. When we came on deck we observed the water had changed still more, and was very green, as if from the bottom. The fish had all disappeared, which caused us to think we were certainly on soundings. The deep lead was thrown about noon, but they went at it in such a grumbling and growling manner, and the ship going ahead, that nothing resulted from it. We had made only twelve or sixteen miles sailing, and yet we were again an entire degree further north, for on taking an observation we found we were in latitude 40° 25′, and, in point of fact, not far from land. The longitude obtained was 306° 40′. All this made us think of what the Englishman had said yesterday, but, under the circumstances, we thought we could not be where he said — the strong current, and the chopping of the sea, and its color — which made us consider whether we might not be about Cape Cod or Sandy Hook, as my *bestek* stood on the chart. I believed we were on the shoals of Cape Cod, fifty or sixty miles from land, as the result proved. The waves beat against each other very much from the northwest and south, and by evening the sky became overcast on all sides. We were apprehensive of a storm, and therefore took in all the sails; but it turned into a very heavy rain, without much wind, which, however, was northeast, and we had necessarily to keep off shore. We set our course S. W., and S. W. by S. The wind began to blow towards evening, and increased in the first part of the night. It rained nearly all night, which made us sail close and go ahead bravely.

13*th*, *Wednesday*. The wind and our course remained the same, under a stiff topsail breeze and a rolling sea, the color of which was changed to black. As soon as it was day we put on all sail until noon. We could obtain no latitude, but reckoned we were in 38° 4′, the progress upwards of an hundred miles, the course S. W. by S., and the longitude 305° 30′. We hoped this wind would carry us over. It was blowing E. by S., and increased so that we had to take in the topsails. It turned into a very severe storm in the night, and the wind gradually veered round to the west.

14*th*, *Thursday*. This hard storm came from the S. S. W. We took in all sail, clewed up the foresail, lowered the yards with great difficulty, struck the mainsail and reefed it, so that we were prepared to lie by. We steered S. S. E., but the wind from the S. W. was exceedingly heavy, and although the sea did not run so high as in the last storm, it was more driving, and short, and gave very severe blows. The large bowline broke into pieces, and we had to strike the mainsail in order to repair it; but as for getting it up again there was little chance, for it struck so frightfully in hoisting it we were afraid the topsail would fall, or the sail itself fly into tatters. We had no opportunity to observe the latitude, but reckoned it to be 38° 30′; our progress was nothing, or 12 or 16 miles further south, and consequently the longitude was the same as before. In the afternoon, about four o'clock, there rose a very heavy sea, which not only threw itself into the mainsail but over the whole deck, so that the ship could hardly rise again. We stretched a bonnet again from the main shrouds to the mizzen shrouds, in order to relieve the ship, and enable her the better to oppose the seas; but about seven o'clock in the evening there came a sea which not only covered the whole ship but it broke with such force it seemed as if the ship would go to the bottom. They did not know how or whence it came, nor how to get rid of the water. From this time the weather seemed to moderate gradually, the wind blowing from the west, and afterwards N. N. W., and thus the storm passed off. I have not described the particulars of this storm, which, although it was not so severe as the other, nevertheless was neither better nor worse, because the other storm was high in the air and on deep water, for which reason the sea ran very regularly and slowly, but here the sea ran short and confusedly, hard and pushing. All the power of this storm was below, upon the water, which was not so deep. The sky over head was clear, and was never obscured, during this storm, except towards the horizon, where it was like flying mist. The ship suffered more than she did before, the mast became loose again, the rigging broken in pieces, the vanes flown away, and every thing stripped.

15*th*, *Friday*. The wind which was N. W., and N. W. by N., having subsided, the hatches were opened, the sails spread, and every thing repaired and put in order. It was quite calm, and we sailed S. W., and afterwards W. S. W. The carpenter having to go behind the stern of the ship for the purpose of opening the window of the cabin, discovered that the sternpost was split from top to bottom, so that it hung and swung by the planks of the ship, and when she was moved by the waves, you could thrust your whole hand in, on either side, and tnat whether the rudder or the ship was moved by the sea. He then went into the hold, and found the deck was rent or burst its whole length and drawn off from the sides, although the ship had been repaired the last time she was in Holland. From this circumstance it can be judged whether the last storm was not as severe as the first. When the carpenter communicated to the captain the condition of the sternpost, the latter gave a grim laugh and shook his head, as if it were of no importance; but afterwards, when he went himself to see it, he quickly changed his opinion. It was found to be a matter of serious consideration. Those whose business it was, were called together to devise means how it might be repaired and made fast at once; which it was determined should be done. The day was occupied in restoring lesser articles, every one drying his little goods and drawing his breath. Dolphins came around the ship, some of which we had hold of, but they escaped from us. We saw a vessel ahead of us on the larboard, but we did not

12

go towards her. Our latitude at noon was 37° 36′. We could not calculate our progress. We had first drifted N. W., and then as much N. E., and afterwards, by the stiffening of the wind, south, so that we remained in about the same longitude. In other particulars this storm did not differ from the other. At midnight we had a slight breeze and made sail again, with clear moonshine and fine weather.

16*th*, *Saturday*. The wind gradually shifting to the south and increasing, we went finely ahead. As soon as it was day, all hands began to work in good earnest at the broken sternpost, which was found to be much worse than was supposed yesterday. They worked the more earnestly because it would not have stood long. They put a large iron ringbolt on one side of the stern and a broad iron hook on the other. A good thick rope was then made fast to the ring or the hook, and a small part of the sternpost cut away for the rope, and the rope was thus passed behind the sternpost and taken to the capstan. It was wound round as often as it would conveniently go through the two rings, and then each of tbe coils was spiked upon the sternpost, and thus the sternpost was brought close to the planking. Two pieces of timber were afterwards let into it and well spiked at each end, and this it was believed would hold. In the meanwhile the wind began to blow again from the southwest with a cloudy sky, and we could not obtain the altitude, but we reckoned it the same as before. The course was west, the distance sailed eighty-eight miles, and therefore the longitude had changed 1° 28′. We hoped this wind would have brought us upon the coast, but in the afternoon it increased so much, that we had scarcely finished the sternpost and made fast the iron rudder pin, which had become loose from the beating of tne sea, when we thought the storm was again upon us, from the indications of the sky and the wind. Every thing was accordingly again put in order and made fast, the top gallant mast was taken down in order to prevent the swinging of the mast, as it was loose before; and the topsails were reefed, and afterwards taken in, for the reason that we observed in the N. W. a very black cloud rising against the wind, accompanied with thunder and lightning. The nearer this cloud came up the more it swelled. It struck us amidships, whereby the water chopped and rose very high. We took all sail in and struck the yards. A very heavy rain followed, some of which I caught, and for once refreshed myself by drinking my full; and others followed my example; for we had not much beer, and our water either stunk or was brackish, such of it as was on deck and the sea had beaten upon. It cleared up considerably, however, and the moon shone; but the weather nevertheless continued uncertain, mingled with lightning. A breeze springing up from the the east about nine o'clock, all hands set to work to increase our sails and set them before the wind. At midnight they were all taken in again, as the sky became overcast, and there was much thunder and lightning with rain, which continued till day-light.

17*th*, *Sunday*. About three o'clock in the morning, the wind having changed to the S. W. and W., we again made sail, and the wind then turning further to the north, we changed our course again. We came among many small fish called springers, because they spring out of the water. They were about the size of whiting, but we could not catch any of them. I saw a sea hedge-hog as large as the fist, with prickles on its body in proportion. It was speckled, and provided with four paws, by means of which it swam like a rat. Its head was small, and its body round, but flat underneath, like a St. James's shell. The latitude to-day was 39° 16′, the westing about 24 miles and northing 20 to 24. About six o'clock in the evening the wind shifted more to the north, and we could only sail

N. N. E., so we lay over and sailed S. W. The wind veering still more to the north, we steered gradually more to the west, under reefed topsails. We observed in the evening again that the water was green, a sign we were near the shore.

18*th*, *Monday*. The sea having became somewhat smoother, and the wind coming from the N. and N. N. E. over the land, we sailed due west. The sea was more blue, indicating it was deeper water, and that we had sailed during the night away from the land. At eleven o'clock it became green again, which made us think we were approaching the other shore on the west, or that we were sailing over a shoal. We observed a blue dove flying, which was regarded by all as a sign of our approaching land, and reminded us of the dove coming back to the ark of Noah, as a messenger of the drying up of the earth, and soon to go out of the ark in the liberty of God's favor and peace; and thus we were coming near the land, and would soon go out of our prison, where we had by his will been so long shut up with so many unclean beasts, going out in his favor and peace, wherever he should carry us, and making an offering of ourselves to his service. The latitude at noon was 39° 24′, the distance made good sixty miles, the course held W. by N., and the longitude was 304° 4′. The weather was fine, and the sea rolled no more. The lead was thrown in the evening, but it did not reach the bottom. The wind continued the same all night. We threw the line again at midnight, but without success.

19*th*, *Tuesday*. The wind was still N. E. and E. N. E., and we held on our west course with tolerable progress. The sea was now a paler green. The latitude was 39° 6′, and we had advanced, according to our calculation, upwards of one hundred miles, on a course a little south of west. The longitude was 303° 30′. Some were several days out of their reckoning, and I would have been also if I had not discovered the mistake and rectified it. The lead thrown towards evening did not yet show any bottom, as they said, though it was doubtful. We sailed all night with a light breeze and a clear moonshine, which, indeed, was another mark of God's favor and preserving care towards us, that we should fall upon the coast with a full moon, and not when there was no moon. Certainly he watches over us in our sleep, and nothing can happen otherwise than according to his providence.

20*th*, *Wednesday*. The wind continued easterly, and our course westerly. We saw again several signs of being near land, such as different kinds of snipe and other small birds; also stubble; sea weed; little red strings, like coral, a sea plant which grows on the coast; rock weed, and other weeds floating on the water. About ten o'clock a cloud of mist came in from the N. W., which demonstrated pretty well to my mind Long Island and the part of the mainland south of the bay towards the South river. I thought whether it might not be the dew drawn up by the sun from the land there, and driven over our heads by the wind. The wind changed to the north, but when these clouds had passed by us, it shifted again to the east. We had had for a day or two warmer weather. The air from the land smelt entirely different, sweet and fresh, and not so saltish as the sea air. We set our course W. by N. The water changed from a dark green to a lighter, which gave us all no bad spirits. Others with myself were constantly on the lookout for land, but we discovered none. The latitude we obtained to-day was 39°. We had gone a little south, to about the latitude of the South river, and should be opposite its north cape. We reckoned the distance sailed to be from 92 to 96 miles. As our heaviest deep lead was too light, and we could not keep the vessel still, she either sailing too rapidly or drifting too much, and as the weather was favorable, we resolved to launch the jolly-boat in order to take soundings. The tub with the lead and line were put on board, and the mate and boatswain went off in her, although, in fact, the jolly-boat remained quiet on the water, and did not drift off far. They rowed off a piece, and let the line run out, when they soon cried out "bottom, bottom." It must not be asked whether this did not send a thrill of joy through the ship, where every one jumped up and clapped his hands, which was answered from the jolly-boat like an echo. On being asked, how deep it was, they said about 34 fathoms, at which we were rejoiced, and, at the same time, surprised that we had not found bottom before, as we were certainly near enough. The jolly-boat was hoisted on board again, and the lead, which had been greased over so that it might take an impression of the bottom, was examined by every one. We observed upon it a mixture of pebbles and shells, all grown over with green, of the same color as the sea. This occurred about 4 o'clock in the afternoon. Our course was then directed as much as possible to the north. We sailed N. by E. and N. N. E. Two hours afterwards we threw the lead again, and had 25 fathoms. At sunset we thought we saw land, and although others thought differently, I cannot rid myself of the idea that it was land. I looked at it long enough, and perceived no motion, as would have taken place if it were clouds. From the soundings I supposed we were near the north cape of the South river, and I also thought I saw a clove or double hill, as laid down at that point on the chart, a little south of west of us. The chart indicates a row of hills there. It was nevertheless contradicted. In the mean time our hearts ascended with thankfulness to God, adoring and admiring his goodness and fatherly guidance. The weather was fine, and the moon clear. Not the smallest cloud obscured the sky, and the sea was as smooth as if it were a river. God's blessing was so visibly over us, that the most brutal were touched after their own way. Oh! those wretched, wicked, yea, truly wicked people.

21*st*, *Thursday*. The hatches of the hold were all opened yesterday evening, and we began to make the cables fast to the anchors, which we finished this morning. As soon as the sun rose, every one climbed aloft in order to look for land and some of them immediately cried out "land," but they soon discovered they were mistaken. Our course was north, with the wind E. N. E. I said the land we would see was in front of us, and we could not see it yet because it was in latitude 40° 20′, and we had 39°, a difference of eighty miles, and as we had sailed only from twenty-four to twenty-eight miles at the most during the night, we were still fifty-two to fifty-six miles off, and if we continued to sail as we were doing, it would be noon or two o'clock before we would see it. I must say a word here in relation to our cat; how she was always sick and lame for some days before a storm, and could not walk, and when the storm was over, was lively and nimble again. She had now been very playful for several days, running here and there over the ship, but this morning she was unusually gay. She came running with a spring, leaping into the rigging and going far aloft, turning her head about and snuffing the land, as much as to say, there is the land you should look out for; and causing great laughter among the folks, who said the cat was on the lookout for land. When she came down she mewed. But a thick fog coming from the land, cut off all view and hopes of going inside, as we turned at once from the shore. I obtained, however, the altitude, to wit: 40° 5′. The distance was reckoned to be sixty-four miles. In the mean time the deep lead was thrown many times, and 22, 21, 19, 17, 16, 14 fathoms of water found, at one time more and at another less, for the bottom is uneven. We did this in order not to run ashore during the fog. It, however, cleared away, and we wore over again, and immediately saw the land distinctly, which caused new rejoicing. We perceived clearly that we had been sailing, since yesterday, along the shore, although it was too far off to be seen. *Rensselaer's* Hook,[1] which adjoins Sandy Hook, was in front or north of us; and we had sailed N. N. E. and N. by E. It was about one o'clock when we first saw the land. It is not very high, but like a dome, only it is a little higher. Long Island is not very high; Rensselaer's Hook, which is the most westerly point of the bay, is the highest of all. Sandy Hook is low, and stretches out about three miles eastwardly from Rensselaer's Hook, and makes the channel. You must be close on Sandy Hook before you can see Long Island. We intended to run in, but could not well do so this evening, in consequence of the mist continually intercepting the sight of the land. As the weather was calm, and the sea smooth, we came to anchor, in thirteen fathoms of water, and lay there quietly all night.

22*d*, *Friday*. When the day began to break, they were all in an uproar; but the weather continued misty, with a northeast wind, for which reason we judged we could not make the channel. All those who were so joyful and merry yesterday, were now more sober, as we were compelled to keep off land, so as not to be caught on a lee shore, from which it is very difficult to get away. The fog cleared up a little about ten o'clock, and we sailed again towards the shore, when we perceived we were approaching the west side. It rained a part of the time, and was misty, so that sometimes we could only see the land dimly, and for a moment, and Sandy Hook hardly at all. We durst not yet venture to run in, and wore off again. About noon we saw a ketch to the sea-ward of

[1] Nevesink.

us, but we did not speak to her. She was laying her course to the west. This coast surely is not very easy to enter, especially in the autumn. Our captain had trouble enough, though our mate did not agree with him. Sailing onward, we had 13, 14, 15, 16 fathoms of water, but very uneven bottom as we approached the shore. We laid our course N. N. E. and N. E. by N. and from the shore, S. S. W. and S. At four o'clock in the afternoon we determined to run in, if it were possible. We could see the land a little better, and also Rensselaer's Hook. Everybody, therefore, was very industrious, some in looking after the sails, ropes and tackle, so as to be able to turn and tack ship quickly; others were constantly on the lookout for land and especially to discover Sandy Hook, in order to secure the best channel which is next to that point; for not far from it, on the other side, are the east banks, which are very dangerous. We did our best, first in a calm, then with a little breeze, to enter. We caught sight of Sandy Hook at last, but it was soon hid by the fog. We observed how the land lay by the compass, and so sailed accordingly, expecting a good flood tide which would begin to make at six o'clock. The deep lead was thrown constantly, and we found five and four fathoms in the shallowest places, near the channel. It was low water, and the wind was N. E. and E. N. E., which took us soon inside, short around the point of Sandy Hook, into the bay towards the highlands of Rensselaer's Hook. Upon passing the Hook which was now west of us, we found deeper water 5, 6, 7 and 8 fathoms, and ran, as I have said, immediately for the highlands, and came to anchor in ten fathoms of water, praising the Lord again, and thankful for the many instances of his goodness towards us. This is a very fine bay, where many ships can lie, protected from all winds, except the S. E., which, however, cannot do much damage, because the east banks lie before it: and at the worst, the ship can only be driven in the wind. They determined this evening, to go up early in the morning, in the jolly-boat, to Staten Island or Long Island, for a pilot.

23*d*, *Saturday*. It rained the whole night. Our ship lay as quiet as if she were made fast to the piles at Amsterdam, which was very unusual for us. The wind being west in the morning, they changed their resolution of going up for a pilot, and as the wind was so favorable determined to take her up themselves. The anchor was therefore raised, and we sailed on, for the purpose of passing between Staten Island and Long Island, where there are two high points of land, for that reason called the *Hoofden* (headlands).[1] We turned gradually from Sandy Hook to the right, in order to avoid the shoals of the east bank, and so sailed to the Hoofden. We had a good flood tide, and four to five fathoms of water at the shoalest part; but the wind shifted again to the north, and we were compelled to tack, which rendered our progress slow, for it was quite calm. Coming to the Hoofden, and between them, you have 10, 11, and 12 fathoms of water. As soon as you begin to approach the land, you see not only woods, hills, dales, green fields and plantations, but also the houses and dwellings of the inhabitants, which afford a cheerful and sweet prospect after having been so long upon the sea. When we came between the Hoofden, we saw some Indians on the beach with a canoe, and others coming down the hill. As we tacked about we came close to this shore, and called out to them to come on board the ship, for some of the passengers intended to go ashore with them; but the captain would not permit it, as he wished, he said, to carry them,

---

[1] The name of "De Hoofden" was derived as the journalist subsequently informs us from the resemblance of the shores to the Hoofden or headlands of Dover and Calais.

according to his contract, to the *Manathans*, though we understood well why it was. The Indians came on board, and we looked upon them with wonder. They are dull of comprehension, slow of speech, bashful but otherwise bold of person, and red of skin. They wear something in front, over the thighs, and a piece of duffels, like a blanket, around the body, and this is all the clothing they have. Their hair hangs down from their heads in strings, well smeared with fat, and sometimes with quantities of little beads twisted in it out of pride. They have thick lips and thick noses, but not fallen in like the negroes, heavy eyebrows or eyelids, brown or black eyes, thick tongues, and all of them black hair. But we will speak of these things more particularly hereafter. After they had obtained some biscuit, and had amused themselves a little, climbing and looking here and there, they also received some brandy to taste, of which they drank excessively, and threw it up again. They then went ashore in their canoe, and we having a better breeze, sailed ahead handsomely. As soon as you are through the Hoofden, you begin to see the city, which presents a pretty sight. The fort, which lies upon the point between two rivers, is somewhat higher; and as soon as they see a ship coming up, they raise a flag on a high flag-staff, according to the colors of the sovereign to whom they are subject, as accordingly they now flew the flag of the king of England. We came up to the city about three o'clock, where our ship was quickly overrun with people who came from the shore in all sorts of craft, each one inquiring and searching after his own, and his own profit. No custom-house officers came on board, as in England, and the ship was all the time free of such persons. We came to anchor, then, before the city at three o'clock. Every one wanted to go ashore immediately. We let those most in a hurry go before us, when, leaving our property in charge of Robyn, we also went in company with a passenger, named Gerrit, who took us to the house of his father-in-law, where we lodged.

It is not possible to describe how this bay swarms with fish, both large and small, whales, tunnies and porpoises, whole schools of innumerable other fish, and a sort like herring, called there *marsbanckers*, and other kinds, which the eagles and other birds of prey swiftly seize in their talons when the fish come up to the surface, and hauling them out of the water, fly with them to the nearest woods or beach, as we saw.

We had finally arrived where we had so long wished to be, but from whence we were soon to depart, because we had come only to do the will of him who watches over us, and who after our longest voyage, will cause us to arrive, by his favor, as it pleases him. Meanwhile unto him be given all honor, and praise and glory for what he does, to all eternity. Amen; yea, amen.

Leaving the ship on our arrival, it would seem proper that this narrative concerning the voyage should here be brought to an end; but as the sea over which we passed is wide and broad, and various things are to be noted, which could only be found out in process of time, I will here add them each by its kind.

Observations upon the Sea and the Voyage.

1. I have uniformly found it true, that the bottom causes the change in the color of the sea, and makes the color lighter or darker according as it may happen to be; as we experienced from the beginning to the end of our voyage. And this is the reason; the water of itself has no color, but, as it is transparent, the bottom shows itself, such as it is, through the clearness of the water, according to

its depth: but something must be allowed for the sky, clouds and other bodies in the atmosphere, which, although they do not change the water, nevertheless shine in it, and throw a shadow or reflection.

2. The banks or shoals of Newfoundland extend further south than they are laid down on the charts, and as far as 36° or less of latitude, as we observed from the color of the water, although it may be deeper there than about Newfoundland.

3. There is a stream running from the river Amazon, along the coast of Guiana, through the Gulf of Mexico and the channel of the Bahamas, along the coast of Florida, Virginia and New Netherland, to the banks of Newfoundland, where, uniting with another stream, coming from the north out of Davis's strait and river St. Lawrence, goes again south, and afterwards S. W., to the Bermudas, but mostly to the east of them, the particular causes and reasons of which we will notice in its proper place.

4. This stream has its course along the gulfs, capes and bays of the coast, the same as we experienced near or west of Cape Cod or Staten Hook, where for two days successively, without headway on the ship, and in a calm, we were carried by it a degree to the north. This should be kept in mind, and one should regulate himself accordingly.

5. The storm of the Bermudas has been mentioned in its place.

6. I have heretofore exposed mistakes on the large plane chart, and it is not material to enter further into that subject.

7. After we approached and passed the Bermudas, the wind did not turn round the compass with the sun, which happened to us four or five times, and frequently does so, as is said by experienced persons.

8. Therefore, in navigating this passage for this place, it

is best, when there are no reasons to the contrary arising from the Turks or otherwise, to run just above or below the Azores, to latitude 34 and 33, and even to 32 and 31, in order to get into the stream, and yet I also consider it well to sail to the eastward of these islands; or if you avoid the Azores, then to sail from Newfoundland or its latitude, due south, or S. S. E., to the before mentioned latitude; but, in returning, it is best to follow the coast to Newfoundland, in order to fall into the stream and wind. The home voyage is most always the shortest, inasmuch as the stream runs mostly along the coast.

9. When a change occurs in the color of the water, and at other times, the deep lead should be much used. It should be of 25 or 30 pounds weight. The ship or vessel should lie as still as possible, or the jolly-boat should be used, whether the lead be thrown with a certainty as to where you may be, or for the discovery of other bottom.

10. In storms or hurricanes never be without stern-sails, however small, unless you can sail before the wind, but no longer than that; for it is too dangerous, and too uncomfortable, both for the ship and the persons in her.

Some other observations in regard to the art of navigation and the management of ships, of minor importance we will reserve for another occasion.

The Persons with whom we made our Voyage.

Although this is such a miserable subject, that I deliberated long whether it were worth while to take any notice of it, yet since one does not know when a matter can be serviceable, I will nevertheless say something.

The persons who belonged to the ship were:

The captain, Thomas Singleton, an Englishman, and a

quaker, from London, I believe. He had his wife with him, who was quite young, about 24 or 26 years old, and he was a person of 40 or 45. He was not the best or most experienced seaman by a long distance. He was proud and very assiduous or officious to please men, especially Margaret and her man; yet he had some amiable qualities, he was affable. He was stingy; for when many mackerel were caught, he would not give one to the poor sailors. He was even displeased if the sailors came with their fish lines to fish near the place, where he was, because the fish might come to their lines instead of his. His wife was a young, worldly creature, who had not the least appearance of quakerism, but entirely resembled an English lady fashioned somewhat upon the Dutch model. She was proud, and wore much silver and gold; and when Margaret once spoke to him about it, he said, "I did not give it to her." Whereupon Margaret asked, "Why did you give her money to buy them?" To which he replied, "She wanted it."

The English mate, who afterwards became captain, was a passionate person, inwardly still more than he showed outwardly, a great man-pleaser where his interest was to be promoted. He was very close, but was compelled to be much closer in order to please Margaret.

The Dutch mate, Evert, was a wicked, impious fellow, who also drank freely. He was very proud of his knowledge and experience, which were none of the greatest.

The boatswain, Abram, of Plymouth, was rough and wicked in his orders, but he was a strong and able seaman. Robyn was the best.

I cannot permit myself to go further; it is too unpleasant a subject.

The passengers and crew were a wretched set. There was no rest, night or day, especially among the wives — a rabble I cannot describe. It was as if they were in the fish market or apple market, night and day, without cessation; where, indeed, some of them had obtained their living, and even in worse places. There were nine or ten of them always together. Among the men there were some persons who drank like beasts, yes, drank themselves dead drunk, as you may judge from the fact that two or three of them drank thirty-five gallons of brandy, besides wine from the time we left England or Holland. It is not to be told what miserable people Margaret and Jan were, and especially their excessive covetousness. In fine, it was a Babel. I have never in my life heard of such a disorderly ship. It was confusion without end. I have never been in a ship where there was so much vermin, which were communicated to us, and especially not a few to me, because being in the cordage at night I particularly received them. There were some bunks and clothes as full as if they had been sown. But I must forbear.

When we first came on board the ship we eat where we were, and with those we found there, but afterwards the messes were regulated, and we were placed on deck with five or six uncouth youngsters; where, nevertheless, we continued. This so exercised the other passengers, seeing us submit so willingly, that they themselves could no longer endure it, and desired us to come with them, and make a mess of eight. We had been compelled to buy our stores in England, as what we had were spoiled, or not sufficient. There was not a bit of butter or vinegar on the food during the whole voyage, except what we had purchased at Falmouth. I do not know how long it was we had nothing to eat except heads of salt fish, and those spoiled for the most part. We had to eat them till they were thrown overboard. Most of the time we had white peas, which our cook was too lazy to clean, or were boiled in stinking water, and when they were brought on the table we had to throw them away. The meat was old and tainted; the pork passable, but enormously thick, as much as six inches; and the bread was mouldy or wormy. We had a ration of beer three times a day to drink at table. The water smelt very bad, which was the fault of the captain. When we left England they called us to eat in the cabin, but it was only a change of place and nothing more. Each meal was dished up three times in the cabin, first for the eight passengers, then for the captain, mate and wife, who sometimes did not have as good as we had, and lastly for Margaret and Mr. Jan who had prepared for them hardly any thing else except poultry and the like. But this is enough.

After we left England, I took upon myself, out of love of the thing, and because there were so few persons to work the ship, namely, ten in all, including the captain, to watch and attend the rudder, as well as to make observations in navigation; but when I perceived the sailors, on this account, became lazy and depended upon me, I left the rudder-gang. Nevertheless, when an English ship came near running us down in the watch off Cape Cod, causing thereby much uproar and confusion in our ship, I did my best to unfasten a rope which they could not make loose, at which the mate raved and swore, and for which he would have almost struck or killed me. When my comrade heard of it he wished me not to do any thing more, and that was my opinion. I could not, however, refrain from helping to the last, but I abandoned the watch, and so caused the mate to feel that we were not insensible, for there was nothing else to be done to him. He, nevertheless, invited us daily more than any one else. Finally, when the voyage was completed, there was no one, either captain, or mate, or sailor, or Margaret, who said "We thank you," except our poor Robyn. We had a little package put in the ship at Falmouth, about a foot and a half square, on which the captain charged us four guilders freight, in the money of Holland. We represented to Margaret how we had managed with only one chest between us, although each passenger was entitled to have one of his own, but it was all to no purpose. Four guilders it must be. It was not that we had any difficulty in giving it, but it was only to be convinced of her unblushing avarice. The mate's wife was the least evil-inclined, and listened most to what was said to her, which we hope will bear fruit. We have truly conducted ourselves towards all in general and each one in particular, so that not only has every one reason to be edified and convinced, but, by the grace of God, every one renders us testimony that we have edified and convinced them as well by our lives as our conversation. Let him alone who is the author of all grace, receive therefor all the glory, to all eternity. Amen.

JOURNAL

OF OUR

TRAVELS THROUGH NEW NETHERLAND,

FROM

THE TIME OF OUR ARRIVAL UNTIL OUR DEPARTURE FOR THE FATHERLAND.

NEW YORK AND ITS VICINITY.

Having then fortunately arrived, by the blessing of the Lord, before the city of New York, on Saturday, the 23d day of September, we stepped ashore about four o'clock in the afternoon, in company with Gerrit,[1] our fellow passenger, who would conduct us in this strange place. He had lived here a long time and had married his wife here, although she and his children were living at present, at Zwolle. We went along with him, but as he met many of his old acquaintances on the way, we were constantly stopped. He first took us to the house of one of his friends, who welcomed him and us, and offered us some of the fruit of the country, very fine peaches and full grown apples, which filled our hearts with thankfulness to God. This fruit was exceedingly fair and good, and pleasant to the taste; much better than that in Holland or elsewhere, though I believe our long fasting and craving of food made it so agreeable. After taking a glass of Madeira, we proceeded on to Gerrit's father-in-law's, a very old man, half lame, and unable either to walk or stand, who fell upon the neck of his son-in-law, welcoming him with tears of joy. The old woman was also very glad. This good man

---

[1] Gerrit Cornelius Van Duyne, the common ancestor of the Van Duyne family in this country. He died in 1706. For further particulars in relation to him the reader may consult the *Genealogy of the Bergen Family*, by Hon. Teunis G. Bergen: New York, 1866, pp. 221.

was born in Vlissingen, and was named Jacob Swart.[1] He had been formerly a master carpenter at Amsterdam, but had lived in this country upwards of forty-five years. After we had been here a little while, we left our traveling bag, and went out to take a walk in the fields. It was strange to us to feel such stability under us, although it seemed as if the earth itself moved under our feet like the ship had done for three months past, and our body also still swayed after the manner of the rolling of the sea; but this sensation gradually passed off in the course of a few days. As we walked along we saw in different gardens trees full of apples of various kinds, and so laden with peaches and other fruit that one might doubt whether there were more leaves or fruit on them. I have never seen in Europe, in the best seasons, such an overflowing abundance. When we had finished our tour and given our guide several letters to deliver, we returned to his father-in-law's, who regaled us in the evening with milk, which refreshed us much. We had so many peaches set before us that we were timid about eating them, though we experienced no ill effects from them. We remained there to sleep, which was the first time in nine or ten weeks that we had lain down upon a bed undressed, and able to yield ourselves to sleep without apprehension of danger.

24*th*, *Sunday*. We rested well through the night. I was surprised on waking up to find my comrade had already dressed himself and breakfasted upon peaches. We walked out awhile in the fine, pure morning air, along the margin of the clear running water of the sea, which is driven up this river at every tide. As it was Sunday, in order to

---

[1] Jacob Swart and Truytje Jacobs, his wife, were still living in 1686, in the Smits valley (Pearl street, between Wall street and Franklin square), according to Domine Selyns' list of members of the Dutch church.—I *New York Historical Society Collections*, new series, 398.

avoid scandal and for other reasons, we did not wish to absent ourselves from church. We therefore went, and found there truly a wild worldly world. I say wild, not only because the people are wild, as they call it in Europe, but because most all the people who go there to live, or who are born there, partake somewhat of the nature of the country, that is, peculiar to the land where they live. We heard a minister preach, who had come from the up-river country, from fort Orange, where his residence is, an old man, named Domine Schaats, of Amsterdam. He was, it appears, a Voetian, and had come down for the purpose of approving, examining, ordaining and collating a student; to perform which office the neighboring ministers come here, as to the capital, and, in order that the collation may be approved by the governor, who, at this time, was not at home, but was at *Pemequick*, in the northerly parts of New England.[1] This student, named *Tessemaker*, from Utrecht, I believe, was a Voetian, and had found some obstacles in his way, because the other ministers were all Cocceians, namely: Do. *Niewenhuisen*, of (New) Amsterdam, (Do. Van Zuren), of Long Island, and Do. *Gaesbeek*, of Esopus, whose son is sheriff of this city. He was to minister at the South river, near the governor there, or in the principal place, as he himself told us. The governor was expected home every day, and then Tessemaker supposed he would be dispatched.

The governor is the greatest man in New Netherland, and acknowledges no superior in all America, except the viceroy, who resides upon Jamaica.

---

[1] The governor here alluded to was Sir Edmund Andros, who was commissioned as such by the Duke of York over all the territories granted and confirmed to the duke by Charles I, embracing not only the conquered province of New Netherland, extending from the Connecticut river to the Delaware, but also a portion of the province of Maine lying between the Kennebec and St. Croix, of which tract Pemaquid was the principal point. Andros had built a fort there two years before this time.

This Schaats, then, preached. He had a defect in the left eye, and used such strange gestures and language that I think I never in all my life have heard any thing more miserable; indeed, I can compare him with no one better than with one Do. Van Ecke, lately the minister at Armuyden, in Zeeland, more in life, conversation and gestures than in person. As it is not strange in these countries to have men as ministers who drink, we could imagine nothing else than that he had been drinking a little this morning. His text was, *Come unto me all ye, &c.*, but he was so rough that even the roughest and most godless of our sailors were astonished.

The church being in the fort, we had an opportunity to look through the latter, as we had come too early for preaching. It is not large; it has four points or batteries; it has no moat outside, but is enclosed with a double row of palisades. It is built from the foundation with quarry stone. The parapet is of earth. It is well provided with cannon, for the most part of iron, though there were some small brass pieces, all bearing the mark or arms of the Netherlanders. The garrison is small. There is a well of fine water dug in the fort by the English, contrary to the opinion of the Dutch, who supposed the fort was built upon rock, and had therefore never attempted any such thing. There is, indeed, some indication of stone there, for along the edge of the water below the fort there is a very large rock extending apparently under the fort, which is built upon the point formed by the two rivers, namely, the East river, which is the water running between the *Mahatans* and Long Island, and the North river, which runs straight up to fort Orange. In front of the fort, on the Long Island side, there is a small island called *Noten* island (Nut island), around the point of which vessels must go in sailing out or in, whereby they are compelled to pass close by the point of the fort, where they can be flanked by several of the batteries. It has only one gate, and that is on the land side, opening upon a broad plain or street, called the Broadway or Beaverway. Over this gate are the arms of the Duke of York. During the time of the Dutch there were two gates, namely, another on the water side; but the English have closed it, and made a battery there, with a false gate. In front of the church is inscribed the name of Governor *Kyft*, who caused the same to be built in the year 1642. It has a shingled roof, and upon the gable towards the water there is a small wooden tower, with a bell in it, but no clock. There is a sun-dial on three sides. The front of the fort stretches east and west, and consequently the sides run north and south.

After we had returned to the house and dined, my comrade not wishing to go to church, sat about writing letters, as there was a ship, of which André Bon was master, about to leave in a few days for London; but in order we should not be both absent from church, and as the usual minister was to preach in the afternoon, I went alone to hear him. He was a thick, corpulent person with a red and bloated face, and of very slabbering speech.[1] His text was, *the elders who serve well, &c.*, because the elders and deacons were that day renewed, and I saw them admitted. After preaching, the good old people with whom we lodged, who, indeed, if they were not the best on all the *Manathans*, were at least among the best, especially the wife, begged we would go with their son Gerrit, to one of their daughters, who lived in a delightful place, and kept a tavern, where we would be able to taste the beer of New Netherland, inasmuch as it was also a brewery. Some of their friends passing by requested Gerrit and us to accompany them, and so we went for the purpose of seeing what was to be seen; but when we arrived there, we found our-

[1] The minister here referred to was the Rev. William Nieuenhuisen.

selves much deceived. On account of its being, to some extent a pleasant spot, it was resorted to on Sundays by all sorts of revellers, and was a low pot-house. Our company immediately found acquaintances there and joined them, but it being repugnant to our feelings to be there, we walked into the orchard to seek pleasure in contemplating the innocent objects of nature. Among other trees we observed a mulberry tree, the leaves of which were as large as a plate. The wife showed us pears larger than the fist, picked from a three year's graft which had borne forty of them. A great storm of rain coming up in the evening compelled us to go into the house, where we did not remain long with the others, but took our leave of them, against their wishes. We retraced our steps in the dark, exploring a way over which we had gone only once in our life, through a *valey* (salt meadow) and over water, upon the trunk of a tree. We nevertheless reached home, having left the others in their revels. While in their company we conversed with the first male born of Europeans in New Netherland, named Jean Vigné. His parents were from Valenciennes and he was now about sixty-five years of age. He was a brewer and a neighbor of our old people.[1]

---

[1] This is an interesting statement, which may not only be compared with that hitherto received, attributing to Sarah de Rapalje, who was born on the 9th of June, 1625, the honor of having been the first born Christian child in New Netherland, but is to be considered in other respects. According to the data given by our travelers, who, writing in 1679, make Jean Vigné sixty-five years old at that time, he must have been born in the year 1614, eleven years before Sarah de Rapalje, and at the very earliest period compatible with the sojourn of any Hollanders upon our territory. Jean Vigné belonged to the class of great burghers in New Amsterdam, and was one of the schepens of the city in the years 1655, 56, 61 and 63.—*O'Callaghan's Register of New Netherland*, 61-3, 174. He was twice married.—*New York Manual*, 1862. Valentine says (*History of New York*, 73), that he died in 1691 without issue. In this statement in regard to his being the first person of European parentage born in New Netherland there are some notable points. The first trading voyages to Hudson's

A ketch came in from sea this evening, of which David Jochemsen was the master. She left England three weeks before us, and was the same one we saw the day we came in. The captain said he recollected to have seen us, but observing us tacking several times, he did not dare follow us, for fear of being misled.

25*th*, ***Monday***. We went on board the ship this morning in order to obtain our traveling bag and clothes for the purpose of having them washed, but when we came on board we could not get ashore again, before the afternoon, when the passengers' goods were to be delivered. All our goods which were between decks, were taken ashore and carried to the public storehouse, where they had to be examined; but some time elapsed before it was done in consequence of the examiners being elsewhere. At length, however, one Abraham Lennoy,[1] a good fellow

---

river were made by the Dutch in 1613–14, and the first wintering or habitation there was in 1614–15. There must have been, therefore, one European woman at least in the country at that early period. Whether Jean Vigné's parents returned to Holland or remained here during the obscure period between the time of his birth and the occupation of the country by the West India Company, it is impossible to determine. Either may have been the case. If the statement, however, be correct, and there is nothing inconsistent in it, with the history of the colony as far as known, Jean Vigné was not only the first born of European parents in New Netherland but as far as known in the whole United States north of Virginia. We deem it of sufficient importance to give here the statement of our travelers in regard to him in the original language: *Wijhadden ind it geseltschap gesproken den eerst geboren mans-persoon van Europianen in Nieu Nederlant, genoemt Jean Vigné. Sijne ouders waren van Valencijn, en hij was nu ontrent* 65 *jaer out, synde ook een brouwer en buerman van onse oude luij.*

[1] Peter La Noy, or De la Noy, is here meant, as is evident from what is said subsequently in this journal under the date of the fifth of October. Peter was at this time book-keeper to the collector of the port. He was afterwards collector and was mayor of the city under Leisler, and a member of his council.—*New York Colonial History*, vol. III, 302, 596, 645. Abraham was his brother, and a schoolmaster.

apparently, befriended us. He examined our chest only, without touching our bedding or any thing else. I showed him a list of the tin which we had in the upper part of our chest, and he examined it and also the tin, and turned up a little more what was in the chest, and with that left off, without looking at it closely. He demanded four English shillings for the tin, remarking at the same time, that he had observed some other small articles, but would not examine them closely, though he had not seen either the box or the pieces of linen. This being finished we sent our goods in a cart to our lodgings, paying for the two heavy chests and straw beds, and other goods from the public storehouse, to the Smit's *valey*, sixteen stuivers of zeewan, equal to three stuivers and a half in the money of Holland.[1] This finished the day and we retired to rest.

26th, Tuesday. We remained at home for the purpose of writing, but in the afternoon finding that many goods had been discharged from the ship, we went to look after our little package, which also came. I declared it, and it was examined. I had to pay 24 guilders in zeewan or five guilders[2] in the coin of Holland. I brought it to the house and looked the things all over, rejoicing that we were finally rid of that miserable set and the ship, the freight only remaining to be paid which was fixed at four guilders in coin. We went first to Margaret in relation to the freight, who said she had nothing more to do with it, and that we must speak to her husband about it, which it was not convenient to do that evening, and we therefore let it go, waiting for an opportunity to speak to her and her husband with the captain and perhaps also Mr. Jan.

27th, Wednesday. Nothing occurred to-day except that I went to assist Gerrit in bringing his goods home, and

---

[1] Three cents and a half.

[2] Two dollars.

declaring them, which we did. We heard that one of the wicked and godless sailors had broken his leg; and in this we saw and acknowledged the Lord and his righteousness. We visited Jean Vigné in order, as he was one of the oldest inhabitants, to obtain from him information on various matters relating to the country.

28*th*, *Thursday*. We remained at home to-day. I performed some little errands. *Monsieur La Grange*[1] called upon us, dressed up like a great fop, as he was. My comrade did not fail to speak to him seriously on the subject. He requested us to go with him immediately to his house, as I at length did. His house was not far from our lodgings on the front of the city. He had a small shop, as most all the people here have, who gain their living by trade, namely, in tobacco and liquors, thread and pins and other knick-knacks. His wife welcomed me, and instantly requested that we would come to their house and stay there as long as we were here, for which I thanked them. They had lost a child by the small pox, and they had been sick with the same disease. He said he intended to go to the South river within three weeks, and hearing we were inclined to travel, he desired our company, being willing to take us every where and to give us every information. I thanked him, but gave him no assurances, telling him we would see what the Lord would will of us.

29*th*, *Friday*. We finished our letters, and intended to go to-day over to Long Island. At noon a person came to us in our chamber and requested that we would be pleased to go to their minister, who was in the next house, as he was desirous of seeing and conversing with us, having already heard much good of us. We excused ourselves on the ground that we were busy writing,

---

[1] La Grange seems to have been one of the persons to whom the travelers brought letters.

endeavoring to finish our letters, in order, if it were possible, to go over to Long Island in the afternoon, with which he went away.

As soon as we had dined we sent off our letters; and this being all accomplished, we started at two o'clock for Long Island. This island is called Long Island, not so much because it is longer than it is broad, but particularly because it is the longest island in this region, or even along the whole coast of New Netherland, Virginia and New England. It is one hundred and forty-four miles in length, and from twenty-four to twenty-eight miles wide, though there are several bays and points along it, and, consequently, it is much broader in some places than others. On the west is Staten island, from which it is separated about a mile, and the great bay over which you see the *Neresincke.* With Staten island it makes the passage through which all vessels pass in sailing from or to the *Mahatans*, although they can go through the *Kil van Kol*, which is on the other side of Staten island. The ends of these islands opposite each other are quite high land, and they are, therefore, called the *Hoofden* (Headlands), from a comparison with the Hoofden of the channel between England and France, in Europe. On the north is the island of *Mahatans* and a part of the mainland. On the east is the sea, which shoots up to New England, and in which there are various islands. On the south is the great ocean. The outer shore of this island has before it several small islands and broken land, such as Coney island,[1] a low sandy island of about three hours' circuit, its westerly point forming with Sandy Hook, on the other side, the entrance from the sea. It is oblong in shape, and is grown over with bushes. Nobody lives upon it, but it is used in winter for keeping cattle, horses, oxen, hogs and others,

[1] *'t Conijnen Eylant*, Rabbit's island.

which are able to obtain there sufficient to eat the whole winter, and to shelter themselves from the cold in the thickets. This island is not so cold as Long Island or the *Mahatans*, or others, like some other islands on the coast, in consequence of their having more sea breeze, and of the saltness of the sea breaking upon the shoals, rocks and reefs, with which the coast is beset. There is also the Bear's island[1] and others, separated from Long Island by creeks and marshes overflown at high water. There are also on this sea coast various miry places, like the Vlaeck,[2] and others, as well as some sand bays and hard and rocky shores. Long Island stretches into the sea for the most part east by south and east southeast. None of its land is very high, for you must be nearly opposite Sandy Hook before you can see it. There is a hill or ridge running lengthwise through the island, nearest the north side and west end of the island. The south side and east end are more flat. The water by which it is separated from the *Mahatans*, is improperly called the East river, for it is nothing else than an arm of the sea, beginning in the bay on the west and ending in the sea on the east. After forming in this passage several islands, this water is as broad before the city as the Y before Amsterdam, but the ebb and flood tides are stronger. There is a ferry for the purpose of crossing over it, which is farmed out by the year, and yields a good income, as it is a considerable thoroughfare, this island being one of the most populous places in this vicinity. A considerable number of Indians live upon it, who gain their subsistence by hunting and fishing, and they, as well as others, must carry their articles to market over this ferry, or boat them over, as it is free to every one to use his own boat, if he have one, or to borrow

---

[1] *'t Beeren Eylant.* Now called Barren island.

[2] The Wieringen shoals in the Zuyder Zee are probably meant.

or hire one for the purpose. The fare over the ferry is three stuivers[1] in zeewan for each person.

Here we three crossed over, my comrade, Gerrit, our guide, and myself, in a row-boat, as it happened, which, in good weather and tide, carries a sail. When we came over we found there Jan Teunissen, our fellow passenger, who had promised us so much good. He was going over to the city, to deliver his letters and transact other business. He told us he would return home in the evening, and we would find him there. We went on, up the hill, along open roads and a little woods, through the first village, called Breukelen, which has a small and ugly little church standing in the middle of the road.[2] Having passed through here, we struck off to the right, in order to go to *Gouanes.* We went upon several plantations where Gerrit was acquainted with most all of the people, who made us very welcome, sharing with us bountifully whatever they had, whether it was milk, cider, fruit or tobacco, and especially, and first and most of all, miserable rum or brandy which had been brought from Barbadoes and other islands, and which is called by the Dutch *kill-devil.* All these people are very fond of it, and most of them extravagantly so, although it is very dear and has a bad taste. It

---

[1] Less than half a cent in our money.

[2] Breukelen, now Brooklyn, was so called from the village of that name in the province of Utrecht. The church here referred to was built in 1666, and was the first one in Brooklyn. When it was taken down does not appear. "A second church," says Furman, in his *Notes relating to Brooklyn*, 76, "was erected on the site of that built in 1666, which second church continued standing until about 1810, when a new and substantial church was erected on Joralemon street, and the old one taken down. This old church was a very gloomy looking building, with small windows, and stood in the middle of the highway, about a mile from Brooklyn ferry." Of this second church a view is given in the *Brooklyn Manual*, of 1863.

is impossible to tell how many peach trees we passed, all laden with fruit to breaking down, and many of them actually broken down. We came to a place surrounded with such trees from which so many had fallen off that the ground could not be discerned, and you could not put your foot down without trampling them; and, notwithstanding such large quantities had fallen off, the trees still were as full as they could bear. The hogs and other animals mostly feed on them. This place belongs to the oldest European woman in the country. We went immediately into her house, where she lived with her children. We found her sitting by the fire, smoking tobacco incessantly, one pipe after another. We enquired after her age, which the children told us was an hundred years. She was from Luyck (Liege), and still spoke good Waalsche (old French), with us. She could reason very well sometimes, and at other times she could not. She showed us several large apples, as good fruit of that country, and different from that of Europe. She had been about fifty years now in the country, and had above seventy children and grandchildren. She saw the third generation after her. Her mother had attended women in child-bed in her one hundred and sixth year, and was one hundred and eleven or twelve years old when she died. We tasted here, for the first time, smoked *twaelft*[1] (twelfth), a fish so called because it is caught in season next after the *elft*[2] (eleventh). It was salted a little and then smoked, and, although it was now a year old, it was still perfectly good, and in flavor not inferior to smoked salmon. We drank here, also, the first new cider, which was very fine.

We proceeded on to *Gouanes*, a place so called, where we arrived in the evening at one of the best friends of Gerrit,

---

[1] The striped bass.

[2] The shad.

named Symon.[1] He was very glad to see us, and so was his wife. He took us into the house, and entertained us exceedingly well. We found a good fire, half-way up the

[1] This settler was Simon Aertsen De Hart, who immigrated to this country in 1664. His wife, at this time, was Geertie (Gertrude) Cornelissen. Upon her death he married the widow of William Huycken, of Gowanos, on June 19, 1691. The house in which he entertained our travelers is still standing, in 1866. We are indebted to the Hon. Teunis G. Bergen, son of the late Garret Bergen, of Gowanos, for the following interesting particulars in relation to this ancient dwelling and its several proprietors, showing it to have been in the same family ever since the visit of the travelers.

"Simon Aertsen De Hart settled in Brooklyn subsequently to his arrival in this country, in 1664, upon a portion of a tract of land of 930 acres, bought by William Arianse Bennet and Jacques Bentyn of the Indians in 1636, extending from the vicinity of 27th street, in Brooklyn, to the New Utrecht line at Bay ridge. This entire tract was surveyed May 21, 1666, by Augustus Graham, surveyor general of the colony, and the map of his survey is on file in the office of the secretary of state at Albany. Two dwelling houses are represented upon it, one where the present Schermerhorn house is situated, and the other west of the first meadow, where the present house, partially of stone, stands, on Gowanos cove, near 28th street, and on the parcel designated on the map as land said to be sold to Simon Arison. Governor Fletcher issued a confirmatory grant or patent, on 2d November, 1696, to Simon Arison, for 303 acres, embracing the two parcels designated on the map as "the land in difference between Simon Arison and Adriaen Bennet," and "the land said to be sold to Simon Arison." Tradition has handed down the house still standing on the cove near 28th street as the one occupied by Simon Arison. The main building is of stone. The wing, which is built entirely of wood, has probably been added since the main house was erected, which has undoubtedly been several times altered and materially repaired. About fifty years ago Simon Bergen, its owner at that time, proposed to take it down, on account of its general decay, but upon the persuasion of Garret Bergen, his adjoining neighbor, he was induced to put it in repair, and place a new roof upon it; and so it has remained to the present day. The children of Simon Aertsen De Hart were Simon (2), who inherited this plantation, Elias and Annetje. Simon (2) had only one son, Simon (3), who also inherited the land, and several daughters, one of which, Geertje, married Simon Bergen. Simon (3) had no children, and by will devised the property to his sister Geertje, wife of Simon Bergen. Simon Bergen, Jun., son of Simon and Geertje Bergen, took the portion of the land where the house stands; and his daughter Leah, who married Jacob Morris, is now the owner for life, with remainder over to her issue, under the will of her father." A copy of the map made by Mr. Graham is preserved in the *Brooklyn Manual* for 1863, p. 360.

chimney, of clear oak and hickory, of which they made not the least scruple of burning profusely. We let it penetrate us thoroughly. There had been already thrown upon it, to be roasted, a pail-full of *Gouanes* oysters, which are the best in the country. They are fully as good as those of England, and better than those we eat at Falmouth. I had to try some of them raw. They are large and full, some of them not less than a foot long, and they grow sometimes ten, twelve and sixteen together, and are then like a piece of rock. Others are young and small. In consequence of the great quantities of them, everybody keeps the shells for the purpose of burning them into lime. They pickle the oysters in small casks, and send them to Barbadoes and the other islands. We had for supper a roasted haunch of venison, which he had bought of the Indians for three guilders and a half of *seewant*, that is, fifteen stuivers of Dutch money (fifteen cents), and which weighed thirty pounds. The meat was exceedingly tender and good, and also quite fat. It had a slight spicy flavor. We were also served with wild turkey, which was also fat and of a good flavor; and a wild goose, but that was rather dry. Every thing we had was the natural production of the country. We saw here, lying in a heap, a whole hill of watermelons, which were as large as pumpkins, and which Symon was going to take to the city to sell. They were very good, though there is a difference between them and those of the Caribly islands; but this may be owing to its being late in the season, and these were the last pulling. It was very late at night when we went to rest in a Kermis bed, as it is called, in the corner of the hearth, along side of a good fire.

30*th, Saturday.* Early this morning the husband and wife set off for the city with their marketing; and we, having explored the land in the vicinity, left after breakfast. We went a part of the way through a woods and fine, new made land, and so along the shore to the west end of the island called *Najack*.[1] As we proceeded along the shore, we found, among other curiosities, a highly marbled stone, very hard, in which we saw Muscovy glass lying in layers between the clefts, and how it was struck or cut out. We broke off a small piece with some difficulty, and picked out a little glass in the splits. Continuing onward from there, we came to the plantation of the *Najack* Indians, which was planted with maize, or Turkish wheat. We soon heard a noise of pounding, like thrashing, and went to the place whence it proceeded, and found there an old Indian woman busily employed beating Turkish beans out of the pods by means of a stick, which she did with astonishing force and dexterity. Gerrit inquired of her, in the Indian language, which he spoke perfectly well, how old she was, and she answered eighty years; at which we were still more astonished that so old a woman should still have so much strength and courage to work as she did. We went from thence to her habitation, where we found the whole troop together, consisting of seven or eight families, and twenty or twenty-two persons, I should think. Their house was low and long, about sixty feet long and fourteen or fifteen feet wide. The bottom was earth, the sides and roof were made of reed and the bark of chestnut trees; the posts, or columns, were limbs of trees stuck in the ground, and all fastened together. The top, or ridge of the roof was open about half a foot wide, from one end to the other, in order to let the smoke escape, in place of a chimney. On the sides, or walls, of the house, the roof was so low that you could hardly stand under it. The entrances, or doors, which were at both ends, were so

[1] Fort Hamilton, which is surrounded, in a great measure, by a marsh, and hence is here called an island.

small and low that they had to stoop down and squeeze themselves to get through them. The doors were made of reed or flat bark. In the whole building there was no lime, stone, iron or lead. They build their fire in the middle of the floor, according to the number of families which live in it, so that from one end to the other each of them boils its own pot, and eats when it likes, not only the families by themselves, but each Indian alone, according as he is hungry, at all hours, morning, noon and night. By each fire are the cooking utensils, consisting of a pot, a bowl, or calabash, and a spoon also made of a calabash. These are all that relate to cooking. They lie upon mats with their feet towards the fire, on each side of it. They do not sit much upon any thing raised up, but, for the most part, sit on the ground or squat on their ankles. Their other household articles consists of a calabash of water, out of which they drink, a small basket in which to carry and keep their maize and small beans, and a knife. The implements are, for tillage, a small, sharp stone, and nothing more; for hunting, a gun and pouch for powder and lead; for fishing, a canoe without mast or sail, and without a nail in any part of it, though it is sometimes full forty feet in length, fish hooks and lines, and scoops to paddle with in place of oars. I do not know whether there are not some others of a trifling nature. All who live in one house are generally of one stock or descent, as father and mother with their offspring. Their bread is maize, pounded in a block by a stone, but not fine. This is mixed with water, and made into a cake, which they bake under the hot ashes. They gave us a small piece when we entered, and although the grains were not ripe, and it was half baked and coarse grains, we nevertheless had to eat it, or, at least, not throw it away before them, which they would have regarded as a great sin, or a great affront. We chewed a little of it *with long teeth*, and managed to hide it so they did not see it. We had also to drink out of their calabashes the water which was their drink, and which was very good. We saw here the Indians who came on board the ship when we arrived. They were all very joyful at the visit of our Gerrit, who was an old acquaintance of theirs, and had heretofore long resided about there. We presented them with two jewsharps, which much pleased them, and they immediately commenced to play upon them, which they could do tolerably well. Some of their *patroons* (chiefs), some of whom spoke good Dutch, and are also their medicine-men and surgeons as well as their teachers, were busy making shoes of deer leather, which they understand how to make soft by continually working it in their hands. They had dogs, fowls and hogs, which they learn by degrees from the Europeans how to manage better. They had, also, peach trees, which were well laden. Towards the last, we asked them for some peaches, and they answered: "Go and pick them," which showed their politeness. However, in order not to offend them, we went off and pulled some. Although they are such a poor, miserable people, they are, nevertheless, licentious and proud, and given to knavery and scoffing. Seeing a very old woman among them, we inquired how old she was, when some young fellows, laughing and jeering, answered twenty years, while it was evident to us she was not less than an hundred. We observed here the manner in which they travel with their children, a woman having one which she carried on her back. The little thing clung tight around her neck like a cat, where it was kept secure by means of a piece of daffels, their usual garment. Its head, back and buttocks were entirely flat. How that happened to be so we will relate hereafter, as we now only make mention of what we saw.

These Indians live on the land of Jaques (Cortelyou),

brother-in-law of Gerrit.[1] He bought the land from them in the first instance, and then let them have a small corner, for which they pay him twenty bushels of maize yearly, that is, ten bags. Jaques had first bought the whole of *Najack* from these Indians, who were the lords thereof, and lived upon the land, which is a large place, and afterwards bought it *again*, in parcels. He was unwilling to drive the Indians from the land, and has therefore left them a corner of it, keeping the best of it himself.[2] We arrived then upon this land, which is all good, and yields large crops of wheat and other grain. It is of a blackish color, but not clayey, and almost like the garden mould I have seen in Holland. At length we reached the house, where we found *Mons. Le Grange*, who had come there in search of us, to inform us further concerning his departure for the South river, and to take us to his house. We spoke to him in regard to this and other matters, as was proper, and shortly afterwards he left. Jaques is a man advanced in

---

[1] Jacques Cortelyou came from Utrecht to this country in 1562, in the quality of tutor to the children of Cornelis van Werckhoven, of that city, first patentee direct from the West India company, of Nyack, or Fort Hamilton. He married Neeltje Van Duyne, and died about 1693. The Indians received six coats, six kettles, six axes, six chisels, six small looking-glasses, twelve knives and twelve combs, from the West India company, in 1645, for all the land extending along the bay, from Gowanus to Coney island, embracing the present town of New Utrecht. Van Werckhoven went to Holland, after attempting a settlement at Nyack, but with the intention of returning. He died there, however, in 1655; and Cortelyou, who remained in possession of Nyack as his agent, obtained permission, in 1657, from the director and council, to lay out on the tract, the town of New Utrecht, so named in compliment to the birth-place of Van Werckhoven — *N. Y. Doc. Hist.*, I, 413; *O'Callaghan's New Netherland*, II, 185; *Brodhead's New York*, I, 410. *Bergen Genealogy*, 90.

[2] The journalist, as we have seen, mistakes in supposing the first purchase of Nyack from the Indians to have been by Cortelyou; but is probably correct in stating a second purchase by him, which might have been made for the purpose of aiding him with a title by possession against the heirs of Van Werckhoven, who actually did subsequently claim this inheritance.

years. He was born in Utrecht, but of French parents, as we could readily discover from all his actions, looks and language. He had studied philosophy in his youth, and spoke Latin and good French. He was a mathematician and sworn land-surveyor. He had also formerly learned several sciences, and had some knowledge of medicine. The worst of it was, he was a good Cartesian and not a good Christian, regulating himself, and all externals, by reason and justice only; nevertheless, he regulated all things better by these principles than most people in these parts do, who bear the name of Christians or pious persons. His brother-in-law and ourselves were welcomed by him and his wife. He treated us with every civility, although two of his sons being sick, and he very much confined in attending upon them, he was much interrupted in attending to us, since they more than we afflicted his head and that of his wife. We went looking around the country, and towards evening came to the village of New Utrecht, so named by him. This village was burned down some time ago, with every thing about it, including the house of this man, which was almost an half an hour distant from it. Many persons were impoverished by the fire. It was now almost all rebuilt, and many good stone houses were erected, of which Jaques's was one, where we returned by another road to spend the night. After supper, we went to sleep in the barn, upon some straw spread with sheep-skins, in the midst of the continual grunting of hogs, squealing of pigs, bleating and coughing of sheep, barking of dogs, crowing of cocks, cackling of hens, and, especially, a goodly quantity of fleas and vermin, of no small portion of which we were participants; and all with an open barn door, through which a fresh northwest wind was blowing. Though we could not sleep, we could not complain, inasmuch as we had the same quarters and kind of bed that their own son usually had, who had now on our arrival crept in the straw behind us.

OCTOBER 1*st*, *Sunday*. We went, this morning, on a tour of observation of the country and of the neighbors, some of whom were better situated than others, but all of them had more or less children sick with the small pox, which, next to the fever and ague, is the most prevalent disease in these parts, and of which many have died. We went into one house where there were two children lying dead and unburied, and three others sick, and where one had died the week before. This disease was more fatal this year than usual. We spoke to these afflicted people what was suitable and they could bear.

Finding myself afterwards alone upon a small eminence, I made a sketch, as well as I could, of the land surrounding the great bay, that is, Coney island, the entrance from the sea, *Rensselaer's* hook, and so further to the right, towards *Kil van Kol*.

After dinner we intended to leave for a place called the bay,[1] where *Jan Theunissen*, our fellow passenger, lived, who had made us great promises of friendship; besides, my companion was desirous, as they said there would be preaching, to hear the minister of the island, who was very zealous and a great Cocceian, and, perhaps, a Cartesian. But Jaques persuaded us from it, because the house where Jan Theunissen lived with his father was so full of people on Sundays, who came from all directions to attend preaching, that you could scarcely get in or out. As the minister was not in the village where he dwelt, he remained over with many other persons; and he (Jaques) said he would accompany us there the next morning. So we let it pass, and took another walk to New Utrecht, where we drank some good beer a year old, and coming back again

[1] Flatlands, the residence of Elbert Elbertsen Stoothoff, the father-in-law of Jan Theunissen.

to the house, indulged in peaches on the road. I went along the shore to Coney island, which is separated from Long Island only by a creek, and around the point, and came inside not far from a village called *Gravesant*, and again home. We discovered on the road several kinds of grapes still on the vines, called *speck* (pork) grapes, which are not always good, and these were not; although they were sweet in the mouth at first, they made it disagreeable and stinking. The small blue grapes are better, and their vines grow in good form. Although they have several times attempted to plant vineyards, and have not immediately succeeded, they, nevertheless, have not abandoned the hope of doing so by and by, for there is always some encouragement, although they have not, as yet, discovered the cause of the failure.

2d, Monday. Having slept the night again at *Najack*, we four went, after breakfast, to the bay, where we arrived about ten o'clock. We did not find Jan Theunissen at home, as he had driven to the city to bring his goods; but the father and mother bade us welcome, and took us around into their orchards to look at them. My comrade spoke to him as opportunity offered of godly things, but he seemed to be a little disposed to play the part of a religious and wise man, and he defended himself and the evil as much as he could, going to work somewhat coldly with us. We took the time, however, to go around and see every thing thoroughly, and found the land, in general, not so good as that at *Najack.* There is towards the sea, a large piece of low flat land which is overflown at every tide, like the *schorr* (marsh) with us, miry and muddy at the bottom, and which produces a species of hard salt grass or reed grass. Such a place they call *valey*[1] and mow it for hay, which cattle would rather eat than fresh hay or

[1] Pronounced *fly*.

grass. It is so hard that they cannot mow it with a common scythe, like ours, but must have the English scythe for the purpose. Their adjoining corn lands are dry and barren for the most part. Some of them were now entirely covered with clover in blossom, which diffused a sweet odor in the air for a great distance, and which we discovered in the atmosphere, before we saw the fields. Behind the village, inland, are their meadows, but they also were now arid. All the land from the bay to *'t Vlacke Bos*[1] is low and level, without the least elevation. There is also a tract which is somewhat large, of a kind of heath, on which sheep could graze, though we saw none upon it. This meadow (*schorr*), like all the others, is well provided with good creeks which are navigable and very serviceable for fisheries. There is here a grist-mill driven by the water which they dam up in the creek; and it is hereabouts they go mostly to shoot snipe and wild geese. In the middle of this meadow there is a grove into which we went, and within which there was a good vale cleared off and planted. On our return from this ramble we found Jan Theunissen had come back with his company. He welcomed us, but somewhat coldly, and so demeaned himself all the time we were there, as to astonish my comrade at the change, but not me entirely, for I had observed this falling off while we were yet at sea and were approaching the land and even before that, and had remarked it to my colleague, but he had more confidence in him. The day having been thus passed, we remained here for the night to sleep. In the evening we made the acquaintance of one *Jean Poppe*, formerly a skipper in the West Indies, whom I had known when I lived there. He did not know me by name or by vocation, but only that I lived there, and had conversed with him there, but not much. He was tired of

[1] Flatbush.

the sea, and not having accumulated much, he had come to settle down here, making his living out of the business of a turner, by which he could live bountifully.

3*d*, *Tuesday*. This whole day it did nothing except rain, with an E. and E. N. E. wind, so that we were compelled to sit in their house, as in a prison all the time; and it was so much the worse because the house was constantly filled with a multitude of godless people; for this father or father-in-law of Jan Theunissen, being the principal person in the place, was their captain, and having many children of his own besides, there was a continual concourse at his house. We had to remain, although it grieved us a great deal. But as we had heard that there was an Englishman residing at Gravesend, named Bowman, who went every year about this time with horses and sheep to the South river, and would probably go there again in about three weeks time, we resolved, when the rain was partly over, to go and talk to him, which we did, arriving there towards evening. We found him at home, and inquired of him as to the situation. He said, he intended to leave in fourteen days or at the longest in three weeks, with horses, and would be happy to have our company on the road. He told us several things touching the situation of the South river, where he had a large tract of land which he intended soon to put under cultivation. It being evening, and nearer Jaques's house than the bay, we determined to go there as we had previously intended. Mr. Bowman had the kindness to conduct us a portion of the way so that we could not go astray. We arrived at Jaques's house, where we were welcome. The land around Gravesend is also flat, but not so flat or so barren as in the bay, and yields good crops.

4*th*, *Wednesday*. We slept for the night in our old place. In the morning the horses were harnessed to the wagon for the purpose of carrying us to the city, and bringing back some medicines which had arrived for him (Jaques) from Holland in our ship. We breakfasted to our full, and rode first to the bay, where we had left our traveling bag. Seeing there was nothing to be accomplished with our Jan Theunissen, all his great promises having vanished without the least result, though they had cost us dearly enough, we let that rest quiet, and taking our leave, rode on to *'t Vlacke Bos*, a village situated about an hour and a half's distance from there, upon the same plain, which is very large. This village seems to have better farms than the bay, and yields full as much revenue. Riding through it, we came to the woods and the hills, which are very stony and uncomfortable to ride over. We rode over them, and passed through the village of *Breukelen* to the ferry, and leaving the wagon there, we crossed over the river and arrived at home at noon, where we were able to rest a little, and where our old people were glad to see us. We sent back to Jaques half of our tincture calimanaris, and half of our balsam sulphureus and some other things. He had been of service to us in several respects, as he promised to be, and that with perfect willingness.

5*th*, *Thursday*. We remained at home this morning, my comrade having been a little indisposed the preceding day and night, and betook ourselves to writing. At noon we visited *Mons. de La Grange*, who was busily employed in his little shop, packing and marking a parcel of ribbons which he was going to send to Barbadoes, because, as he said, he could not dispose of them here to advantage, that is, with sufficient profit. We let him first finish his work, and after that he took us to his counting room, where his wife was. We did not fail to converse kindly with him and his wife in relation to those matters in which we believed they were sinning, notwithstanding all the little reasons which pious people of that description are accustomed to advance in extenuation of their sin and avarice.

As there were plenty of books around, my comrade inquired of him what book he liked or esteemed the most. Upon this he brought forward two of the elder Brakel, one of which was, *De Trappen des Geestelycken Leven* (the gradations of spiritual life).[1] He also took down another written by a Scotchman, of whom my comrade had some knowledge, and translated by Domine Koelman. On my return home, the son of our old people asked me if I would not go to their usual catechizing, which they held once a week at the house of *Abraham Lanoy*, schoolmaster, and brother of the commissary in the custom house. I accompanied him there, and found a company of about twenty-five persons, male and female, but mostly young people. It looked like a school, as indeed it was, more than an assembly of persons who were seeking after true godliness; where the schoolmaster, who instructed them, handled the subject more like a schoolmaster in the midst of his scholars than a person who knew and loved God, and sought to make him known and loved. They sung some verses from the psalms, made a prayer, and questioned from the catechism, at the conclusion of which they prayed and sung some verses from the psalms again. It was all performed without respect or reverence, very literally, and mixed up with much obscurity and error. He played, however, the part of a learned and pious man, *enfin le suffisant et le petit precheur*. After their departure, I had an opportunity of speaking to him and telling him what I thought was good for him. He acknowledged that I con-

---

[1] By Theodorus a-Brakel, father of the more distinguished divine, William a-Brakel. He was descended from Roman Catholic stock in the province of Brabant, but was born at Enkhuisen in North Holland in 1608. He was educated at Franeker, and called to minister first at Beers in Friesland, then at the Burgh on the island of Texel, and finally at Makkum, where he died in 1699. Like his son he was in strict orthodoxy with the Reformed church of Holland.—Kok. *Vad. Hist.*

vinced him of several things; and thus leaving him I returned home.

6th, Friday. We remained in the house during the forenoon, but after having dined we went out about two o'clock to explore the island of *Manathans.* This island runs east and west, or somewhat more northerly. On the north side of it is the North river, by which it is separated from the main land on the north; on the east end it is separated from the main land by a creek, or rather a branch of the North river, emptying itself into the East river. They can go over this creek at dead low water, upon rocks and reefs, at the place called *Spyt den duyvel.* This creek coming into the East river forms with it the two *Barents islands.*[1] At the west end of these two running waters, that is, where they come together to the east of these islands, they make, with the rocks and reefs, such a frightful eddy and whirlpool that it is exceedingly dangerous to pass through them, especially with small boats, of which there are some lost every now and then, and the persons in them drowned; but experience has taught men the way of passing through them with less danger. Large vessels have always less danger because they are not capable of being carried along so quickly. There are two places where such whirling of the stream occurs, which are on account of the danger and frightfulness called the Great and Little Hellgate. After these two streams are united, the island of *Manathans* is separated on the south from Long Island by the East river, which, beginning at the bay before New York, runs eastwardly, after forming several islands, again into the sea. This island is about seven hours' distance in length, but it is not a full hour broad. The sides are indented with bays, coves and creeks. It is almost entirely taken up, that is, the land is held by private owners, but not half of it is

[1] Now called Great and Little Barn islands.

cultivated. Much of it is good wood land. The west end on which the city lies, is entirely cleared for more than an hour's distance, though that is the poorest ground; the best being on the east and north side. There are many brooks of fresh water running through it, pleasant and proper for man and beast to drink, as well as agreeable to behold, affording cool and pleasant resting places, but especially suitable places for the construction of mills, for although there is no overflow of water, yet it can be shut off and so used. A little eastward of *Nieu Haerlem* there are two ridges of very high rocks, with a considerable space between them, displaying themselves very majestically, and inviting all men to acknowledge in them the majesty, grandeur, power and glory of their creator, who has impressed such marks upon them. Between them runs the road to *Spyt den duyvel.* The one to the north is most apparent; the south ridge is covered with earth on its north side, but it can be seen from the water or from the main land beyond to the south. The soil between these ridges is very good, though a little hilly and stony, and would be very suitable in my opinion for planting vineyards, in consequence of its being shut off on both sides from the winds which would most injure them, and is very warm. We found blue grapes along the road which were very good and sweet, and as good as any I have tasted in the Fatherland.

We went from the city, following the Broadway, over the *valey*, or the fresh water. Upon both sides of this way were many habitations of negroes, mulattoes and whites. These negroes were formerly the proper slaves of the (West India) company, but, in consequence of the frequent changes and conquests of the country, they have obtained their freedom and settled themselves down where they have thought proper, and thus on this road, where they have ground enough to live on with their families. We left the village, called the *Bouwerij*, lying on the right hand, and went through the woods to New Harlem, a tolerably large village situated on the south side of the island, directly opposite the place where the northeast creek and the East river come together, situated about three hours journey from New Amsterdam, like as old Harlem, in Europe, is situated about three hours distance from old Amsterdam. As our guide, Gerrit, had some business here, and found many acquaintances, we remained over night at the house of one *Geresolveert*,[1] scout (sheriff or constable), of the place, who had formerly lived in Brazil, and whose heart was still full of it. This house was constantly filled with people, all the time drinking, for the most part, that execrable rum. He had also the best cider we have tasted. Among the crowd we found a person of quality, an Englishman, named Captain Carteret, whose father is in great favor with the king, and he himself had assisted in several exploits in the king's service. He was administrator, or captain general, of the English forces which went, in 1660, to retake St. Kitts, which the French had entirely conquered, and were repulsed. He had also filled some high office, during the war, in the ship of the Duke of York, with two hundred infantry under his command. The king has given to his father, Sir (George) Carteret, the entire government of the lands west of the North river, in New Netherland, with power to appoint as governor whom he pleases; and at this present time there is a governor over it, by his appointment, another Carteret, his nephew, I believe, who resides at Elizabethtown, in New Jersey.[2]

---

[1] *Resolved*, a christian name.

[2] Philip Carteret, the brother, not the nephew, of Sir George, is the person here meant. He was appointed governor of New Jersey under the joint proprietorship of Lord Berkeley and Sir George Carteret, in 1664, and of East Jersey in 1674, under the sole grant to Sir George. He resigned in 1682, and died in December of that year, in this country,

From this Carteret, in England, the quakers have purchased the privilege of a government of their own, over a large tract of territory which they have bought and settled within his dominion; and it is but little different from their having bought the entire right of government of the whole of his land. This son is a very profligate person. He married a merchant's daughter here, and has so lived with his wife that her father has been compelled to take her home again. He runs about among the farmers, and stays where he can find most to drink, and sleeps in barns on the straw. If he conducted himself properly, he could be not only governor here, but hold higher positions, for he has studied the moralities, and seems to have been of a good understanding; but that is all now drowned. His father, who will not acknowledge him as his son, as before, allows him yearly as much only as is necessary for him to live.[1]

7th, Saturday. This morning, about half-past six, we set out from the village, in order to go to the end of the island; but before we left we did not omit supplying ourselves with peaches which grew in an orchard along the road. The whole ground was covered with them and with apples, lying upon the new grain with which the orchard was planted. The peaches were the most delicious we had yet eaten. We proceeded on our way, and when we were not far from the point of *Spyt den duyvel,* we could see on our left hand the rocky cliffs of the main land on the

---

leaving a widow, the daughter of Richard Smith, of Smithtown, on Long island. — *Whitehead's East Jersey under the Proprietors*, 36, 84.

[1] Captain James Cartaret, here described, was an illegitimate son of Sir George. He was chosen governor of East Jersey, in 1672, by the deputies of the disaffected inhabitants of Middletown and other towns, which resisted the payment of rent to the co-proprietors. He enjoyed this barren honor only a short time, as the opposition was completely overcome in the following year. The mention of him in this journal seems to be the only account of him afterwards. — *Whitehead's East Jersey*, &c., 55, 58.

other side of the North river, these cliffs standing straight up and down, with the grain, just as if they were antimony. We crossed over the *Spyt den duyvel* in a canoe, and paid nine stuivers fare for us three, which was very dear. We followed the opposite side of the land, and came to the house of one *Valentyn*, a great acquaintance of our Gerrit. He had gone to the city, but his wife, though she did not know Gerrit or us, was so much rejoiced to see Hollanders, that she hardly knew what to do for us. She set before us what she had. We left after breakfasting there. Her son showed us the way, and we came to a road which was entirely covered with peaches. We asked the boy why they left them lie there, and they did not let the hogs eat them. He answered, we do not know what to do with them, there are so many; the hogs are satiated with them and will not eat any more. From this we may judge of the quantity of them. We pursued our way now a small distance through the woods and over the hills, then back again along the shore to a point, where one *Webblingh*, an Englishman, lived, who was standing ready to cross over. He carried us over with him, and refused to take any pay for our passage, offering us at the same time some of his rum, a liquor which is everywhere. We were now again at New Harlem, and dined with *Geresolveert*, at whose house we slept the night before, and who made us welcome. It was now two o'clock; and leaving there, we crossed over the island, which takes about three quarters of an hour to do, and came to the North river, which we followed a little within the woods, to *Sappokanikke*[1]. Gerrit having a sister and friends there we rested ourselves, and drank some good beer, which refreshed us. We continued along the shore to the city, where we arrived in an hour in the

---

[1] According to Judge Benson this was the Indian name of the point, afterwards known as Greenwich, on the north side of the city.—*New York Historical Collections*, second series, 84.

evening, very much fatigued, having walked this day about forty miles. I must add, in passing through this island we sometimes encountered such a sweet smell in the air that we stood still, because we did not know what it was we were meeting.

8th, Sunday. We staid home this morning for the purpose of writing and resting ourselves. Gerrit requested me to shave him, as did also an old countryman of *Neresinck* who lodged at our house, which was the first time in my life that I had ever shaved any one. It afforded us an opportunity of speaking to this countryman about various matters touching the country. We intended in the afternoon to attend the English service, but, on going to the fort, the sentinel told us there was no English preaching in the afternoon, and we returned home.

9th, Monday. We remained at home to-day, except I went out to ascertain whether there was any way of going over to Staten island. Meanwhile we began to dispose of some of our large merchandise. Gerrit went out to *Sapokan*, to do some carpenter's work. We tasted to-day some very fine grapes.

10*th, Tuesday.* Finding no opportunity of going to Staten island, we asked our old friend Symon, who had come over from *Gouanes*, what was the best way for us to get there, when he offered us his services to take us over in his skiff, which we accepted; and at dusk accompanied him in his boat to *Gouanes*, where we arrived about eight o'clock, and where he welcomed us and entertained us well.

11*th, Wednesday.* We embarked early this morning in his boat and rowed over to Staten island, where we arrived about eight o'clock. He left us there, and we went on our way. This island is about thirty-two miles long and four broad. Its sides are very irregular, with projecting points and indented bays, and creeks running deep into the country. It lies for the most part east and west, and is somewhat triangular. The most prominent point is to the west. On the east side is the narrow passage which they call the channel, by which it is separated from the high point of Long Island. On the south is the great bay which is inclosed by *Nayaq*, *t' Conijnen* island, *Rentselaer's* Hook, *Neversinck*, &c. On the west is the *Raritans*. On the north or northwest is New Jersey, from which it is separated by a large creek or arm of the river, called *Kil van kol*. The eastern part is high and steep, and has few inhabitants. It is the usual place where ships, ready for sea, stop to take in water, while the captain and passengers are engaged in making their own arrangements and writing letters previous to their departure. The whole south side is a large plain, with much salt meadow or marsh, and several creeks. The west point is flat, and on or around it is a large creek with much marsh; but to the north of this creek it is high and hilly, and beyond that it begins to be more level, but not so low as on the other side, and is well populated. On the northwest it is well provided with creeks and marshes, and the land is generally better than on the south side, although there is a good parcel of land in the middle of the latter. As regards the middle or most hilly part of the island, it is uninhabited, although the soil is better than the land around it; but, in consequence of its being away from the water, and lying so high, no one will live there, the creeks and rivers being so serviceable to them in enabling them to go to the city, and for fishing and catching oysters, and for being near the salt meadows. The woods are used for pasturing horses and cattle, for being an island, none of them can get off. Each person has marks upon his own by which he can find them when he wants them. When the population of the country shall increase, these places will be taken up. Game of all kinds is plenty, and twenty-five and thirty deer are sometimes seen in a herd. A boy who came in a house where we were, told us he had shot ten the last winter himself, and more than forty in his life, and in the same manner other game. We tasted here the best grapes. There are now about a hundred families on the island, of which the English constitute the least portion, and the Dutch and French divide between them about equally the greater portion. They have neither church nor minister, and live rather far from each other, and inconveniently to meet together. The English are less disposed to religion, and inquire little after it, but in case there were a minister, would contribute to his support. The French and Dutch are very desirous and eager for one, for they spoke of it wherever we went, and said, in the event of not obtaining Domine Tessemaker, they would send, or had sent, to France for another. The French are good Reformed churchmen, and some of them are Walloons. The Dutch are also from different quarters.

We reached the island, as I have said, about nine o'clock, directly opposite *Gouanes*, not far from the watering place. We proceeded southwardly along the shore of the high land on the east end, where it was sometimes stony and rocky, and sometimes sandy, supplied with fine constantly-flowing springs with which at times we quenched our thirst. We had now come nearly to the furthest point on the southeast, behind which I had observed several houses when we came in with the ship. We had also made inquiry as to the villages through which we would have to pass, and they had told us the *Oude Dorp* would be the first one we would come to; but my comrade finding the point very rocky and difficult, and believing the village was inland, and as we discovered no path to follow, we determined to clamber to the top of this steep bluff, through the bushes and thickets, which we accomplished with great difficulty and in a perspiration. We found as little of a road above as below, and nothing but woods, through which one could not see. There appeared to be a little foot-path along the edge which I followed a short distance to the side of the point, but my comrade calling me and saying that he certainly thought we had passed by the road to the *Oude Dorp*, and observing myself that the little path led down to the point, I returned again, and we followed it the other way, which led us back to the place from where we started. We supposed we ought to go from the shore in order to find the road to the *Oude Dorp*, and seeing here these slight tracks into the woods, we followed them as far as we could, till at last they ran to nothing else than dry leaves. Having wandered an hour or more in the woods, now in a hollow and then over a hill, at one time through a swamp, at another across a brook, without finding any road or path, we entirely lost the way. We could see nothing except a little of the sky through the thick branches of the trees above our heads, and we thought it best to break out of the woods entirely and regain the shore. I had taken an observation of the shore and point, having been able to look at the sun, which shone extraordinarily hot in the thick woods, without the least breath of air stirring. We made our way at last as well as we could out of the woods, and struck the shore a quarter of an hour's distance from where we began to climb up. We were rejoiced, as there was a house not far from the place where we came out. We went to it to see if we could find any one who would show us the way a little. There was no master in it, but an Englishwoman with negroes and servants. We first asked her as to the road, and then for something to drink, and also for some one to show us the road; but she refused the last, although we were willing to pay for it. She was a cross woman. She said she had never been in the village, and her folks must work, and we would certainly have to go away as wise as we came. She said, however, we must follow the shore, as we did. We went now over the rocky point, which we were no sooner over than we saw a pretty little sand bay, and a small creek, and not far from there, cattle and houses. We also saw the point to which the little path led from the hill above, where I was when my comrade called me. We would not have had more than three hundred steps to go to have been where we now were. It was very hot, and we perspired a great deal. We went on to the little creek to sit down and rest ourselves there, and to cool our feet, and then proceeded to the houses which constituted the *Oude Dorp*. It was now about two o'clock. There were seven houses, but only three in which any body lived. The others were abandoned, and their owners had gone to live on better places on the island, because the ground around this village was worn out and barren, and also too limited for their use. We went into the first house which was inhabited by English, and there rested ourselves and eat, and inquired further after the road. The woman was cross, and her husband not much better. We had to pay here for what we eat which we had not done before. We paid three guilders in zeewan, although we only drank water. We proceeded by a tolerably good road to the *Nieuwe Dorp*, but as the road ran continually in the woods, we got astray again in them. It was dark, and we were compelled to break our way out through the woods and thickets, and we went a great distance before we succeeded, when it was almost entirely dark. We saw a house at a distance to which we directed ourselves across the bushes. It was the first house of the *Nieuwe Dorp*. We found there an Englishman who could speak Dutch, and who received us very cordially into his house, where we had as good as he and his wife had. She was a Dutch woman from the *Manhatans*, who was glad to have us in her house.

12*th*, *Thursday*. Although we had not slept well, we had to resume our journey with the day. The man where we slept set us on the road. We had now no more villages to go to, but went from one plantation to another, for the most part belonging to French, who showed us every kindness because we conversed with them in French, and spoke of the ways of the Lord according to their condition. About one-third part of the distance from the south side to the west end is still all woods, and is very little visited. We had to go along the shore, finding sometimes fine creeks well provided with wild turkeys, geese, snipes and wood hens. Lying rotting upon the shore were thousands of fish called *marsbancken*, which are about the size of a common carp. These fish swim close together in large schools, and are pursued so by other fish that they are forced upon the shore in order to avoid the mouths of their enemies, and when the water falls they are left there to die, food for the eagles and other birds of prey. Proceeding thus along we came to the West point where an Englishman lived alone some distance from the road. We eat something here, and he gave us the consolation that we would have a very bad road for two or three hours ahead, which indeed we experienced, for there was neither path nor road. He showed us as well as he could. There was a large creek to cross which ran very far into the land, and when we should get on the other side of it, we must, he said, go outward again along (the shore). After we had gone a piece of the way through the woods, we came to a valley with a brook running through it, which we took to be the creek or the end of it. We turned round it as short as we could, in order to go back again to the shore, which we reached after wandering a long time over hill and dale, when we saw the creek, which we supposed we had crossed, now just before us. We followed the side of it deep into the woods, and when we arrived at the end of it saw no path along the other side to get outwards again, but the road ran into the woods in order to cut off a point of the hills and land. We pursued this road for some time, but saw no mode of getting out, and that it led further and further from the creek. We, therefore, left the road and went across through the bushes, so as to reach the shore by the nearest route according to our calculation. After continuing this course about an hour, we saw at a distance a miserably constructed tabernacle of pieces of wood covered with brush, all open in front, and where we thought there were Indians; but on coming up to it we found in it an Englishman sick, and his wife and child lying upon some bushes by a little fire. We asked him if he were sick. "Do you ask me whether I am sick? I have been sick here over two months," he replied. It made my heart sore indeed, for I had never in all my life seen such poverty, and that, too, in the middle of a woods and a wilderness. After we obtained some information as to the way, we went on, and had not gone far before we came to another house, and thus from one farm to another, French, Dutch and a few English, so that we had not wandered very far out of the way. We inquired at each house the way to the next one. Shortly before evening we arrived at the plantation of a Frenchman, whom they called *Le Chaudronnier* (the coppersmith), who was formerly a soldier under the Prince of Orange, and had served in Brazil. He was so delighted, and held on to us so hard, that we remained and spent the night with him.

13*th*, *Friday*. We pursued our journey this morning from plantation to plantation, the same as yesterday, until we came to that of *Pierre le Gardinier*, who had been a gardener of the Prince of Orange, and had known him well. He had a large family of children and grand-children. He was about seventy years of age, and was still as fresh and active as a young person. He was so glad to see strangers who conversed with him and his in the French language about the good, that he leaped for joy. After we had breakfasted here they told us that we had another large creek to pass called the Fresh kil, and there we could perhaps be set across the *Kil van Kol* to the point of Mill creek, where we might wait for a boat to convey as to the *Manhatans*. The road was long and difficult, and we asked for a guide, but he had no one, in consequence of several of his children being sick. At last he determined to go himself, and accordingly carried us in his canoe over to the point of Mill creek in New Jersey behind Kol (*achter Kol*).[1] We learned immediately that there was a boat up this creek loading with brick, and would leave that night for the city. After we had thanked and parted with Pierre le Gardinier, we determined to walk to Elizabethtown, a good half hour's distance inland, where the boat was. From the point to this village there is a fine wagon road, but nowhere in the country had we been so pestered with mosquitos (*muggen*) as we were on this road. The land about here is very poor, and is not well peopled. We found the boat, and spoke to the captain who left about two hours afterwards; but as the wind was against going out of the creek, he lay by and waited for the tide. We returned by evening to the point where we were to stay until morning. There was a tavern on it, kept by French papists, who at once took us to be priests, and so conducted themselves towards us in every respect accordingly, although we told them and protested otherwise. As there was nothing to be said further we remained so in their imaginations to the last, as shown both in their words and actions, the more

---

[1] "*En bracht ons met syn canoo tot op de hoeck van de molen kil aen Nieu Jarnesee achter kol.*" The term *achter kol*, literally *behind kol*, that is, back of the kol, a name given to the river or kil between Staten island and the main land from its peculiar shape, was applied to all the territory west of that river or kil and the Hackensack. Kol is here used as an abbreviation of *kil van kol*. Mill creek seems to have been the stream now known as Elizabethtown creek.

certainly because we spoke French, and they were French people. We slept there this night, and at three o'clock in the morning we set sail.

14*th*, *Saturday*. Being under sail, as I have said, it was so entirely calm that we could only float with the stream until we came to the *Schutters* island, where we obtained the tide again. It was now about four o'clock. In order to protect ourselves from the air which was very cold and piercing, we crept under the sail which was very old and full of holes. The tide having run out by daylight, we came under sail again, with a good wind which brought us to the city at about eight o'clock, for which we were glad, and returning thanks to God, betook ourselves to rest.

15*th*, *Sunday*. We went at noon to-day to hear the English minister, whose services took place after the Dutch church was out. There were not above twenty-five or thirty people in the church. The first thing that occurred was the reading of all their prayers and ceremonies out of the prayer book, as is done in all Episcopal churches. A young man then went into the pulpit and commenced preaching, who thought he was performing wonders; but he had a little book in his hand out of which he read his sermon which was about a quarter of an hour or half an hour long.[1] With this the services were concluded, at which we could not be sufficiently astonished. This was all that happened with us to-day.

16*th*, *Monday*. I was occupied to-day in copying my

---

[1] The only English minister in the whole province at this time was attached to the garrison at the city of New York. This was the Rev. Charles Wooley, a graduate of Emanuel College, Cambridge, in 1677. He came to New York in August, 1678, and left there for England in July, 1680. He was the author of a small volume with the title of *A Two Years' Journal in New York*, &c., published in 1701, and recently republished, with notes by Dr. E. B. O'Callaghan, in Mr. Gowans' interesting series of early works on the colonies.

journal. In the morning there came an Indian to our house, a man about eighty years of age, whom our people called Jasper, who lived at *Ahakinsack* or at *Akinon*. Concerning this Indian our old people related that when they lived on Long Island, it was once a very dear time; no provisions could be obtained, and they suffered great want, so that they were reduced to the last extremity; that God the Lord then raised up this Indian, who went out a fishing daily in order to bring fish to them every day when he caught a good mess, which he always did. If, when he came to the house, he found it alone, and they were out working in the fields, he did not fail, but opened the door, laid the fish on the floor, and proceeded on his way. For this reason these people possess great affection for him and have given him the name of Jasper, and also my *nitap*, that is, my great friend. He never comes to the *Manhatans* without visiting them and eating with them, as he now did, as among his old friends. We asked him why he had done so much kindness to these people. "I have always been inclined," he answered, "from my youth up to do good, especially to good people, known to me. I took the fish to them because *Maneto* (the devil) said to me, you must take fish to these people, whispering ever in my ear 'you must take fish to them.' I had to do it, or *Maneto* would have killed me." Our old woman telling us he sometimes got drunk, we said to him he should not do so any more, that the great *Sakemacker* (the Lord) who is above, was offended at such conduct and would kill him. "No," said he, laughing as if that were a mistake of ours, "it is *Maneto* who kill those who do evil, and leaves those who do good at peace." "That is only" we replied, "because *Maneto* is the slave and executioner of the great Sakemacker above;" and we then asked him if he believed there was such a great and good Sakemacker there? "Undoubtedly," he said, "but he remains above, and does not trouble himself with the earth or earthly things, because he does nothing except what is good; but *Mancto*, who also is a Sakemacker, and is here below, and governs all, and punishes and torments those men who do evil and drink themselves drunk." Hereupon we inquired of him why he did so then. "Yes," he said, "I had rather not, but my heart is so inclined that it causes me to do it, although I know it is wrong. The Christians taught it to us, and give us or sell us the drink, and drink themselves drunk." We said to him: "Listen! if we came to live near you, you would never see us drunk, nor would we give or sell you or your people any rum." "That," he replied, "would be good." We told him he must not make such a difference between himself and a Christian, because one was white and the other red, and one wore clothes and the other went almost naked, or one was called a Christian and the other an Indian, that this great and good Sakemacker was the father of us all, and had made us all, and that all who did not do good would be killed by *Mancto* whether they were called Christians or Indians; but that all who should do good would go to this good *Sakemacker* above. "Yes," said he, "we do not know or speak to this Sakemacker, but *Mancto* we know and speak to, but you people, who can read and write, know and converse with this *Sakemacker*."

We asked him, where he believed he came from? He answered from his father. "And where did your father come from?" we said, "and your grand-father and great grand-father, and so on to the first of the race?" He was silent for a little while, either as if unable to climb up at once so high with his thoughts, or to express them without help, and then took a piece of coal out of the fire where he sat, and began to write upon the floor. He first drew a circle, a little oval, to which he made four paws or feet, a head and a tail. "This," said he, "is a tortoise, lying in the water around it," and he moved his hand round the figure, continuing, "this was or is all water, and so at first was the world or the earth, when the tortoise gradually raised its round back up high, and the water ran off of it, and thus the earth became dry." He then took a little straw and placed it on end in the middle of the figure, and proceeded, "the earth was now dry, and there grew a tree in the middle of the earth, and the root of this tree sent forth a sprout beside it and there grew upon it a man, who was the first male. This man was then alone, and would have remained alone; but the tree bent over until its top touched the earth, and there shot therein another root, from which came forth another sprout, and there grew upon it the woman, and from these two are all men produced." We gave him four fish-hooks with which he was much pleased, and immediately calculated how much in money he had obtained. "I have got twenty four stuivers worth," he said. He then inquired our names, which we gave him, and wished to know why he asked for them? "Well," he replied, "because you are good people and are true *nitaps;* and in case you should come into the woods and fall into the hands of the Indians, and they should wish to kill or harm you, if I know or hear of it I might help you, for they will do you no injury when they know me." For he was the brother of a Sackemaker. We told him that we did not give them to him on that account, but only from regard because he was a good person, although the good will or thankfulness which he wished to show thereby was good. "Well," he said, "that is good, that is good," with which, after eating something, he departed.

But at noon he returned with a young Indian, both of them so drunk they could not speak, and having a calabash of liquor with them. We chided him, but to no purpose, for he could neither use his reason nor speak so as to be understood. The young Indian with him was a Sackemaker's son, and was bold. He wanted to have a piece of meat that was on the table, and on which we all had to make our dinner, when we told him it was not for him. "Yes," said he, "I see it is so;" nevertheless, and although we offered him something else to eat, he was evilly disposed and dissatisfied, and would take nothing except the piece of meat alone; but that was not given to him. Whereupon Jasper told him he must be quiet, that the old people and we were all his *nitaps*, and by degrees quieted him, they sitting together by the fire and drinking their rum. They left afterwards for Long Island.

17*th*, *Tuesday*. Nothing transpired to-day.

18*th*, *Wednesday*. In the afternoon Jasper, the Indian, came back again, and proceeded confidently to our room in the rear of the house, but sober and in his senses. He told us how he had been with his nephew, the Sackemaker's son to Long Island, among the other Indians; and that he had given away, not only his fish-hooks, but also his shoes and stockings. We found fault with him at first for having become so drunk, contrary to his promise, and when he well knew it was wrong. To which he said he had to buy some nails for an Englishman who lived near him, from another Englishman here, who had sold and given him the rum.

I must here remark, in passing, that the people in this city, who are most all traders in small articles, whenever they see an Indian enter the house, who they know has any money, they immediately set about getting hold of him, giving him rum to drink, whereby he is soon caught and becomes half a fool. If he should then buy any thing, he is doubly cheated, in the wares, and in the price. He is then urged to buy more drink, which they now make half water, and if he cannot drink it, they drink it themselves. They do not rest until they have cajoled him out of all his money, or most of it; and if that cannot be done in one day, they keep him, and let him lodge and sleep there, but in some out of the way place, down on the ground, guarding their merchandise and other property in the meantime, and always managing it so that the poor creature does not go away before he has given them all they want. And these miserable Christians are so much the more eager in this respect, because no money circulates among themselves, and they pay each other in wares, in which they are constantly cheating and defrauding each other. Although it is forbidden to sell the drink to the Indians, yet every one does it, and so much the more earnestly, and with so much greater and burning avarice, that it is done in secret. To this extent and further, reaches the damnable and insatiable covetousness of most of those who here call themselves Christians. Truly, our hearts grieved when we heard of these things, which call so grievously upon the supreme judge for vengeance. He will not always let his name be so profaned and exposed to reproach and execration.

We asked Jasper, why he had given away his hooks and stockings. He said, it was a custom among them, for the lesser to give to the greater. We replied the Sackemaker was richer than he, and he should, therefore, have kept them. "No," he said, "I did it as a mark of respect and obedience." We gave him four more fish-hooks, and told him he must take care of them for himself. "I will bring you fish as soon as I catch any," he said as he went away, promising also that he would get drunk no more.

From this time until the 22d of October, nothing special took place, except that we spoke to one Ephraim, a young trader, who was just married here, and who intended to go with his wife to the South river, where he usually dwelt, for which purpose he was only waiting for horses and men from there.[1] He tendered us his services and his horses,

[1] This person was Ephraim Heermans, son of Augustine Heermans, of both of whom we will hear more in the sequel.

if we would accompany him, and offered to carry us in his own boat everywhere on that river, from the falls (of the Delaware), to which we would have to travel by land, and where the boat would be waiting for him to take him down the river; since he himself would have to touch at many places on the river, in going down. As Bowman, who was going there with horses, did not make his appearance, we accepted the offer with thankfulness, waiting only for the time.

24th, Tuesday. Margaret's ship in which we arrived here, being ready to leave, but she not going in it, as it was said, we set about writing letters, which we might give to our Robyn, and finished them to-day, and also the copying of my journal.

25th, Wednesday. Having closed up our letters, we had Robyn at our house, and gave them to him in his own hands, as we had heard from the supercargo himself that he would run into Falmouth again for the purpose of paying the duties; we gave Robyn money to post our letters over London, together with something for his trouble, and with this, wishing him the blessing of the Lord, we took leave of him; but recollecting afterwards that we had forgotten to put a date to the letters, which was very necessary, I had to go in search of Robyn again, whom I found at last, and took back from him the letters. When we had resealed them, I went after him again, but he had gone on board the ship. I waited for an opportunity and went on board myself, and handed them to him again. He was glad to see me on board; and while there I went looking around to see how the ship was laden, and found her so full that the poor sailors had scarcely room to eat or sleep. The boatswain who had now become mate, because the Dutch mate, Evert, had become captain of a ketch, treated me with much kindness; but as the boat and sailors were continually ashore, it was dark before I could reach the land.

26*th*, *Thursday*. We inquired whether our journey to the south would soon take place, and was informed it would not be this week. We resolved not to remain idle, and to embrace the opportunity to cross to-morrow over the North river opposite the fort to a place called *Gemoenepaen*, as soon as we could find the means of passage.

27*th*, *Friday*. We went after breakfast to see if we could be taken over the river. We found a boat going soon, but we must wait a little. In the meanwhile we made the acquaintance of a person from Zeeland, or who had lived there a long time, for he himself was a Hollander. He had been an apprentice to Jaques Fierens, printer, in the Globe in the Gi street, and, although I had been often enough in that house, and he knew my face, he did not know me particularly. He came to this country with *Cornelis Everts* of Zeeland, and had assisted in taking it from the English in 1674. He had remained here since and married. He sometimes bound old books, and was the only bookbinder in the country.

It was about noon when we crossed over. Our old woman at the house had told us of another good woman who lived at this place, named *Fitie*, from Cologne, and recommended us to visit her, which we did as soon as we landed. We found her a little pious after the manner of the country, and you could discover that there was something of the Lord in her, but very much covered up and defiled. We dined there and spoke to her of what we deemed necessary for her condition. She has many grandchildren, all of whom are not unjust. We continued our journey along a fine broad wagon road to the other village, called Bergen, a good half hour or three-quarters, inland from there, where the villagers, who are most all Dutch, received us well, and were rejoiced to see us. They inquired and spoke to us about various things. We also found there the cook of the vessel in which we came over. He was sick of the ship, and was stopping ashore with his relations here in order to recruit himself. He entertained us according to his ability, and gave us some *Hespaen* (raccoon) to eat, a wild animal somewhat larger than a cat. It was very fat, and of a good flavor, almost like a pig. The skins of these animals are good peltry, and are sent in great quantities to Europe. We had also some good cider. Our cook took a small walk with us over the country, and showed us the situation of the plantations around there, as he had lived there a long time, and consequently was acquainted with all these farms. The soil was very good, and indeed of the best that we had seen anywhere. This good ground was for the most part on the declivities of the hills, and so on below. The *Slangen Bergh* (Snake's Hill) of which I had heard much, and which I had imagined to myself was a large projecting hill, lies close by and is only a small round hill; and is so named on account of the numerous snakes which infest it. It stands quite alone, and is almost entirely encircled by the North kil.[1] It is nothing but rocks and stones, with a little earth up above where a plantation could be formed. We returned to the village by evening, and lodged with one *Claes Fransen*, who had brought us over the river. He had a good old mother, and also a brother living there. His other brothers were married, and lived in the same village. We conversed with these people about spiritual things, and had great enjoyment therein. We were entirely welcome. We slept upon some straw on the floor, and it was lucky for us that he sold blankets, some of which he used to cover us. We have nowhere, to my knowledge, seen or eaten finer apples. One kind was very large, fair,

---

[1] Hackingsack river.

and of good taste, fifty-six of which only could be put in a heaped up bushel (*schepel*), that is, half a bag. Another variety, somewhat smaller, but not less fair in appearance, and of a better flavor, my comrade was acquainted with, and said they were called the *Double Paradise*. He acknowledged they were very delicate.

28*th*, *Saturday*. Early this morning Claes prepared to cross over to the *Manhatans*, to carry to market some fine fat mutton from a sheep which he had killed the night before. He sold it for three cents (*twee blanken*) a pound, reckoned in Holland money and Amsterdam weight. It was rainy the whole morning, and it had stormed so hard in the night that we could not find a dry place in the house to lie in. We were apprehensive of hearing of some misfortune to the ships, especially two lying under Staten island, one of which was Margaret's, and was bound for Holland. Claes was alarmed for his boat, in which we had to cross over; but going to the shore about eleven o'clock, he found it there, but half full of rain water. The mast which he had left standing was overboard, and to be looked for, but was afterwards found, and the mast bench and socket were out of their places, and in pieces. He had, therefore, some repairs to make. It cleared up gradually, and he resolved to cross over, which he was the more anxious to do, because he was going to bring back Domine *Tessemaker*, who had promised to come the next day and preach for them before his departure; for although there is a considerable congregation in this vicinity, and they are abundantly able to support a minister, they have none; for it is not easy to obtain one, and there is no probability of their doing so as long as the country belongs to the English, though they intend to build a church next spring. For the present they have nobody except a *voorleser* (clerk), who performs his service for them on Sundays, in the school house, where they assemble. They have, however, agreed with the minister of the city to administer there the Lord's Supper three times a year, for which he receives thirty bushels or fifteen bags of wheat. This service he performs on week-days, because he cannot be absent from the city on Sundays, where he is the only minister. This *Gmoenepaen* is an *arm* of the main land on the west side of the North river, beginning at Constable's Hook, directly opposite Staten island, from which it is separated by the *Kil van Kol.* On the east is the North river; on the north the main land *Pavoni* or *Haverstroo*, or indeed *Hackingsack*, and on the west, the North kil, which separates it from New Jersey and Elizabethtown. It is almost an hour broad, but has large salt meadows or marshes on the kil. It has many bays and inlets, and lies very commodiously for the inhabitants, because it is everywhere accessible by water from the city. The village of *Bergen* lies about in the middle of the tract, *and has been reasonably strong in time of the war with the Indians.*[1] It has very fine farms which yield well.

As we were about to cross, an Indian came up, who also desired to be carried over. He asked the skipper whether he might go over with him, who replied he had too much freight. "Well," said he, "I will pay you for that. How

---

[1] This passage is obscure. The original reads as follows: *Het dorp Bergen leijt omtrent op het midden van de streek, en is redelijck vast geweest in tyde van oorlogh met de wilde.* The Indian war here referred to was probably that of 1655, when the Indians made a descent upon New Amsterdam, and after being driven from that city, crossed over to Pavonia, and destroyed the buildings, and killed or captured the inhabitants. *O'Callaghan's New Netherland*, II, 290-1. When Bergen was first settled, is not positively known, but it was recognized as an existing village by the director-general and council of New Netherland in 1661. *Taylor's Annals of the Classis of Bergen*, 50-51. It would seem, therefore, to have been settled before the last mentioned year, and it may have been "reasonably strong;" that is, *settled* at the time Pavonia was burned. The word *vast* which we have rendered by *strong*, may, however, have another signification.

much freight do the people give you?" The skipper answered six cents in seewan." "Well then," said the Indian, "I will give you seven." This made us all laugh, because he valued himself less and bound himself to pay more than the others. We, therefore, took him with us. The river here is full four miles wide, and when it blows, especially from the north or northwest, there is sometimes a rolling sea, making it dangerous to cross over, particularly in small boats. While we were in the village of Bergen, a person came to us who was willing to take us up through the *Northwest kil*, where we were inclined to go, because Jaques of Long Island and his associates, had bought for a trifle, a piece of land there of twelve thousand *morgen*[1] and he had related wonders to us about it; and that above his land, and above the falls which are more than an hour's distance from it, there was another tract still better, which was corroborated by almost every one, especially in Bergen, whose inhabitants were very well acquainted there, and some of whom had bought a large piece of land close by. The before mentioned tract was considered by them the best in all New Netherland. We, therefore, did not reject the offer of this person, but only postponed it until a later opportunity, perhaps after our return from the South river. They said this piece of land was very large, and could be increased to twenty-five or thirty thousand *morgen*, which the Indians were disposed to sell, and we could buy for a small price. When we reached home we showed our old people the apples which we had brought with us, and

---

[1] A *morgen* is about two acres of land. Smith, in his *History of New Jersey*, 159, alluding to the earliest settlements on the Passaic river, says that above an island there belonging to Christopher Hoogland, of Newark, was "a large tract belonging to Jaques Cartelayne (Cortelyou) and partners, who now (1682), made some settlement. These tracts were within the jurisdiction of Newark." Cortelyou's purchase was at Aquackanonk.

they confessed that as long as they had lived in the country, they had never seen any finer or larger.

29th, Sunday. We had been last Sunday to hear the quakers, but the greater portion of them were on Long Island, so that nothing was done. My comrade had a mind to go again to-day, but I remained at home. After waiting two hours, he went to hear the episcopalians and then returned to the quakers, who had remained all this time sitting silent and gazing. He then took a walk out for a considerable time, and went back again and found them still in the same position. Being tired out, he would wait no longer, and came home. We went in the afternoon to see Ephraim for the purpose of inquiring of him how soon our journey to the South river would commence, and whether we would have time first to take a trip to *Aquakenon* with the man from Bergen, of whom we have spoken above; but we did not find him at home.

30th, Monday. We went again this morning to speak to him. He said we would have time to go there, and allowing the utmost it might take us, he would still wait a day or two. We went immediately to *Sapokanikke*, where (Gerrit) was engaged in building, whom we wished to accompany us, because he knew several of those Indians and spoke their language, and because he had said all along that he wished to see the land of his brother-in-law, since Jaques had promised him as much of it as he would cultivate; but we found him indisposed with a sore leg, and unable to go. Nevertheless, we crossed over the river in the evening, at the same time the two ministers were returning, namely, *Tessemaker* who preached there on Sunday as we have stated, and *Niewenhuise* who had administered the Lord's Supper there to day. We went over with Claes, and it was dark when we arrived at *Gmoenepaen.* We followed Claes, who took us to his house, where we were made welcome by his old mother. My comrade went with Claes, yet this evening, to see the man who was to take us up the kil, so that in case he had any thing to make ready it might be done this evening. He said it would be noon before the tide would serve to-morrow and that he had nothing else to do in the morning. We learned he was a most godless rogue, which caused us to be cautious in what we had to do with him. We conversed this evening with the old woman in whose house we slept, and this poor woman seemed to have great enjoyment and fruition, as did also her sons and others with whom we occasionally conversed. It appeared, indeed, as if the Lord might have there the seed of the elect, which he will bring forth in his own time, if it please him. Truly these are the best people whom we have found in these parts.

31*st*, *Tuesday*. We went this morning to look about the country a little, which pleased us very much, and thus occupied ourselves until noon, when we proceeded to look after our guide and arrange matters with him. As soon as he came in the house, we inquired of him what he wanted for his trouble for the journey. He demanded a cloth *innocent* or coat, and that not of the poorest. His wife, who was the worst woman, I think, I have ever beheld in my life, did the best also to cheat us. We asked him what he thought such a coat would cost. "Well," said he, "call it a hundred guilders." We told him we did not intend to give so much. He replied, "I cannot take less for so long a time." "And how long do you expect to be gone," we asked. "You must not, "he said, "think of being back before Monday." We then asked him how much he demanded a day, and he said eight guilders. We made an agreement with him for seven guilders a day, that is, twenty-eight stuivers, Holland money. We then started to get some provisions, which the old woman, where we slept, had cheerfully given us; but we took nothing, except two half loaves of rye bread, and some apples in our traveling bag, but this Dirck provided himself better for making the journey. When we were ready, we went over the salt meadow or marsh to the kil, which was full an half an hour's distance; but when we came to the canoe, the ebb tide was still running strong, and we required the flood. The canoe lay in a bend of a small creek, and it was impossible to get it out of this bight and over the mire, except at high water, which would not take place until evening. We were, therefore, brought to a stand, whether to proceed in the evening, to which we were not much inclined, or await until the next morning, which was too much of a delay in view of our journey to the south. We had, besides, felt some misgivings in our hearts on account of the godlessness of the person who was to conduct us. We saw that the Lord plainly shewed what we had to do, and we, therefore, abandoned the trip, and told him we had not so much time to lose, and should embrace another opportunity. He cursed and swore at those who had told him the tide would serve at noon. In truth he had not been careful and had nobody to blame but himself. We were glad we were rid of him. We gave our apples and bread back to the old woman, who, as well as all the villagers, who heard we were not going up, were rejoiced, and declared we would not have been satisfied. Afterwards, several others offered their services to accompany us by land, either on foot or horseback, or otherwise, and go with us themselves, which we did not reject, but only postponed until we should see what the Lord would do in his time.

We went immediately to the strand to see whether we could still cross over to the other side; but Claes had left for the city, and did not return until evening, and there was no other boat. We were, therefore, compelled to remain; but, in the meantime, we visited the before mentioned Fytie, where we met several Indians, who lived upon and owned the very land we had intended to visit. They had heard we had gone up to look at their land, and wondered at seeing us back there. They manifested pleasure at our wishing to visit them, and examine their land; shook hands with us, and said we were great and good *nitaps*. They were in hopes we would come and live on their lands, where we would always be good *nitaps*. Meanwhile Claes having arrived, we went back with him to Bergen, and passed the night again at his house.

November 1*st*, *Wednesday*. As soon as Claes had taken his freight on board, we crossed over with him to the city. Our old people where we lodged were glad we had not gone with that person, for they also knew him well. About noon Claes came to the house, wishing to buy something of us, which he did. We presented him and the good people of this place with *The Christian Principles*,[1] in Low Dutch, because we hoped, after what we had seen, it would serve for their instruction and edification, and the glory of God, who will bring forth the fruits thereof in his own time if it please him.

2*d*, *Thursday*. This day, and for the rest of the week, nothing transpired worthy of note, except we informed Ephraim that our trip was not to take place, and therefore he need not wait on our account. I have wished several times that I could sketch in order to employ the art sometimes when it might be serviceable, especially upon this voyage. I, therefore, have practised it some, because it was convenient, and I thought I succeeded in it reasonably well, but I have done it, without any regularity or assiduity, and only to amuse myself occasionally.

---

[1] A publication of the Labadists.

5th, Sunday. My comrade, who was exercising himself in the English language, went again to hear the English minister preach.

6th, Monday. We went again to ascertain whether our journey to the South river would soon be undertaken; for although this opportunity would suit us very well and we should not miss it, nevertheless the best time was passing by, and the winter was close at hand. There was a horse offered us elsewhere, which had to be taken to the South river; and a yacht also was ready to sail there. The time, therefore, was to be looked to; and we went again to Ephraim, who assured us that he would not delay it longer than the ensuing Thursday. But we heard that Domine *Tessemaker* was going with him, by which we were entrapped, for it was one of the reasons why we did not leave with La Grange, who had now been gone fourteen days, that he always told us Domine Tessemaker and some other persons would accompany him. However, as the Lord had thus ordered it, we were glad to submit to his will, who always knows why he does thus and so.

Nothing worth mention happened between this and Thursday. Meanwhile, however, Domine Tessemaker had abandoned the journey with Ephraim, and resolved to proceed by sea in the yacht or boat, in which he sailed the next day. Whether he had some special reasons for going by water we do not know, although we guessed so. Ephraim had ordered a shallop or yacht, which was to land us at the *Raritans*, and was to be ready, he said, Thursday evening or Friday morning without fail, but of that he would give us timely notice. We, therefore, remained at home until Friday morning, the

10*th*, when, as we did not see him, we went to ascertain the cause and why the journey was not begun. He said it was not his fault, but that his mother-in-law could not leave so soon, and he had given her time until next Monday, and had, therefore, let the sloop make a trip. This did not please us very much, for our time was fast running away, and we were able to accomplish nothing. We bethought ourselves, therefore, whether we could not make some progress, and as our Jaques (Cortelyou), had promised to show us the laws of the country, we determined to go and see whether we could not abstract from them what we had to do therein before our departure. We both left about noon to go over to Long Island, and passed through *Breukelen* and *Vlacke Bos*, over *Nieu Uytrecht* on a large, fine wagon road to *Najack*, where we arrived about three o'clock. It had been very warm during the day, and we were all in a perspiration and fatigued. Jaques's wife bade us welcome, but he himself was in the fields. After we had rested ourselves and eaten something, we went outside upon the banks of this beautiful bay, to breathe a little air, and look at several vessels, going and coming. In the meantime he came with his son to meet us. They had been to the fish *fuyck*, which they had lying there upon the shore and out of which they had taken at noon some fine fish, but at present the water was too high. Another of his sons had been out shooting, but had not shot anything; though the day before he had shot a woodcock and a partridge before the door of the house, which we must taste this evening with some other things. While we were standing there, the fuyck was lifted again, from which they took out two fine bass, of a kind we had not yet seen. They are quite large, and of a good shape. They have seven black stripes on the body, extending from the head to the tail. We eat of them also in the evening, and found them very fine, and had not yet tasted any better in the country. They were fat and hard, with a little of the flavor of the salmon. The game suited us very well.

We had much conversation together, and informed ourselves in relation to various matters. He gave us some medicinal roots. He also let us look at the laws, which were written in a folio volume, but in very bad Dutch, for they had been translated from English into Dutch. As it was a large book, and we saw we could not copy it there, we requested him to let us take it home with us for that purpose. He consented upon condition that if we left for the south, we would then deliver it to his brother-in-law, Gerrit, who intended to come over shortly, and would hand it to him. We lodged this night somewhat better than we had done before in the barn, for we slept in his dwelling, and could feel where we had slept.

11*th*, *Saturday*. As soon as we awoke we determined to return home and finish up some matters in the little time remaining. We left, therefore, about eight o'clock, after taking some breakfast. He conducted us to New Utrecht. We lent him *Les Pensées de Pascal* which we judged would be useful to him. We returned by the same roads as we came, and reached home about eleven o'clock. We had observed that although the previous day had been pretty warm, the night had not only been frosty but ice had formed as thick as the back of a knife. We commenced at noon copying the most necessary laws, and afterwards the rest of them.

12*th*, *Sunday*. We continued making extracts, and finished about the middle of the day all that we deemed it necessary to make, omitting minor matters pertaining to the duties of particular officers. What we copied were the laws and nothing else.

13*th*, *Monday*. We took care that Jaques should receive the papers back again, and then went to see whether our journey with Ephraim would be made. We found the boat lying at the dock, laden with fire-wood, and that the day would necessarily be occupied in discharging, so that at the best, it could not be undertaken before the next day. The time was finally fixed for the journey for the next day, and every thing was this day arranged.

JOURNEY TO THE DELAWARE.

14*th*, *Tuesday*. Having taken leave of all our acquaintances, we set off at ten o'clock, this morning, in company with Ephraim, his wife, his wife's mother, two of her sisters, and a young brother, who where to accompany her as far as *Pescattaway*. We stepped into the boat, where we found three horses, two quakers and another Englishman. We were not long in starting. The wind was from the west, which is a head wind for sailing to *Achter Kol*. The sky began to be heavily overcast, and the wind to freshen up more, so that we had to tack. Ephraim being afraid the wind might shift to the northwest, and blow hard, as it usually does when it is from that quarter, wished to return, and would have done so, if the skipper had not tried to go ahead more than he did. The tide running out, and the boat advancing but little, and being fearful of the flood tide, which would delay us, if it did not drive us back, and as there was room to work with the rudder, I went and took hold of the tiller myself, and brought the boat, with the flood tide, just within the point of Staten island, where we found a ketch bound for *Achter Kol*, and further up to the *Slangenbergh*. Having now the tide with us, we tacked about, and quickly passed by the *Schutter's* island, lying in the mouth of a kil, on the north side of the *Kil achter Kol*. This island is so called, because the Dutch, when they first settled on the North river, were in the practice of coming here to shoot wild geese, and other wild fowl, which resorted there in great numbers. This kil,[1] when the water is high, is like a large river, but at low water, it is dry in some places. Up above it divides itself into two branches, one of which runs about north to the *Slangenbergh* and *Ackingsak*; and the other called the Northwest kil, because it extends in that direction, runs to *Aquakenom*, of which we will speak hereafter. We sailed inside of *Schutter's* island, although the passage is very small, and thus obtained the in-running current; because, the flood tide which came from *Achter Kol*,[2] and that from the North river, strike each other here, and thus shoot together in this kil. With much effort we reached the point of Elizabeth's kil, where we were compelled to come to anchor, at four o'clock. We all went ashore, and lodged for the night in the house of the French people, of whom we have spoken before, and who were not yet rid of the suspicion they had conceived, notwithstanding the declarations we had made to the contrary. We all slept on the floor, and supped upon what we had brought with us. We were no sooner in the house, than it began to rain and blow hard from the northwest, and to be very cold. We saw herein the good providence of the Lord again, whom we had so many times, during our journeying, so visibly perceived, watching and protecting so faithfully those who cared for nothing, except for him and to do his will.

15*th*, *Wednesday*. It still blew stiff out of the northwest, so that our skipper had little disposition to weigh anchor and get under sail, especially with the horses on board, although we would have willingly proceeded. It was, therefore, determined that the horses should go by land with the

---

[1] *Kil achter Kol*, Staten island sound.

[2] Newark bay.

servant and brother of Ephraim, and the quakers resolved to do the same. The rest of the company went on board the boat, and after taking in a large reef, we got under sail, with a head wind, but ebb tide. It blew hard and squally, and we had to look out well, with sheets in hand. We made good progress, and came to *Smokers Hoeck*, which is about half way of *Kil achter Kol.* We came to anchor here, because the next reach was directly against the wind, and it blew too hard to tack. We all stepped ashore here, and went on foot to an English village called Woodbridge, where we should find the horses. Smoker's Hook is the easterly point of the kil, which runs up to Woodbridge, and we would have sailed up this creek, but it was ebb tide. We passed over reasonably fair and good land, and observed particularly fine salt meadows on the creek, on which there was built a good grist mill, and over which we had to cross. We arrived about noon or one o'clock, at this English village. Ephraim, not wishing to go with his family to the ordinary tavern, went to another house or tavern, where he had been many times before, and where the people were under some obligations to him. But he could not lodge there now; and we were, therefore, compelled to go to the common tavern, which was full of persons, sitting drinking, and where nothing was to be obtained except that vile rum. Nevertheless, we had to pass the day there, waiting for the boat and the baggage; but these did not come up to-day, in consequence of the hard wind. We had, therefore, to lie down here upon the ground all together, on a little hay, as we had done last night.

16*th*, *Thursday.* The weather moderated and it cleared up, but we had to wait till about noon, before the goods arrived from the boat, which the skipper had to bring up in a canoe, because the boat could not come. We obtained here another horse, making five horses we had, and another servant of Ephraim. We then dined, and politely took our leave of Madam *Van Burgh*, the mother of Ephraim's wife, and of her two sisters, who had come to conduct her. as far as here, and from here were to return home again in the same boat, but the little brother went with us to the south, to live with Ephraim. It was then about three o'clock, when we mounted the horses, namely, Ephraim and his wife upon the best one, my comrade and myself each upon the one we had obtained at Woodbridge, his brother and servant on one, and the other servant upon another. *Our* horses, like the riders, were very poor. We proceeded on, however, and about four o'clock arrived at *Pescatteway*, the last English village in New Jersey, for thus the government of my Lord Carteret is called; which begins on the west side of the North river, and extends about half way to the South river, though this division did not seem to me to be well made. We rode about two English miles through *Pescatteway*, to the house of one Mr. Greenland,[1] who kept an *ordinary* (tavern) there. We had to pass the night here, because it was the place of crossing the Millstone river, which they called the falls. Close by there, also, was the dwelling of some Indians, who were of service to this Mr. Greenland, in many things. We were better lodged and entertained here, for we slept upon a good bed, and strengthened ourselves against the future.

17*th*, *Friday*. As the water was high in the kil or Millstone river, Ephraim would not ride over the fall, on account of the current of water, which made it dangerous. He, therefore, determined after breakfast we should be set across in a canoe, and the horses should swim across, as they did. We reached the other side about nine o'clock, and proceeded on horseback. The road from here to the

---

[1] See *Whitehead's Early History of Perth Amboy, &c.*, 402.

falls of the South river, runs for the most part W. S. W., and then W. It is nothing but a foot-path for men and horses, between the trees and through the small shrubs, although we came to places where there were large plains, beset with a few trees, and grown over with long grass, which was not the worst. When you have ridden a piece of the way, you can see over the lands of the Nevesink, far off on the left hand, into the ocean, affording a fine view.[1] The land we rode over was neither the best, nor the worst. The woods consist of reasonably straight oak and hickory, with some chestnut, but they are not very close. They would, therefore, afford tolerably good tillable land; but we observed the best pieces lay here and there, along the creeks. We saw many deer running before us, out of the road, sometimes five or six together, starting off at the sound of the horses. When about half way, you come to a high, but very *rocky hill*, which is very difficult for man or beast to walk upon. After crossing it, you come to a large valley, the descent to which, from this hill, is very steep, by a very shrubby road; and you must dismount, in order to lead your horses down carefully, as well as to descend carefully yourselves. We were in the middle of this valley, when a company met us on horseback, from the South river. They were acquaintances of Ephraim, and some of them were his relations. They wished each other welcome, and mutually inquired after various matters, after which we separated, exchanging one of our horses, which Ephraim's brother rode, and was to be sent back to the *Manathans*, for one of theirs, which must return to the South river. We rode on a little further, and came to Millstone river again, which runs so crookedly, that you cross it at three different places. After

[1] The highlands of Nevesink are 281 feet above the level of the sea, at their highest point.

we crossed it now, we took the bridles from the horses, in order that they might eat something, while we sat down and dined together, upon what we had in our traveling bags. We remounted in about an hour, and rode on, continuing our way and course as before. About three o'clock we came again to Millstone river, which we again waded over, but it had gradually become smaller. Resuming our route, we arrived at the falls of the South river about sundown, passing a creek where a new grist-mill was erected by the quakers, who live hereabouts in great numbers, and daily increase. But it seemed to us as if this mill could not stand long, especially if the flow of water were heavy, because the work was not well arranged. We rode over here, and went directly to the house of the person who had constructed it, who was a quaker, where we dismounted, and willingly dismissed our horses. The house was very small, and from the incivility of the immates and the unfitness of the place, we expected poor lodgings. As it was still daylight, and we had heard so much of the falls of the South river, or, at least, we ourselves had imagined it, that we went back to the river, in order to look at them; but we discovered we had deceived ourselves in our ideas. We had supposed it was a place, where the water came tumbling down in great quantity and force from a great height above, over a rock into an abyss, as the word *falls* would seem to imply, and as we had heard and read of the falls of the North river, and other rivers. But these falls of the South river are nothing more than a place of about two English miles in length, or not so much, where the river is full of stones, almost across it, which are not very large, but in consequence of the shallowness, the water runs rapidly and breaks against them, causing some noise, but not very much, which place, if it were necessary, could be made navigable on one side. As no Europeans live above the falls, they may so remain. This miller's house is the highest up the river, hitherto inhabited. Here we had to lodge; and although we were too tired to eat, we had to remain sitting upright the whole night, not being able to find room enough to lie upon the ground. We had a fire, however, but the dwellings are so wretchedly constructed, that if you are not so close to the fire as almost to burn yourself, you cannot keep warm, for the wind blows through them everywhere. Most of the English, and many others, have their houses made of nothing but clapboards, as they call them there, in this manner: they first make a wooden frame, the same as they do in Westphalia, and at Altona, but not so strong; they then split the boards of clapwood, so that they are like cooper's pipe staves, except they are not bent. These are made very thin, with a large knife, so that the thickest end is about a *pinck* (little finger) thick, and the other is made sharp, like the edge of a knife. They are about five or six feet long, and are nailed on the outside of the frame, with the ends lapped over each other. They are not usually laid so close together, as to prevent you from sticking a finger between them, in consequence either of their not being well joined, or the boards being crooked. When it is cold and windy the best people plaster them with clay. Such are most all the English houses in the country, except those they have which were built by people of other nations. Now this house was new and airy; and as the night was very windy from the north, and extremely cold with clear moonshine, I will not readily forget it. Ephraim and his wife obtained a bed; but we passed through the night without sleeping much.

18*th*, *Saturday*. About ten o'clock, after we had breakfasted, we stepped into a boat, in order to proceed on our journey down the river. The ebb tide was half run out. Although there is not much flood tide here, as it is stopped by the falls, yet, the water rises and falls with the ebb or flood, or, through the ebb or flood, because, the water, although it runs down, increases through the flood, in consequence of its being forced up, and is diminished with the ebb, because the ebb gives it so much the more course to run down. We went along, then, moving with the tide; but as Ephraim was suffering with the quartan ague, and it was now its time to come on, we had to go and lie by the banks of the river, in order to make a fire, as he could not endure the cold in the boat. This continued for about an hour and a half. The water was then rising, and we had to row against the current to *Burlington*, leaving the island of *Matinakonk*,[1] lying on the right hand. This island, formerly, belonged to the Dutch governor, who had made it a pleasure-ground or garden, built good houses upon it, and sowed and planted it. He also dyked and cultivated a large piece of meadow or marsh, from which he gathered more grain than from any land which had been made from woodland into tillable land. The English governor at the *Manathans*, now held it for himself, and had hired it out to some quakers, who were living upon it at present. It is the best and largest island in the South river; and is about four English miles in length, and two in breadth. It lies nearest to the east side of the river. At the end of this island lies the quakers' village, Burlington, which east side of the river the quakers have entirely in their possession, but how they came into its possession, we will show in another place. Before arriving at this village, we stopped at the house of one *Jacob Hendricks*, from Holstein, living on this side. He was an acquaintance of Ephraim, who would have gone there to lodge, but he was not at home. We, therefore, rowed on to the village, in search of lodgings, for it had been dark all of an hour or more; but

[1] Burlington island, formerly also called Chygoe's island. It contains about 300 acres of land.

proceeding a little further, we met this Jacob Hendricks, in a canoe with hay. As we were now at the village, we went up to the ordinary tavern, but there were no lodgings to be obtained there, whereupon we reëmbarked in the boat, and rowed back to Jacob Hendricks', who received us very kindly, and entertained us according to his ability. The house, although not much larger than where we were the last night, was somewhat better and tighter, being made according to the Swedish mode, and as they usually build their houses here, which are block-houses, being nothing else than entire trees, split through the middle, or squared out of the rough, and placed in the form of a square, upon each other, as high as they wish to have the house; the ends of these timbers are let into each other, about a foot from the ends, half of one into half of the other. The whole structure is thus made, without a nail or a spike. The ceiling and roof do not exhibit much finer work, except among the most careful people, who have the ceiling planked and a glass window. The doors are wide enough, but very low, so that you have to stoop in entering. These houses are quite tight and warm; but the chimney is placed in a corner. My comrade and myself had some deer skins, spread upon the floor to lie on, and we were, therefore, quite well off, and could get some rest. It rained hard during the night, and snowed and froze, and continued so until the

19*th*, *Sunday*, and for a considerable part of the day affording little prospect of our leaving. At noon the weather improved, and Ephraim having something to do at Burlington, we accompanied him there in the boat. We went into the meeting of the quakers, who went to work very unceremoniously and loosely. What they uttered was mostly in one tone, and the same thing, and so it continued, until we were tired out, and went away. We tasted here, for the first time, peach brandy, or spirits, which was very good, but would have been better if it had been more carefully made. Ephraim remained there for the evening, and we returned back to our former lodgings, where we slept on a good bed, the same that Epraim and his wife had the night before. This gave us great comfort, and recruited us greatly.

20th, Monday. We went again to the village this morning, and entered the ordinary exhorters' house, where we breakfasted with quakers, but the most wordly of men in all their deportment and conversation. We found lying upon the window a volume of Virgil, as if it were a common hand-book, and also Helmont's book on *Medicine*[1], whom, in an introduction, which they have made to it, they make pass for one of their sect, although in his life time he did not know any thing about quakers; and if they had been in the world, or should have come into it, while he lived, he would quickly have said, no, to them; but it seems these people will make all those who have had any genius, in any respect, more than common, pass for theirs; which is certainly great pride, wishing to place themselves far above all others; whereas, the most of them, whom I have seen as yet, are miserably self-minded, in physical and religious knowledge. It was almost noon before we left. The boat in which we had come as far as there with its owner, who intended to return in it, was exchanged for

---

[1] Jean Baptiste van Helmont, born in Brussels, in 1577; died in Holland in 1644. He was a distinguished alchemist and physician, and after studying different systems of medicine, old and new, came to the conclusion that wisdom in that science and in others, was to be acquired by prayer. He was the first person to designate the elastic fluids, other than air, by the term *gas*. The results of his treatment of patients committed to his charge, may not be peculiarily his own; but it is acknowledged by his biographer, that the sick never languished in his hands, being always killed or cured in three days. The work of his, on medicine, referred to in our text, was probably his, *Ortus Medecinæ, id est, initia physica inaudita, progressus medicinæ novus in morborum ultionem ad vitam longam.* Amsterdam, 1615.

another, belonging to Upland, of which a quaker was master, who was going down with several others of the same class; but as it was half ebb tide, and the shallop was lying far up in the mud, no one of these zealous people was willing to bring her through it, into the water. Ephraim, in order to get started, and to shame them, did not hesitate long, and followed by his servant and both of us, very soon had the boat afloat in the water. Pursuing our journey, we arrived about two o'clock at the house of another quaker, on the west side of the river, where we stopped to eat our dinner and dry ourselves. We left there in an hour, rowing our best against the flood tide, until, at dark, we came to *Takanij*, a village of Swedes and Fins, situated on the west side of the river. Ephraim being acquainted, and having business here, we were all well received, and slept upon a parcel of deer skins. We drank very good beer here, brewed by the Swedes, who, although they have come to America, have not left behind them their old customs.

21*st*, *Tuesday*. The tide falling, we set out with the day, and rowed during the whole ebb and part of the flood, until two or three o'clock, when we arrived at the island of *Tynakonk* (Tinicum), the fifth we had passed. *Mantinakonk* and this *Tinakonk*, are the principal islands, and the best and the largest. The others are of little importance, and some of them, whose names we do not know, are all meadow and marsh, others are only small bushes. The pleasantest thing about them is, they afford an agreeable view and a variety to the traveler, and a little *divertissement* to those who go up and down the river; also some conveniences for fishing in the river, and other accommodations for the planters.

This *Tinakonk*, is the island of which M. Arnout de la Grange had said so much; but we were much disappointed in comparing it with what he had represented, and what

M. la Motte has written about it. The first mistake is in the name, which is not *Matinakonk* — the name probably of the island of which we have spoken before, but *Tinakonk*. It lies on the west side of the river, and is separated from the west shore, not as he said, by a wide running branch of the river, as wide as the Eemster, near Amsterdam, but by a small creek, as wide as a large ditch, running through a meadow. It is long and covered with bushes, and inside somewhat marshy. It is about two miles long, or a little more, and a mile and a half wide. Although there are not less miles than he said, he did not say they were English miles, which are only one-fourth the length of Dutch miles, of fifteen to a degree. The southwest point, which only has been and is still cultivated, is barren, scraggy and sandy, growing plenty of wild onions, a weed not easily eradicated. On this point three or four houses are standing, built by the Swedes, a little Lutheran church made of logs, and the remains of the large block-house, which served them in place of a fortress, with the ruins of some log huts. This is the whole of the manor. The best and pleasantest quality it has, is the prospect, which is very agreeable, and one of the principal things for which Mons. la Motte recommends it, namely, *belle videre*. I have made a sketch of it, according to my ability. But as to there being a mine of iron ore upon it, I have not seen any upon that island, or elsewhere; and if it were so, it is of no great importance, for such mines are so common in this country, that little account is made of them. Although Ephraim had told us every thing in regard to the condition of the land, as well as the claim which Mons. de la Grange makes to it, yet we ourselves have observed the former, and have ascertained the latter, from a person who now resides there, which is as follows: When the Swedish colony was flourishing under its own government, this island belonged a lord *Papegay* (Papegoia), the Swedish governor, who lived upon it, and cultivated it, the church and the fort, still existing there as monuments to prove the fact. Although the Swedes have had fortresses, from time to time, in several other places, at this time, this was called New *Gottenburgh*. This governor died, leaving a widow; and she, Madam *Papegay*, sold the island, which was then very flourishing, to the father of de la Grange, for six thousand guilders, in the money of Holland, though the person who now lives upon it says it was seven thousand guilders, to be paid in several installments, here in New Netherland. Some of the first payments were duly made by de la Grange, but the last two, I think, he was not so ready to make, as he had to procure the money from Holland, and that, I know not why, did not come. Thereupon Mons. de la Grange, determined to go to Holland, himself, and bring the money with him; but he died on the voyage, and the payments were not made. It remained so for a long time, and, at length, the widow Papegay, cited the widow de la Grange, before the court, claiming as her right, payment in full, or restitution of the land, as de la Grange had been in possession of the land for some years, and had enjoyed the profits, and the time for the last payment had also expired some years before. In the mean time comes one Mons. la Motte, who it seems was to assist Madam de la Grange, either by discharging the debt, or by defending the suit, and in order the better to do so, he buys the island from the widow de la Grange, seeking her also in marriage. But as Madam Papegay persevered, and the affair of Mons. la Motte, and the widow de la Grange, came to nothing, and on the other hand the widow de la Grange could not deliver the land to M. la Motte, and la Motte could not pay. The widow de la Grange was, therefore, condemned to restore the island to Madam Papegay, and pay her costs, and also to pay the income which she had received from the island, for the time she had lived upon it, and for the buildings which she had allowed to go to waste. Madam de la Grange, conceiving this decree to be unjust, appealed to the high court — the country having in the mean time been taken by the English — and was again condemned, and therefore, had to deliver up the land. Now, in this last war with Sweden, Madam Papegay, who has two brothers in Sweden, in the service of the crown, was sent for by them to come home, whereupon, she sold the island to Mr. *Otto Kuif*[1] a Holsteiner, who now lives upon it, for fifteen hundred guilders in *zeewant*, as it was very much decayed and worn out. This is three hundred guilders in the money of Holland. Hereupon, Madam Papegay delivered full possession thereof, to this Otto. Now, M. Arnout de la Grange, as heir of his father, when he was here last year, laid claim to the island from Mr. Otto, who told him he did not know him in the matter, and if M. de la Grange had any lawful claim, he must not apply to him, but to the court, as his possession was under its judgment; but if M. de la Grange wished to buy it from him, he would let him have it for three hundred pounds sterling, or as they might agree. Whereupon, de la Grange flew into a passion, and threatened to appeal to London. "That you can do," said Otto, "if you have money enough. All this affects me not, since I have bought and paid for it, and have been put in possession of it by order of the court." De la Grange has not proposed to purchase the island again of Mr. Otto, although he could do it very favorably, notwithstanding Mr. Otto asked so much for it. Ephraim told me that Mr. Otto had said to him, confidentially, that in case he could obtain for it what it had cost him, he would let it go, as he had other land lying elsewhere, and that he had asked so much for it, merely to hear what he (de la Grange) would

---

[1] Otto Ernest Koch or Kock. He was one of the justices on the Delaware.

say, and in order to scare him. Should you lay out three hundred guilders in Holland for merchandise, and sell it here, which usually yields an hundred per cent profit, or is so reckoned in barter, you could have this island almost for nothing, or at least for very little. But there is better land to be bought cheaper. De la Grange has let this slip by, and it seems as if he had not much inclination to stir the subject any more. He has given me to understand that he disregards it, or at least regards it as little now, as he formerly prized and valued it; as indeed he shows, for he has now bought land on Christina creek, consisting of two or three old plantations, which, perhaps, are not much better than this island, and cost him enough. He has obtained another piece from the governor, lying between Burlington and the falls, on the west side, but will not accomplish much with it. I forgot to mention that de la Grange, four years ago when he was in Holland, gave one Mr. Peter *Aldrix*, who now resides on the South river, and is one of the members of the court, authority to make this man, Otto, deliver the island to him, which *Aldrix* refused, and advised him that he was well assured he could not accomplish any thing with it. Yet to satisfy la Grange he laid the matter before Mr. Otto, who gave him the same answer he had given la Grange. As I understand and have heard, la Grange bases his claim under the English law, that the son is the heir of the father's possessions; but the possession of the father being disputed, and he himself disinherited by two courts, the claim is null and of no value.[1]

---

[1] The accuracy of this long statement in regard to Tinicum, its settlement and fortification by the Swedes, and the dispute as to the title, is not less remarkable than its minuteness. Much of the detail given here is new, but many of the leading points are corroborated by the records of the country, and by judicious writers, early and late, and entire confidence is established, therefore, in the whole account. The reader may consult

When we arrived at this island, we were welcomed by Mr. Otto, late *medicus*, and entertained at his house according to his condition, although he lives poorly enough. In the evening there also arrived three quakers, of whom one was their greatest prophetess, who travels through the whole country in order to *quake*. She lives in Maryland, and forsakes husband and children, plantation and all, and goes off for this purpose. She had been to Boston, and was there arrested by the authorities on account of her quakery. This worthy personage came here in the house where we were, although Ephraim avoided her. They sat

---

Campanius by Du Ponceau, 79; *Aerelius*, 35-6; *Clay's Annals*, 23-5; *Ferris's Original Settlement on the Delaware*, 61; *Record of Upland Court*, 152-3; *Dr. Smith's Hist. of Delaware Co., Pa.*, 58, 97, 110, 123, 145, 519; and *Hazard's Annals of Pa.*, 400-1. Two last named writers give us some minutes of the trial in the suit of Madam Papegay, against Madam de la Grange, then the wife of Andrew Carr, which took place in New York, in October, 1672, and lasted three days. We also learn from the same authorities that the controversy in relation to Tinicum, did not end there, as our journalist supposed it would. Three or four years after he wrote the above account, a suit was brought by M. Arnout or Arnoldus de la Grange, against Mr. Otto Ernest Cock, for the possession of the island, the plaintiff claiming as heir-at-law of his father, and setting forth that at the time of the former trial he was under age, and in Holland, and, therefore, could make no defense; and that he was not a party to the action which was commenced against Andrew Carr and Priscilla, his wife mistaken in the execution for the plaintiff's mother, whose name was Margaretta. The parties entered into an agreement, however, pending the trial, in accordance with which the jury rendered their verdict in favor of M. de la Grange, with costs and forty shillings damages, "the plaintiff paying to the defendant thirty-seven pounds and ten shillings, and also delivering the *block-house* and timbers in the same agreement mentioned." The last trial took place before the court at Chester, under the jurisdiction of William Penn, who had in the meantime obtained the grant of Pennsylvania. Madam Papegay was the daughter of Governor Printz, the second governor of the Swedish settlements, on the Delaware, who returned to Sweden in 1653, leaving his son-in-law John Papegay or Papegoia in charge of the place, who was superseded on the arrival of Governor Rising, in May, 1654.

by the fire, and drank a dram of rum with each other, and in a short time afterwards began to shake and groan so, that we did not know what had happened, and supposed they were going to preach, but nothing came out of it. I could not endure them, and went out of doors. They left for Upland, which is three or four miles from there on the same side of the river, in the same boat in which we came.

22*d*, *Wednesday*. It was rainy all this day, which gave us sufficient time to explore the island. We had some good cider which he had made out of the fruit from the remains of an old orchard planted by the Swedish governor. The persons of whom we have before spoken, having left for Upland, Ephraim did not wish to go there because he thought they would preach; and it being rainy, and no fit boat at hand, we remained here the whole day. We saw an ox as large as they have in Friesland or Denmark, and also quite fat—a species of which we have observed more among the Swedes, and which thrive well. It clearing up towards evening, we took a canoe and came after dark to Upland. This is a small village of Swedes, although it is now overrun by English. We went to the house of the quaker who had brought us down, and carried the other persons from Tinakonk. His name was Robert Williamson or *Weert*.[1] We found here the prophetess or *apostle-ess*, with her company. Among others, there were two widows, who were at variance, and whom the prophetess with all her authority and spiritual power could not reconcile, or had not endeavored to do so. They would have

---

[1] Robert Wade is the person meant. He came over to this country in 1675, in company, it would seem, with John Fenwick, the early proprietor and settler in West Jersey, but leaving his company, settled at Upland (now Chester), in the same year, upon land of Madam Papegay, called Printzdorp. His house was the one used for the meetings of the quakers. *Smith's History of Delaware County*, 103, 134, 549. *Record of Upland Court*, 79.

been compelled to have gone before the court, unless Ephraim had striven his best to make them adjust the matter, and brought them to a settlement. One of these widows, named *Anna Salters*, lived at *Takany*, and was one of those who, when a certain person gave himself out as the Lord Jesus, and allowed himself to be carried around on an ass, shouted Hosanna as he rode over their garments, for which conduct he was arrested, his tongue bored through with a red-hot iron, and his forehead branded with a B, for blasphemer. She was not only one of those, but she annointed his head and feet, and wiped them with her hair. The other widow, named Elizabeth, was also one of the principal persons. She lived a little lower down than *Takoney*, on the same side of the river. The state of the difference between them was this. They had agreed between themselves to exchange or barter their plantations, and each made a writing and each kept her own. Anna Salters afterwards repented her bargain, and went to Elizabeth, and desired that each should take back the writing subscribed by her; but it so happened that Anna Salters went away, having given up hers, and the other not being then to be found. She had given hers to Elizabeth, supposing she would afterwards obtain the other; but when she went again to demand it, Elizabeth said the paper had become wet, and in her attempting to dry it, was burnt up. It was believed that Elizabeth had the two writings in her possession, and consequently both plantations, which, they said, she wanted to sell privately. Whereupon Anna called upon her to restore either the deed or the plantation. Elizabeth charged that Anna was indebted to her for a certain amount of tobacco, which she had taken to England for her, and of which she had never been able to obtain a correct account. It was really confusion and rascality. Elizabeth, who was a bad person, appealed always to some papers which she said she had not with her. Ephraim who was clerk of both the courts, namely, of Upland and New Castle,[1] wrote down separately from the beginning the claims which they set up against each other, and decided that the plantations should be mutually restored, and the debts balanced, and he made them agree to it, although Elizabeth was very unwilling. Robert Wade, who is the best quaker we have yet seen, and his wife, who is a good woman, were both troubled, as they said, as also was the prophetess, that such things should take place among their people before strangers, and be settled through them, and when there were other strangers present. Whereupon Ephraim said, "Who do you suppose we are? Possibly we are as good Christians as you are." And certainly he exhibited something more christianly in reconciling and pacifying them than they who brewed this work had done, or those who would be so very devout that they would neither speak to them authoritatively nor admonish them with kindness to any effect. The Lord has caused us to see this example that we might know that these people are still covetous, and that almost all of them are attached to the world and to themselves—that is, they are worldly people, which shows the holiness of the spirit by which they are actuated! As regards Anna Salters, it was said she was mundane, carnal, covetous, and artful, although she appeared to be the most pious. Her sayings and discussions were continually mixed up with protestations of the presence and omniscience of God, and upon the salvation of her soul, so truly gross that if the ordinary boors had talked so, they would have been punished and expelled. But what are not those people capable of, who present themselves to be carried away as

[1] Ephraim Hermans was appointed "clerk of the court of Newcastle in Delaware, and of Upland in the river," by Governor Andros, on the 23d September, 1676. *Breviate*, Penn. *vs.* Calvert, 45.

we have mentioned above; as well as others in this country, who publish and declare one, that she is Mary the mother of the Lord; another, that she is Mary Magdalen, and others that they are Martha, John, &c., scandalizers, as we heard them in a tavern, who not only so called themselves, but claimed to be really such. For this reason, Mr. Wade would no longer have them in his house, making them leave, although it was well in the evening; for the Wades said they could not endure it. Indeed, God the Lord will not let that pass by, for it is not far from blasphemy. He will bring them to justice, if they be of his elect.

It was very late in the evening, in consequence of this dispute, before we supped and went to sleep. We were taken to a place to sleep directly before an open window, to which there was no shutter, so that it could not be closed, and as the night was very cold, and it froze hard, we could scarcely keep ourselves warm.

23*d*, *Thursday*. It was late before we left here, and we therefore had time to look around a little, and see the remains of the residence of Madame Papegay, who had had her dwelling here when she left *Tinakonk*. We had nowhere seen so many vines together as we saw here, which had been planted for the purpose of shading the walks on the river side, in between the trees. The dinner being ready, I was placed at the table next to the beforenamed prophetess, who while they all sat at the table, began to groan and quake gradually until at length the whole bench shook. Then rising up she began to pray, shrieking so that she could be heard as far as the river. This done, she was quickly in the dish, and her mouth began immediately to prate worldly and common talk in which she was not the least ready. When the meal was finished, Ephraim obtained a horse for himself and his wife, and we followed him on foot, carrying our traveling bags. Our host took us to the path, and Ephraim's servant was to act as our guide. In traveling along we observed the difference between the soil on the North river and this, and also that this difference was not so great as is usually asserted. After we had proceeded about three hours, our guide missed the way, and we had gone a good distance before he became aware of it, and would have gone on still further if we had not told him that we thought the course we were going was wrong. We therefore left one road, and went straight back in search of the other which we at length found. A man overtook us who was going the same way. and we followed him. We crossed the *Schiltpadts kil* (Tortoise or Turtle creek), where there was a fall of water over the rocks, affording a site for a grist-mill which was erected there. This *Schiltpadts kil* is nothing but a branch or arm of *Christina kil*[1] into which it discharges itself, and is so named on account of the quantities of tortoises which are found there. Having crossed it we came to the house of the miller who was a Swede or Holsteiner whom they usually call *Tapoesie.* He was short in person, but a very friendly fellow. Ephraim had told us we would find him such as we did, for he had ridden there before us. He had, as it appeared, several well-behaved children, among whom was a little girl who resembled very much our little Judith in her whole countenance and figure, and was about the same age, and had she met us by our house, I should have considered her Judith. Her name was Anne Mary. We were welcome here, and were entertained according to the man's circumstances.

24th, Friday. Ephraim having some business here, we did not leave very speedily. This miller had shot an animal they call a muskrat, the skin of which we saw hanging up to dry. He told us they were numerous in the creeks. We asked

---

[1] The *Shelpot* is evidently a corruption of this name, though probably the Brandywine is here meant.

them why they gave them that name, and he said because they smelt so, especially their testicles, which he had preserved of this one, and gave my comrade, remarking that they were intended for some amateur or other, and he could do little with them. The muskrat is not larger than the common rat. It has gray hair, and the fleece is sometimes sold with other peltries, but it is not worth much, although it has some odor. It was about noon when we were set across the creek in a canoe. We proceeded thence a small distance over land to a place where the fortress of Christina had stood which had been constructed and possessed by the Swedes, but taken by the Dutch governor, Stuyvesant, and afterwards, I believe, demolished by the English. We went into a house here belonging to some Swedes, with whom Ephraim had some business. We were then taken over Christina creek in a canoe, and landed at the spot where Stuyvesant threw up his battery to attack the fort, and compelled them to surrender. At this spot there are many medlar trees which bear good fruit from which one *Jaquet*, who does not live far from there, makes good brandy or spirits, which we tasted and found even better than French brandy. Ephraim obtained a horse at this *Jaquet's*, and rode on towards *Santhoek*, now Newcastle, and we followed him on foot, his servant leading the way. We arrived about four o'clock at Ephraim's house, where we congratulated each other, and were glad, thanking the Lord in our hearts for his constantly accompanying grace. We found here the young brother of the wife with the servant, who had come with the horses from the falls overland, and had been at the house several days. We also saw here Ephraim's sister, Miss Margaret Hermans, who showed us much kindness. She was a little volatile, but of a sweet and good disposition. She had been keeping house during the absence of Ephraim. Truly the Lord has in all these things been very good to us, for we knew not where to go, and he has directed us among these people, who have done out of love what they have shown us. We knew not where to lodge, and he has provided us lodgings where we were so free and had, according to the circumstances of the time, what we desired. We hope and doubt not the Lord will visit that house in grace, and even gives us some assurances in what we have seen.

25th, Saturday. We rested a little to-day. Ephraim and his wife and we ourselves had several visits from different persons who came to welcome us, as *Mons. Jan Moll,*[1] whom we had conversed with in New York, and who now offered us his house and all things in it, even pressing them upon us. But we were not only contented with our present circumstances, but we considered that we would not be doing right to leave Ephraim's house without reason. We therefore thanked him, but nevertheless in such a manner, that we took notice of his kindness, and answered accordingly.

---

[1] Mr. John Moll was a person of considerable distinction in the affairs of Newcastle and the Delaware, for many years. He was one of the justices of the court at Newcastle during the whole period of the Duke of York's government, and was for some time its presiding justice. That court was an appellate tribunal from all the other courts on the river. He was named as commissioner in conjunction with Ephraim Hermans, in the deed of feoffment from the Duke of York to William Penn, to give possession and seisin of the town of Newcastle, and a circle of land twelve miles around it, a duty which they performed. His account of the ceremony is curious. He certifies that on the first arrival of Mr. Penn from England at Newcastle in October, 1662, and after considering for twenty-four hours the deeds which Mr. Penn showed him from the Duke of York, we did "by virtue of the powers given us by the said letters of attorney, give and surrender in the Duke's name to Mr. Penn, actual and peaceable possession of the fort at Newcastle, by giving him the key thereof to lock upon himself alone the door; which, being opened by him again, we did deliver to him again also one turf, with a twig upon it, a porringer with river water and soil, in part of all that was specified in the said indenture and according to the true intent and meaning thereof." *Breviate*, Penn *vs.* Calvert, 52-4-5. *Hazard's Annals of Penn*, 606-7. Our journalist subsequently furnishes some particulars in relation to Mr. Moll and his family.

Peter *Aldrix*[1] also showed us much attention, as did others, to all of whom we returned our thanks. We went out to view this little place, which is not of much moment, consisting of only forty or fifty houses. There is a fine prospect from it, as it lies upon a point of the river where I took a sketch.

26*th*, *Sunday*. We went to the church, but the minister, Tessemaker, who has to perform service in three places, over the river, Newcastle, and *Apoquemene*[2] was to-day over the river, and there was, therefore, nothing done, except what was done by a poor limping clerk, as he was a cripple and poor in body. He read from a book a sermon, or short explanation, and sung and made a prayer, if it may be called such, and then the people went home. In the afternoon there was a prelection again about the catechism.

27*th*, *Monday*. The weather was sharp and windy. We had intended to proceed on our journey but we could not very well do so. My comrade had also been indisposed in the night. We therefore waited for the opportunity which the Lord would present. Meanwhile we had another visit. Ephraim advised us to wait a day or two until his brother, Casparus Hermans, whom he expected there, should arrive, and who would conduct us farther into Maryland.

28*th*, *Tuesday*. Little transpired while we were waiting to-day, except that we spoke to several persons of the way of the Lord, and particularly to the sister of Ephraim, Miss Margaret, who received with some favor what was

---

[1] Peter Aldricks or Alrichs was the nephew of Jacob Alrichs, first vice director of the colony established at New Amstel, afterwards Newcastle, by the city of Amsterdam, in 1657, and probably came over with him. He was commissary at that colony at the time of the English conquest, and was subsequently appointed by Governor Colve, commander and schout of the South river. His lands were confiscated by the English government. *Colonial History*, II, 111, 114; III, 115.

[2] Apoquinimink.

said to her, and also to Ephraim and his wife, who we hope will bring forth the seed the Lord has sown in them, in his own time.

29th, Wednesday. We were still waiting, although Ephraim had sent for his brother; but we obtained tidings that he had gone to Maryland, and was coming back home immediately, as he had gone to visit his father who lives at the entrance into Maryland and was sick.

30th, Thursday. The weather had been cold and windy, but had now cleared up; so that some of the servants of Casparus came, who confirmed the account that their master had gone to Maryland, but they were expecting him home. Whereupon Mons. Moll who had to go to one of his plantations lying on the road leading to Casparus's house, requested us to accompany him, so that the servants of Casparus on their return home would find us at his place and take us on to the house of Casparus. We accordingly started, Mr. Moll riding a horseback and we following him on foot, carrying our traveling sacks, but sometimes exchanging with him, and thus also riding a part of the way. This plantation of his is situated about fifteen miles from Newcastle. It was about ten o'clock in the morning when we took leave of our friends and left. We passed through a tolerably good country, but the soil was a little sandy, and it was three o'clock in the afternoon when we reached the plantation. There were no persons there except some servants and negroes, the commander being a Parisian. The dwellings were very badly appointed, especially for such a man as Mons. Moll. There was no place to retire to, nor a chair to sit on, or a bed to sleep on. For their usual food the *servants* have nothing but maize bread to eat, and water to drink, which sometimes is not very good and scarcely enough for life, yet they are compelled to work hard. They are brought from England in great numbers into Maryland, Virginia and the *Menades* and sold each one according to his condition, for a certain term of years, four, five, six, seven or more. And thus they are by hundreds of thousands compelled to spend their lives here and in Virginia, and elsewhere in planting that vile tobacco, which all vanishes into smoke, and is for the most part miserably abused. It is the chief article of trade in the country. If they only wished it they could have every thing for the support of life in abundance, for they have land and opportunity sufficient for that end; but this insatiable avarice must be fed and sustained by the bloody sweat of these poor slaves. After we had supped, Mr. Moll, who would be civil, wished us to lie upon a bed that was there, and he would lie upon a bench, which we declined; and as this continued some length of time I lay down on a heap of maize, and he and my comrade afterwards did the same. This was very uncomfortable and chilly, but it had to go so.

DECEMBER 1*st*, *Friday*. Mr. Moll wishing to do us every kindness, as he indeed did do many, wrote addresses which might be serviceable to us in Maryland, for he was not only very well known there, but had influence among the people by reason of the trade they had with each other, and of his being a member of the court, and having some authority. He also gave us some letters of recommendation and credit in case we might have any necessity for the latter, in all which he indeed showed he had an affection for us. After we had breakfasted, the servants of Casparus not having arrived, he himself conducted us to one of the nearest plantations where his cooper was, who had also something to do for Casparus, and would conduct us farther on, as took place; and we arrived about three o'clock at the house of Casparus. But he had not yet come home nor had the servants arrived, for whom we had been waiting.

2*d*, *Saturday*. We waited here all this day, and had time

and opportunity to explore this place, which they call Augustine. We found it well situated, and *would not badly suit us*. There are large and good meadows and marshes near it, and the soil is quite good. It has much good timber and a very fine prospect, for looking from the strand you can see directly south into the mouth of the bay, as this place lies on the west side of the river in a bend. There is much land attached to it, which he purchased from the Indians for almost nothing, or nothing to signify. Towards evening two Englishmen and a quaker stopped here to pass the night who were also going to Maryland.

3d, Sunday. The Englishmen left this morning at daylight, and after breakfast we determined also to leave, delivering a letter, which Ephraim had given us for his brother, to his wife. We started at nine o'clock, and followed a large broad wagon road, which Casparus had made through the woods, from his house to his father's who lived in the uppermost part of Maryland, that is, as high up as it is yet inhabited by Christians. This road is about twenty-two miles long, and runs almost due west, but a little more northerly than southerly. When we were about half way we met Casparus on horseback with a cart, his wife having described him to us. We told him we had been to his house waiting for him, and had left a letter there for him from his brother. He regretted, he said, he had not known it and was not at home, but he hoped, and so did we, that we would be able to converse together on our return, and with this we pursued our respective roads. It was very warm to-day, and we were all in a perspiration. We reached *Augustynus Hermans* the father of these two brothers, about three o'clock. Augustine Hermans is a Bohemian, and formerly lived on the *Manathans*, and had possessed farms or plantations there, but for some reason, I know not what, disagreeing with the Dutch governor, Stuyvesant, he repaired to this place, which is laid down upon a complete map, which he has made of Maryland and Virginia, where he is very well acquainted, which map he has dedicated to the king. In consequence of his having done the people of these two countries a great service, he has been presented with a tract of land of about a thousand or twelve hundred acres, which he, knowing where the best land was, has chosen up here, and given it the name of Bohemia. It is a noble piece of land, indeed the best we have seen in all our journey south, having large, thick, and high trees, much black walnut and chestnut, as tall and straight as a reed.

It was, then, on this day and at this plantation, that we made our entry into Maryland, which was so named, I believe, in the time of Queen Maria,[1] when it was discovered or began to be settled. It is a large territory, but has as yet no fixed boundaries, except only on the south where it is separated from Virginia by a straight line running westerly from [2]——— to the river. All north of this line is Maryland, and all south of it Virginia. On the east it is bounded by New Netherland, but that line is undefined; and on the north and west indefinitely by the Indians. The principal rivers are on the east side of the bay.

Maryland is considered the most fertile portion of North America, and it were to be wished that it was also the most healthy, though it is more healthy than its neighbor, Virginia, which has to give passage by water through the great bay of (the Chesapeake), to Maryland. It is also

---

[1] Henrietta Maria, consort of Charles I.

[2] This point could not well have been given at that time by the journalist or any body else, and therefore is left blank by him. According to the description of this line in the charter of Maryland to Lord Baltimore by Charles I, it is, "a right line drawn from the promontory, or headland, called Watkins Point, situated upon the bay aforesaid (Chesapeake) near the river Wighco, on the west unto the main ocean on the east." *Bozman*, II, 10.

very rich in fish as well as in all kinds of water fowl. There are few Indians in comparison with the extent of country. When the English first discovered and settled Virginia and Maryland, they did great (wrong) to these poor people, and almost exterminated them.

To return to Augustine Hermans, he was sick when we arrived at his house. We found there the three Englishmen before mentioned, who had left the house of Casparus in the morning. They were about proceeding further on their journey. We delivered to Augustine a letter from his son Ephraim, and related to him how we had traveled with him from the Manathans, and how he was, which rejoiced him. Becoming thus acquainted he showed us every kindness he could in his condition, as he was very miserable, both in soul and body. His plantation was going much into decay, as well as his body for want of attention. There was not a Christian man, as they term it, to serve him; nobody but negroes. All this was increased by a miserable, doubly miserable wife; but so miserable that I will not relate it here. All his children have been compelled on her account to leave their father's house. He spoke to us of his land, and said he would never sell or hire it to Englishmen, but would sell it to us cheap, if we were inclined to buy. But we satisfied ourselves and him by looking at it then, hoping that we might see each other on our return. We were directed to a place to sleep, but the screeching of the wild geese and other wild fowl in the creek before the door, prevented us from having a good sleep, though it answered.

4*th*, *Monday*. After breakfast we were set over this creek, or Bohemia river, in a canoe, after Augustine had, as the head man of the place, signed the passport which Mr. Moll, Ephraim and Aldrix had given us. Our first address was to one Mr. *Van Waert*, who had arrived from England the day before, and who gave us little news, except that a certain skipper Jacob, who lived at the *Manathans*, had left England some days before him, bound there. We were glad of this, thinking we would receive some letters from Fatherland, as we had, when we were at New Castle, written to our hostess at New York, that in case the skipper Jacob had letters for us, she should send them to the South river. Towards evening we came to a Swede's, named *Mouns*, where we had to be put across a creek, after we had mistaken the road. We spent the night with him, and were entirely welcome. He and his wife and some of his children spoke good Dutch, and conversed with us about various matters concerning the country.

5*th*, *Tuesday*. We left after breakfast, and he took us upon the road to go to Captain *Frisby's*. Leaving Mr. *Blackstone's* plantation on the right hand of Frisby's, we came to the court house standing on the Sassafras river, which is also an ordinary. We requested to be taken over the river, as there is a ferry here, which they did, and it cost us each an English shilling. We then traveled along the river until we came to a small creek, which runs very shallow over the strand into the river. Here we had to take off our shoes and stockings in order to cross over, although it was piercing cold. We continued some distance further, along the river, to the *Great bay*, when we came to another creek and called out to be taken across, which was done. The road was shown us further on to Mr. *Howel's*, where we had a letter of recommendation and credit to deliver Captain *Seybry*, who was not at home, but had gone to the ships which had arrived. So we gave the letter to Mr. *Howel*, to hand to Mr. Seybry. We slept here this night, and were welcome.

6*th*, *Wednesday*. This morning we crossed a creek, and were shown the way to another plantation, where we would be set over still another. To this plantation we soon came, but the people excused themselves from taking us over, saying that their canoe was not at home, and sent us to another plantation on the right. We crossed there and saw on almost every tree one or two grape vines, and that for a long distance along the road until we reached the plantation of one *Hendrick Hendricksen*, where no one was at home except a woman, who nevertheless lent us a canoe with which we might not only cross over, but go a considerable distance down the creek, trusting her canoe to us. We arrived in this at the plantation of Mr. *Hopkins*, who was not at home. Being fatigued, and not having yet breakfasted, we asked for something to drink that clear water from, and afterwards for something to eat; but we could obtain nothing except a piece of maize bread with which we satisfied ourselves. The worst was, she would not show us the way, which, however, we found ourselves. We arrived at noon at *Salsberry's*, who also was not at home. They had all sailed down below to the ships. But we found a good old woman who immediately put before us something to eat, and gave us some exceedingly good cider to drink. We were, therefore, somewhat strengthened. This plantation is one of the most pleasantly situated I have seen, having upon the side of the great bay a fine prospect, and a pretty view in the distance, as the sketch shows. We left here about three o'clock, and were taken across the creek and put upon the road, and at evening came to the house of one *Richard Adams*, an Englishman, who had a Dutch wife born at Deventer. The husband was not at home, and she had almost forgotten her Dutch. However, we were welcome, and we remained there for the night, and rested reasonably well.

7th, Thursday. We left there after breakfast, and were put across a creek which runs by the door, and shown the road to go to an English plantation. The owner was not at home, but we first passed a small plantation where an Amsterdamer was engaged in carpenter work, who very willingly pointed out the road. We found at the Englishman's a young man from Middleburgh, who had been sold as a servant, but had served out his time. He was in the last English war, had been taken by a privateer and carried to Virginia, and there sold for four years, which having expired, he thought of returning to Fatherland next year. We were mutually unacquainted with each other, but he was glad to see one of his countrymen. He took us to the road, and we proceeded on to a plantation where the people were in the woods working, to whom we went to inquire the way. The master of the plantation came to meet us, accompanied by his wife and a person who spoke high Dutch. The owner's name was *Miller*. We told him we wished to learn the road to Mr. *Hosier's*. He was about to show us the way, but as this was far around, his wife said he had better let us be taken over a creek which ran in front of his plantation, and we would have a less distance to go, whereupon he gave us directions that it should be so done. We thanked him, and went to his plantation for the purpose of going over, but we were not there soon enough, for there was a man gone over who was now almost on the other side, who called out to us that he was not coming back, because there was another canoe on this side where there was a woman. This I immediately launched in the water, as we had permission, and went over, and the woman took it back. We had here as company the man who had crossed over before us, for a piece of the way, and he directed us to another plantation, also with a creek in front of it where we had to cross. There was no one here except some women attending upon another sick woman. The man who had traveled with us a part of the way, afterwards came up and again directed us, but we came to a different plantation from what we intended. If we had gone to the right hand, we should have proceeded straight, for we would then have found Mr. *Commegys*, a Dutchman, whom we were in search of according to the address Mr. Moll had given us, and for whom we had inquired. We should have found him with many of his people bringing slaughtered meat over the creek. The owner of the plantation we had come to, had no canoe at home; but he assisted us by going with us himself, where a son of Mr. Commegys, as he said, worked a plantation, who, if he heard us call, would certainly come and take us over. But when we came to the creek we saw all those people who had carried the meat over in the boat, but this man did not know them, and doubted whether they were Commegys's men. We arrived at last at Cornelis's, the son of Commegys and called out to him, and he brought a canoe which relieved us, as it was close on to evening. We thanked the person who had brought us, and stepped into the canoe. Cornelis, who was an active young man, was pleased to meet Hollanders, although he himself was born in this country. We found Mr. Commegys on the next plantation, who bade us welcome, and after we had drank some cider, accompanied us with one of his company to Mr. Hosier's, who was a good generous-hearted man, better than any Englishman we had met with in this country. He had formerly had much business with Mr. Moll, but their affairs in England running behindhand a little, they both came and settled down here; and, therefore, Mr. Moll and he had a great regard for each other. He showed us very particular attention, although we were strangers. Something was immediately set before Mr. Commegys and ourselves to eat, in which the wife manifested as much kindness as the husband. This was not unacceptable, for we had eaten nothing all day. They requested Mr. Commegys and us very urgently to stay all night, but he desired to go home, although it was two or three hours distant from there, and it already began to grow dark. However, we left with him on foot, but he obtained a horse on the road which enabled him to travel better than we could with our wearied feet. We reached his house about eight o'clock, where he and his wife bade us welcome. We were well entertained, and went easily to sleep, having traveled during the day a great distance.

8th, Friday. We advised this morning with Mr. Commegys as to proceeding further down to Virginia, and crossing the bay, in pursuance of the address which we had received from Mr. Moll, and our recollection, to wit, that arriving at Mr. Commegys's we should then consult him, and he would give us further information. In talking the matter over with him, he said, he saw no probability of our being able to accomplish this, and advised us against it, for several reasons. First, the country below there was full of creeks and their branches, more so than that we had passed over, and it was difficult to get across them, as boats were not always to be obtained, and the people were not very obliging. As to going by water, either down or across the bay, there was not much navigating at this time of year, the winter being so close at hand, and the worst of it would be to get back again. To go by sea to the South river, or New York, there was not much opportunity, and it was attended with great danger and inconvenience. As to exploring the land, he assured us we had seen the best; the rest of it was poor and covered with bushes, especially in Virginia. It would cost us much at this time, and we would have to do with a godless and very crafty people, who would be the more so towards us, because we were strangers who could not speak their language, and did not understand the customs of the country, and so forth, all which we took into consideration. After breakfast a man arrived with a letter from Mr. Miller, requesting Commegys to go with him in his boat across the bay to the ships. Commegys not wishing to go, answered the letter, and said to us in general terms something about a man who wished to cross the bay in a boat, but he did not express himself fully, and we also did not understand him well. We supposed the man was at his plantation with a boat, and after waiting awhile without perceiving any thing of him, we asked him where the man was with the boat. He said he was not there, but that it was Captain Miller's boat which was going, and he lived about ten or twelve miles off. We immediately resolved to go there, which we did, about noon, after having breakfasted and dined together. Mr. Commegys was from Vienna, and had had a Dutch woman for a wife, who had taught her children to speak the Dutch language; they therefore had a kind disposition towards Hollanders. After her death he married an English woman, and he had himself learned many of the English maxims, although it was against his feelings; for we were sensible that he dared not work for us with an open heart. He told us he would rather live at the Cape of Good Hope than here. "How is that," said I, "when there is such good land here?" "True," he replied, "but if you knew the people here as well as I do, you would be able to understand why."

We departed from his house over the same road by which we had come, thinking that if nothing more should result from this opportunity, we would at least have advanced so far on our way back. We arrived at about three o'clock at Mr. *Hosier's*, who received us kindly, and would have cheerfully kept us all night, but understanding our intention, he not only let us go and showed us the road, but went with us himself in order to facilitate our getting over the creek; but on arriving at the next plantation on the creek, there was no canoe to put us over, and he therefore took us to another, the same one where we had found the Commegys, and where we now found his son, of whom I have before spoken, who soon had his boat ready, when thanking Mr. Hosier, and taking our leave of him, we crossed over. Young Commegys showed us the road, which we followed to a creek, where we found a canoe, but no person with it. We took ourselves over in it, and came to the house where we left the sick woman before spoken of. There were now some men at home whom we requested to show us the road, and the same person who brought us here over the same road, accompanied us a part of the way, and gave us directions how to proceed. We struck the creek directly opposite Mr. Miller's plantation, as it began to get dark, and on calling out were taken over. We inquired of Mr. Miller whether he intended to cross the bay in his boat and when, and whether he would take us with him. He said yes, but he did not know whether he would leave the next day or not. He would start as soon as the weather would permit, as he had some casks of tobacco to carry over, with which we might help him; but he did not know how we would manage on the other side, as he had to go further up the river from there, and he saw no chance for us to go down the bay or to cross back again. We finally concluded we would go with him, and remain on board the ships until he came back to take us with him, he promising not to leave there without coming for us. We also found here the person who spoke high Dutch, and of whom we have before said a word. We were able to converse with him, but my companion could do so the best. He resided on this plantation, and was a kind of proctor or advocate in the courts. We passed the evening with him. We were well entertained here, and had a good bed to sleep on, which was very agreeable.

9th, Saturday. We expected the trip would be made this morning, but no mention was made of it, and we asked him at last whether it would not be proceeded with. He said the weather was not fit, and that as soon as it was suitable we would start. But about noon the wind blowing very fresh from the west, which was straight ahead, we gave up all hope of going to-day. Seeing that the same difficulty might exist on Monday and the following days, as he said he would not go over on Sunday, we determined to proceed, after we had dined, with our journey back to New Castle, which we did, excusing ourselves on the ground that we could not wait so long, and that time pressed us. So we took our leave and went to Richard Adams's as we had promised his wife when we went on, to stop there on our return; but missing the way, or not knowing it we came to a plantation and house about three o'clock, where there was neither man nor beast, and no one from whom we could inquire the road. We chose the one we thought best, and walked on till evening. We came to a plantation on the point of the creek where Richard Adams lived on the opposite side, being now on the great bay about four miles below where we had to be. We were strangers here, and had no address to these people, who, nevertheless, showed us every kindness and treated us well. They told us we had lost the way at the empty house, by taking the road to the left instead of the right.

10*th*, *Sunday*. The son who went out to shoot at daylight, put us on the road which would lead us to the creek directly opposite Richard Adams's house, taking us back to the empty plantation which we now left on the right hand. We arrived at the place about eight o'clock, and were taken over the creek by Richard Adams himself. He and his wife were glad to see us, and bade us welcome. As it was Sunday, and we had promised to write a letter to Holland for his wife, we remained there this day, writing the letter after dinner, and having time also to look around a little. These people were so delighted at the service we were to do them in Holland, of posting a letter to Steenwyk, and sending an answer back to them, that they did not know what to do for us. He gave us some French brandy to drink, which he had purchased of the captains of the ships who had brought it from England; but as it was an article prohibited on pain of forfeiture, it was not to be bought here, and scarcely any thing else, for he had made an useless journey below, not being able to obtain shoes and stockings for his little children who were bare-legged.

I have nowhere seen so many ducks together as were in the creek in front of this house. The water was so black with them that it seemed when you looked from the land below upon the water, as if it were a mass of filth or turf, and when they flew up there was a rushing and vibration of the air like a great storm coming through the trees, and even like the rumbling of distant thunder, while the sky over the whole creek was filled with them like a cloud, or like the starlings fly at harvest time in Fatherland. There was a boy about twelve years old who took aim at them from the shore, not being able to get within good shooting distance of them, but nevertheless shot loosely before they flew away, and hit only three or four, complained of his shot, as they are accustomed to shoot from six to twelve and even eighteen and more at one shot. After supper we eat some Maryland or Virginia oysters which he had brought up with him. We found them good, but the *Gouancs* oysters at New York are better.

11*th*, *Monday*. We left there after breakfast, the man conducting us to the path which led to the plantation of Mr. *Stabley*, whose address we had from Mr. Moll, but he was sick. We were here a little while, but nothing was offered us to eat, and we only asked to drink. We wished to be put across the Sassafras river here, but could not accomplish it, although we were upon the bank of the river. We were directed to the ferry at the court house, which was about two miles west, but difficult to find through the woods. A person gave us a letter to take to the *Manathans*, who put us in the path leading to the ferry, where we arrived about two o'clock, and called out to them to come and take us over. Although the weather was perfectly still and they could easily hear us, we were not taken over, though we continued calling out to them until sundown. As no one came for us, we intended to go back to the plantation of Mr. Stabley, or one of those lying before us, and to proceed there along the strand, but a creek prevented us, and we had to search for the road by which we came. We missed this road, although we were upon it, and could not find that or any other plantation, and meanwhile it became dark. Although the moon shone we could not go straight, for it shone above, and did not give us light enough to see through the trees any houses or plantations at a distance, several of which we passed as the result proved. We were utterly perplexed and astray. We followed the roads as we found them, now easterly and then westerly, now a little more on one side, and then a little more on the other, until we were completely tired out, and wished ourselves back again upon the strand. We had to keep on, however, or remain in the woods, and as the latter did not suit us, we chose the former, fatigued as we were, and uncertain as was the issue. I plucked up courage and went singing along, which resounded through the woods, although I was short of breath through weariness. My comrade having taken his compass out of his sack in order to see how we were going, had put it back again, and we were walking on, when he discovered he had by that means lost his *degen*,[1] (sword); though we had gone some distance, we returned again to look for it, and I found it at last. We continued on westerly again, but as we came to no end, we determined to go across, through the thickets and bushes, due north, in order if we could not discover any plantation,

---

[1] This word is possibly erroneously written. Its meaning here cannot even be conjectured.

we might at least reach the strand. It was now about nine o'clock in the evening. After having proceeded about an hour in that direction, we heard directly in front of us, a dog barking, which gladdened us. It was a remarkable circumstance, as dogs are used to keep men away from dwellings, but served to bring us to them, and was remarkable also for the providence of the Lord, who caused this dog to bark, who, the nearer we approached, heard more noise made by us among the leaves and bushes, and barked the more, calling to us as it were, to come straight up to him, which we endeavored to do. We soon came, however, to a very deep hollow, where we could see over the tops of the trees in it, and on the other side what seemed to be a shed of a plantation in which the dog was barking. This encouraged us, but we had yet to go through the hollow, where we could see no bottom, and the sides were steep. We scrambled down I know not how, not seeing whether there was water or a morass there; but on reaching the bottom, we found it was a morass grown up with bushes. My comrade who followed me, called out to know whether we could not pass round it, but we had to go through it. We came at length to a small brook, not broad, which we crossed and clambered up the side again, when we came to the shed where the dog continued barking, and thus led us to the house. His master was in bed, and did not know what noise it was he heard. On our knocking, he was surprised to hear such strange people at the door, not knowing whether we were few or many, or whether he dared invite us in or not, but he did. We had then little trouble. When we entered the house he was astonished to see us, inquiring what people we were, where we came from, where we were going, but especially how we reached there. No one, he said, could get there easily in the day time, unless he were shown or knew the way well, because they were very much hidden, and he would come to all the other plantations sooner than this one. We told him our adventures, at which he was as much astonished as we were rejoiced. We had reasons to behold the Lord in all this, and to glorify him as we did silently in our hearts. The wife arose and offered us a little to eat of what she had, and afterwards gave me some deer skins, but they were as dry and hard as a plank. I lay down upon them, and crept under them, but was little covered and still less warmed by them. My companion went to lie with a servant in his bunk, but he did not remain there long before a heavy rain came — before which the Lord had caused us to enter the house against all appearances — and compelled him to evacuate his quarters very quickly. The water entered in such great quantities that they would otherwise have been wet through, though already it did not make much difference with my comrade. We passed the night, however, as well as we could, sitting, standing, or lying down, but cold enough.

12*th*, *Tuesday*. This plantation was about four miles below the court house or ferry, westerly towards the bay, and we did not know if we went to the ferry that we would not be compelled again to remain there calling out, uncertain when we would be carried over. We therefore promised this servant if he would put us across we would give him the money, which we would otherwise have to pay at the ferry. The master made some objections on account of the servant's work and the distance from the river, and also because they had no canoe. The servant satisfied him on these points, and he consented. We breakfasted on what we could get, not knowing how or where we would obtain any thing again. We three, accordingly, went about two miles to the strand, where we found a canoe, but it was almost entirely full of water, and what was the worst of it, we had nothing with which to bale it out. However, by one means and another we emptied it and launched the canoe. We stepped in and paddled over the river to the plantation of a Mr. *Frisby.* I must not forget to mention the great number of wild geese we saw here on the river. They rose not in flocks of ten or twelve, or twenty or thirty, but continuously, wherever we pushed our way; and as they made room for us, there was such an incessant clattering made with their wings upon the water where they rose, and such a noise of those flying higher up, that it was as if we were all the time surrounded by a whirlwind or a storm. This proceeded not only from geese, but from ducks and other water fowl; and it is not peculiar to this place alone, but it occurred on all the creeks and rivers we crossed, though they were most numerous in the morning and evening when they are most easily shot.

Having crossed this river, which is of great width, we came to the plantation of Mr. Frisby, which stands upon an eminence and affords a very pleasant prospect, presenting a view of the great bay as well as the Sassafras river. When we first came on, we stopped here, but the master was not at home; and as we had a letter of recommendation and credit to him, he found it at his house when he returned. When we arrived there now, we intended merely to ask his negroes for a drink, but he being apprised of our arrival, made us go into the house, and entertained us well. After we had partaken of a good meal, he had horses made ready for us immediately to ride to Bohemia river, which hardly deserves the name of a river in respect to other creeks. We mounted on horseback, then, about ten o'clock, he and one of his friends leading a piece of the way. Upon separating, he left us a boy to show us the path and bring back the horses. This boy undertaking more than he knew, assured us he was well acquainted with the road; but after a while, observing the course we rode, and the distance we had gone, and that we had ridden as long as we ought to have done, if we had been going right, we doubted no longer we had missed the way, as truly appeared in the end; for about three o'clock in the afternoon we came upon a broad cart road, when we discovered we had kept too far to the right and had gone entirely around Bohemia river. We supposed we were now acquainted with the road, and were upon the one which ran from Casparus Hermans's to his father's, not knowing there were other cart roads. We rode along this fine road for about an hour or an hour and a half, in order to reach Augustine Hermans, when we heard some persons calling out to us from the woods, "Hold, where are you riding to?" Certain, as we supposed we were, in our course, we answered, "to Augustine Hermans." "You should not go that road then," they rejoined, "for you are out of the way." We therefore rode into the bushes in order to go to them, and learned that we were not upon the road we thought we were, but on the road from *Apoquemene*, that is, a cart road made from *Apoquemene*, a small village situated upon a creek, to Bohemia creek or river. Upon this road the goods which go from the South river to Maryland by land, are carried, and also those which pass inland from Maryland to the South river, because these two creeks, namely, the Apoquemene, and the Bohemia, one running up from Maryland, and the other from the Delaware river, as the English call the South river, come to an end close to each other, and perhaps shoot by each other, although they are not navigable so far; but are navigable for eight miles, that is two Dutch miles of fifteen to a degree. When the Dutch governed the country the distance was less, namely, six miles. The digging a canal through was then talked of, the land being so low; which would have afforded great convenience for trade on the South river, seeing that they would have come from Maryland to buy all they had need of, and would have been able to transport their tobacco more easily to that river, than to the great bay of Virginia, as they now have to do, for a large part of Maryland. Besides, the cheap market of the Hollanders in the South [river] would have drawn more trade; and if the people of Maryland had goods to ship on their own account, they could do it sooner and more readily, as well as more conveniently in the South [river] than in the great bay, and therefore, would have chosen this route, the more so because as many of their goods, perhaps, would for various reasons be shipped to Holland, as to England. But as this is a subject of greater importance than it seems upon the first view, it is well to consider whether it should not be brought to the attention of higher authorities than particular governors. What is now done by land in carts, might then be done by water, for a distance of more than six hundred miles.

We had, then, come on this road with our horses to the carrying-place into Maryland and more than three miles from where we supposed we were. To go there we would have had to pass through woods and over small morassy creeks. The sun was nearly down, and we therefore advised with the persons before mentioned. One of them was a quaker who was building a small house for a tavern, or rather an ale house, for the purpose of entertaining travelers, and the other was the carpenter who was assisting him on the house, and could speak good Dutch, having resided a long time at the *Manathans.* We were most concerned for the young man and the horses. The quaker, who had put up a temporary shed, made of the bark of trees, after the manner of the Indians, with both ends open, and little larger than a dog's kennel, and where at the best, we three might possibly have been able to lie, especially when a fire was made which would have to be done, offered us his lodgings if we wished, and as good accommodations as he had, which were not much. He had nothing to eat but maize bread which was poor enough, and some small wild beans boiled in water; and little to lie on, or to cover one, except the bare ground and leaves. We would not have rejected this fare if the Lord had made it necessary, and we were afterwards in circumstances where we did not have as good as this; but now we could do better. The other person, an Irishman, who lived about three miles from there, did not urge us much, because, perhaps, he did not wish us to see how easily he would make two English shillings for which we had agreed with him to take the horses and boy to the creek, and put them on the path to reach home. We were to walk to his house, conducted by the quaker, while he rode round the creek with the horses. We had to cross it in a canoe, which, when we were in it, was not the breadth of two fingers above water, and threatened every moment to upset. We succeeded, however, in crossing over, and had then to make our way through bushes by an untrodden path, going from one newly marked tree to another. These marks are merely a piece cut out of the bark with an axe, about the height of a man's eyes from the ground; and by means of them the commonest roads are designated through all New Netherland and Maryland; but in consequence of the great number of roads so marked, and their running into and across each other, they are of little assistance, and indeed often mislead. Pursuing our way we arrived at the house of Maurice, as the carpenter was called, where he had already arrived with the horses, and had earned two shillings sooner than we had walked three miles, and more than he had made by his whole day's work. We went into the house and found his Irish wife, engaged in cooking, whereby we made reprisals in another way. After we had thus taken a good supper, we were directed to a place to sleep which suited us entirely and where we rested well.

13*th*, *Wednesday*. As soon as it was day we eat our breakfast and left, after giving this man his two shillings, who also immediately rode off with the young man and the horses, to put him on the path to Sassafras river, while the quaker who had remained there during the night, was to take us to the broad cart road where he had found us. But neither he nor we, could follow the new marked trees so well in the morning light, and we soon missed the way, and no wonder, for we now had the marks behind the trees. We went again through the thickets and bushes of the woods, to and fro, for full three hours without any prospect of getting out, and that within a distance of not over three-quarters of an hour. We struck a foot-path at last which led us to Bohemia creek, directly opposite the house which was being built. We descended in order to wade over it, the bottom appearing to be hard on this side, and promising a good passage; but when we were in the middle of it, we sank up to our knees in the mud. When we were over we went into the quaker's hut, who warmed-up some beans, and set them before us with maize bread. Not to leave him like an empty calabash, we gave him an English shilling for leading us astray, and other things. We had now a fine broad cart road to follow, eight miles long, which would lead us to *Apoquemene*, as it did, and where we arrived about noon. They are most all Dutch who live here, and we were again among the right kind of people, with whom we could at least obtain what was right. We stepped into a house and were welcome. Some food was immediately set before us to eat, and among other things butter, cheese, and rye bread which was fresh and so delicious that my companion said it was to him like sweet cake. We left there after we had taken dinner, a boy leading us upon the way as far as a long wooden bridge or dam over a meadow and creek, and proceeded on to Casparus Hermans's, the brother of Ephraim, about six miles from there, where we arrived at three o'clock, but again found him absent from home. As the court was sitting at Newcastle he had to be there as one of its members. We were, however, welcomed by his wife. Her name was Susanna, and his, Casparus or Jasper; which led my thoughts further, communing with God in his love, who makes the past as well as the future to be present, and who consumes the present in him with the future and the past, as it proceeds from him with all our sensations. We passed the night there, and had to sleep with a quaker who was going next day to Maryland.

14*th*, *Thursday*. While we were waiting for Casparus, we embraced the opportunity to examine his place again, which pleased us in all respects, and was objectionable only because it lay on the road, and was therefore resorted to by every one, and especially by these miserable quakers. He returned home in the afternoon, and was glad to find us. We spoke to him in relation to a certain tract of land which we wished to look at, and Ephraim and his father had told us of; and when we heard what it was, it was a part of Bohemia, which we had already tolerably well looked at on our way to Maryland, being that which lies on the creeks and river, and which, on our return and twice losing the way, lay higher up in the woods; but we reserved the privilege in case we should winter on the South river, of riding over it thoroughly on horseback, with him and his brother Ephraim.[1] For the present, time compelled us to see if we could not yet reach the *Manathans* for the winter; and we were the more induced to the attempt because a servant of Ephraim had arrived this evening by water in a boat, and would be ready to return with it to Newcastle early in the morning. We therefore excused ourselves and let the subject rest. We

[1] It was upon the piece of land here alluded to that the colony of the Labadists was afterwards planted.

heard here that his father Augustine Hermans was very sick and at the point of death, and that Miss Margaret had gone there to attend upon him in that condition.

15*th*, *Friday*. It was flood tide early this morning, and our servant slept a little too long, for it was not far from high water when he appeared. We hurried, however, into the boat and pushed on as hard as we could, but the flood stopped running, when we were about half way. We continued on rowing, and as the day advanced we caught a favorable wind from the west and spread the sail. The wind gradually increasing brought us to Newcastle about eight o'clock among our kind friends again, where we were welcome anew. We were hardly ashore before the wind, changing from the west to the northwest, brought with it such a storm and rain that, if we had still been on the water, we would have been in great peril, and if we had been at Casparus's we would not have been able to proceed in such weather. We here again, so clearly perceived the providence of the Lord over us, that our hearts were constrained to ascend to him, and praise him for what he is and does, especially towards his children. As we have confined ourselves quite strictly to the account of our journey, we deem it serviceable to make some observations upon some general matters concerning Maryland, in addition to what we have before remarked.

As regards its first discoverer and possessor, that was one Lord Baltimore, an English nobleman, in the time of Queen Maria. Having come from Newfoundland along the coast of North America, he arrived in the great bay of Virginia, up which he sailed to its uppermost parts, and found this fine country which he named Maryland after his queen. Returning to England he obtained a charter of the northerly parts of America, *inexclusively*, although the Hollanders had discovered and began to settle New Netherland. With this he came back to America and took possession of his Maryland, where at present his son, as governor, resides.[1]

Since the time of Queen Elizabeth, settlers have preferred the lowest parts of the great bay and the large rivers which empty into it, either on account of proximity to the sea, and the convenience of the streams, or because the uppermost country smacked somewhat of the one from whom it derived its name and of its government. They have named this lower country Virginia, out of regard to Queen Elizabeth. It is the most populous, but not the best land, and has a government distinct from that of Maryland. A governor arrived while we were there, to fill the place made vacant by the death of his predecessor.[2]

As to the present government of Maryland, it remains firm upon the old footing, and is confined within the limits

---

[1] Charles Calvert, was at this time both proprietor and governor of Maryland. He came out first in 1662 as governor under his father Cecilius, the first proprietor, upon whose death in 1675 he succeeded to the title of Lord Baltimore, and the estates in this country. He went to England upon the happening of this event, and returned in February, 1680, to Maryland, where he continued in the administration of the government personally until 1684, when he again visited England. By the revolution which soon after followed, the province was lost to the family, and was not fully restored until 1715, when its heir had changed his religious faith and adopted that of the established church of England. Cecilius and Charles Calvert, Lords Baltimore, were Catholics. *McMahon's History of Maryland,* 216, *et seq.*

[2] Lord Culpepper came over as governor of Virginia, in 1679 or 1680, although he had been appointed some time previously. Sir William Berkeley, whom he succeeded, and whose administration of the unequaled duration of forty years, had terminated in a sea of blood, upon the suppression of Bacon's rebellion, having been recalled, returned to England in 1677, where he died shortly after his arrival there. Colonel Jeffries discharged the duties of the place as lieutenant governor during a portion of the interval until the arrival of Lord Culpepper; but he also dying in 1678, the government devolved upon Sir H. Chickerly for the rest of the period. *Burk's History of Virginia,* II, 203, 223. Chalmers says, Lord Culpepper arrived here in May, 1680. *Annals,* I, 340.

before mentioned. All of Maryland that we have seen, is high land, with few or no meadows, but possessing such a rich and fertile soil, as persons living there assured me, that they had raised tobacco off the same piece of land for thirty consecutive years. The inhabitants who are generally English, are mostly engaged in this production. It is their chief staple, and the means with which they must purchase every thing they require, which is brought to them from other English possessions in Europe, Africa and America. There is, nevertheless, sometimes a great want of these necessaries, owing to the tobacco market being low, or the shipments being prevented by some change of affairs in some quarter, particularly in Europe, or to both causes, as was the case at this time, when a great scarcity of such articles existed there, as we saw. So large a quantity of tobacco is raised in Maryland and Virginia, that it is one of the greatest sources of revenue to the crown by reason of the taxes which it yields. Servants and negroes are employed in the culture of tobacco, who are brought from other places to be sold to the highest bidders, the servants for a term of years only, but the negroes forever, and may be sold by their masters to other planters as many times as their masters choose, that is, the servants until their term is fulfilled, and the negroes for life. These men, one with another, each make, when they are able to work, from 2,500 pounds to 3,000 pounds, and even 3,500 pounds of tobacco a year, and some of the masters and their wives who pass their lives here in wretchedness, do the same. The servants and negroes after they have worn themselves down the whole day, and gone home to rest, have yet to grind and pound the grain, which is generally maize, for their masters and all their families as well as themselves, and all the negroes, to eat. Tobacco is the only production in which the planters employ themselves, as if there were nothing else in the world to plant but that, and while the land is capable of yielding all the productions that can be raised anywhere, so far as the climate of the place allows. As to articles of food, the only bread they have is that made of Turkish wheat or maize, and that is miserable. They plant this grain for that purpose everywhere. It yields well, not a hundred, but five or six hundred for one; but it takes up much space, as it is planted far apart like vines in France. The corn, when it is to be used for men, has to be first soaked, before it is ground or pounded, because the grains being large and very hard, cannot be broken under the small stones of their light hand-mills; and then it is left so coarse it must be sifted. They take the finest for bread, and the other for different kinds of groats, which, when it is cooked, is called *sapaen* or *homma*. The meal intended for bread is kneaded moist without leaven or yeast, salt or grease, and generally comes out of the oven so that it will hardly hold together, and so blue and moist that it is as heavy as dough; yet the best of it when cut and roasted, tastes almost like warm white bread, at least it seemed to us so. This corn is also the only provender for their horses, oxen, cows, hogs and fowls, which generally run in the woods to get their food, but are fed a little of this morning and evening during the winter when there is little to be had in the woods; though they are not fed too much, for the wretchedness, if not *cruelty*, of such living, affects both man and beast. This is said not without reason, for a master having a sick servant, and there are many so, and observing from his declining condition, he would finally die, and that there was no probability of his enjoying any more service from him, made him, sick and languishing as he was, dig his own grave, in which he was laid a few days afterwards, the others being too busy to dig it, having their hands full in attending to the tobacco.

A few vegetables are planted, but they are of the coarsest

kinds and are cultivated in the coarsest manner, without knowledge or care, and they are, therefore, not properly raised, and do not amount to much as regards the production, and still less as to their use. Some have begun to plant orchards, which all bear very well, but are not properly cultivated. The fruit is for the greater part pressed, and makes good cider, of which the largest portion becomes soured and spoiled through their ignorance or negligence, either from not putting it into good casks, or from not taking proper care of the liquor afterwards. Sheep they have none, although they have what is requisite for them if they chose. It is matter of conjecture whether you will find any milk or butter even in summer; we have not found any there at this season of the year. They bestow all their time and care in producing tobacco; each cask or hogshead, as they call it, of which pays two English shillings on exportation, and on its arrival in England, two pence a pound, besides the fees for weighing and other expenses here, and freight and other charges beyond sea. When, therefore, tobacco only brings four or five pence, there is little or nothing left for the owner.

The lives of the planters in Maryland and Virginia are very godless and profane. They listen neither to God nor his commandments, and have neither church nor cloister. Sometimes there is some one who is called a minister, who does not as elsewhere, serve in one place, for in all Virginia and Maryland there is not a city or a village — but travels for profit, and for that purpose visits the plantations through the country, and there addresses the people; but I know of no public assemblages being held in these places; you hear often that these ministers are worse than anybody else, yea, are an abomination.

When the ships arrive with goods, and especially with liquors, such as wine and brandy, they attract everybody, that is, masters, to them, who then indulge so abominably together, that they keep nothing for the rest of the year, yea, do not go away as long as there is any left, or bring any thing home with them which might be useful to them in their subsequent necessities. It must, therefore, go hard with the household, and it is a wonder if there be a single drop left for the future. They squander so much in this way, that they keep no tobacco to buy a shoe or a stocking for their children which sometimes causes great misery. While they take so little care for provisions, and are otherwise so reckless, the Lord sometimes punishes them with insects, flies and worms, or with intemperate seasons, causing great famine, as happened a few years ago in the time of the last Dutch war with the English, when the Lord sent so many weevils (*eenkorentjes*) that all their grain was eaten up as well as most all the other productions of the field, by reason of which such a great famine was caused that many persons died of starvation, and a mother killed her own child and eat it, and then went to her neighbors, calling upon them to come and see what she had done, and showing them the remains of her child, whereupon she was arrested and condemned to be hung. When she sat or stood on the scaffold, she cried out to the people, in the presence of the governor, that she was now going to God, where she would render an account, and would declare before him that what she had done she did in the mere delirium of hunger, for which the governor alone should bear the guilt; inasmuch as this famine was caused by the *eenkorens*, a visitation from God, because he, the governor, undertook in the preceding summer, an expedition against the Dutch, residing on the South river, who maintained themselves in such a good posture of defense, that he could accomplish but little; when he went to the *Hoere-kil* on the west side of that river, not far from the sea, where also he was not able to do much; but as the people subsisted there only by cultivating wheat, and had at this time a fine and abundant harvest in the fields — and from such harvests the people of Maryland generally and under such circumstances as these particularly, were fed — he set fire to it, and all their other fruits, whether of the trees or the field; whereby he committed two great sins at the same time, namely, against God and his goodness, and against his neighbors, the Dutch, who lost it, and the English who needed it; and had caused more misery to the English in his own country, than to the Dutch in the enemy's country. This wretched woman protesting these words substantially against the governor, before heaven and in the hearing of every one, was then swung up.[1]

In addition to what the tobacco itself pays on exportation, which produces a very large sum, every hundred acres of land, whether cultivated or not, has to pay one hundred pounds of tobacco a year, and every person between sixteen and sixty years of age must pay three shillings a year. All animals are free of taxation, and so are all productions except tobacco.

It remains to be mentioned that those persons who pro-

---

[1] The *Hoerekil*, in English Whore creek, is on the west side of Delaware bay, about three miles inside of Cape Henlopen. This distinctive name first appears in the *Vertoogh van Nieu Nederlant*, written in 1649 (*N. Y. Historical Society Collections*, second series, II, 281). It would seem to have been first applied in the preceding year from a circumstance which is related in *N. Y. Colonial History*, III, 342. This spot was first attempted to be settled by the Dutch in 1631, when a colony of thirty-four persons sent out by Godyn, Van Rensselaer, Bloemart, De Laet, and David Pietersen De Vries as patroons, was landed there, but was a few months afterwards in the same year destroyed, and the colonists all murdered by the Indians. It then, in common with the whole territory, on both sides of the mouth of Delaware bay, for thirty-two miles up from the sea, bore the name of Swanendael. It remained unsettled until 1659, when it was purchased of the Indians a second time by the Dutch West India Company, and was by the company transferred immediately to the city of Amsterdam, although it had been purchased of the Indians by Godyn and others in 1629, and by them assigned to the West India Company in 1535. *Hazard's Annals of Pennsylvania*, 23, 39, 255-7. A colony of Mennonists, directed

fess the Roman Catholic religion, have great, indeed, all freedom in Maryland, because the governor makes profession of that faith, and consequently there are priests and other ecclesiastics who travel and disperse themselves everywhere, and neglect nothing which serves for their profit and purpose. The priests of Canada take care of this region, and hold correspondence with those here, as is supposed, as well as with those who reside among the Indians. It is said there is not an Indian fort between Canada and Maryland, where there is not a Jesuit who teaches and advises the Indians, who begin to listen to them too much; so much so, that some people in Virginia and Maryland as well as in New Netherland, have been apprehensive lest there might be an outbreak, hearing what has happened in Europe, as well as among their neighbors at Boston; but they hope the result of the troubles there will determine many things elsewhere. The Lord grant a happy issue there and here, as well as in other parts of the world, for the help of his own elect, and the glory of his name.

We will now leave Maryland, and come back to New

---

by Peter Cornelisen Plockhoy, left Holland, and established itself at the Hoerekil in 1662, under the authority of the city of Amsterdam. This new colony was plundered by the English on the conquest of New Netherland in 1664.

The transaction to which the journalist refers happened eight years afterwards. It was perpetrated by the proprietor of Maryland in vindication of his title, though it seems to have been ruthlessly done, and without justification. It occurred in the summer of 1672, when Lord Baltimore sent an expedition to the Hoerekil, consisting of sixty men at first, but afterwards reduced to thirty men and horse, under one Jones, who, "in derision and contempt of the Duke's authority, bound the magistrates and inhabitants, despitefully treated them, sifted and plundered them of their goods, and when it was demanded by what authority he acted, answered in no other language but a cocked pistol to his breast, which if it had spoken, had forever silenced him." *Hazard's Annals*, 398. *N. Y. Colonial Manuscripts*, XX, 37.

The name of the town of Hoerekil was changed to Deal in 1680, and subsequently to Lewes, and is now Lewis or Lewiston.

Castle (*Sandhock*), on the South river, where, in the house of our friend Ephraim Hermans, the Lord had brought us, and our friends received and lodged us with affectionate hearts.

16*th*, *Saturday*. Mr. Moll, who is the president [of the court] and one of the principal men in the South [river,] having finished his business in the court which was now ended, had intended to ride this morning to a plantation which he had recently purchased on Christina kil, and would have been pleased to have had us accompany him, and look at the lands about there, which he said were very good; but as the hard and rainy weather of yesterday had not yet cleared up, he put off the journey until Monday, in hopes he would then have our company, when he would provide a horse for each of us, and Ephraim would also go with us. Meanwhile we went to see whether there would be any means of returning to the *Manathans* notwithstanding the ice, either by land or sea. If we should return by water, we would be able to see the lower parts of this river, the Hoere-kil and others; but no opportunity presented itself, because it was so late in the year, there being no navigating in consequence of every one being afraid of the ice.

17*th*, *Sunday*. We had an opportunity to-day to hear Domine Tessemaker, which we did, but never heard worse preaching, and I, therefore, had little desire to go again in the afternoon, though I was misled by the ringing of the bell. He is a man who wishes to effect some *etablissement* or reform here, but he will not accomplish much in that respect, as he not only has no grace therefor, but there seems to be something in his life which will hereafter manifest itself more. For the present we can say with truth that he is a perfect worldling.[1] It seems that in these

---

[1] Domine Peter Tessemaker remained in charge of the church at New Castle until 1682, when he accepted a call to Schenectady, where he fell a victim to the massacre perpetrated by the French and Indians in February, 1690. His head was cloven open, and his body burnt to the shoulder blades.

spiritually, as well as physically, waste places, there is nevertheless, a craving of the people to accept any thing that bears even the name of food, in order to content rather than satisfy themselves therewith. Nevertheless the Lord will take pity upon these his lands, as we hope, for it appears indeed that the seed of the elect is here, especially among those of European descent.

18*th*, *Monday*. We four, namely, Mr. Moll, Ephraim, my comrade and myself, after we had breakfasted, started about nine o'clock, on horseback, from New Castle for Christina kil. We observed the land through which we rode was sometimes only common soil, until we reached a plantation which Mr. Moll and Ephraim owned together, lying on a branch of that creek, and which was a good piece of land. Ephraim having finished the business for which he had come here, of having planks sawed for boarding a new clap-board house he had built, left us and rode back to New Castle, and we continued on after we had looked at a grist-mill which the Swedes had constructed upon one of the branches of the creek, a considerable distance along another of them. We discovered here and there pieces of good land, but they were not large, and were along the creek. The greater portion of the country was only common land. Evening coming on, we rode back to the plantation of a Mr. Man, lying upon a neck of land called Cheese-and-bread (*Caes-en-broot*) island, which is a good piece of ground, and up to which the creek is navigable for large boats or barks. This man is a great friend of Mr. Moll. We were, therefore, very welcome, and slept there this night.

19*th*, *Tuesday*. After breakfast we rode out in company with Mr. Man, to look at several pieces of land which they very highly recommended to us, but it was because, as they said, they wished to have good neighbors, though sometimes neighbors did not amount to much. It was now in the afternoon, and we rode towards home, over a plain where the deer ran out of the road in herds. Coming to the large creek, which is properly called Christina kil, we found Mr. Moll had not correctly calculated the tide, for he supposed it would be low water or thereabouts, whereas the water was so high that it was not advisable to ride through it with horses, and we would have to wait until the water had fallen sufficiently for that purpose. While we were waiting, and it began to get towards evening, an Indian came on the opposite side of the creek, who knew Mr. Moll, and lived near there at that time, and had perhaps heard us speak. He said that we would have to wait there too long; but if we would ride a little lower down, he had a canoe in which he would carry us over, and we might swim the horses across. We rode there at once, and found him and his canoe. We unsaddled the horses, and he swam them over one by one, being in the canoe and holding them by the bridle. When we were over, we quickly saddled them and rode them as fast as they could run, so that they might not be cold and benumbed. It was entirely dark, and we remarked to each other the providence of the Lord in this Indian coming there; for otherwise we would not have known how to find the way through the woods in consequence of the great darkness. It was bad enough as it was, on a path that both the horses and Mr. Moll were acquainted with, for we could scarcely see each other sometimes. We reached New Castle happily about eight o'clock in the evening, much rejoiced, and thanking Mr. Moll.

20*th*, *Wednesday*. While we were in Maryland, and were crossing over the Sassafras river, we saw a small English ship lying there, which they told us would leave about the English Christmas. We now learned from Mr. Moll, that he was going to write by her, and was willing if we wrote, to allow our letters go to London under cover of his; and also that he should soon go to Maryland to attend the court now about to be held there. We determined, therefore, not to permit the opportunity to pass by of writing home.

21*st*, *Thursday*. We finished our letters to-day. We perceived it would be in vain to wait for a chance to go to the *Manathans* by sea, and there would be no opportunity to go up the river. We, therefore, finally concluded to hire a canoe and a person to take us up the river; and accordingly agreed with one *Jan Boeyer*, for fifty guilders in zeewan, and a dollar for the canoe a day, to leave the next day if it were possible. Whereupon, Ephraim and his wife, who had done their best herein, as well as other friends, set about writing letters for us to take to the *Manathans*. Meantime, Ephraim received news that his father was near his end, and had to be handled by one or two men to turn him in bed, and that he desired once more to speak to him.

22*d*, *Friday*. It had frozen some this morning, and Jan Boeyer manifested little disposition to go up the river, declaring that with such a frost as this, the river above was all frozen up; and though there was no probability of it, we had to wait. Ephraim and Mr. Moll, left together for Maryland to see Ephraim's father, who wanted to speak to him, as we heard, in relation to the land or manor which he possessed there; for while he had given portions to all his other children, namely, one son and three daughters, he had made Ephraim, his oldest son, heir of his rank and manor, according to the English law, as *fils de commys*, that is, Ephraim could enjoy the property during his life, and hire or sell it for that period, but upon his death, it must go to his oldest son, and so descend from heir to heir. Mr. Moll was the witness of this, and had the papers in his care. It seemed that the father wished to make some change because we had been there, and he had offered us a part of the land. We, therefore, think we will hear what he shall have done in the matter.

Although it had frozen hard, yet when the sun rose high about nine o'clock, it was ordinarily pleasant and handy weather, but there was no decision on the part of our skipper to leave. In the meantime we had the house with Ephraim's wife alone, and, therefore, more freedom and opportunity to speak to her of God, and godly things, which she well received. We expect something good from her as well as from Ephraim.

23*d*, *Saturday*. The weather was milder, and there was some fog which cleared away as the sun rose. We went to see Jan Boeyer again, but he had no intention to make the journey. We heard it was not so much on account of the ice, as of the small-pox, which prevailed very much up the river, and which he had never had. There was no use of striving with him, and we determined, therefore, to hire somebody else, if we could find any person. Mr. Peter Aldrix made inquiry for us, but to no purpose, and we had to wait and depend upon God's providence. We heard, however, of some people who had arrived in a canoe from Christina kil, and that even in that creek there was no ice yet, or up the river.

24*th*, *Sunday*. Domine Tessemaker being at Apoquemene there was no preaching to-day at New Castle but prelecting. We went, however, to the church, in order not to give offense. Much of the reading we could not bear, but we hope others were more edified than we expected to be.

It was very fine weather and it annoyed us that we had to wait so. This evening there arrived a canoe with Swedes, who had come from half way below the falls, and of whom we inquired whether there were any ice up the river. They said there was not, and they were going back the next day. We endeavored to make an agreement with them to carry us, but they asked entirely too much, namely, an anker of rum, which would amount to about 120 guilders in zeewan; whereupon we rebuked them for their exorbitancy. The Swedes and Fins, particularly, have this fault, and generally towards strangers; but as it seemed to me they had drank a little too much, we let the matter rest in the hope they would talk more reasonably to-morrow.

25th, Monday. The weather being good, we spoke again to our Swedes, but they continued obstinate; and also to Jan Boeyer, but nothing could be done with him either. While we were standing on the shore talking with them about leaving, I saw coming down the river a boat which looked very much like that of the quaker of Upland, as indeed it was. He landed at New Castle and was going to Ephraim's house, where he had some business to transact, intending to leave the next day. We asked him if he was willing to take us with him, and he said, he would do so with pleasure. We were rejoiced, observing the providence of the Lord who took such fatherly care of us. There stood Jan Boeyer and the Swedes cheated by their own covetousness. Robert Wade and his wife lodged at Ephraim's, which assured us our journey would be commenced the next day.

26th, Tuesday. All the letters having been collected together, which we were to take with us and deliver, and the quaker having finished his business, we breakfasted together, and courteously took leave of all our acquaintances; but especially with some love, of Madam Ephraim, named *Elizabeth van Rodenburgh.* She had shown us much kindness, and given us good hope that the Lord will not forget her therein.

We will observe before leaving *Sand-hoek*, that it has always been the principal place on the South river, as well in the time of the English as of the Dutch. It is now called New Castle by the English. It is situated on the west side of the river upon a point which extends out with a sandy beach, affording a good landing place, better than is to be found elsewhere on that account. It lies a little above the bay where the river bends and runs south from there, so that you can see down the river southerly, the greater portion of it, which presents a beautiful view in perspective, and enables you to see from a distance the ships which come out of the great bay and sail up the river. Formerly all ships were accustomed to anchor here, for the purpose of paying duties or obtaining permits, and to unload when the goods were carried away by water in boats or barks, or by land in carts. It was much larger and more populous at that time, and had a small fort called Nassau; but since the country has belonged to the English, ships may no longer come here, or they must first declare and unload their cargoes at New York, which has caused this little place to fall off very much, and even retarded the settlement of plantations. What remains of it consists of about fifty houses, most all of wood. The fort is demolished, but there is a good block-house, having some small cannon, erected in the middle of the town, and sufficient to resist the Indians or an incursion of Christians; but it could not hold out long. This town is the capital of justice, where the high court of the South river is held, having three other courts subordinate to it, from which appeals lie to it, as they do from it to New York, and from New York to England. These three minor courts are established, one at Salem, a small village of quakers newly commenced on the east side of the river not far from New Castle; another is at Upland, on the west side above New Castle, a Swedish village, and the third is at Burlington, a new quaker village on the east side of the river above New Castle. New Castle is about eighty miles from the falls, and the same distance from the mouth of the river or the sea. The water in the river at New Castle, at ordinary flood tide is fresh, but when it is high spring tide, or the wind blows hard from the south or southeast, it is brackish, and if the wind continues long, or it is hard weather it becomes a little saltish. With a new or full moon it makes high water at New Castle at five o'clock. The principal persons whom we have seen are Mr. Moll and his wife, Ephraim Hermans and his wife, Peter Aldrix and his wife, and Domine Tessemaker.

As regards Mr. Moll, he lived in his youth at Amsterdam, in order to learn business. He afterwards went to Bristol, in England, where he carried on a reasonably large business which he had begun to do at Amsterdam. In the war between England and Holland, he lost so much that he failed, or made an agreement with his creditors. He, therefore, immigrated to this country, and after trading in Virginia and Maryland some time, came to New Castle to live, where he has two or three plantations, upon which he raises tobacco, more for the purpose of paying his creditors, as he himself informed me, than because he seeks this manner of gain and life, intending, as soon as he can release himself, to go and live upon the land, and support himself by what God may be pleased to give him.[1] Touching the hope of grace discoverable in him it is very slight, although he has listened with attention to all we have said to him, requesting us to continue, and that he might be favored with a letter from us on the subject, or some books such as we might deem necessary, and willing, with a full heart, to do us every service in his power in these quarters or elsewhere, as he had done many, and endeavored to do still more. The Lord will do for him as it pleases him.

The wife of Mr. Moll is an English woman, a pious independent. When he married her, she lived in a large house where many persons dwelt together, separate from all other assemblies and the attachments of the world, seek-

[1] See note on page 180, *ante*.

ing nothing except to serve God in peace and uprightness, and having their own preacher and other ministers. But with all this she remains a great *mundane*, as to which we have spoken to her. They have only one son.

Ephraim Hermans is the oldest child of Augustine Hermans, there being two brothers and three sisters, one of whom lives now at Amsterdam. They are all of a Dutch mother, after whose death their father married an English woman, who is the most artful and despicable creature that can be found. He is a very godless person, and his wife, by her wickedness, has compelled all these children to leave their father's house and live elsewhere.[1] Ephraim, the oldest, having gone into business, settled at New Castle, his oldest sister keeping house for him. He had for a long time sought in marriage at New York, a daughter of the

---

[1] Augustine Hermans, or Heermans, called also Harman, was a Bohemian by birth, but came from Holland to New Amsterdam in or before 1647, in which year he was appointed by the director and council of New Netherland, one of the Nine Men, a body of citizens selected to assist the government by their counsel and advice. He came over to this country as a clerk to John and Charles Gabry, of Amsterdam. He was sent, in company with Resolved Waldron, by the Dutch governor, to the governor of Maryland, to confer in relation to the claim of title of the proprietor of Maryland to the South river. This no doubt led to his subsequent settlement on Bohemia river, so named by him, in that province. He seems to have been a surveyor and draughtsman. In addition to the map of Maryland, stated by our journal to have been made by him, which seems to have been the consideration for the grant of Bohemia manor, he made a sketch of the city of New Amsterdam, which was engraved on Nicolas Jan Visscher's map *Novi Belgii Novæque Angliæ nec non partis Virginiæ*, published in 1650-6, and also on a reduced scale from Visscher's map on the map prefixed to the second edition of *Vanderdonk's Description of New Netherland*. His first wife was Janneken Verlett of Utrecht, whom he married at New Amsterdam, December 10, 1650, and by whom he had children: 1, Ephraim George, baptized September 1, 1652; 2, Casparus, baptized July 2, 1656; 3, Anna Margaretta, baptized March 10, 1658; Judith, baptized May 9, 1660, and Francina, baptized March 12, 1662. *New York Manual* 1863, 723. *Brodhead*, 475, 561, 621, 666. *Asher's List of Maps and Charts of New Netherland*, 12, 21.

late governor of the island of Curaçoa, in the Caribbean sea, belonging to the Dutch West India Company, whose name was *Johan van Rodenburgh.*[1] She lived with her mother on the *Manhatan*, who, after the death of her husband, Rodenburgh, married one *Joannes van Burgh*, by whom she had several children.[2] Her daughter, Elizabeth van Rodenburgh, being of a quiet turn of mind, and quite sickly, had great inclination to remain single. Ephraim, however, finally succeeded in his suit, and married her at New York.[3] He brought her with him to New Castle on the South river, and we accompanied them on the journey. Ephraim had been a bad, artful fellow in his youth, and lived in all godless ways, but the Lord seized his heart, whereby he began to repent, and saw that he must live otherwise, the Lord compelling him. He found, however, no ground or strength, but having a good conception of spiritual matters or religion, as far as could be the case in such a man, he saw nothing but untruth, falsehood and deception in all that was done in relation to God and godly things, and great hypocrisy in the best persons with whom he was acquainted. Convinced of this, and seeing no better result, he remained in suspense, although he professed the doctrines of the reformed, and was a member of their church. Seeing our life, and hearing us speak, he has begun to see the difference, and discover the truth received in the heart. He has examined himself in several things, and corrected them, and was disposed to do more,

---

[1] According to the Caraçoa papers at Albany, *Lucas Rodenburgh* was appointed provisional director of Curaçoa August 22, 1644. He was succeeded, probably on his death, by Mr. Beek in December, 1655. *O'Callaghan's Calendar of Dutch Manuscripts*, 329, 330. *N. Y. Colonial History*, II, 46.

[2] See *Calendar of Dutch Manuscripts*, 331.

[3] The bans of this marriage were published 3d September, 1677. *New York Manual*, 1862, 593.

as we had persuaded him. May the Lord bestow upon him his true grace, who puts it in our hearts to beseech this for him with confidence. We commit all to him.[1]

His wife, Elizabeth van Rodenburgh, has the quietest disposition we have observed in America. She is politely educated. She has had through her entire youth a sleeping sickness of which she seems now to be free. She has withdrawn herself much from the idle company of youth, seeking God in quiet and solitude. She professes the reformed religion, is a member of that church, and searches for the truth which she has found nowhere except in the word and preaching, which she, therefore, much attended upon and loved, but which never satisfied her, as she felt a want and yearning after something more. She was so pleased at our being near her, and lodged at her house, she could not abstain from frequently declaring so, receiving all that we said to her with gratitude, desiring always to be near us; and following the example of her husband, he corrected many things, with the hope and promise of persevering if the Lord would be pleased so to give her grace. We were indeed comforted with these two persons, who have done much for us out of sincere love. The Lord pities them, and will keep his promise to this house.

Margaret Hermans possesses a good disposition, although a little wild, according to the nature of the country. She

---

[1] In addition to the clerkship of the courts at New Castle and Upland, Ephraim Hermans filled other places of trust and confidence on the Delaware. Like his father he was a surveyor. He was clerk of permits, entries, and clearings of customs on the Delaware, and receiver of quit-rents on that river within the jurisdiction of the courts above mentioned. In 1679, he was sent to New York in company with Mr. John Moll and Captain Cautwell by the justices at New Castle to represent certain grievances to the governor. He had four children at least, as we find that number baptized in the church at New York, namely, Augustine, Augustina, Samuel and Ephraim. *Breviate*, Penn *vs.* Calvert. *Hazard's Annals.* *N. Y. Manual*, 1863.

complained that she was like a wild and desolate vine, trained up in a wild and desolate country; that she had always felt an inclination to know more of God quietly, and to serve him, hoping the Lord would be merciful to her. She treated us with great affection, and received thankfully and acceptably what we said to her. We did not see her on our return, as she had gone to attend upon her father; and we, therefore, have not conversed much with her. The Lord will do with her as it pleases him.

Peter Aldrix came from Groningen to this country in the year '63 or '64, for the Lord Burgomasters of Amsterdam, as chief of their cargoes and storehouse in respect of the trade with the Indians, and thus was at the head of their office on the South river. Whether he had been in this country before or not, I do not know.[1] He did not occupy his place long, for the English shortly afterwards took the country and deprived him of all he had; yet he has remained here, gaining his livelihood by various means as well as he can, and seems to have gradually succeeded. He had a ketch made for the purpose of trading to the [West India] Islands, and elsewhere. He has a large family of children, and others. He sought to render us as much service as he could, but for the things of grace he is not inclined. He is a mundane, but is not vicious. The Lord can use him as it pleases him.

These are the persons at New Castle with whom we have some acquaintance, and such the hope they have given us. We have promised them to continue it, and write to them, and send them such books as we might deem necessary for them.

Returning now to our boat, it left about ten o'clock for a place a little higher up the river where they had to take in some wheat, and where we were to go on foot, with the

[1] See note on page 190, *ante*.

quaker's wife. We reached it about noon, and found the boat laden, and lying high up on the land, so that we had to wait until the tide was half flood. We saw there a piece of meadow or marsh, which a Dutch woman had dyked in, and which they assured us had yielded an hundred for one, of wheat, notwithstanding the hogs had done it great damage. The boat getting afloat, we left about three o'clock, and moved up with the tide. The weather was pleasant and still, with a slight breeze sometimes from the west, of which we availed ourselves; but it did not continue long, and we had to rely upon our oars. We arrived at Upland about seven o'clock in the evening, and it was there only half flood, so much later does the tide make there than at New Castle. The quaker received us kindly, gave us supper, and counseled with us as to how we should proceed further. We were shown a better place to sleep than we had when we were here before.

27*th*, *Wednesday*. It rained some during the night and it was very misty early in the morning. Before the tide served to leave, we agreed with this man who had brought us up, to send us in his boat to Burlington, with two boys to manage it, paying him twenty guilders for the boat, and three guilders a day to each of the boys for three days, amounting in the whole to thirty-eight guilders; but one of the boys wishing too much, he determined to take us up himself. A good wind coming out of the south, we breakfasted and dined in one meal, and left about ten o'clock, with a favorable wind and tide, though at times the wind was quite sharp. We sailed by *Tinakonk* again, but did not land there. It began at noon to rain very hard, and continued so the whole day, and also blew quite hard. We ran aground on the lee shore upon a very shallow and muddy place, from which we got off with difficulty. On account of this and other accidents, if we had had the boys it would have been bad for us. We arrived at *Wykakoe*, a

Swedish village on the west side of the river, in the evening at dusk, where we went, all wet, into the house of one Otto, who had three children lying sick with the small-pox. We dried ourselves here partly. He gave us supper and took us to sleep all together in a warm stove room, which they use to dry their malt in and other articles. It was very warm there, and our clothes in the morning were entirely dry.

28*th*, *Thursday*. It was flood at daylight when we left, but had not gone far before I discovered I had left one of my gloves behind, whereupon we ran the boat ashore, and I went back and found it. My comrade was more unfortunate, for after we had proceeded full two hours, and when we were going to breakfast on what our female friend had given us, he found he had left his knife and fork; but we had gone too far to lose the time to go back for them. The weather was foggy, but when the sun had risen a little, it cleared away and became pleasant and calm. We therefore advanced rapidly, rowing with the tide, and reached *Takany* of which we have before spoken, about ten o'clock, and where we landed a person who had come up with us. We continued on, and as the tide just commenced rising there we had a constant flood tide with us to Burlington, where we arrived about two o'clock. We were put ashore on an island of Peter Aldrix who had given us a letter of recommendation to a person living there, and working for him. We paid Robert Wade who and his wife are the best quakers we have found. They have always treated us kindly. He went immediately over to Burlington where he did not stop long, and took the ebb tide and rowed with it down the river. It was not high tide for an hour and a half after we arrived at the island, and there is, therefore, a difference of eleven hours or more in the same tide from New Castle.

The man who lived on this island was named Barent,

and came from Groningen. He was at a loss to know how to get us on further. Horses, absolutely, he could not furnish us; and there was no Indian about to act as a guide, as they had all gone out hunting in the woods, and none of them had been at his house for three weeks. To accompany us himself to *Achter kol* or the *Raritans*, and return, could not be accomplished, in less than four days, and he would have to leave his house meantime in charge of an Indian woman from Virginia, who had left her husband, an Englishman, and with two children, one of which had the small-pox, was living with him; and she could be of no use to any one, whether Indians or other persons who might come there. We were compelled again to wait upon the providence of the Lord.

About three o'clock in the afternoon a young Indian arrived with whom we agreed to act as our guide, for a dufflels coat which would cost twenty-four guilders in *zeewant*, that is, about five guilders in the money of Holland; but he had a fowling-piece with him which he desired first to take and have repaired at Burlington, and would then come back. He accordingly crossed over, but we waited for him in vain, as he did not return. The greatest difficulty with him was, that we could not speak the Indian language, and he could not speak a word of any thing else. He not coming, we asked Barent if he would not undertake the task, which, after some debate, he consented to do. He arranged his affairs accordingly, and prepared himself by making a pair of shoes or foot-soles of deer skin, which are very comfortable, and protect the feet. That was done in half an hour. We were to give him thirty guilders in zeewant, with which he was satisfied.

29*th*, *Friday*. We breakfasted, and left about ten o'clock in a canoe, which set us on the west side of the river, along which a foot path runs a part of the way, in an east northeast direction, and then through the woods north northeast. We followed this path until we came to a plantation, newly begun by a quaker, where we rested and refreshed ourselves. We agreed with this man, who came in the house while we were there, that he should put us over the river for three guilders in zeewant.[1] We crossed over about one o'clock, and pursued a foot path along the river, which led us to a cart road, and following that we came to the new grist-mill at the falls, which, in consequence of the great flow of water, stood in danger of being washed away.[2] Crossing here, we began our journey in the Lord's name, for there are no houses from this point to *Peskatteway*, an English village on the Raritans. We had now gone twelve or thirteen miles from Peter Aldrix's island, and it was about two o'clock in the afternoon.

We must here make some general observations in relation to the South river. The Dutch, who first discovered and took possession of it, so named it, undoubtedly because it empties into the sea in the most southerly part of New Netherland, to wit, in latitude 39° north, being one degree and twenty minutes, or more, further south, than the mouth of the North river. It runs up from the sea northwesterly, making a fine, large bay, much better than that of the North river, or Godyn's bay. It is not only of greater length, which is about forty miles, with a breadth of six or seven miles; but it has a fine bottom of sand, and gravel reefs all along the banks. The water is purer up above. From the inside or middle of the bay, its course to the narrow part, or river is mostly south [north] or bent gradually from northwest to north, with here and there a small bay, and it continues running so, from twenty to twenty-four miles, or more, to New Castle, where it bends to the east to northeast, with several bays on both sides, to Upland and *Tinakonk*, a distance of twenty-four miles. At

---

[1] This was at or near Bordentown.

[2] At or near Trenton.

Tinakonk, it runs about east or east northeast, but having passed that island it bears off again, north to northeast; also, with several bays to *Wykakoe* about twenty miles, and continuing so to Takany, sixteen miles. From Takany to Burlington, it runs again more easterly and east northeast twenty miles, thence due east six miles, where there is a round bay turning north to north northwest to the falls four miles, so that from the falls to the sea coast it is about eighty English miles, or twenty Dutch miles, from New Castle each way. It has numerous fine navigable creeks on both sides of it, which are like small rivers running far inland, but how far is not yet known; nor is it known how far the south river extends above the falls, as they have not explored above them. This river is generally very clear. I do not know that there is any thing above to be avoided, except occasionally a muddy point on the margins. Heavy ships, drawing 10, 12 and 14 feet water, go up the river as far as Burlington, and higher; but in the great bend where it runs to the falls, it can be navigated close to the falls by boats, drawing five and six feet and more. The land on the east side is generally lower than on the west, and is not so good. It continues very flat, deep into the country, as you go far down. On the west side the land is tolerably high, immediately off from the river, and is generally good all the way down. Both sides being low this river is better to navigate than the North river, for that has very high banks, which being frightfully steep and rocky, it is subject to great whirlwinds and squalls, which, coming suddenly over the hills, fall upon the river, which is no small inconvenience. The water which comes over the falls is pure and clear, and is quite blue, but running lower down, it gradually becomes muddy, but is entirely clear again at *Takany*, and reasonably so at *Wikakoe;* further on it becomes thick, but it is always good. As to the salubrity of the climate of which we did not say any thing when we spoke of Maryland, it is certain that Virginia being the lowest on the sea, is the most unhealthy where they [die] by thousands sometimes of the epidemical disease of the country. In Maryland, which lies higher up from the sea than Virginia, it is more healthy, although it is subject to the epidemic. Therefore, all those who come into the country, must undergo this sickness without escape. Even the children, who are born there, are not excepted, as those who live there and have experienced it, told us when we were there. And although their manner of life is the cause of much irregularity in their health, there is, nevertheless, something in the atmosphere which produces disease: but this will become gradually better, as the country is measurably populated, and thereby becomes more cleared, as experience shows is true of all the lands in America, which have been unhealthy. The uppermost parts of Maryland are more healthy than those lowest down. The South river is more salubrious than Maryland, as it lies higher. It partakes, however, somewhat of the nature of Maryland, especially below, but with great difference, which every year increases. The higher the more healthy; although at the *Hoerekil* which is near the sea, it is as healthy as anywhere, because it is well populated. In the upper part of the river, it is as healthy as it can be anywhere, and for myself, I believe that New Netherland has not a place in it which is not healthier than any part of old Netherlands in the United Provinces, and is becoming every day more salubrious, especially if they live here as they do in Holland. The North river is entirely healthy, for it lies much higher up than the South river, that is further to the north, and although it is nearer the sea than where they live in Maryland and on the South river, it is, nevertheless, more wholesome, which shows that it is not the air of the sea which causes the insalubrity, but other reasons which I will not consider at present.

As the Hollanders were the first discoverers of this river, they were also the first residents, settling themselves down in small numbers at the *Hoerekil*, and thereabouts, and at *Santhoeck*, though the most people and the capital of the country were at the *Manhatans*, under the rule and authority of the West India Company. The Indians killed many of them because they did not live well with them, especially with their women, from which circumstance this kil derives its name. Others fled to the *Manhatans*, but afterwards returned, and have since continued in possession of the river, although in small numbers and with little strength. Meanwhile, some Swedish soldiers, who had been in the service of the West India Company, went to Sweden, and there made known the fact that the country was so large the Hollanders could not possess it all, especially the river called the South river, lying next to Virginia, their old friends, and that it was only necessary to go there with a small number of people to take possession of it, as no one in that country was powerful enough to prevent it. They accordingly ordered a levy to be made of men, half of them under the name of soldiers, and half of boors, and sent them under a certain commander, to settle on the west side of the river, well knowing where the best and healthiest climate was, namely, up the river, and being thus near their friends, the English. Whether these good friends here or in Europe, have not assisted them in this matter, is not known. They thus established themselves there, the Hollanders either being not strong enough or too negligent to prevent them, whilst the West India Company began gradually to fail, and did not hinder them. The Swedes, therefore, remained, having constructed small fortresses here and there, where they had settled and had Swedish governors.

The Hollanders did not abandon this river, but they, as well as the Swedes, sought to advance their settlements; but although the whole country belonged to them, they were, nevertheless, unable to possess it, the company either having too much to do elsewhere, or not ability sufficient, or sending over too few people. They have, always, however, had their forts, without hindrance or molestation from the Swedes, or being brought under their dominion. This continued during the time the burgomasters of the city of Amsterdam had this territory under their protection, up to the year 1664, when Governor Stuyvesant went there with a large force, planted himself before the fortress of Christina on Christina kil, cannonaded it and compelled them to surrender it with all their government to him, in the name of the city of Amsterdam.[1] In that year the whole country was reduced under the dominion of the crown of England, which put an end to the rule of the Hollanders, who had then recently conquered the Swedes.

The east side of the river, which is now entirely in the possession of the quakers, has never been claimed by any one, although here and there lived a Swede, as also among the Swedes, here and there dwelt a Hollander. But when the whole country, in the year 1664, came to the crown of England under the Duke of York, the duke or the king gave the land lying between the two rivers, namely, the North river and the South river, the easterly part to my Lord Carteret, and the westerly part to my Lord Berkeley, but without a boundary line between them. This remained so a long time when Mr. Byllinge, a brewer of London, failed there. Berkeley, who was a great friend of his, as

---

[1] It seems hardly necessary to mention that the journalist has fallen into an error in regard to the time of the expedition of Stuyvesant against the Swedes on the Delaware, and that it took place in 1655, and not in 1664. Otherwise his statement is quite accurate.

well as many other courtiers, and frequented his brewery daily, came to his brewery and told him that as he, the brewer, was a broken man, he could advise him how to recover his fortune; that if he would furnish him a sum of money, he would, by authentic writings, make over to him a tract of land which the king had given him. This suited the brewer very well, who succeeded in obtaining the money from his friends, and this land was accordingly transferred to him. But as the affairs of the brewer would not permit him to act himself, he had a friend named Fenwick, also a quaker, who was to transact the business in his own name, for him the brewer, in consideration of which Fenwick was to enjoy a tenth of the whole westerly part. Fenwick managed it in his name so well that he would soon have stripped the other of all, but means were afterwards employed to compel him to be satisfied with his tenth. Fenwick had letters printed and circulated everywhere, in which he described this portion of the country in glowing colors; that it was the *luij lekkerland*,[1] especially for those who were of the same religious sentiments as himself. Many persons of this belief thereupon bought pieces of land, parceled out only on the map, according to the imperfect knowledge which they then possessed, first into tenths, of which Fenwick had one, and then each tenth into hundredths, embracing water, morasses, swamps and marshes, so that these poor people bought they knew not what. Fenwick hereupon came over to this country, with a portion of these people, in order to take possession of what they had bought; but he, being in debt in England, was arrested on the eve of departure, and compelled to leave the original letters of authorization in the hands of his creditors, and could obtain himself nothing but copies

[1] A kind of paradise,—literally a land where there is nothing to do, and every delicacy to be enjoyed.

thereof. With these he arrived in the South river, and demanded the country from the chief rulers there, who required the production of his authority, which he refused a long time, but not being able to obtain justice, he brought forward his copies to show them, whereupon these principal men referred him to their sovereign governor at New York, who has not yet been able either to reject or admit the claim. They landed, however, after some tumult, but without bloodshed, and have remained there, constantly bringing more people, and the governor tolerating them.[1] Every one of the purchasers who arrives here is at a loss to know where he has bought, and so settles down where he thinks best, leaving it to be determined hereafter; and finding more land has been sold than can be delivered, looks out for himself. Inasmuch as they are thrown under the government of New York, they have two small courts to decide trifling cases, in order thereby to save travel. Meanwhile the country was recovered by the Hollanders in 1673, and then again, by treaty of peace, surrendered to the crown of England, whereby the Dutch lost all their right to the westerly part a second time, unless the provision in the treaty that all things should remain as before the war, should restore them their pretended right. But if this clause only relates to the two peacemaking parties, it remains justly with the crown of England. Finally, there is the utmost confusion without any good foundation for it.

---

[1] Fenwick, holding West Jersey in trust for Edward Byllinge by deed from Lord Berkeley, as stated by our journalist, arrived in the Delaware in June, 1675, and landed, says Smith, the early historian of New Jersey, "at a pleasant, rich spot, situated near Delaware, by him called Salem, from the peaceable aspect it then bore." Fenwick was a soldier, and not to be deterred by slight opposition. He commanded the squadron of cavalry which attended at the execution of Charles I. The difficulties as to his title in West Jersey are set forth in *Smith's History of New Jersey*, and *Johnson's Historical Account of Salem*.

There are quakers who either are more wise, or through poverty, act so, who do not buy any land on the east side of the river, but buy on the west side, where it is cheaper in consequence of the Indians being there. The quakers have endeavored to break up the Dutch and others not of their religion, who have lived of old on the east side of the river, but resist them, and are sustained by the authorities. How far this may be carried, and what may be the result, time will show. The Indians hate the quakers very much on account of their deceit and covetousness, and say they are not Englishmen, always distinguishing them from all other Englishmen, as is also done by almost all other persons. The Indians say "they are not Christians, they are like ourselves." The deeds of all lands bought on the South river from the government of New York, contain a provision that they must be settled upon within three years, or they will revert to the king. Every acre of land, whether cultivated or not, pays a bushel, that is, one schepel and a fifth of wheat. The meadows (*valeyen*), pay nothing. The swamps (*creupel bos*), cattle and men, are free.

We will now resume our journey. When we passed by the mill, a quaker was there who gave us a letter, and told us it was difficult traveling, on account of the height of the water in the creeks; that about eight miles further on, some Indians had come to live, a little off the path on the left hand. We thought we would reach there by evening. We left the falls about two o'clock, following the ordinary path, which is the same for men and horses, and is grown up on both sides with bushes, which wore our breeches, stockings and shoes, as much as all the woods in Maryland together. The road runs from here east northeast. When we came upon the land above, we found an extraordinary quantity of water, not only upon the flats and in the valleys, brooks, and morasses, but also upon the high, solid ground. We supposed this was caused by shutting up the creek by the mill dam, whereby the water did not have shoot sufficient to run down, but it was not that alone. We pursued our way, however, courageously, but discovered no Indians up to evening. We called aloud to ascertain whether they were about there, as they would answer if they were; and as our guide could speak the Indian language well, we thought it would all come right. But it was to no purpose; we perceived no Indians. We had gone about twelve miles from the falls, and it began to grow dark, when we came to a hill descending to a creek or small river called Milstone river, whence we saw fire at a distance, and supposed that Indians or other people might be about there. We, therefore, called out again several times, but received no answer. On arriving at the creek we found it so full of water, and running so swiftly, there was no prospect of crossing it that evening, the more so, as it was almost entirely dark. We looked about for some wood, though there was not much at this place, and collected as much as we thought we would want to burn for the whole night. We made a good fire, and after warming and drying ourselves, eat our supper from what we had brought in our traveling bag. At last we lay down around the fire and fell asleep, having traveled twenty-five miles during the day; but our rest did not continue long, as it began to rain hard before midnight, and we soon awoke and arose to attend to our fire, in order that it might not be extinguished. The rain continued so long and increased so that we could not sit down, because the place was so full of water. We had to take care and protect the fire from going out, which gave us enough to do. It was quite calm, or blew very little, the wind coming from all quarters; nevertheless, we could not dry ourselves, although we kept turning continually round towards the fire. We were wet through, and could do nothing better than to stand straight up, whereby from the length of time and the weight of our clothes we became very weary instead of having the repose we so much needed. Walk or sit, we could not, because it was too dark, and the land too full of water for the former, and for the other it was too wet. We were compelled to wait with patience in this position until daylight, which seemed to tarry, because we longed for it so much. It was one of the shortest days in the year, with dark and rainy weather. Each one looked out for the day as if we could thereby cause it to appear sooner. Finally, as our wood was consumed, the day begun.

30*th*, *Saturday*. As soon as we could see, we went to the creek, to ascertain whether we could cross over, but it was as full and the water ran as swiftly as the evening before, because it had rained continually, and was still raining; although we had hoped if the weather had remained dry, the water would have subsided. As it was, there was no other course than to wade over, and although we were stiff and cold, we had to take off our stockings, and put our bare feet in the shoes to protect them from treading on any thing sharp, and our stockings were the dryest articles we had. We bound up our breeches as high as we could. "Now," said I, "let each one of us take a good stick in his hand in order to prop himself up against the current, and prevent his being washed away." Our guide went ahead even before I had found a stick; but when he reached the middle of the creek, he cried out, "Help, help, if you do not help me, I will be carried away." I ran, took off my breeches, placed them on top of my head, and, struggling, stick in hand, with the stones washing from under my feet and stick, went to him and took from him my traveling sack with which he was bent down. I kept on and was nearly across when my foot slipped on a smooth stone, and I fell forward into the water. However, by the aid of the stick, and the short distance to go, I succeeded in crossing, the sack being thoroughly wet. Our guide who had on leather breeches, which became full of the running water, whereby he could not get along, now rolled them up, and by that means the water ran out below and lightened him, and thus he got over. My companion was yet on the other side, with his traveling bag and two *degens* (swords?). He did the same as I had done, and placed his breeches on top of his head, tied the rest on well, and followed us; but he was scarcely in the middle of the creek when he cried out to us to come and meet him, and relieve him of the sack if we wished him to come over, for he could not go any further. Whereupon, I went in the creek again to him, and took from him the sack. Thus we all three waded over. We dressed ourselves quickly, for it was very cold, putting on our stiff legs, the wet stockings, which chafed them, and over them the water soaked shoes and the breeches which were wet through with the rain and very heavy; and then taking a mouth full of rum, we set out again on the way, stiff as we were. We were now anxious in relation to crossing this Milstone at half way, where it would be much broader and fuller of water. We proceeded then badly conditioned, wet, cold and weary enough. We had thirty-six miles to travel to-day and more if we missed the road. We kept up our spirits, however. We found the land above so full of water, that we were most of the time over shoes in it, and sometimes half leg deep. After we had gone four or five miles, we saw the houses of the Indians on the right, and went to them partly for the purpose of drying ourselves, for though the rain seemed at times to abate it still continued, and partly to inquire the best way to go, in order to cross the large creek. We entered their dwelling where we dried ourselves and breakfasted a mouthful out of our traveling sacks. We presented the Indians some fish-hooks which pleased them. As to crossing the large creek, they said it was not advisable to wade over, as the water was as high as our shoulders or higher, as one of them showed us, and the current was so swift as to render it impassible. He said that not far from their house lived a *sackemaker* who had in the creek a canoe with which he had set a man across the day before, who had a horse which he swam over; but the sackemaker was not pleased at his doing so without his permission. We promised him a guilder to take us to the sackemaker. While we were in this house a little naked child fell from its mother's lap, and received a cut in its head, whereupon all who sat around that fire, and belonged to that household, began to cry, husband and wife, young and old, and scream more than the child, and as if they themselves had broken their arms or legs. In another corner of this house, there sat around a fire, forming another household, a party whose faces were entirely blackened, who observed a gloomy silence and looked very singular. They were in mourning for a deceased friend. The Indian having made himself ready, took both our sacks together and tied them on his back for the purpose of carrying them, which did not suit us badly, as we were very tired. He did that without our asking him, and conducted us in a direction more southeasterly to their king or sackemaker, who lived two or three miles from there. On arriving there, they immediately offered us some boiled beans in a calabash, cooked without salt or grease, though they brought us our own kind of spoons to take them out with. It was the queen who did this, who was dressed more than the others. She gave us also a piece of their bread, that is, pounded maize kneaded into a cake and baked under the ashes. We eat some of it, more for the purpose of satisfying her people, than our appetite. Meanwhile we agreed with the sackemaker to set us across the river for three guilders in zeewan. We presented fish-hooks to several of them, but especially to the queen who had entertained us. The *sackemaker* being ready, took one of our sacks to carry, and went on ahead of us; and there went this king, carrying our pack, almost without any clothing on his body. He conducted us to the creek which was two or three miles distant to the north and northeast over a very difficult and rocky hill. On arriving at the creek we saw there certainly would have been no way of going over, for the water was very high, and ran like a sluice. We were then put across, I myself helping the *sackemaker* and our *sack-carrier* in doing it, as it was difficult to go over even in a canoe. He took us a piece of the way, until we came to the right path, and gave us proper directions how to proceed further. He was to come for our guide the next day and carry him back.

We went on through water for the most part east northeast, until about three o'clock in the afternoon, when the rain began to hold up, and we turned into a road on the right, which runs easterly to the *Raritans* kil. We did this because it was nearer, as they said, and also in order to go to a young Dutchman's and secure good lodgings, of which we were truly in want. The other road led to *Piskatteway* to Mr. Greenland's, where we stopped a night in going on; yet this road was so long, and it was so difficult to travel continually through the water, that we could hardly proceed any further, as my comrade was entirely exhausted. We were, therefore, half afraid we would be compelled to pass the night in the woods. We picked up courage, however, as well as we could, and arrived at dusk at the house of Cornelis van Langevelt (Longfield),[1] stepson of Thomas, the baker in New York. He lived in that house alone with an Indian, who assisted him in

[1] Cornelius Longfield was one of the deputies to the general assembly of East Jersey, from Piscataway, in 1696-7. *Whitehead's Contributions to the Early History of Perth Amboy*, 403.

trading with the Indians, but he had some neighbors who were beginning a new village on the land of this Thomas, the baker, directly opposite *Pescatteway*, upon the point where the Milstone river unites itself with the *Raritans kil*, and flows down to *Achter kol*. The begun village had no name yet, but they intended to call it *Nassau*.[1] This Dutchman was a good acquaintance of Barent, our guide, and we were, therefore, welcome. He had heard of our being at the South river, and expected we would come over here, perhaps, he said, to be neighbors. He recommended to us a piece of land here, but we had neither time nor inclination to go and look at it.

We had special reasons to thank the Lord, and let our hearts ascend to him on account of several things which we here take notice of to his glory, and in which his providence and goodness have assisted us. First, if we had taken the before described Indian with us, there is no probability we would have come right, he being a mere boy, without experience, and not well acquainted with the road, especially under such difficult circumstances; and, worst of all, we were not able to speak a word with him. Our guide said several times, and we thought so, too, that when he had seen these difficulties, he would have deserted us in the woods, and run away, as he could easily have done, and we would have been left alone. In the next place, we did not find the Indian dwelling on the other side of the first crossing, as we had wished, and supposed we would do. And if we had, what advice would there have been for our crossing the second place? We would then have been between the two crossings without any help. And thirdly, notwithstanding all our hardships, our

[1] This would seem to have been not far from New Brunswick, if not at that identical spot. The name of Milstone is evidently applied here to a portion of the present Raritan river.

hearts possessed such strength and courage until we happily arrived. To him be glory therefor forever.

Milstone river is not, as is usually supposed, the *Raritans* kil, for that runs near this house on the right hand, due west, and a little more southerly beyond, and this one before the house, runs on the left hand, west-northwest, and a little more northerly beyond. It has its source above the falls of the South river, not far from that river, and runs for the most part north, and coming from thence, makes several great bends, and, therefore, in going from Piscatteway to the South river, you must cross it three times. As far as known, it is about twelve or fourteen Dutch miles to this place on the *Raritans.* The Milstone is not very wide, which causes the current to run so much swifter when there is much upper water. It has several falls, and is shallow in dry weather. It is, therefore, not navigable, though the Indians sometimes come down in their little canoes, made of the bark of trees.

31*st*, *Sunday.* As we proposed to rest ourselves, we kept ourselves quiet to-day. We paid our guide, giving him two ducatoons,[1] that is, thirty-two guilders in *zeewant*, because he had a little more trouble than either he or we had expected, and presented him with one hundred fish-hooks in addition. He was well satisfied and thanked us. He left after breakfast to return home. Meanwhile, we expected a boat which they said was coming to load with wood, but it did not come.

1680, JANUARY 1*st*, *Monday.* The boat not arriving, and Christmas, according to the old style, being near, at which time there is not much boating, every one endeavoring to be at home, we were apprehensive it would not come. We, therefore, made an agreement with one of the neighbors, that he should take us in a canoe to the French

[1] Equal to two dollars and fifty cents in our money.

tavern, which we have mentioned before, at Elizabethtown point, *kil achter kol*, for twelve guilders in zeewant. We accordingly left about ten o'clock in the morning, through a beautiful creek, which is more like a river, with fine large meadows or marshes on both sides of it. We came to a bank, from the broken point of which a beautiful white clay is taken, as fine as I have ever seen anywhere, or as Cologne earth can be. At the same place there are also red earth, and earth entirely black, which would be suitable for various purposes. At the point of the *Raritans* kil, we arrived at a place called Amboy, a very proper site for a city or place of business. From there you can look over the great bay between the *Nevesinck* and the west point of Staten island into the sea. As regard view, therefore, it lies as well as New York, and is quite safe to be reached by ships. The land around it is tolerably good, and therefore, the place is reserved from sale. There is an abundance of oysters on the shore, considered to be of the best. The ebb tide being spent, we entered *kil achter kol* with a good wind and rowing ahead, arrived at about three o'clock at the point of Woodbridge creek. We landed here on Staten island to drink at the house of the Frenchman, *Le Chaudronnier*, where we formerly passed a night in making our tour of Staten island. He set before us something to eat, and related to us what strange opinions, every one, as well as he himself, entertained of us, which were certainly false enough, and whereof we disabused him. From there we made good speed past Smoker's hook, and by evening arrived at the point of Elizabethtown creek, in the tavern before mentioned, where we lodged for the night; but there was nothing to be had there except to warm us. We were no sooner in the house than it began to rain and blow hard. We were, therefore, lucky in being housed, for to be in such weather and darkness upon the water in a canoe, is not without danger. We again perceived the Lord's goodness and care, for which we rendered him thanks. We discovered no chance of going to the city immediately, but heard that two boats had gone down this afternoon, and were expected back the next day, which made us glad. We had something left in our traveling sack, upon which we made our supper, and then laid ourselves down to sleep in our old fashion upon a little hay, before the fire.

2d, Tuesday. On looking out at daybreak, we found quite calm, good weather, but no boats; but when it grew lighter, we saw a boat lying at anchor below the point. She appeared to be laden, and we therefore could not be certain that she would come up further. It was in consequence of her being laden that she had waited there for daylight, although she had a good tide to sail up to the city. We ascertained she was one of those which had gone down the evening before; and thereupon looked about to see how to get on board of her, as it would not be long before she would leave. The landlord took us and another person in a canoe to put on board, but before we had paddled half way, we saw them weigh anchor, and get under sail. We called out, and pulled with all our might, and, as it was calm, overtook her in time, and went on board. They were Dutchmen from the city, and were even our neighbors. They cheerfully received us; we paid our landlord, who immediately rowed back.

The wind began to blow gradually more and more from the west-northwest, so that when we arrived in the North river, we had as much as we could carry. It brought us up to the city about nine o'clock, where we had not yet set a foot on shore, before such a storm burst out of the northwest, of rain, hail and snow together, that every thing seemed to bend and crack. It was at the same time so cold, it appeared as if this weather, whereby the winter was begun, had held back until we had arrived in the city to spend the winter. We cannot pass this circumstance by without some reflections upon the special goodness and providence of the Lord, which we experience so constantly; that he caused us to reach the land and house on the point of Elizabethtown creek before the storm came up there; that the boat came to anchor there and took us on board, when she had a good tide and wind, but the darkness prevented her from keeping on, and we believe no more boats went there afterwards, not only during Christmas, but during the whole winter; and thirdly, that as soon as we had landed in the city, such a great storm and the winter began at the same time; to which may be added a fourth, that we hired the canoe on the *Raritans*, for being in the city, I spoke to the skipper of the boat, and he said he did not expect to go there again during the winter. Certainly if we did not regard all this with an humble and thankful heart, we should he guilty indeed.

But before we depart from New Jersey, we must remark that my Lord Carteret, having obtained this government, sent here his nephew [brother] Carteret, to manage the same in his own way. This Carteret arriving here from England, accordingly, for the purpose of governing it, went first to New England, where he so recommended his plan of government, and promised the people so much if they would go with him, that he caused a large number of persons to follow him here from Piscataway and Woodbridge, two places so called in New England, and settle down in New Jersey, where they have built two villages, called Piscataway and Woodbridge, after the names of the places where they had lived in New England.[1] And

---

"[1] Governor Carteret did not arrive to his government of New Jersey till the latter end of the summer, 1665. With him came about thirty people, some of them servants. They brought goods proper for the planting a new country; and the governor soon afterwards sent persons into New England and other places to publish the proprietor's concessions, and to invite people to settle there; upon which many soon came from thence.

indeed they did not do badly in view of the soil, because it is much richer here than where they were, although they did not choose the best land here by far. Besides these people, he found here already a large number of other persons at *Gmœnepa*, Bergen, &c.

We were welcomed on our arrival by our old people, and we rejoiced and praised God, for we had seen the storm coming while we were on the water. We rested and warmed ourselves, then refreshed ourselves a little, and in the afternoon, delivered a portion of the letters which had been entrusted to us from the South river, and Maryland. Those which we had from Ephraim and his wife, we gave to her mother and father (in-law) who welcomed us. We told them of the good health of their children, and the comfort and hope which they gave us, which pleased them.

3d, Wednesday. We put our chamber in order this morning, and in the afternoon delivered the rest of the letters. We went also to M. de la Grange's, where we saw a newly drawn map of the South river, from the falls to Burlington, made by the land surveyor there. He told us the governor had given him a grant of a piece of land on the South river between those places.

But what grieved us was, on arriving here to find no letters by Captain Jacob, when we had so much expected them, and did not know the cause of there being none. But we consoled ourselves in him who is the consolation of all those who know him and trust in him; as we praised and thanked him for his fatherly protection, his constant care and guidance, through his providence, which has been

---

Some settled at Elizabethtown, and others at Woodbridge, Piscataway and Newark." *Smith's History of New Jersey*, 67. Piscataway was so named from Piscataqua in New England, and Woodbridge, from the Rev. John Woodbridge, of Newbury, Massachusetts, from which two places the first settlers came. *Whitehead's Contributions, &c.*, 359, 401.

so continual and so manifest in our whole journey. He causes us to put our trust in him, to lose ourselves in him, and worthily to walk in such grace that he may be glorified in us and through us here, during our lives, in grace, and hereafter in glory. Amen. So may it be.

It would serve very well to add now a general description of the country through which we have traveled, and of each part in particular; but as we intend to give ourselves expressly to this work, we will omit it here, and proceed, meanwhile, with our journal.

THE HUDSON AND ITS AFFLUENTS.

4*th*, *Thursday*. It was now Christmas, according to the old style. It had frozen very hard during the night. We went to church, in order to hear *Do. Niewenhuise* preach, but more to give no offense to the people, than either on his or our own account.

5*th*, *Friday*. We began writing.

6*th*, *Saturday*. It continued to freeze hard, though during the day the weather was more moderate. The ice was strong and mixed with snow.

13*th*, *Saturday*. It felt like a change of weather. In all this time nothing occurred worthy of note except the ships left the harbor in front of the city, on Thursday, for *Deutel bay*, a cove on the East river, about three miles east of the city, opposite Hellgate, where they lie during the winter, to be out of the way of the floating ice, which is sometimes very great.[1] On Friday, the governor's yacht arrived

---

[1] Deutel bay was a small bight of the East river, nearly opposite the southerly point of Blackwell's island, at the foot of 46th and 47th streets, on the island of New York. Compare Ratzer's map of New York, 1766-7, with Bridge's map of the Commissioners, 1811. Judge Benson, in his memoir, *N. Y. Historical Society Collections*, second series, II, 96, says, "Deutel bay, corrupted to Turtle bay. When the head of the cask was further secured with *pegs*, they would say the cask was *gedeutelt;* the pegs were short, but at the base broad; the bay narrow at its entrance, broad at the bottom; the *supposed* resemblance between the bay and the peg, the *sup-*

from Virginia, having been twenty-two days on the way. They had taken a *sackemaker* there with whom the governor had made a treaty of peace between the Indians and English in that quarter. In all this frost and cold we have discovered little difference from the cold in Holland, except that when the sun is high, that is, about nine o'clock in the morning, it is a little milder here. It thawed every day until the

16*th*, *Tuesday*, when all the ice and snow disappeared. De la Grange having a new small map of a portion of the South river, I copied it.

24*th*, *Wednesday*. *Fred. Flipsen* met me, and told me the governor had been at his house, and spoken to him about us, and that he desired to see us and talk with us. We, therefore, determined to call upon him, and at the expiration of three days of rain and stormy weather, on the

26*th*, *Friday*, we went to *Fredryck Flipsen*, that he might take us to the governor, as he had promised, and as he did do. The governor received us kindly, and told us he had wondered at our being so long in the country without coming to see him. We replied, that we would not have failed in doing so, if he had been in the city, for when we arrived here he was at *Penequik*, and afterwards when he had been only a few days at home, with much business to occupy him, he left for Fort Albany just as we were going to the South river. We separated politely from each other.

30*th*, *Monday*. A person who, they said, was the thief-

---

posed origin of the name. "This derivation of the name is merely hypothetical, as the distinguished writer himself declares. If we may judge from the topographical authorities which we have cited above, of the very highest character, the "supposed resemblance" between the bay and the peg never did exist, and consequently this "supposed origin" of the name has not even this foundation. The name occurs early in our records; a patent was issued for land at Deutal bay to George Homs and Thomas Hall, on 15th November, 1638. *O'Callaghan's Calendar of Dutch Manuscripts*, 365.

catcher (*diefleyer*), came to our house in the evening, and, by order of the governor, summoned us to appear at eight o'clock the next morning at the house of Rombouts,[1] the mayor of the city, and give our names and further information as to our doings and condition, as all strangers now and henceforth, whether men or women, must do. We were somewhat astonished, since they had told us, as was certainly true, that such had never been the custom. What induced them to adopt this course, we do not know.

31*st*, *Tuesday*. We went in company with the old woman where we lodged, to Mayor Rombouts, at the appointed time. When we arrived, there was a magistrate's officer or two in attendance, and some came in while we were there. Addressing us, he said: "Friends, we have summoned you here, not because we have any thing to say to you, or have any debt to claim, or because any one has sought of us to demand of you any such thing, or to summon you." The reason, he said, was because we had been so long in the country without having reported our names, who we were, our profession, trade or business, condition and purpose. We answered, we would by no means have been in default, if there were any law or order which required us to do so, or if we had been informed that it was customary, or had ever been done; and it, therefore, surprised us that they complained and charged us with neglect of duty, or found fault with us, or wished to convict us of a matter where there was no law, obligation, custom, or even precedent; that this treatment struck us as very strange, since there were several foreigners who had come over in the ship with us, from whom they had not required what they required of us. "You know well," he said, "it is the custom in Europe." We replied, "it was

[1] Francis Rombouts was mayor of New York in 1679-80. A brief sketch of his life is contained in the *New York Manual* for 1864, page 609.

not so in any of the United Provinces or any other places except upon the frontiers." "Well," he continued, "we are no frontier, but a capital, and it must and shall be so in the future." He then inquired after our names, trade or profession, and place of residence in Fatherland, all of which we told him, namely, that my comrade was a theologian, and had studied at Leyden; that I was a wine-racker,[1] and that we both lived near Leeuwarden, in Friesland. He asked further what we came there to do, or what was our purpose or intention. We told him it was to look at the country. "How, look at the country?" he asked: "some come here to look at the cities, others at the fortifications; some to learn the mode of government and policy, others the manner of regulating the militia; others again to learn the climate, and times, and seasons, and you run and travel through the country without giving us any notice why." We replied, we had come here and traveled through the country in order to make ourselves acquainted generally with the nature and fertility of the soil, as was convenient, or we might perhaps go around mornings and evenings. He inquired further of us how we wished to be regarded in the future, whether as citizens or foreigners. We answered, as foreigners. "Well then," he proceeded. "You are forbidden to carry on trade, particularly with the inhabitants, that is, to sell any thing to private persons, but you may dispose of it to merchants who sell to private individuals." He said the privilege, or burgher right cost ——— beavers, each beaver reckoned at five guilders in Holland money, or twenty-five guilders in zeewan, and was prohibited to all persons who reside out of the city; and as we resided out of the city, we must be treated like others. We replied to this, we would cheerfully obey the law. We were also told to travel nowhere, particularly

[1] One who put up wine in casks.

to Albany, without special permission from the governor, which we said we would ask from his Excellency, and thereupon we left.

On arriving at our house, we found there Simon of *Gouanes*, who had brought a boat load of wood, and with whom my companion went to Long Island, but I remained at home; the Lord exercising me somewhat, I was rather quiet. We had been to the strand several days, watching for Claes, the ferryman, or some other opportunity to cross over to *Gemoenepaen*, but we found none; and as there was some difficulty between this governor, and the governor of New Jersey, we were contented to wait and follow the providence of the Lord therein, although our purpose in going over was not on that account.

FEBRUARY 1*st*, *Wednesday*. Gerrit, the son-in-law of our host, having been a long time upon Long Island, came over with a cask of tobacco, which he intended to ship in the ship Beaver; he repacked it, and I helped him cooper it. He said he had another one to bring over from the island, and then he would take Simon's boat and go with us to *Ackquakenon*. After he had finished packing this one, the boat going to Gouanes after wood, I left along with him on the

3*d*, *Friday*, at nine o'clock in the morning. I heard that my companion had gone from the Bay to *Najack*, where I proposed to follow him, because we might not be able to obtain these people who, in order to go to *Ackqueqenon*, resolve upon it half a year beforehand, for when one can go, the other cannot, and we were not able to wait. Simon told us now he could not accompany us. The other person was uncertain, and Gerrit was not any more sure. I arrived at Najack in the evening, and my comrade also arrived there from the bay, in company with Jaques. He concluded to return to the city with me in the morning.

4*th*, *Saturday*. Our resolution was defeated. We started on the road, but were compelled to return, as it had rained hard the whole night, and continued to do so all day.

5*th*, *Sunday*. It snowed all night and until about nine o'clock in the morning, when it cleared up, and we set out on our journey. We reached the ferry at one o'clock, where we waited three hours to be taken over by the lame brother-in-law of Jan, the baker, or Jan Theunissen.

6*th*, *Monday evening*. M. de la Grange came to call upon us, being somewhat under concern of mind, and giving us some hope. His wife, being touched also, has been to see us several times; and certainly the Lord will comfort us about his people. I will take some other occasion to speak more particularly in relation to this matter, if the Lord continue it. Meanwhile, I had translated the *Verheffinge des Gestes tot God*, (Lifting up the Soul to God) into Dutch, for Elizabeth Rodenburgh, wife of Ephraim Hermans, in order to send her a token of gratitude for the acts of kindness enjoyed at her house, as she had evinced a great inclination for it, and relished it much, when sometimes we read portions of it to her while we were there. I also began a translation of the last exercise of the *Holy Decades*. Nothing further occurred worthy of mention, except that the snow, frost, rain and inclement weather prevented us from going to *Ackquequenon*.

11*th*, *Sunday*.[1] We received letters from the South river, from Mr. Ephraim Hermans, and Heer *Johan Moll*, which consoled us as to their state, and gave us some hope at least of great progress, as appears by the same. We answered them, and dispatched our letters by the same person who brought theirs, and who was to return on the

[1] The dates of the journal after Friday the 26 of January, appear to have fallen into a little confusion, a day or two having been dropped, probably, in consequence of daily notes being sometimes omitted for lack of incident. The same difficulty occurs the last of March.

14*th*, *Wednesday*, and with whom we sent the translation of the *Verheffinge des Gestes* with a small package of knitted baby-clothes. The ship Beaver came out of *Deutel bay*, and was up for Europe and Holland immediately. Therefore, on the

15*th*, *Thursday*, we began writing to our friends in the Fatherland. The winter gradually passing away, the weather was during the last of February, and first of March, as pleasant as if it were the month of May. I finished the translation of the Decades.

MARCH 2*d*, *Saturday*. M. de la Grange has chartered a yacht to go to the South river, with a lot of merchandise, and to take to his land there the boor, whom he had brought for that purpose from the Fatherland. This person came from Sluis,[1] and had done nothing here as yet, because de la Grange had not gone to *Tinaconcq*, as he had first intended. He designed to take him now to the land he had bought on Christina kil, and have it put in order. He had obtained exemption from tax on his merchandise, and was the first one who had enjoyed this advantage, that is, from the second tax, he having paid the first tax when the goods were unladen here. All merchandise pays a second tax when it is sent to the South river, or Albany. I gave him *Les Paroles de Salut* for *Heer Johan Moll*, who had urgently requested us to send him some religious book or other, writing to him what was necessary on the subject.

We had waited till this time to go to *Ackquekanon*, either on account of the weather, or because it was not convenient for the persons on Long Island. We finally determined to go with Gerrit who could speak very good Indian, and who had sent word to us from Long Island, that we must be at Simon's house in *Gouanes*, for that purpose on Sunday morning in order to go in his boat. We accordingly prepared ourselves.

---

[1] In Zeeland.

3*d*, *Sunday*. We both went over to Long Island, at eight o'clock; and as we were entering the ferry boat, Madame de la Grange came aboard with her nephew, *Kasparus Reinderman*, who, when they had landed, took a wagon, and rode on to the bay. We went through *Breukelen* to *Gouanes*, where we arrived about ten o'clock, and found Gerrit was not yet there. Several families of Indians had erected their huts upon the beach, whereby Simon's house was very accessible. This was done with the consent of his wife, with whom he had left the profit from the Indians. While we were engaged in obtaining some oysters, Gerrit with Jaques and his son and daughter rode up in a wagon. Jaques had come for the purpose of attending to a sick horse of Simon, which had a certain disease, they call here the staggers, to which their horses are subject, and with which the creatures whether going or standing constantly stagger, and often fall; this increasing they fall down at last, and so continue till they die. It is cured sometimes by cutting the tip end of the tail, and letting the blood drip out; then opening a vein, giving the animal a warm drink and making a puncture in the forehead, from which a large quantity of matter runs out. The boat being leaky, and a right calculation not having been made as to the tide, we remained here to-day, intending to leave early in the morning, and, therefore, made every preparation. We had expected another person to go with us, but there were only us three.

4*th*, *Monday*. We left Gouanes bay at high water, about eight o'clock, with a southerly wind, but calm, and rowed with the current to *Gheele hoeck* (Yellow hook), where we made sail, and crossed the bay to *Achter kol*, where we knew there were some Indians lying behind Constable's hook. We sailed there in order to request one of them, named Hans, to go with us as a guide. Hans had long frequented among the Dutch, and spoke the Dutch language tolerable well. He was a great *nietap*, that is, friend of Gerrit. He refused at first to accompany us, saying he had just come from there; and when we urged it upon him, he said, "would you Christians do as much for us Indians? If you had just been there and had come back tired and weary, and some Indians should come and ask you in the midst of your children, in your own houses, while busied with your occupation, would you be ready immediately to go back with them?" We answered yes, upon proper terms. He said, "I do not think so, I know well what you would do." We told him, we would fully satisfy him. He wished to make a bargain beforehand, which we did not, as we wanted to see whether he would earn any thing. He allowed himself to be persuaded; "but," he said, "I will lose so much time in making zeewant," which is their money and consists only of little beads.[1] "I am very cold; you are all well clothed and do not feel the cold; I am an old man (as he was), and have nothing but a little worn out blanket for my naked body." We must give him a blanket and then he would be willing to go with us. We said we had none with us. "Well," he replied, "I do not ask you to give it to me now, but when I come to the city." We told him he should be satisfied, and have no cause of complaint. After he had fitted himself out a little he went with us. We had some of the flood tide left; but before we reached *Schutters* island the wind changed, and it was quite calm. We, therefore, struck our sails and went to rowing in order to strike the current. By scraping along we reached the *Slangenbergh*, on the west point of the *Noord*

[1] It is hardly necessary to mention that these beads were made out of clam shells, those made from the purple part of the shell being more valuable than those made from the white. At the time of the journal three purple, or six white pairs of wampum or zeewan, passed for a stuiver or penny, by express regulation of the governor.

West kil[1] where there is a very large piece of salt meadow, and where the tide ran so strong against us we could not proceed any further. We, therefore, lay to and went ashore, in order to walk about a little. This was the largest, cleanest and most level piece of salt meadow that we had observed anywhere. After having been an hour or a little more on shore, a light breeze sprung up out of the east, when we took the boat again and putting off, came to *Milfort*, an English village, lying upon high land on the south side of the creek, having left *Santfort* on the right hand, which is an English village also, lying on the west side of *Hackingsackse kil.* We then came to high land; and the wind falling, we rowed up against the ebb tide to a house on the northeast side belonging to one Captain *Berry*, where it being evening and commencing to rain, we stopped, made the boat fast, and took every thing out of her.[2] We entered the house which was large enough,

---

[1] The Passaic.

[2] The following description of this part of New Jersey, appeared in 1685, in a work published under the sanction of the proprietors of East Jersey, with the title of *The model of the government of the province of East New Jersey, in America.*

"Newark *alias* Milford, is a town distant to the northward, over land from Elizabethtown, about 6 or 7 miles. It lies on a river called Newark river, which emptieth itself into the bay about 4 or 5 miles down. Opposite to the town, on the north side of the river lyeth a great tract of land belonging to Mr. Kingsland and Captain Sandford, the quit rents whereof are purchased. There is another tract of land taken up higher on the river by Captain Berry, who hath disposed of a part of it. There are several plantations settled there. Its said he hath about 10,000, acres there; further up the water is an island of about 1,000 acres belonging to Mr. Christopher Hoogland, of Newark; if it be not an island it is tyed by a very narrow slip of land to the continent. Above that is a greater tract of land, above 8 or 9,000 acres purchased by lease of the governor according to the concessions by Captain Jacques Castelayne, and partners who have begun some settlement."—*Whitehead's East Jersey under the Proprietors*, 274.

The first settlements at Newark were made in 1666, by immigrants from

but poorly furnished. We found nobody there except a negro who could speak nothing but a little broken French. We warmed ourselves, and eat from what we had brought with us, Hans, the Indian, sharing with us. In the meanwhile, we engaged in conversation with him, and he told us certain things which we had never heard any Indian or European mention, the opinion of the Indians in relation to the Godhead, the creation, and the preservation and government of all things.

We acknowledge, he said, a supreme first power, some cause of all things, which is known by all the Indians of North America, hereabouts, whether *Mahatans*, *Sinnekes*, *Maquaas*, *Minquaas*, southern or northern Indians, not only by the name of *Sackamacher* or *Sachamor* (which the Dutch for the sake of convenience will pervert into *Sackemacher*), that is to say, lord, captain or chief, which all persons bear who have any power or authority among them, especially any government or rule over other persons and affairs, and that name, it appeared to him, was used by others to express God, more than by themselves; but the true name by which they call this Supreme Being, the first

---

Milford, Guilford, and Branford in Connecticut, whence its name of Milford, which seems to have been applied to it for several years, although it bore the name of Newark, in the town records, quite from the first.—*Records of the Town of Newark*, 4, 10.

Captain William Sandford, received his grant July 4, 1668, of all the lands between the Hackingsack and Passaic rivers lying south of a line drawn from one river to the other, seven miles north of their intersection. This gentleman distinguished himself by declining any public office. His tract of land was afterwards called New Barbadoes.—*East Jersey under the Proprietors*, 47–8, 187–8.

Captain John Berry acquired his lands in June, 1669. They adjoined Sandford's, and extended north six miles into the country.—*Ibid*, 48.

Jacques Castelayne, as the reader has learned, was the Long Island settler, Jaques Cortelyou. The error in his name was continued by Smith in his *History of New Jersey*, as before noted, and no doubt from the authority above cited.

and great beginning of all things, was *Kickeron* or *Kickerom*, who is the origin of all, who has not only once produced or made all things, but produces every day. All that we see daily that is good, is from him; and every thing he makes and does is good. He governs all things, and nothing is done without his aid and direction. "And," he continued, "I, who am a captain and *Sakemaker* among the Indians, and also a medicine-man (as was all true), and have performed many good cures among them, experience every day that all medicines do not cure, if it do not please him to cause them to work; that he will cure one and not another thereby; that sickness is bad, but he sends it upon whom he pleases, because those upon whom he visits it are bad; but we did not have so much sickness and death before the Christians came into the country, who have taught the people debauchery and excess; they are, therefore, much more miserable than they were before. The devil who is wicked, instigates and urges them on, to all kinds of evil, drunkenness and excess, to fighting and war, and to strife and violence amongst themselves, by which many men are wounded and killed. He thus does all kind of evil to them." I told him I had conversed with Jasper or *Tantaqué*, another old Indian, on the subject, from whence all things had come, and he had told me they came from a tortoise; that this tortoise had brought forth the world, or that all things had come from it; that from the middle of the tortoise there had sprung up a tree, upon whose branches men had grown. That was true, he replied, but *Kicheron* made the tortoise, and the tortoise had a power and a nature to produce all things, such as earth, trees, and the like, which God wished through it to produce, or have produced.

It was now time to see if we could not take some rest in a place not very well protected against the cold, and where there was nothing to lie upon except the naked floor; but the negro wishing to favor my comrade and myself, showed us a bunk (*koy*), in which there was nothing save a few leaves of maize, and those thin enough. We lay down there, but suffered greatly from the cold. We slept very little, and lay shivering all night, and the slave sometimes shaking us and waking us up. We were so stiff we could not move; but the night passed on as well as it could, and we rose early. It had rained, and we started at daylight to the boat, and rowed into the stream. Gerrit grumbled very much. He was a coarse, ignorant man, and had not well calculated the tide. We went ashore about eight or half-past eight to breakfast, and had great difficulty in making a fire, for all the brush was wet through with the rain. We were fortunate enough, however, at last, to succeed. We took a walk for a short distance into the woods, which were not the poorest. In the meanwhile, the ebb had run out; the water was calm, and taking a little of the flood, we rowed on until we arrived at *Ackquekenon*, about one o'clock in the afternoon. *Ackquekenon* is a tract of land of about twelve thousand *morgen*, which Jaques of *Najack*, with seven or eight associates, had purchased from the Indians, the deed of which we have seen, and the entire price of which amounted to one hundred or one hundred and fifty guilders in Holland money, at the most. It is a fine piece of land, the best tract of woodland that we have seen except one at the south. It is not very abundant in wood, but it has enough for building purposes and fuel. On one side of it is the Northwest kil, which is navigable by large boats and yachts thus far, but not beyond. On the other side, there is a small creek by which it is almost entirely surrounded, affording water sufficient, both summer and winter, to drive several mills.

When we reached here, we took our provisions and whatever was loose out of the boat into a hut of the Indians, of whom there is only one family on this whole tract. We eat our dinner by their fire, and determined to go in the afternoon to the falls, although it had already began to rain. We started off accordingly under the guidance of Hans, the Indian. The rain gradually increased, with snow, and did not hold up the whole day. After we had traveled good three hours over high hills, we came to a high rocky one, where we could hear the noise of the water, and clambering up to the top, saw the falls below us, a sight to be seen in order to observe the power and wonder of God. Behind this hill the land is much higher than on the other side, and continues so as far as is known. A kil or river runs through this high land between the hills, formed by several branches coming down from still higher land. This river, running along the valley to seek the sea, comes to this hill where it runs over a large blue rock, which is broken in two, obliquely with the river. One part is dry, which is the hill before mentioned; the other is, where the river, running over a crevice or fissure between both, appears to be eight or ten feet wide, having on either side smooth precipices like walls, but some parts broken between them. The river finding this chasm pours all its water into it headlong from a height, according to guess, of about eighty feet; and all this pouring water must break upon the undermost piece of stone lying in the crevice, which causes a great roaring and foaming, so that persons standing there side by side, have to call out loud before they can understand each other. By reason of the breaking of the water, and the wind which the falling water carries with it, there is constantly spray ascending like smoke, which scatters itself like rain. In this spray, when the sun shines, the figure of a rainbow is constantly to be seen trembling and shaking, and even appearing to move the rock. The water in this fissure runs out on the south; and there at the end of the rock or point, it finds a basin, which is the beginning of the lower kil. This point, is, I judge, about one hundred feet above the water, and is steep like an upright wall. When the fish come up the river, this basin is so full of all kinds of them, that you can catch them with your hands, because they are stopped there, and collect together, refreshing themselves, and sporting in and under the falling fresh water, which brings with it from above, bushes, green leaves, earth and mire, in which they find food. The water runs hence east and northeast to *Ackquekenon*. The Indians come up this river in canoes to fish, because it is one of the richest fisheries they have; but the river is not navigable by larger boats, though in case the country were settled, the navigation could be improved. The falls lie among high hills, especially on the south, so that the sun does not penetrate there well except in summer. We found heavy ice there at this time, although it had all thawed away below. When I saw this ice at a distance, I supposed it was the foam. I took a sketch as well as I could, very hastily, for we had no time, and it rained and snowed very much. What I did, is not very happily done. I regret I could not crayon it, for it is worth being portrayed. Night coming on, we had to leave. We were very wet and cold, especially in the feet. It was dark, and slippery walking on such precipices, and crossing little streams. Tired and weary, wet and dirty, we reached the place where we had started from, about eight o'clock in the evening, and went into the hut of the Indians, having to-day rowed constantly from early dawn until one or two o'clock, and then walked, through heavy weather, twenty-four to twenty-eight miles.

We endeavored to warm and dry ourselves in this cabin as best we could. We could not stand up on account of the smoke, and there were no means of sitting down unless flat on the ground, which was very bad for us, on account of our being so wet, but we did the best we could. We took our supper, and distributed some of our bread among the Indians, with which they were as much pleased as children with sweet cake. We gave each man four fish-hooks, and the women and children each two. We also gave them two small trumpets, and then they were great *nitaps* or friends. We had to lie down there, and at first, as long as it was warm, it went very well; but the fire being almost burned out, and the hut rather airy, and the wind being no longer kept out by the heat in the opening, through which the smoke escaped, we became stiff in the knees, so that I could not, through weariness and cold, move mine without great pain and difficulty. The longed-for day came, and we went out in the snow to look through the woods, and along the little stream, to see whether it would be worth the trouble to erect a saw-mill there for the purpose of sawing timber for sale, as Jaques had supposed. But although we found the stream suitable for mills, we did not discover proper wood sufficient for the purpose. The soil seemed to promise good, and the place is as well situated as it can be, to make a village or city. The land on both sides of the Northwest kil is all taken up, and the prospect is that the whole region will soon be inhabited. It is already taken up on the south side as high up as the falls. Eating our breakfast about eight o'clock, we went on board of the boat, it being now the

6th, Wednesday. We set off with a westerly wind, though light and gusty. If the wind in this river do not come straight from behind, you cannot derive much benefit from it, in consequence of the land on both sides of it being so high, and the bay so winding. The river is the pleasantest we have yet seen. It is gratifying to look upon the continually changing views which present themselves in going either up or down, with its evergreens of pine and cedar, and other species, the names of which I do not know, and its clean bottom and clear fresh water. We rowed and sailed as well as we could, until the flood tide stopped us, when we went ashore to eat our dinner, and make a good fire to warm ourselves. When the ebb began to make, we proceeded on our way. Our poor Indian who did nothing in the boat, sat all the time benumbed with cold in his poor little blanket. But as the day advanced, it was better. The tide serving us, and the wind being stronger as we came below the high land, we reached *Achter kol* before evening, and set the Indian ashore at his hut, who told us he would come and see us on Monday. It was calm, with the wind more and more favorable, and we crossed over the bay, and arrived at *Gouanes bay* about eight o'clock.

I had asked Hans, our Indian, what Christians they, the Indians, had first seen in these parts. He answered the first were Spaniards or Portuguese, from whom they obtained the maize or Spanish or Turkish wheat, but they did not remain here long. Afterwards the Dutch came into the South river and here, on Noten island,[1] a small island lying directly opposite the fort at New York, and to Fort Orange or Albany, and after them the English came for the first, who, nevertheless, always disputed the first possession. But since the country has been taken several times by the one and the other, the dispute is ended in regard to the right of ownership, as it is now a matter of conquest.

When we arrived at Gouanes, we heard a great noise, shouting and singing in the huts of the Indians, who as we mentioned before, were living there. They were all lustily drunk, raving, striking, shouting, jumping, fighting each other, and foaming at the mouth like raging wild beasts. Some who did not participate with them, had fled with their wives and children to Simon's house, where the drunken brutes followed, bawling in the house and before

[1] Governor's island.

the door, which we finally closed. And this was caused by Christians. It makes me blush to call by that holy name those who live ten times worse than these most barbarous Indians and heathen, not only in the eyes of those who can discriminate, but according to the testimony of these poor Indians themselves. What do I say, the testimony of the Indians! Yes, I have not conversed with an European or a native born, the most godless and the best, who has not fully and roundly acknowledged it, but they have not acknowledged it salutarily, and much less desisted, disregarding all convictions external and internal, notwithstanding all the injury which springs therefrom, not only among the Indians, but others, as we will show in its proper place. How will they escape the terrible judgment of God; how evade the wrath and anger of the Lord and King, Jesus, whom they have so dishonored and defamed, and caused to be defamed among the heathen? Just judgment is their damnation. But I must restrain myself, giving God all judgment and wrath, and keeping only what he causes us to feel therefor. Such are the fruits of the cursed cupidity of those who call themselves Christians for the very little that these poor naked people have. Simon and his wife also do their best in the same way, although we spoke to them severely on the subject. They brought forward this excuse, that if they did not do it, others would, and then they would have the trouble and others the profit; but if they must have the trouble, they ought to have the profit, and so they all said, and for the most part falsely, for they all solicit the Indians as much as they can, and after begging their money from them, compel them to leave their blankets, leggings, and coverings of their bodies in pawn, yes, their guns and hatchets, the very instruments by which they obtain their subsistence. This subject is so painful and so abominable, that I will forbear saying any thing more for the present.

These Indians had *canticoyed* (*gekintekayt*) there to-day, that is, conjured the devil, and liberated a woman among them, who was possessed by him, as they said; and indeed, as they told us, it had that appearance, but I have never seen it.[1]

We fared better this night than the last, and whether from fatigue or other reasons, slept soundly.

7th, Thursday. We had intended to go to *Najacq*, to Jaques's, and afterwards to Elbert's in the bay, in order to report to them how we had found their land, but Gerrit having promised his father-in-law some firewood, he had to take Simon's boat for the purpose, and Simon's wife also had some errands in the city. We, therefore, determined to go with them as we did, leaving Gouanes at ten o'clock, and seeing the Indians putting up their huts which they had entirely thrown down during their intoxication, although it was not much trouble, as it was not much to make them. With a tolerably fair wind we reached the city at noon, where we gave ourselves up to rest.

We wished now to make a voyage to the *Nevesinkx*, *Rentselaer's Hoeck*, and *Sant Hoek*, but we could find no opportunity, for the reason that this route is very little navigated in the winter and spring, because it is somewhat dangerous. Meanwhile, the weather continued very variable; sometimes we had frost and severe cold, then rain and snow, wind and squalls, until the time of the sun's

---

[1] The *Canticoy* appears to have been a dance which the Indians practiced on various occasions. Denton calls it, "a dancing match, where all persons that came were freely entertained, it being a festival time." *Brief Description of New York*, 11. Jacobus Koelman, a Dutch writer, who seems to have seen it, alludes to it in speaking of the dances of the Labadists, as a religious exercise. "I am well aware," he says, "historically of the religious dances of the devotees among the Turks, called *dervises*, and that in the West Indies in New Netherland, a religious dance is performed by the heathen, when they go after the dead, which in their language they call *kintekan*, as I well remember."—*Historisch Verhaal*, 105.

crossing the line, when it began to become warm, but continued still variable, though it improved daily.

20*th*, *Wednesday*. While my comrade sat writing, he observed a change in his vision, being able to see better than before, when he had to look extremely close in writing. It happened thus: writing as he was accustomed to do, his sight in an instant became entirely obscured, so that he had to stop, not being able to write any more. Not knowing what it was, he shut his eyes and rubbed them, as they usually do when any thing obstructs the sight, and then undertook to write as he had done before, but yet he could not see well; when raising his head higher from the paper, he saw much clearer than when he had to look close to it. Had he kept his eyes up so high before, he would scarcely have been able to see at all. You could also perceive that his writing was different afterwards.

A yacht arrived down the river from the *Hysopus*, from which they learned the navigation was open, though boats going up would have to tug through the ice. It brought news of the death of the minister, Domine *Gaesbeck*, a Cocceian, which had caused great sorrow. They had determined to call another minister from Holland, or Tessemaker from the south. They had built a new church in the *Hysopus*, of which the glass had been made and painted in the city, by the father of our mate, *Evert Duiken*, whose other son, Gerrit, did most of the work.[1] This *Gerrit Duiken* had to take the glass to the *Hysopus*, and having heard we had a mind to go there, he requested our company, which we

[1] Evert Duykinck, who came early to New Netherland, and was in the employment of the West India Company, at the fort Good Hope, on the Connecticut, at the time of the troubles with the English there in 1640, was a glazier by trade. By the phrase, *making the glass*, we apprehend glazing is all that is meant by our journalist. His son, Gerrit, was an adherent of Leisler, and a member of his council. *O'Callaghan's Calendar of Dutch Manuscripts*, 44, 326.

would not refuse him when the time came. He promised to teach me how to draw.

23*d*, *Saturday*. The first boat arrived from Fort Orange to-day, bringing scarcely any news except that a great number of Indians had died in the early part of the winter of small pox, and a large party of them had gone south to make war against the Indians of Carolina, beyond Virginia, for which reason the hunting of beaver had not been good, and there would be a great scarcity of peltries this year, which was the chief trade of New Netherland, especially in this quarter.

There was something published and posted by this government to-day against that of New Jersey or *Achter kol*, but I do not know precisely what it was.[1] We found to-day an opportunity to go to *Nevesinck*. An Englishman who had a little boat, and small enough, was going on Monday without fail, and he had, he said, about sixteen passengers.

24*th*, *Sunday*, and 25*th*, *Monday*. It stormed hard from the northwest, and he could not go, but he came to tell us he would give us notice when he would sail.

26*th*, *Tuesday*. He came and told us he would leave next day at sunrise, and in passing by the house, he would come in and call us.

27*th*, *Wednesday*. We waited for him from an early hour, but it was nearly ten o'clock before we saw him. We went to his boat which was poor enough, very small, light, and lank, though it had been repaired some; it had an old sail and piece of a foresail, and yet this captain was as

---

[1] This was the proclamation of Governor Andros against Governor Carteret's assuming to exercise the powers of governor of East Jersey, to be found in *Leaning and Spicer's Grants and Concessions of New Jersey*, 675. We are enabled to identify it from the date, which is the 13th of March old style, corresponding with that of our journalist, who adopts the new style, which had already been introduced at that time into Holland.

stern and arrogant with his boat, as if it were a ship-of-war. We waited there for the passengers, but they had melted away to three, my comrade, myself and one other person. We started about eleven o'clock with a good wind and tide, though it was almost low water. When we reached the Narrows (*de Hoofden*), the wind veered round to the southeast, which was against us. We discovered the boat to be so leaky that she had a foot or two of water in her, which he sought to excuse, but every word he said on the subject was untrue. The pump was stopped up, and we had to help him clear it out, which was accomplished after much trouble and bungling. We cleared it out, but we had that to do three times, because in repairing the boat they had left all the chips and pieces of wood lying in the hold between the planks, and when we pumped, this stuff would continually obstruct the pump, though we succeeded in getting out most of the water. Meanwhile the wind changed to the south and southwest, with which there was every prospect of getting outside. We tacked about and reached Coney (*Conijnen*) island, a low, sandy island, lying on the east side of the entrance from the sea. We came to anchor under its outermost point, when we should have gone inside of Sandy Hook (*Sant Hoeck*), in a creek, as we were able yet to do; but he said, we must go outside of Sandy Hook, round by sea, and then make for a creek there. I began now to have other thoughts. To put to sea in such a light, low, decayed and small boat, with rotten sails, and an inexperienced skipper, and that at night, did not suit me very well. The sea began already to roll round the point of Coney island, and I apprehended bad weather from pain in my breast and other indications. He said the place where we were lying was entirely shoal, and he, therefore, dared not go near the shore, as there was only eight or ten feet water. But he was much mistaken, for when he let the anchor fall, it ran out six fathoms of rope before it struck the bottom. I had seated myself all the time at the helm, and observed he was a miserable person. It was then about half flood, and having put things somewhat in order, he asked us if we would go ashore with him. I said yes, and I did so for the purpose of ascertaining how the westerly point of this island was situated on the sea entrance. My comrade and the other passenger having no wish to go, remained on board. Upon reaching the shore, we saw immediately a large ship coming up the bay from Sandy Hook, which we supposed to be Margaret's ship, which she had left to be repaired at Falmouth, as we have before mentioned. I wondered why our skipper did not return on board, but he not only remained ashore, and left his boat with two inexperienced persons, but he had not hauled up on the beach his small canoe in which we came ashore, or made it fast. I went with him along the strand, on the sea side, and saw that, close by Coney island, a strong flood tide was running, which was pressed between the east bank and the island, and that led us to think there was an opening there through which you could sail out and in, which is the fact, as I was afterwards informed by one who was very well acquainted with the place; but it is only deep enough for boats, yachts, and other small craft. This island, on the sea side, is a meadow or marsh intersected by several kils or creeks. It is not large, being about half an hour or three quarters long, and stretching nearly east and west. It is sandy and uninhabited. They generally let their horses run upon it to feed, as they cannot get off of it. We found good oysters in the creek inside, and eat some of them, but seeing his carelessness, I could not remain longer from the boat, as the canoe might be carried off, on the rise of the water, by the tide or the wind, and my comrade and the other passenger who was sea-sick, not know what to do, the more so, looking at the inexperience and carelessness of the captain. I, therefore, hurried to the boat, running across the island. On the inside of the island, I found a sandy elevation like a dune or high dyke which became gradually lower towards Long Island, and that is all which shows itself here. This elevation is on the land side, and is mostly covered with hollies, which, according to my recollection, I have never seen growing in this region except on dry and very fine sand. When we reached the canoe, it was not only afloat, but it had been thrown across the beach by the sea, and was full of water. If it had moved off, we certainly would have been at a loss. The water being high, the sea came rolling in heavily around the point into the bay, and caused the boat lying in the current, which ran strong here, to pitch greatly. We were even fearful about getting on board again, for the canoe could scarcely hold us both. I told him to go on board first, and bring the boat nearer the shore, and then he could take me aboard, but he would not do so, we must go on board together. We, therefore, both went into it, and reached the boat, though it was very dangerous. As soon as we came aboard, our skipper spoke about leaving there, as we could not lie there well. I asked him where he would go to. He said to the city, which I did not much oppose, and was secretly glad of, seeing it was from the Lord. We, therefore, had to abandon our design of going to the *Nevesinckx* at this time. The large ship which we had seen, sailed before us; and we found that we had not been mistaken in our supposition, as it was the same vessel we had left in Falmouth. It commenced blowing hard in the evening, and we had as much as we could stand, but we reached the city while it was yet in the evening, very much rejoiced.

28th, Thursday, and 29th, Friday. There was a severe storm, accompanied with much rain, from the south-east, it being about new moon. Certainly, if we did not see in this, the continual care of the Lord, in his providence, we were worse than beasts, for it was too manifest not to be touched by it. He gives us grace only to lose ourselves more and more in him, and to offer ourselves up to his service.

30*th*, *Sunday*. The storm continued the whole day.

31*st*, *Monday*. We determined to make a journey to Albany the first opportunity, but this could not be done without the special permission of the governor. Although a regulation exists that no one shall go up there unless he has been three years in the country, that means for the purpose of carrying on trade; for a young man who came over with us from Holland, proceeded at once to Albany, and continues to reside there. We went accordingly to request permission of the governor. After we had waited two or three hours, his excellency came in and received us kindly. We made our request, which he neither refused nor granted, but said he would take it into consideration. Meanwhile, we inquired after vessels of which there were plenty going up this time of year.

APRIL 2*d*, *Wednesday*. We went again to the lord governor for permission, who received us after he had dined. He inquired for what purpose we wished to go above; to which we answered, we had come here to see the country, its nature and fertility; and that we had heard there were fine lands above, such as *Schoonechten*, *Rentselaersvyck*, and the *Hysopus*. "Those are all small places," he said, "and are all taken possession of; but I am ashamed I did not think of this." He then requested us to come some morning and dine with him, when he would talk with us. We thanked him, and took our leave, reflecting whether it would be advisable to trouble his excellency any more about the matter, as it was not of such great importance to us, and he, perhaps, considered it of more moment than we did. We then felt inclined to leave the country the very first opportunity, as we had nothing more to do here, and it was the very best time of year to make a voyage. As we had some of our goods left after we were forbidden to sell any more, we went to see if we could get rid of what we had kept for Ephraim. As there was no prospect of seeing him, we proposed to do the best we could with one of our neighbors, named *Cornelis van Kleif*, to whom my comrade had spoken, and who was inclined to trade. He entered into negotiations, but was a little timorous. We offered to let him examine the bills of the persons from whom we had bought the goods, and also of the freight and custom-house duties, and he should give us an advance of thirty per cent on their amount; or, he might see what they were worth, and could be sold for, and we would divide the profits equally with him. After he had looked at them, he did not dare to take them himself alone, but said he would bring another person, in order that with the two of them, they could make it safe. He did not say he had no means of payment, though he did remark he had no peltries, which we would willingly have taken in payment. The other person had the means to pay. We told him we would wait until de la Grange returned from the South river; that I had spoken to his wife on the subject, and that he was expected back every day; at all events, that we would wait until we had spoken to some other person. Van Kleif's wife, however, took some fine thread, ribbons, pins, and what she wanted for herself.

7th, Sunday. M. de la Grange arrived home from the South river, and came with his wife in the afternoon to visit us, both being under concern of mind. We addressed to them what we thought necessary. He stated he had agreed with his nephew to go in partnership with him, and could not withdraw therefrom, unless God did something special. They both hoped that God would have pity upon them.

We spoke of the remnant of our little stock, and of the

time advancing when we must be rid of it, so as to be prepared to leave the country. He said as soon as the boat, which he had chartered, returned from the South river, in which he had some peltries, we would see what we could do with each other.

8*th*, *Monday*. Van Kleif came to examine the goods again. He had the disposition, but not the means to buy, and wished to bring still another person to make the purchase, whom he named, and who was one of the most miserly persons in the city, which was not agreeable to us. We, therefore, told him we had already spoken to M. de la Grange.

10*th*, *Wednesday*. The boat of de la Grange arrived from the South river, bringing a letter for us from Ephraim, in which he informed us of his intention to come and visit us the last of April or the first of May, which we much desired.

The governor of Hartford, a place situated to the north, arrived in the city from the West Indies. Our governor entertained him nobly, and parted with him with great civility.

Two vessels sailed for Boston, where we much desired to go, but we were not prepared. The governor investigated whether either of them had taken any thing on board below the city.

We left a small piece of brown serge, which stood us in rather dear, but was very fine and strong, and which on account of its high price, we had not been able to dispose of, to be cut up for a coat, waistcoat and breeches for both of us, with fur in front, so that almost the whole piece was used, de la Grange taking the remnant, with which he was much pleased, for a coat, because he did not know where to obtain such goods in this country. Meanwhile, the barter of our few goods was going on with him at the rate of fifty per cent profit on the invoices, upon which condition he took almost all of them.

13*th*, *Saturday*. We called upon the governor, and requested permission to leave. He spoke to us kindly, and asked us to come the next day after preaching, thus preventing our request.

14*th*, *Sunday*. About five o'clock in the afternoon, we went to the lord governor, who was still engaged, at our arrival, *in the Common Prayer;* but as soon as it was finished, he came and spoke to us, even before we had spoken to him, and said of a person who was with him, "This is Captain Deyer,[1] to whom I have given directions to write a permit or passport for you to go to Albany." He again asked us where we came from, and where we lived, which we told him. He also inquired something about the prince of Friesland, and the princess, and also about the differences of the people of Friesland and his Royal Highness and their High Mightinesses, which we told him. We then thanked him for his favor, and said the object of our visit was not only to ask permission to go up the river, but also to leave the country. He thereupon stated that there would be no boat going to Boston for two or three weeks, but he intended to send one himself soon to *Pennequicq*, which was at our service, and we could easily get to Boston from there by a fishing boat or some other vessel. We thanked him for the honor and kindness he had shown us, and further inquired of him whether it would be necessary to have a passport at our departure. He replied no. We inquired, also, whether it would be necessary to post up our names, as there is an established regulation that it should be done six weeks before leaving. To this he replied, if we were merchants, and owed any body, it

[1] William Dyer, gent., was commissioned by the Duke of York in 1674, collector of the customs at New York, in which capacity he acted during Andros's first term as governor of the province. He was mayor of New York in 1680-1.—*New York Colonial History*, III, 221, 304.

would be proper to do so, and then asked if such was the case with either of us. We answered no; then, he continued, it is not necessary. For all which we thanked his excellency, and took our leave.

Reflecting upon this matter, we thought whether it would not be more respectful to make the voyage to Albany, than to leave, since we had several times requested permission to do so, and he had now granted it. Should we not go, it would, perhaps, not be well received by him, the more so as there would not be any vessel going to Boston for some weeks. Nevertheless, it was not bad that we had shown his excellency it was not so important to us that we could not let it pass.

15*th*, *Monday*. We went in search of a boat to go to Albany, and found one ready to leave immediately. The name of the skipper was *Meus*[1] *Hoogboom*, to whom we agreed to pay, for the passage up and down, one beaver, that is, twenty-five guilders in zeewant, for each of us, and find ourselves. We gave him our names, to have them inserted in the passport.

Meanwhile we disposed of all our goods to M. de la Grange, upon the terms before mentioned, and received in pay peltries of every description. But, as we were not experienced in merchandise, and much less in peltries, we deemed it proper to have what we received, examined and valued against the goods sold, by Van Kleif, before named. He valued some of the peltries much less than they had been charged to us. But as there are few merchants who do not *hatchel* each other a little, so standing near this merchant you could see he was not free from this feeling, and you would believe, if he had owned our goods and been free to receive payment for them, in such kind of pay, he would have valued them much higher.

[1] *Meus* is a contraction of Bartholomeus.

However, there were three beavers among them which were not current; these Mr. de la Grange cheerfully took back, as they were not his, but had been borrowed by him of his nephew, in consequence of his not having enough of his own.

He was about to return to the South river, in order to bring on more goods, which he had there. His wife was going with him, to see if she would live there; for she seemed to take the subject to heart of separating herself from the sinful attachments of the world, giving up trade, and going to live upon the land and out of the land. His nephew was also going with them, for a pleasure trip, and to see the country, and especially to learn the way of trading. They were to leave this evening, having already dispatched the boat on Monday last.

16*th*, *Tuesday*. Before we proceed any further, I must here insert a very remarkable circumstance, for the comfort and joy of God's children, who rejoice with the holy and blessed angels over the repentance of one poor great sinner, more than over ninety and nine just men, who need no repentance. The old man and his wife with whom we lodged had several children, the husband and wife each three by former marriages, and one between themselves. The husband's children by his former wife were two daughters and one son. One of the daughters was married to Gerrit, the wheelwright, who had married her in New Netherland, but upon the first change in the government [1664], she left for Holland, and he followed her there after a little time, and kept house at Zwolle; but not being able, after several years, to succeed very well in the Netherlands, he came back in the same ship with us, leaving his wife and children behind at Zwolle. Finding matters go on here to his wishes, he sent for his family by Captain Jacob, of the ship Beaver. This is Gerrit the wheelwright, or carpenter, whom we have mentioned several times in our journal. Another daughter lived still at Amsterdam, for whom he has given us several messages and a letter to take when we leave. His son is a carpenter in the East Indies. The children of the old woman were a daughter named *Geesie*, married here, in New York, to one *Peter Denis*,[1] weighmaster; another daughter, named *Rebecca*, was also married here with one *Arie*,[2] who gained his livelihood by cultivating land and raising cattle, but kept a tavern, or drinking house, having a situation therefor, and living upon a delightful spot at the *Vers Water* (Fresh Water), a little out of town; and a son, named *Theunis*,[3] who was married and had six children, and who supported himself by farming at *Sapokanike*. The old couple had one child between them, named *Willem*, now about twenty-three years old, a carpenter by trade, a little rough and coarse, but otherwise not an unjust kind of a person, according to the world. He lived at home with his parents, where we lodged. He was somewhat wronged in his inheritance, as the old people acknowledged, and we reproved them for it. They promised amendment.

Now the before named Theunis had led a very godless life, and had been wild and reckless, extraordinarily covetous, addicted to cursing and swearing, and despising all religious things; but he was not a drunkard, nor was

---

[1] Peter Denyse; who was farmer of the weigh house. He died soon after this time.— *O'Callaghan's Calendar of English Manuscripts*, 66, 96.

[2] Arie, or Adrian Cornelisen, who, with *Rebecca Idensen*, his wife, was, according to Domine Selyn's list of church members, still residing in 1686, over the Fresh Water, afterwards called the *Kolk*, and now Centre street. He was living there as early as 1664. — *Calendar of Dutch Manuscripts*, 265. For his children, see *New York Manual*, of 1863, p. 753. It was to his house the travelers went on the first Sunday afternoon after their arrival in New York.

[3] Theunis Idensen. The names and times of baptism of his six children are given in *New York Manual of* 1863, p. 779.

he unchaste, though he previously had taken something that did not belong to him. In a word, he was ignorant of the truth and a godless man, yet his evil and wickedness were more in the spirit than in the flesh. Nevertheless, it appears that God had purposes of grace in regard to him, and the time was approaching when God would touch him and draw him to him. He had long since felt his conscience gnawing him for his godless life, and that with a strength which very much increased his *chagrin.* He became meagre in body, his eyes were sunken in his head, he was sombre of speech, he sought solitude in order to fly from the evil, but found it was augmented manifold; and gradually began to long for deliverance and a better life. The devil had been assailing him for six years past, and he was, therefore, in a miserable state, of both soul and body. Thus he was, when, by God's providence, we arrived in the country, and went to lodge at his mother's house, as we have related. We had been at the house only two or three days, when he also came there. I was writing in the front room, and my comrade was with me. He heard us talking together about God, and the Christian life in general, which, so affected him, that he said to himself, "O, God! what men are these? Where did they come from? Are there such people still in the world?" This he told us afterwards. However, it took such hold of his heart, that he more earnestly resolved to reform his life, while the devil, being more displeased, assailed him the more violently. His wife was a very ill-natured women, scolding, growling, cursing and swearing at him, as well as at their children, and constantly finding fault with him, through her avarice, because he did not do more work, although he wrought continually, and as much as three other men. Their children, collectively, were very bad and saucy, and cursed and swore at each other, except the oldest, a daughter, who appeared to be the best of them. This man being in such a state was pressed on all sides. He sometimes, but not often, came to our house, and as we knew nothing of his condition, we only addressed to him, occasionally, a general remark. However, his time and that of the Lord were approaching. He heard a sermon upon the requisites of communicants of the Lord's supper, which he had never, as yet, enjoyed; and was thrown very much aback, abhorring himself and many others, who went to it, yet pursued as wicked lives as he did. For himself, he saw no probability of his ever being able to partake of it, conscious as he was of his being wicked and unworthy. He saw no means of release, and found no help or consolation wherever he went or came. To go to his minister, would, he thought, render him little good, as he knew by several examples. He kept his condition concealed from us, and did not dare speak to us, so that he was in distress for himself, his family, and his entire state, and often wishing to die. This caused him to live in continual variance and quarrelling with his neighbors. He lost several cows and other cattle, by which he suffered great damage. A little daughter, about fourteen years old, who lived with her grandmother, was so badly ruptured, that there was no probability of her being cured, or ever being fit to be married. He had bought a piece of land, in common with Arie, his brother-in-law, to make tillable land out of the rough woods. It was to him like dead fruit. He worked on it three times as much as the other did, in felling and chopping trees, and making the best of it into timber, which was carried to the city with little or no profit to him, but to the people to whom Arie was indebted. Differences arose between them as to the land and labor, and it was, therefore, proposed to divide it, and separate; but, as has been before mentioned, they had begun to clear off a part of it, and they could not agree which should have the cleared land, where he had bestowed so much labor. Great bitterness sprung out of it, when the mother and friends interposed, and settled the difficulty as well as they could. Theunis obtained the cleared land on condition he should make some indemnity to the other; and a part of the land, where he had worked like a mole, and bought and paid for, should be given up by him. He had a very large and beautiful canoe, which was worth much to him, and had been very serviceable to him; this was entirely dashed to pieces by a northwest storm, as *Sapocanikke*, where he resided and the canoe lay, makes with this wind a flat lee shore. Although his neighbors could have prevented the breaking of the canoe, if they had done as they ought to have done, they had not at least attempted to prevent it. He had a fine large negro, a slave, whom he had long possessed, and taught to work and speak good Dutch; who had done him great service, and he had much love for him. The negro was riding on horse-back, when the horse ran away with him, and he fell and was injured internally in the breast. He became sick, supposing it was a cold, and died in a few days. This event caused great sorrow to him, his wife, and his whole family, as also to all his friends; for it was a severe blow and damage to him. He was once working in the field, and his wife was called to help one of the cows which was sick and in a bad condition. This happened eight or ten times at night as well as in the day, whereby he and his wife had no rest night or day. He was on one occasion attending her, when word came to them that one of their little daughters had fallen dead in the barn, and indeed they knew no better, for she lay in a swoon as if dead; at which they were all much frightened and out of their senses. Thus he had one blow after another. The child, who was about nine or ten years old, came to, when they thought her arm was broken, or at least her shoulder out of joint, for she had fallen from a great height. She was brought in that condition to her grandmother's, at our lodgings, to be cured, which was effected after some time. He has also had several mishaps in the woods in chopping and felling trees; and had about this time an accident which broke him down. Having felled a tree, it remained hanging with its branches in the limbs of another one, and in endeavoring to pull it out his whole hand was crushed so that all his fingers festered. This happened shortly after the others. All these misfortunes depressed this poor man very much, and daily increased his anguish. He could not sleep, and found rest nowhere. He did nothing but sigh and complain of inward trouble. When we heard all these things, we said several times to each other, the Lord has certainly some intention in regard to this man and this household: the Lord visits this man; although we did not doubt there was something of the evil one.

About this time he came to our house, and we embraced the opportunity to speak to him, which we did with great earnestness and affection, by which he was strengthened, and went home contented. But it did not continue long. He became very much disturbed and troubled. He went in the fields to plough, and the horses began to neigh and bellow, and would not stand still an instant, springing and jumping, entangling themselves together, foaming and fuming so that he did not know what course to pursue. As to himself, he became so frightened and perplexed, so confused that he did not know what he did or where he was; he was bewildered, and his whole understanding lost; he was like one blind; he wanted to go to the house, and ran hither and thither, through water and everywhere, his hat off his head, and across the fields, and thus reached home. His wife and children were frightened because he looked so horrible and disfigured. He demanded a rope and wanted to harm himself, for he said he could live no longer. The wife and children cried; neighbors were sent for; one of the children brought the grandmother and Rebecca, his sister, from the city. This was on Tuesday, the 16th of April, in the afternoon. My comrade was in the front room when the news came, though there were no particulars. He came to me in the back room sorrowful, and said to me, *vous ne savez que le malin a eu possession sur nostre pauvre homme.* What man? I asked. "Our Theunis," he replied, "word came that he had hanged himself, and afterwards that they did not know whether he was alive." We were alarmed; the old woman, his mother, had gone to him; and after waiting a little time, we also determined to go, and as we were a little quicker on foot we reached *Sapocanike* almost as soon as she did. As we approached the house we heard the lamentations of the women and children, and on entering we found there no one, except the mother, the sister Rebecca, and a female neighbor who was a *faus pieuse.* As soon as we came in, he stood up and came to meet us, holding out his hand, and calling out: "Friends, is there still grace with God, is there still grace for me with God?" We grasped his hand and said: "Yes, there is grace for you with God, and for all repentant sinners." He exclaimed, "What wickedness have I committed! how have I sinned! how have I stolen God's honor, his name profaned with vile oaths, his sabbaths violated, his word despised! how godless have I lived, and run from him! But he has overtaken me. How has the devil troubled and tempted me, how has he for six years assailed me, seeing that I no longer wished to serve him! And now when God comes to touch me and draw me, he seeks to devour me; but he shall not have me. God who protects me is stronger than he," and much more of similar import. We then spoke to him according to his state and condition, which did him much good. This *pieuse* prated also after her manner, but we tempered her down a little. She had urged him very strongly to go and sit down and read I know not what kind of a book; for, she said, she had also been in such a state, and that reading had done her much good. She was much astonished at our saying he should not read, which could be done afterwards, and would benefit him when he should be well and quiet, and felt a desire and longing for it; that he should now, if he could, go to work at what had to be done or he had an inclination to do, whether in the barn among the grain or in the stalls among the cattle, or any other necessary work. We exhorted him to put his trust in God, to pray to him and cleave to him; the devil would then have no more power over him, as this perhaps was his last attack. He said, "I fear him no more, God will protect me; I feel more tranquil, I will not yield." We told him what he must do in future. He answered, "I hope and trust it will go well." He thanked us very much and added, "Friends you are the cause that I still live and of my preservation." We told him it was God to whom he must give the honor and thank for his grace and mercy; and that we would perhaps call the next day, if we did not leave, at which he was glad. We wanted to give a strong admonition to his wife and children, for they had great need of it, and in order that a greater impression might be made upon them by this circumstance. Returning home we were affected by the grace of God towards a poor sinner, who truly told us things from the bottom of his heart which were from God and his Spirit, according to his word and our experience. In leaving we told his wife how she must keep her eye on him, and conduct herself towards him.

17*th*, *Wednesday*. We went to inquire whether the boat was going up the river to day, but it could not be got ready. In the afternoon we went to visit Theunis again, whom we found at home quiet and calm. He received us kindly, and we asked him how he was. Very well, he said, "I am as much relieved as if I had a great burden taken from my shoulders." He had rested well during the night. We praised God, and exhorted him to perseverance, and to trust in him. "Trust in him," he said. "I know as well that I am a child of God as that I stand here, and I have no fear of the devil any more. I know he can trouble me, but he shall no longer have power over me." We told him he must take care of his affairs, and work when he felt inclined. "Work," he said, "I have no more work." It is as if it were Sunday. I know that the cattle must be taken care of and other things must be done, but that concerns me not. I have no work, and will not work again as I have done before. God will take care of me. We admonished him that he himself and his whole family ought to go learn and be reformed. "That I will do," he replied, "if it please God, and if she only will listen and learn; but if she will not I cannot help it." We read to him some portions of scripture, as Matt. v, 6. John xvi, 17. Matt. vii, 8, of the carefulness of the world, by which he found himself comforted, and promised he would avoid the world as much as he could, and wished he could fulfill his inclination and go and live alone in the woods, away from wicked men, for it was impossible to live near them and not sin as they do. "Could I only go up the river," said he, "with you and everywhere you go! Oh, that I were a young man I would not leave you." You could see that he spoke with earnestness and from the uprightness of his soul.

19*th*, *Friday*. We had been several times for our passport, which we supposed would be a special one granted by his excellency to us, but in that we were mistaken. Our names were merely added to the common passport to go up and down the river, as the names of all the passengers were written on it. We left New York about three o'clock in the afternoon with a southerly wind, in company with about twenty passengers of all kinds, young and old, who made great noise and bustle in a boat not so large as a common ferry-boat in Holland; and as these people live in the interior of the country somewhat nearer the Indians, they are more wild and untamed, reckless, unrestrained, haughty and more addicted to misusing the blessed name of God and to cursing and swearing. However there was no help for it; you have to go with those with whom you are shipped. We were scarcely in the North river when we saw a ship coming through the Narrows, but as it was so far off we could not discern what vessel it was. Each passenger had his own opinion on the subject. After we had sailed along an half an hour we heard five or six guns fired from the fort and otherwise, which was a proof that she was from sea. As we were sailing along a boat came up to us but lost her mast in boarding us. She was to the leeward and we were sailing before the wind with a good headway. She came too near our yard-arm which carried away her mast, and it was lucky she was not upset. They put on board some tons of oysters, which are not to be found at Fort Albany or away from salt water. In passing *Sapocanike* we saw Theunis standing upon an eminence where he was busy ploughing, and observing us as long as he could. We made rapid progress, but with the night the wind slackened, and we were compelled to come to anchor in order to stem the tide.

20th, Saturday. When the day broke we saw how far we had advanced. We were at the entrance of the Highlands which are high and rocky, and lie on both sides of the river. While waiting there for the tide and wind another boat came alongside of us. They had a very fine fish, a striped bass, as large as a codfish. The skipper was a son-in-law of Dr. Schaats, the minister at Albany, a drunken, worthless person who could not keep house with his wife, who was not much better than he, nor was his father-in-law. He had been away from his wife five or six years, and was now going after her.[1] The wind coming out of the south about nine o'clock we weighed anchor, and got under sail. It gradually increased until we had drifted through the Highlands, which is regarded no small advantage whenever they wish to sail up or down the river; because, if they do not have a fresh breeze aft, they cannot have much favorable wind, as in blowing crosswise over the Highlands, it blows above the vessel, and sometimes comes down in whirlwinds which are dangerous. In the evening we sailed before the Hysopus, where some of the passengers desired to be put ashore, but it blew too hard and we had too much headway. It did not seem to be very important. In consequence of the river above the Hysopus being difficult to navigate, and beset with shoals and passages, and of the weather being rainy with no moon, we could not proceed without continual danger of running aground, and so came to anchor.

21*st*, *Easter Sunday*. The wind was against us and calm, but we advanced as far as the *Noorman's kil*,[2] where we were compelled to come to anchor, on account of the strong current running down the river. We went ashore here to walk about a little. There are two high falls on this kil, where the beautiful green water comes falling over incessantly, in a manner wonderful to behold, when you consider the power, wisdom and directions of God. The water was the greenest I had observed, not only on the

---

[1] Domine Schaats had one daughter, Anneke or Annatje, who married Thomas Davidse Kikebell, the skipper above referred to. Some account of her may be found in *O'Callaghan's History of New Netherland*, II, 568. It appears she was ordered away from Albany by the magistrates, and her husband was now on his way to take her to New York.

[2] Not to be confounded with Norman's kil, adjoining Albany. This was a stream below Kinderhook, the Cats kil.

South river, but in all New Netherland. Leaving the cause of it for further inquiry, I mention it merely in passing. At the falls on this river stands a fine saw-mill which has wood enough to saw. The man who lives there, although not the mildest, treated us, nevertheless, reasonably well. He set before us shad which had been caught the day before, and was very good, better, we thought, than the same fish in Fatherland.[1] I observed along the shore, trees which they call in Holland, the tree of life,[2] such as we have in our garden, but they grow here beautiful and large, like firs. I picked up a small stone in which there was some crystal, and you could see how the crystal was formed in the stone.

A breeze springing up from the south caused us to hurry on board the yacht, which we saw was making sail. We reached her after a good time of hard rowing, and were quite tired before we did so. The breeze did not continue a long time, and we came to anchor again. After several stoppages we proceeded to-day as far as *Kinderhook.*

22*d*, *Monday*. We had again this morning a southerly breeze, which carried us slowly along until noon, when we came to anchor before the *Fuyck*, and Fort Albany or Orange. Every one stepped ashore at once, but we did not know where to go. We first thought of taking lodgings with our skipper, but we had been warned that his house was unregulated and poorly kept. Mons. van Cleif, wishing to do us a kindness, had given us a letter of recommendation to Mr. Robert Sanders, and M. de la Grange had also presented us to the same friend. We went ashore

---

[1] The shad in Holland have larger bones, and a coarser flesh than ours, although they are the same species. The feeding grounds are said to cause the difference.

[2] Arbor vitæ.

just as preaching was over, to deliver our letter. This person as soon as he saw us at his house, was pleased and received us with every attention, and so did all his family, giving us a chamber for our accommodation. We did not remain his debtors in heartily serving him in what was necessary, whether by instruction, admonition or reproof, which he always received kindly, as it seemed, promising himself as well as all his family to reform, which was quite necessary.[1]

23*d*, *Tuesday*. Mr. Sanders having provided us with horses, we rode out about nine o'clock, to visit the *Cahoos* which is the falls of the great *Maquas kil* (Mohawk river), which are the greatest falls, not only in New Netherland, but in North America, and perhaps, as far as is known, in the whole New World.[2] We rode for two hours over

---

[1] Robert Sanders, of Albany, was a distinguished and intelligent Indian trader. He became well versed in the languages, both of the Mohawks and the River Indians, two languages radically different, and acted as interpreter between them and the English authorities, on several occasions. He was particularly designated by Mr. Miller, as a proper person to furnish the government information in relation to the condition of Canada. He rendered himself so obnoxious to the French governor there, in consequence of his opposition to the Jesuit missionaries among the Five Nations, that he was the subject of special complaint in the letter of that functionary, M. Denonville, to Governor Dongan, in 1687.— *Colonial History*, III, 469, 483, 485; VI, 46, 63.—*Miller's Description of New York* (Gowans's Edition), 81.

[2] The Cohoes falls certainly affords a sublime sight when the flow of water is at its height, as it generally is at the time of year when they were visited by our travelers. It is not surprising that they should have considered them the largest in America. As far as the topography of this continent was then generally known, they were undoubtedly correct. The falls of Niagara, it is true, were then known to Europeans, but they had not been particularly described, and had been only obscurely mentioned by Champlain, Sagard and Father Ragueneau in the *Huron Relation of* 1647-8. Father Hennepin visited them in 1678-9, a year or two before our travelers were at the Cohoes, but his account did not appear in print until 1683.

beautiful, level, tillable land along the river, when we obtained a guide who was better acquainted with the road through the woods. He rode before us on horseback. In approaching the Cahoos from this direction, the roads are hilly, and in the course of half an hour you have steep hills, deep valleys and narrow paths, which run round the precipices, where you must ride with care, in order to avoid the danger of falling over them, as sometimes happens. As you come near the falls, you can hear the roaring which makes every thing tremble, but on reaching them, and looking at them you see something wonderful, a great manifestation of God's power and sovereignty, of his wisdom and glory. We arrived there about noon. They are on one of the two branches into which the North river is divided up above, of almost equal size. This one turns to the west out of the high land, and coming here finds a blue rock which has a steep side, as long as the river is broad, which, according to my calculation is two hundred paces or more, and rather more than less, and about one hundred feet high.[1] The river has more water at one time than another; and was now about six or eight feet deep. All this volume of water coming on this side, fell headlong upon a stony bottom, this distance of an hundred feet. Any one may judge whether that was not a spectacle, and whether it would not make a noise. There is a continual spray thrown up by the dashing of the water, and when the sun shines the figure of a rainbow may be seen through it. Sometimes there are two or three of them to be seen, one above the other, according to the brightness of the sun and its parallax. There was now more water than usual in consequence of its having rained hard for several days, and the snow water having begun to run down from the high land.

---

[1] Actual measurement makes the width of the Cohoes, nine hundred feet, the total descent 78 feet and the perpendicular fall 40.

On our return we stopped at the house of our guide, whom we had taken on the way up, where there were some families of Indians living. Seeing us, they said to each other, "Look, these are certainly real Dutchmen, actual Hollanders." Robert Sanders asked them, how they knew it. We see it, they said, in their faces and in their dress. "Yes," said one, "they have the clothes of real Hollanders; they look like brothers." They brought us some ground nuts, but although the Dutch call them so, they were in fact potatoes, for of ground nuts, or *mice with tails*[1] there are also plenty. They cooked them, and gave us some to eat, which we did. There was a canoe made of the bark of trees, and the Indians have many of them for the purpose of making their journeys. It was fifteen or sixteen feet or more in length. It was so light that two men could easily carry it, as the Indians do in going from one stream or lake to another. They come in such canoes from Canada, and from places so distant we know not where. Four or five of them stepped into this one and rowed lustily through the water with great speed, and when they came back with the current they seemed to fly. They did this to amuse us at the request of Mr. Sanders. Leaving there for home, we came again to the house of one *Fredrick Pieters*, where we had stopped in riding out. He is one of the principal men of Albany, and this was his farm; he possesses good information and judgment. My comrade had some conversation with him. He expected us, and now entertained us well. My comrade was in pain from eating the ground nuts. On arriving home in the evening, the house was full of people, attracted there out of curiosity, as is usually the case in small towns, where every one in particular knows what happens in the whole place.

[1] Pea-nuts.

24*th*, *Wednesday*. My comrade's pain continued through the night, although he had taken his usual medicine, and he thought he would become better by riding on horseback. The horses were got ready, and we left about eight o'clock for *Schoonechtendeel*,[1] a place lying about twenty-four miles west or north-west of Albany towards the country of the Mohawks (*Maquaas*). We rode over a fine, sandy cart road through a woods of nothing but beautiful evergreens or fir trees, but a light and barren soil. My companion grew worse instead of better. It was noon when we reached there, and arrived at the house of a good friend of Robert Sanders. As soon as we entered my comrade had to go and lie down. He had a high fever, and was covered up warm. I went with Sanders to one Adam,[2] and to examine the flats which are exceedingly rich land. I spoke to several persons of the Christian life, each one according to his state and as it was fit.

25*th*, *Thursday*. We had thought of riding a little further on, and so back to Albany; but my comrade was too sick, and had the chills and fever again. The weather, too, was windy and rainy. We concluded, therefore, to postpone it till the following day; and in the meantime I accompanied Sanders to the before mentioned Adam's. While we were there, a certain Indian woman, or half-breed, that is, from an European and an Indian woman, came with a little boy, her child, who was dumb, or whose tongue had grown fast. It was about four years old; she had heard we were there, and came to ask whether we knew of any advice for her child, or whether we could not do a little something to cure it. We informed her we were not doctors or surgeons, but we gave her our opinion, just as we thought.

---

[1] This seems to be an effort to transmute the Indian name of Schenectady into a Dutch word, meaning the *beautiful portion*.

[2] See the note on a subsequent page in relation to the burning of Schenectady and the massacre of the inhabitants by the French and Indians.

Sanders told me aside that she was a Christian, that is, had left the Indians, and had been taught by the Christians and baptized; that she had made profession of the reformed religion, and was not of the unjust. Not contenting myself with this account, and observing something in her that pleased me, I asked her to relate to me herself how it had gone with her from the first of her coming to Christendom, both outwardly and inwardly. Looking at me she said, "How glad am I that I am so fortunate; that God should permit me to behold such Christians, whom I have so long desired to see, and to whom I may speak from the bottom of my heart without fear; and that there are such Christians in the world. How often have I asked myself, are there no other Christians than those amongst whom we live, who are so godless and lead worse lives than the Indians, and yet have such a pure and holy religion? Now I see God thinks of us, and has sent you from the other end of the world to speak to us." She had heard me give reasons to the others, and address them generally, before I made this request of her. I answered, that all who professed the Christian religion did not live as that religion required, that such were false professors, and not Christians, bearing the name only, but denying the truth. She had said all this with a tender and affectionate heart, and with many tears, but tears which you felt proceeded from the heart, and from love towards God. I was surprised to find so far in the woods, and among Indians; but why say among Indians? among Christians ten times worse than Indians, a person who should address me with such affection and love of God; but I answered and comforted her. She then related to me, from the beginning, her case, that is, how she had embraced Christianity. She was born of a Christian father and an Indian mother, of the Mohawk tribes. Her mother remained in the country, and lived among the Mohawks, and she lived with her, the same as

Indians live together. Her mother would never listen to any thing about the Christians, or it was against her heart, from an inward, unfounded hate. She lived then with her mother and brothers and sisters; but sometimes she went with her mother among the Christians to trade and make purchases, or the Christians came among them, and thus it was that some Christians took a fancy to the girl, discovering in her more resemblance to the Christians than the Indians, but understand, more like the Dutch, and that she was not so wild as the other children. They, therefore, wished to take the girl and bring her up, which the mother would not hear to, and as this request was made repeatedly, she said she would rather kill her. The little daughter herself had no disposition at first to go; and the mother did nothing more with the daughter, than express continually her detestation and abhorrence of the Christians. This happened several times, when the daughter began to mistrust the Christians were not such as the mother told her; the more so, because she never went among them without being well treated, and obtaining something or other. She, therefore, began to hearken to them; but particularly she felt a great inclination and love in her heart towards those Christians who spoke to her about God, and of Christ Jesus and the Christian religion. Her mother observed it, and began to hate her and not treat her as well as she had done before. Her brothers and sisters despised and cursed her, threw stones at her, and did her all the wrong they could; but the more they abused and maltreated her, the more she felt something growing in her that attracted and impelled her towards the Christians and their doctrine, until her mother and the others could endure her no longer; while she, feeling her love of the Christians, and especially of their religion, which she called their doctrine, to increase more and more, she could no longer live with the Indians. They ceased not seeking to wrong her, and compelled her to leave them, as she did, and went to those who had so long solicited her. They gave her the name of *Eltie* or *Illetie* (Alice). She lived a long time with a woman, with whom we conversed afterwards, who taught her to read and write, and do various handiwork, in which she advanced so greatly that everybody was astonished. She had especially a great desire to learn to read, and applied herself to that end day and night, and asked others, who were near her, to the vexation and annoyance of the other maids, who lived with her, who could sometimes with difficulty keep her back. But that did not restrain her; she felt such an eagerness and desire to learn that she could not be withheld, particularly when she began to understand the Dutch language, and what was expressed in the New Testament, where her whole heart was. In a short time, therefore, she understood more about it than the other girls with whom she conversed, and who had first instructed her, and, particularly, was sensible in her heart of its truth. She had lived with different people, and had very much improved; she spoke of it with heart-felt delight. Finally, she made her profession, and was baptized. Since that time, she said, the love she felt in her heart had not diminished, but had increased, and she sighed to live near Christians, who were good and faithful, and lived up to their religion. Therefore it was, that she was so glad to see us, and that God, who had so loved her before, still so loved her as to permit her to see and speak to us, "*me*," she said, "who have been such a heathen." I told her that God had showed her still more love, as she well knew. She believed it, she said, melting into tears, but she could not express her heart. "Might I only live with such people, how would my heart do good." "Blessed are they who hunger and thirst after righteousness, for they shall be satisfied," I repeated to her, and further expressed what was necessary. "How many times," said she, "have I grieved over these Christians, not daring to speak out my heart to any one, for when I would sometimes rebuke them a little for their evil lives, drunkenness, and foul and godless language, they would immediately say: 'Well, how is this, there is a sow converted. Run, boys, to the brewer's, and bring some swill for a converted sow,' words which went through my heart, made me sorrowful and closed my mouth. But I see that God still thinks of me and loves me, now that he causes me to see and converse with such people as you." We told her she must so much the more receive with love and affection what we said to her, out of regard to God and her soul. "Oh!" said she, "what you have told me is as dear to me as my heart," and she spoke with such feeling and tenderness, such depth of love, that I cannot describe it, and it affected me. Yes, she expressed to me more reality of the truth of Christianity, through the emotions of her heart, although in language according to the genius of the person, which, nevertheless, was nothing but loving—more, I said, than any one, whether minister or other person, in all New Netherland. She had a brother who was also a half-breed, who had made profession of Christianity, and had been baptized, and who was not by far as good as she, but, on the contrary, very wicked; though, I believe, he has been better, and has been corrupted by the conversation of impious Hollanders; for this place is a godless one, being without a minister, and having only a homily (*postyl*) read on Sundays. He was married, and so was she. She has some children; her husband is not as good as she is, though he is not one of the worst; she sets a good example before him, and knows how to direct him.

She has a nephew, a full blooded Mohawk, named *Wouter* (Walter). The Lord has also touched him, through her instrumentality. Wouter speaks no Dutch, or very little. He has abandoned all the Indians, and his Indian friends and relations, and lives with his uncle, the brother of Illetie. He has betaken himself entirely to the Christians and dresses like them. He has suffered much from the other Indians and his friends. He has such a love and comprehension of God, such reverence and humility towards him and what is godly, that it is a joy to hear him speak. His thoughts are occupied night and day with God and Jesus Christ, wondering about God and his mercy, that he should cause him to know him, to comprehend him and to serve him. He is endeavoring to learn the Dutch language, so as to be instructed in Christianity, and to be among good Christians who live like Christians. That was all his desire, thinking all the time about it, speaking always with Illetie about it, who assisted and instructed him as much as she could, and always with love, with which God much blessed her. His uncle, with whom he lived, was covetous, and kept him only because he was profitable to him in hunting beaver. He, therefore, would hardly speak a word of Dutch to him, in order that he might not be able to leave him too soon, and go among the Christians and under Christianity. He sent him to the woods and among the Indians, for the sake of the devilish profit of the world — these are the words of Robert Sanders, and Illetie said not much less; yet this poor creature has, nevertheless, such a great inclination and longing after Christianity.

Besides this inward desire, propensity and feeling, God, the Lord, has given him outward proofs of his love and protection, and among other instances I will relate these two which I well remember. It happened once that his uncle went out a shooting with him in the woods, when the uncle began to sneer at him, saying, that he, a mere stupid Indian, could not shoot, but a Christian was a different character and was expert and handy: that he, Wouter, would not shoot any thing that day, but he himself would have a good hunt. To which Wouter replied; "it is well, I cannot help it; I will have whatever God sends me." Upon this they separated from each other in the woods, and each went where he thought best. "Now when I was tired out," said Wouter, for we heard it from him himself, as well as from his aunt, "and had traveled and hunted the whole day without finding any game, with the evening approaching, grieved that I had shot nothing and troubled at the reproach of my uncle, my heart looked up to God; I fell upon my knees and prayed to him, that although I was no Christian (he meant baptized), I loved God, and only longed to learn the language in order to be instructed in Christianity, and would receive it with my whole heart; that God would be pleased to send to me a wild animal to shoot, so that the slur, which my uncle had thrown upon me, might be wiped off." While thus down on his knees, with his hat hanging upon a bough which was bent down,[1] his prayer not finished, there comes and stands before him a very young deer, not twenty paces off; it comes softly up to him; his gun rests along side of him loaded; he takes aim, shoots, and hits the deer in the breast, and the creature drops before him on its two fore feet and there remains. Without going to the deer, he thanks God upon his knees that he had heard his prayer and had turned back the reproach. "Oh," said he, "now do I know there is a God, who is in the woods also, and hears, loves and thinks of me there." He comes to the deer, which is a young buck two or three years old, as fat and beautiful as he had ever seen in his life, and takes it upon his shoulders and goes with joy to his uncle, whom he found,

---

[1] Methinks he was moved by seeing this bended branch, to bend himself before God, and, therefore, hung his hat upon it; though I dare not so affirm certainly.—*Note of the journalist.*

and asked where was his good hunt and the game he had shot. His uncle was angry and spoke angrily, saying he had been going the whole day, tired and weary, without seeing or shooting any thing, and had come there to look after chestnuts. "That is well, that is good," said Wouter, "reproach the Indians no more for not being good shooters. Look at what God has given me upon my prayer;" for he was very glad at what had occurred. The uncle stood and looked, and knew not what to say, being ashamed at what he heard and saw, and of himself. Wouter said further; "I know there has been no wild animal round about here, for I have explored the whole place, far and near, without being able to discover any; and now in so short a time this one presented itself before me, and it is, therefore, certain that God placed it there or caused it to come there. I have no doubt of it." Although the uncle was ashamed, he was not much affected by the circumstance, and still less humiliated or improved. But Elletie had taken it strongly to heart, and when they both told it to us, we were affected by it ourselves, and saw God in it more than he had done.

Another occasion was during the last harvest, in the year 1679, while he was out in the woods hunting beavers. He had then had a successful time and had killed some beavers, the flesh of which he used for food, and had nothing else to eat. The flesh of the beaver, although we never relished it, is esteemed by others a great delicacy. Nevertheless, as we have been told by those who are well acquainted with it, it is a kind of food with which they soon become satiated. He also became tired of it; and not having any thing else became sad. He felt his heart boil — this is his own expression, and fell down upon his knees and prayed that God who had heard him before, might be pleased now again to hear him and give him other food, not so much to satisfy him, as to show that he was God and loved him — a God whom the Indians did not know, but for whom he felt he had a greater hunger than his hunger for outward food, or for what the Indians usually were satisfied with, which is beaver and beaver meat, that is, to hunt successfully and trade the skins, which is all they go out hunting for; but that he felt something else, a hunger which could not be satisfied with this food and such like; that he felt more hunger after other food than what the Indians satisfied themselves with; and sought to be a Christian, and no longer to be an Indian.

While in the midst of his prayer, there stood a fine deer before him, which he aimed at and felled at one shot. He quickly loaded his gun again, and had scarcely done so, when he saw close to him a young buffalo.[1] He levelled his gun and brought it down; but on running up to it, he came to himself his heart was disturbed, and he became anxious and ashamed in considering his covetousness; that he had not thanked God for the first small animal, so that he could go no further from joy and fear. He fell upon his knees before God, in great humility, shame, and reverence, confessing his fault and his want of gratitude, praying God to forgive him, and thanking him now for both; saying that through his unthankfulness for the first one, he was not worthy to have the second and larger one.

This may be believed as the true meaning and almost the very words of the Indian, for they were repeated to us from him in his presence, Illetie, who first told us, interpreting after him in the presence of five or six persons who were well versed in the Mohawk language, and bore testimony that he said what she interpreted, and that it was not enlarged.

---

[1] There is nothing in this statement inconsistent with the fact that the buffalo is not now to be found in this state. Vanderdonk says, buffaloes were plenty when he wrote, twenty-five years before the date in the text, and it is not probable they had all disappeared in that brief interval.

Thus continuing to long after something which he did not have, and being yet in the woods returning home, he came to a bush which was growing in the shape of a man's hand, and which he stopped to look at and speculate upon. He wondered at it, and his heart was disturbed and began to *boil.* He fell down upon his knees by the bush striking his hands into it, and prayed: Oh God! you cause to come before me a sign or image of what I want and for which I hunger and long. It is true I have two hands with which I hunt and shoot and do other things, but I feel I still require a hand to help me, more serviceable than those I have and use, and stronger and wiser than mine. I am in want of a third hand. It is true I have forsaken the Indians and have come among Christians, but this cannot help me unless a third power make me a true Christian, and enable me to learn the language, that I may inquire, read and enter into the grounds of Christianity." This he did with great tenderness and love; and being so much affected, he cut off the bush and took it with him in remembrance of his feelings and the outpouring of his heart to God, more than for the rarity of the figure in which it had grown. This stick or bush we have seen ourselves and had in our hands. He presented it to Robert Sanders, who carried it to Albany.

His aunt, Illetie, had taught him as well as she could, how he must pray, which she recommended to him to do every time he returned home, morning or evening, or on any other occasion which might happen to him, which he always did with concern and anxiety of heart. He always rejoiced at the proofs of God's [care] over him, and was sorry that he could not improve them, hoping and believing that God would yet give him what he still wanted and hungered after. I asked Illetie, who first told me all this, why they did not take him to some place, where he could learn the language, and some handiwork, with reading and writing and the like, and especially where he might be brought to the knowledge and practice of Christianity. She said there were two impediments, first his uncle, whom we have mentioned, who only kept him as a kind of servant, such as the English have, for the sake of vile gain; and, although he was free, and bound to nobody, would never speak a word of Dutch to him, so that he might not lose him. The other difficulty was, that as he was of age, 24 or 26 years old, or thereabouts, no one would receive him for his board and clothing, fearful he would not learn the one or other handiwork, and would, therefore, be a loss to them. Whereupon I said if he would go with us we would give him board and clothing for all his life, and he should never be our servant or slave, and would be free and clear of all obligation; and if God should give him further the grace he would be our brother and as free as we were. "Oh," said she, "how happy he would be if he should be so fortunate, and God so honored him, as I must shame myself for the honor and happiness he causes me in enabling me to speak with you about these things." I spoke to her further what I thought would serve for her edification and consolation; and told her as my comrade was sick and not able to go out, and weather was too rainy, she must come to us in the evening, and bring Wouter with her, that we might see him, and converse with him.

I thereupon went home and told my comrade my adventure, who was rejoiced at it, and would expect her in the evening. Meanwhile he had become stronger. The parish reader (*voorleser van de plaets*), who is the son of minister *Schaets*, came to visit my comrade, and said he had heard of us, and had been desirous to converse with us. He was a little conceited, but my comrade having heard that he was the *voorleser*, gave him a good lesson, at which he was not badly content, and with which he went away.

When evening came, so came Illetie with her husband,

and Wouter, and Adam and his wife, with two or three others besides. We conversed together through Illetie, who interpreted to him from us, and to us from him, and he himself repeated all that Illetie had told me, as before related. We spoke to him from the bottom of our hearts, and he to us from the bottom of his heart and out of love to us. We exhorted, encouraged and comforted him as much as he required, and his condition would permit. He thanked us with tenderness, that God had vouchsafed to cause him to see and speak with true Christians, with people whom he had so longed for, and with whom he wished to spend his life. "What would you be willing to give to do so," my comrade asked. Oh, said he, all that I have in the world, and more if I had it, or it were in my power. We told him he must leave it to God's liberty, who would do what he pleased, would hear him, and release him when his time should come. After several episodes, we inquired of him what was his greatest wish and desire, his greatest hunger and strongest longing. "I know not justly what it is," he replied, "but I am like a person who has three knives or some other articles which are valuable, useful and necessary, but has lost the one he has most need of, or is the most serviceable and necessary, and without which the others are of little service. Thus I have forsaken my relatives, and all my friends, my nation and country, which is good, and that is one of the articles. Moreover, I have come among Christians, and Dutch, and begun to know something of God, and that also is good, and is the second one. But I am wanting something more than these, and without which they are of no service to me, namely, a knowledge of the Dutch language, ability to enter into the grounds of Christianity, and become a good Christian." We encouraged him, and assured him of the way of the Lord, that God would hear his prayer, and fulfill his desire, according to the words of the Lord Jesus :

"Blessed are they who hunger and thirst after righteousness, for they shall be satisfied." "Oh," said he to Illetie, "how I love people who speak so kindly and mildly, and know how to utter such sweet and beautiful comparisons. Oh, what love I have for them!"

After we had addressed him and her, earnestly and in love; and also the bystanders, to their shame and conviction, for their godless lives, whereby they repelled the heathen and wronged such as begun to be drawn [to God] like these, and as having a terrible judgment to expect which they could not escape, Illetie, said, yes, there were many Mohawk Indians, who, if they were taught, as they seek to be, and had good examples set before them by the Christians, by their lives, and were not so deceived and cheated by the Christians who ought to assist them, would listen; but now they were repulsed, and the Jesuits who were among them, and whom Wouter had heard preach several times in his own language, corrupted them all. Having said all that was proper to them at this time, we invoked upon them the blessing of God.

26*th*, *Friday*. Wouter was early at our house, in order to assist in getting the horses ready. My comrade finding himself better, but still weak, we determined to leave, two of us on horseback and he in a wagon belonging at Albany, which we had the good fortune of meeting at *Schoonechten*, and in which he could ride over a very comfortable road. It had frozen quite hard during the night, but when the sun rose a little, it became warm enough, especially in the woods, where the wind, which was northwest, could not blow through. I went to take my leave of several persons with whom I had conversed, and also of Illetie, consoling and strengthening her once more and committing her to God and his grace, and she leaving us with tenderness and many tears. At a place where we were taking our leave, the uncle of Wouter had come, who commenced saying in very good Dutch: "Well, gentlemen, I understand Wouter is going to Holland with you." We answered, we did not know it, nor had we thought of it, but nevertheless, our hearts were good and tender enough to help him, both body and soul, in whatever the Lord had wrought in him, or should work in him, as far as we could, which we considered to be our duty, and not only our duty, but the duty of all Christians. If he wished to go to Holland, we would not prevent him, because any person who is free, may go there if he chooses; and if he wished to go with us in the same ship in which we should go over, he was free and might act his mind; yes, if he wished to be in our company we would not be able to hinder him, and while he was free no one could prevent him, or ought to, but on the other hand should aid him; especially as all who bore the name of Christians ought to assist in bringing to Christ any one who hungered and thirsted after him as Wouter did. Well, he asked, without any feeling, what trade would you teach him. Whatever God wished, we answered. And if he should be taken by the Turks, he continued, who would be his security, and who would redeem him. Well, we asked, if we were taken by the Turks who would be our security and redeem us? God gives no security and makes no agreement. Whoever wishes to be a Christian must believe and trust in him, and follow him in faith, and so must you, and I, and every one, who wishes to be a Christian. Some hard words passed also between Robert Sanders and him, about something relating to himself, namely, that Sanders had said the uncle only sought to keep Wouter, on account of the profit to him. As the time called us to depart, we took our leave and left him standing there abashed. Having mounted our horses and entered the wagon, we rode from there about ten o'clock, over a smooth sandy road, and arrived at half-past three at

Albany, or Fort Orange, where Sanders's wife was glad to see us, and where we were well received by his whole family.

This *Schoonechtendeel*, is situated, as we have said, twenty-four miles west of Fort Albany, toward the country of the Mohawks, upon a good flat, high enough to be free from the overflowing of the water of the river, which sometimes overflows their cultivated lands which lie much lower. Their cultivated lands are not what they call in that country *valleyen*, but large flats, between the hills, on the margin, or along the side of the rivers, brooks or creeks, very flat and level, without a single tree or bush upon them, of a black sandy soil which is four and sometimes five or six feet deep, but sometimes less, which can hardly be exhausted. They cultivate it year after year, without manure, for many years. It yields large crops of wheat, but not so good as that raised in the wood land around the city of New York and elsewhere, nor so productively, but it makes white flour. The wheat which comes from this place, the Hysopus and some other places is a little blue. Much of the plant called dragon's blood, grows about here, and also yearly a kind of small lemon or citron, of which a single one grows upon a bush. This bush grows about five feet high, and the fruit cannot be distinguished from any other citron in form, color, taste or quality. It grows wild about the city of New York, but not well. I have not heard of its growing in any other places.

The village proper of Schenectady, is a square, set off by palisades. There may be about thirty houses which are situated on the side of the Mohawk river (*Maquas kil*), a stream they cannot use for carrying goods up or down in yachts or boats.[1] There are no fish in it except trout, sunfish

---

[1] Charlevoix, corroborating the above description, describes Schenectady as being in the form of a long square and entered by two gates. This was at the time of the surprise and massacre of its inhabitants by a party of French and Indians in February, 1690.— *Nouvelle France*, II, 45. Sixty-

and other kinds peculiar to rivers, because the Cahoos stops the ascent of others, which is a great inconvenience for the *menage* and for bringing down the produce.

As soon as we arrived in Albany we went to our skipper *Meus Hooghboom*, to inquire when he was going to the city. He said to-morrow, but he said he would come and notify us of the time. We saw it would run on a much longer time, as it usually does in these parts.

27th, Saturday. We went to call upon a certain Madam *Rentselaer*, widow of the Heer *Rentselaer*, son of the founder

---

three of the inhabitants, including Domine Tessemaker, were murdered on that occasion, in cold blood, while they were sleeping in their beds, and twenty-seven were carried into captivity.—*Colden's Five Nations*, 115. Schenectady is said to be an Indian name, signifying in the Mohawk dialect, *beyond the pine plains;* it was also called Corlaer after one of the early settlers. From the circumstance that our journalists were in company with Mr. Robert Sanders, who took them to the most considerable persons of the place, we are inclined to believe that the resident named Adam, at whose house they met Illetie and Wouter, was Adam Vrooman, of whom we have the following account on the occasion of the massacre: "To some of the inhabitants this assault was not altogether unexpected, and they had for some time previously taken the necessary precautions to prevent surprise. Among those who made a successful defense, and kept the foe at bay was Adam Vrooman. Being well supplied with ammunition and trusting to the strength of his building, which was a sort of fort, he formed the desperate resolution to defend himself to the last extremity; and if it should prove to be his fate to perish in the flames of his own domicil, to sell his own life and that of his children as dearly as possible. His house was soon filled with smoke; his wife, nearly suffocated with it, cautiously yet imprudently placed the door ajar. This, an alert Indian perceived, and firing through the aperture killed her. In the meantime, one of his daughters escaped through the back hall door with his infant in her arms. They snatched the little innocent from her arms, and dashed out its brains; and, in the confusion of the scene, the girl escaped. Their triumph here, was, however, of short duration. Mr. Vrooman succeeded in securely bolting the door, and preventing the intrusion of the enemy. On witnessing Mr. Vrooman's courage, the enemy promised, if he would desist, to save his life, and not set fire to his building. This promise they fulfilled, but carried off two of his sons in captivity."—*Yates, in Dunlap's New York*, I, 176–7. See *ante*, p. 301.

of the colony of Rentselaerswyck, comprising twelve miles square from Fort Orange, that is, twenty-four miles square in all. She is in possession of the place, and administers it as *patronesse*, until one Richard Van Rentselaer, residing at Amsterdam, shall arrive in the country, whom she expected in the summer, when he would assume the management of it himself. This lady was polite, quite well informed, and of good life and disposition. She had experienced several proofs of the Lord. The breaking up of the ice had once carried away her mansion, and every thing connected with it, of which place she had made too much account. Also, in some visitations of her husband, death, and others before. In her last child-bed, she became lame or weak in both of her sides, so that she had to walk with two canes or crutches. In all these trials, she had borne herself well, and God "left not himself without witness" in her. She treated us kindly, and we eat here exceedingly good pike, perch and other fish, which now began to come and be caught in great numbers. We had several conversations with her about the truth, and practical religion, mutually satisfactory. We went to look at several of her mills at work, which she had there on an ever-running stream, grist-mills, saw-mills and others. One of the grist-mills can grind 120 schepels[1] of meal in twenty-four hours, that is five an hour. Returning to the house, we politely took our leave. Her residence is about a quarter of an hour from Albany up the river.

28*th*, *Sunday*. We went to church in the morning, and heard Domine Schaats preach, who, although he is a poor, old, ignorant person, and, besides is not of good life, yet had to give utterance to his passion, having for his text, "whatever is taken upon us," &c., at which many of his auditors, who knew us better, were not well pleased, and

---

[1] One hundred and forty-four bushels.

in order to show their condemnation of it, laughed and derided him, which we corrected.

In the afternoon, we took a walk to an island upon the end of which there is a fort built, they say, by the Spaniards. That a fort has been there is evident enough from the earth thrown up, but it is not to be supposed that the Spaniards came so far inland to build forts, when there are no monuments of them to be seen down on the sea coasts, where, however, they have been according to the traditions of the Indians. This spot is a short hour's distance below Albany, on the west side of the river.

29th, Monday. We should have left to-day, but our skipper said he could not obtain his passport. We called upon several persons, and among others, upon the woman who had brought up Illetie, the Indian woman, and had first taken her from the Indians, and to whom we have alluded before. This woman, although not of openly godless life, is more wise than devout, although her knowledge is not very extensive, and does not surpass that of the women of New Netherland. She is a truly worldly woman, proud and conceited, and sharp in trading with *wild*[1] people, as well as *tame* ones, or what shall I call them, not to give them the name of Christians, or if I do, it is only to distinguish them from the others. This trading is not carried on without fraud, and she is not free from it, as I afterwards observed. She has a husband, which is her second one, who is a papist, I believe. He remains at home quietly, while she travels over the country to carry on the trading. In fine she is one of the Dutch female traders, who understand the business so well. If these be the persons who are to make Christians of the heathen, what

---

[1] *Wild* is the term used in the Dutch language to denote an Indian, in the same sense as we use the word savage. So understood, the play upon the words *wild* and *tame* in the place in the text, is the same both in English and Dutch.

will the latter be? But God employs such means as pleases him to accomplish his purposes. He had given Illetie more grace than to her, we are very certain.

We were invited to the fort by the Heer commandant, who wished to see us, but left it to our convenience. We went there with Robert Sanders, who interpreted for us. This gentleman received us politely. He said he was pleased to receive us, and to learn how we liked the lands up above, and made a few such common observations. He seemed to be not unreasonable, and a reliable person. If he was not a Scotchman, he seemed, nevertheless, to be a good Englishman, and, as we thought, a presbyterian. We soon took a friendly leave, and returned home.

We spoke seriously to Robert Sanders about his pride, arrogance, temper and passion, although according to the world's reputation he was not a bad man. His wife is more simple and a better person; we spoke to her also, as well as to their children, especially to the oldest, named Elizabeth, who was tender-hearted and affectionate. He and all of them promised to reform, and we saw with consolation that they in some things commenced to do so.

30*th*, *Tuesday*. We were ready to leave early, but it ran well on towards noon, when with a head wind, but a strong current down, we tacked over to *Kinderhoeck*, lying on the east shore sixteen miles below Albany.

Before we quit Albany, we must say a word about the place. It was formerly named the *Fuyck*, by the Hollanders, who first settled there on account of two rows of houses standing there, opposite to each other, which being wide enough apart in the beginning, finally ran quite together like a *fuyck*,[1] and, therefore, they gave it this name,

---

[1] The *fuyck* is a hoop-net used for the purpose of catching fish, which gradually diminishes in circumference from the opening until it terminates in a small aperture through which the fish passes into a close net. The body of it is in shape somewhat like a truncated cone.

which, although the place is built up, it still bears with many, especially the Dutch and Indians living about there. It is nearly square, and lies against a hill, with several good streets, on which there may be about eighty or ninety houses.[1] Fort Orange, constructed by the Dutch, lies below on the bank of the river, and is set off with palisades, filled in with earth on the inside. It is now abandoned by the English, who have built a similar one back of the town, high up on the declivity of the hill, from whence it can command the place. From the other side of this fort the inhabitants have brought a spring of water, under the fort, and under ground into the town, where they have in several places always fountains of clear, fresh, cool water. The town is surrounded by palisades, and has several gates corresponding with the streets. It has a Dutch reformed, and a Lutheran church. The Lutheran minister lives up here in the winter, and down in New York in the summer. There is no English church, or place of meeting, to my knowledge. As this is the principal trading post with the Indians, and as the privilege of trading is granted to certain merchants there, only as a special benefit, who know what every one must bring there, there are houses or lodges erected on both sides of the town, where the Indians, who come from the far interior to trade, live during the time they are there. This time of trading with the Indians is at its height in the months of June and July, and also in August, when it falls off; be-

---

[1] A ground plan of Albany as it was in 1695, when the number of the houses had doubled, but when the arrangement of the streets, gates, churches and fortifications were not apparently altered from what they were at this time, is preserved in *Miller's Description of New York*, London, 1843, Fig. 3. The new fort was built at the head of State street, which then extended to Lodge street. The name of State street at that time is not given, but Broadway is laid down and called Handelaer's street, that is, *Trader's* street, and would seem from its shape then, and as it remains at the present day, to have been the original *fuyck*.

cause it is then the best time for them to make their journeys there and back, as well as for the Hollanders, on account of their harvests.

We came to anchor at Kinderhook, in order to take in some grain, which the female trader before mentioned [Illetie's mistress], had there to be carried down the river.

MAY 1*st*, *Wednesday*. We began early to load, but as it had to come from some distance in the country, and we had to wait, we stepped ashore to amuse ourselves. We came to a creek where near the river, lives the man whom they usually call *The Child of Luxury*, (*'t Kind van Weelde*), because he formerly had been such an one, but who now was not far from being the Child of Poverty (*'t Kind van Armoede*), for he was situated poorly enough. He had a saw-mill on the creek, on a water fall, which is a singular one, for it is true that all falls have something special, and so had this one, which was not less rare and pleasant than others. The water fell quite steep, in one body, but it came down in steps, with a broad rest sometimes between them. These steps were sixty feet or more high, and were formed out of a single rock, which is unusual. I reached this spot alone through the woods, and while I was sitting on the mill, my comrade came up with the Child of Luxury, who, after he had shown us the mill and falls, took us down a little to the right of the mill, under a rock, on the margin of the creek, where we could behold how wonderful God is even in the most hidden parts of the earth; for we saw crystal lying in layers between the rocks, and when we rolled away a piece of the rock, there was, at least, on two sides of it, a crust or bark, about as thick as the breadth of a straw, of a sparkling or glassy substance, which looked like alabaster, and this crust was full of points or gems, which were truly gems of crystal, or like substance. They sparkled brightly, and were as clear as water, and so close together that you could obtain hundreds of them from one piece of the crust. We broke some pieces off, and brought them away with us as curiosities. It is justly to be supposed that other precious stones rest in the crevices of the rocks and mines as these do. I have seen this sort of crystal as large and pointed as the joint of a finger. I saw one, indeed, at the house of Robert Sanders as large as your fist, though it was not clear, but white, like glassy alabaster. It had what they call a table point. Robert Sanders has much of this mountain crystal at his farm, about four miles from Albany, towards the Cahoos, on the east side of the river, but we have not been there.

On returning to the boat, we saw that the woman-trader had sent a quantity of bluish wheat on board, which the skipper would not receive, or rather mix with the other wheat; but when she came she had it done, in which her dishonesty appeared, for when the skipper arrived at New York, he could not deliver the wheat which was under hers. We set sail in the evening, and came to *Claver rack* (Clover-reach), sixteen miles further down where we also took in some grain in the evening.

2d, Thursday. We were here laden full of grain, which had to be brought in four miles from the country. The boors who brought it in wagons, asked us to ride out with them to their places, which we did. We rode along a high ridge of blue rock on the right hand, the top of which was grown over. This stone is suitable for burning lime, as the people of the Hysopus, from the same kind, burn the best. Large, clear fountains flow out of these cliffs or hills, the first real fountains, and only ones which we have met with in this country. We arrived at the places which consist of fine farms; the tillable land is like that of *Schoon echten deel*, low, flat, and on the side of a creek, very delightful and pleasant to look upon, especially at the present time, when they were all green with the wheat coming up. The woodland also, is very good for [making] tillable land, and it was one of the locations which pleased me most, with its agreeable fountains. Coming back to the shore, I made a sketch, as well as I could, of the Catskil mountains, which now showed themselves nakedly, which they did not do to us when we went up the river. They lie on the west side of the river, deep in the country, and I stood on the east side of it. In the evening, we obtained a still more distinct view of them.

3d, *Friday*. We took on board early the rest of our lading. Our tradress left us here in order to go back to Albany, and we received two other passengers in her stead, a young man of this place, named *Dirck* (Diederic), to whom we made mention of our crystal. He said they had at his place, a rock, in which there was a yellow, glittering substance like gold, as they firmly believed it was; he did not know we were there, otherwise he would have presented us with a specimen. We spoke to him, as he was a good hearted youth, several times of God and Christ, and of the Christian life, and each time he was much concerned. Truly we discover gradually more and more there is here a hunger and thirst after God, and no one to help them. They go everywhere wandering without a shepherd, and know not where they shall turn. We also spoke to the skipper's daughter, a worldly child, who was not affected by what we said. The Lord will, in his own time, gather together those who are of his elect.

We sailed from there about nine o'clock, but after going eight or twelve miles, got aground in consequence of our heavy lading, where we were compelled to remain until four o'clock in the afternoon, waiting for high water. But what was unfortunate, we missed a fine, fair wind, which sprung up about eleven o'clock. Meanwhile, the passengers went ashore. I walked a small distance into the country, and came to a fall of water, the basin of which was full of fish, two of which I caught with my hands. They were young shad. I went immediately after the other passengers for assistance to catch more, but when they came, they made such an agitation of the water, that the fish all shot to the bottom, and remained there under the rocks. We therefore, could obtain no more; but if we had had a small *schep-net* (casting net), we could have caught them in great numbers, or if I had remained there quiet alone. But as it was, we had to abandon it. These fish come at high water from the North river into these little streams, where they find clear, fresh water, and weeds and herbs. They remain there eating and sporting, and, in the meantime, at low water they are left in these holes or basins, and they are thus caught in great numbers in many of the streams by the Indians.

The water having risen, and the wind being favorable, we went on board, and as soon as we were afloat, got under sail. We proceeded rapidly ahead, and at sundown came to anchor before the *Hysopus*, where we landed some passengers who lived there.

4*th*, *Saturday*. We went ashore early, and further inland to the village. We found Gerrit, the glass-maker there, with his sister. He it was who desired to come up here in company with us, and he was now happy to see us. He was engaged putting the glass in their new church, but left his work to go with us through the country, where he was better acquainted than we were. We found here exceedingly large flats, which are more than three hours ride in length, very level, with a black soil which yields grain abundantly. They lie like those at *Schoon ecte* and *Claver rack*, between the hills and along the creek, which sometimes overflows all the land, and drowns and washes out much of the wheat. The place is square,[1] set off with

[1] A ground plan of Esopus or Kingston, showing the stockade with its gates, and the houses and fortifications as they are here described, may be found in *Miller's Description of New York*.

palisades, through which there are several gates; it consists of about fifty houses within the stockade. They were engaged in a severe war with the Indians during the administration of the Heer Stuyvesant, which is, therefore, still called the Hysopus war, partly because it was occasioned on account of the people of Hysopus, and because they have had to bear there the largest burden of it. In returning to the village, we observed a very large, clear fountain bubbling up from under a rock. When we arrived there, we went to the house of the person who was the head of the village where some people had assembled, who, having no minister, and hearing my comrade was a theologian, requested him to preach for them the next day. But our skipper having finished what he had to do, we left there. Here and in Albany, they brew the heaviest beer we have tasted in all New Netherland, and from wheat alone, because it is so abundant. The glass-maker informed us that Willem, the son of our old people, was going to follow the sea, and had left for Barbadoes; that *Evert Duyckert*, our late mate on our voyage out, who had gone as captain of a ketch to Barbadoes and Jamaica, had arrived; that it was his ship we had seen coming in, when we were leaving the city, and that, perhaps, he would go with her to Holland. This place is about three-quarters of an hour inland. At the mouth of the creek on the shore of the river, there are some houses and a redoubt, together with a general storehouse, where the farmers bring in their grain, in order that it may be conveniently shipped when the boats come up here, and wherein their goods are discharged from the boats, as otherwise there would be too much delay in going back and forth. The woodland around the *Hysopus* is not of much value, and is nothing but sand and rock. We had hardly reached the river, when a man came running up to us as hard as he could, requesting to speak to us. We inquired of him what he desired, when he complained of being sorely afflicted with an internal disease, and said he had heard we well understood medicine, and knew what to prescribe for him. We told him we were no doctors, and had only brought a few medicines with us for our own use, and most of them we had given away. My comrade told him what he thought of his disease, and that we could not help him: whereupon, this poor wretched man went sorrowfully back again, for he had spent much to be cured. We told him, however, we would send him a brackish powder which had done good in several cases, and which, if it pleased God to bless it, would perhaps help him. We went on board the boat, and immediately got under sail, with a favorable but light wind, and by evening arrived at the entrance of the Highlands.

5*th*, *Sunday*. The wind was ahead, but it was calm. When the tide began to fall, we tacked, or rather drifted along, but with little progress. We passed through the Highlands, however, and came to anchor by the time the ebb was spent. The weather was very rainy.

6*th*, *Monday*. The wind was still contrary, and blew hard, therefore, we tacked, but in consequence of our being very heavily laden, we advanced but little. We anchored again when we went ashore at a place on the east side of the river, where there was a meadow on fire. We saw there a beautiful hard stone, as white and as clean as I have ever seen either here or in Europe, very fine for building; and also many cedar trees of beautiful color and strong perfume. Some Indians came alongside of us in their canoes, whom we called on board, and bought from them a very large striped bass, as large as a codfish in the Fatherland, for a loaf of stale bread worth about three stuivers, Holland money, and some other fish, for a little old salt meat.

7*th*, *Tuesday*. At daylight the tide served, but the wind was still ahead, though steady. We continued tacking with considerable progress, and at ten o'clock, arrived before the city of New York, where we struck upon a rock. The water was falling, and we, therefore, immediately carried out an anchor, and wore the yacht off. A slight breeze soon afterward sprung up, and took us to the city. The Lord be praised and glorified for his grace. We delivered our letters, and executed the orders which were committed to us. We inquired for Ephraim and de la Grange, but they had not yet arrived.

8*th*, *Wednesday*. We had now nothing more to do, except to get ready with all speed to leave for Boston. As we had ordered some clothes, as we have said, to be made, we urged the tailor to finish them. We inquired for a boat going to Boston, and found there were two, but the time was up the next day for leaving, and we could not be ready so soon. We went first to visit Theunis, concerning whom there had been great talk during our absence. Even the minister *Niewenhuyse*, dared to say that we had misled him; and he intended to visit Theunis, for he had been to our house. But Theunis anticipated him, and said he need not give himself so much trouble, as he could go to him, which he did. When the domine asked him about these things, he told the domine he must not have any such opinion; that we had not misled him, but had led him straight; that he was not able to compensate us for the good we had done him, since he was more edified, instructed, strengthened, and comforted by us, than he had been by any one in his whole life. The domine, therefore, had to be satisfied, and said, " 'tis well then, 'tis well then, I did not know that." Our old woman told us Theunis had been so sad and oppressed again, they did not know what to advise him. We, therefore, went to see him, and found him home, in as good a frame of mind as could be wished for one in such a condition. We asked him how he got along. He said very well; that God was good to him, and then related to us about his going to the minister, and his standing upon the eminence when we were sailing by, looking after us. We spoke to him affectionately, exhorting him to faithfulness; that he must instruct his wife and children, and set them a good example. He informed us that his wife was as changed as day from night in many respects, and he hoped she would improve still more; that he would instruct his children as well as he could, if it pleased the Lord they should be instructed, which comforted us, and we returned home.

The North river is the most navigated, and frequented river in these parts, because the country about it, is the most inhabited. Its larger population as compared with other places is owing for the most part, first to the fact that the capital was originally established here, and has ever since remained here, under whatever government has prevailed, although the South river was first discovered; secondly, because it is the most convenient place for the purposes of navigation, I mean the capital, and is the middle and centre of the whole of New Netherland; and thirdly, because this place, and indeed the river, possess the most healthy and temperate climate. We will hereafter speak of New York, and confine ourselves now to the North river; which was so called for two reasons, and justly so: the first of which is because, as regards the South river, it lies in a more northerly latitude, the South river lying in 39°, and the North river in 40° 25′, and being also thus distinguishable from the East river, which although, it is more easterly, as its name denotes, nevertheless, lies in the same parallel. The other reason is because it runs up generally in a northerly direction, or between north by east and north northeast. It begins at the sea in a bay; for the sea coast, between the North and South rivers, stretches northeast by north and northeast, and southwest and southwest by south; and from the

North river, along Long Island for the most part east and west. Besides this name which is the most common and the best, it bears several others; such as *Maurits* river, because it was discovered, and taken possession of in the time of Prince Maurice; *Montagne* river because one *de la Montagne* was one of the first and principal settlers,[1] and lastly, *Manhattans* river, from the *Manhattans* island, or the *Manhattan* Indians, who lived hereabouts and on the island of Manhattans, now the city of New York. To be more exact, its beginning it seems to us, ought to be regarded as at the city of New York, where the East river, as well as *Kil achter kol* separate from the North river. The waters below the city are not commonly called the river, but the bay; for although the river discharges itself into the sea at Sandy hook, or Rentselaer's hook, this discharge is not peculiarly its own, but also that of the East river, Achter kol, Slangenbergh bay, Hackingsack creek, Northwest creek, Elizabeth creek, Woodbridge creek, Milstone river, Raritan river and Nevesinck creek, all of which deserve the name of rivers, and have nothing in common with the North river, but with Long Island on one side and Staten Island on the other. The water below the Narrows to Sandy hook, are usually called the Great bay; and those of the Narrows and above them as far as the city, and up to, and beyond *Sapocanikke*, the Little bay.

---

[1] This origin of the name of Montagne, as applied to the North river, is perhaps apocryphal; yet it is a singular fact, that it is the only derivation of the word given by any of the early Dutch writers, by whom alone it seems to have been used; probably because it is obvious enough that it is intended to be *Mountain river*. De Laet, who first mentions it in his *Nieuwe Werldt*, 1625, says the North river is called by some *Rio de Montaigne*, which is partly Spanish and partly French, but he attempts no explanation of its meaning in any of the editions, Dutch, Latin or French, of his work: though in a subsequent page he calls the river the great *rieviere de Montaines*. On many of the earlier maps preceding the work of De Laet the region of this river is designated as *Montana*, a ridge of mountains, evidently on Spanish authority. Hence probably De Laet derived the name of Rio de Montaigne.

Although the Great bay is so called, it is not by any means as large as that of the South river. Above Sapocanikke the river is about two miles wide, and is very uniformly of the same width as far up as the *Hysopus* and higher, except in the Highlands, where there are here and there a narrow strait and greater depth. Above the *Hysopus*, which is 90 to 96 miles from the city, it still maintains a fair width, but with numerous islands, shoals and shallows, up to Fort Albany, where it is narrower. It is easily navigable to the *Hysopus* with large vessels, and thence to Fort Albany with smaller ones, although ketches and such craft can go up there and load. It carries the ordinary flood tide into the Highlands, but with much of a down flow of water, only up to them; though with an extraordinary flow down and a dead neap-tide, the water becomes brackish near the city. With a slight flow of water down, and a spring tide, accompanied by a southeast storm, the flood tide is carried quite through the Highlands, and they said they had had a change in the water even as far up as the *Hysopus*. The land on both sides of the river is high and rocky, but higher in some places than others, as at the Highlands, eminently so called because they are higher than the others. In passing by the *Hysopus* you see the *Katskil* mountains, a little inland, which are the highest in this region, and extend from there, in the form of a crescent, into the country of the *Maquaas*. Although these mountains are from 112 to 120 miles distant from the sea, there are skippers, who in clear weather have seen them while sailing along the coast.[1] All the reaches (*racken*), creeks (*killen*), headlands (*hoeken*), and islands, bear the names which were accidentally given them in the first instance: as ANTONIS NEUS (Anthony's nose) a headland and high hill in the Highlands, because it has a sharp

---

[1] The highest mountains in the Catskill range is that called Round Top which is 3,804 feet above tide water. *Moulton's Hist. of New York*, 243, note.

edge running up and down in the form of a man's nose; DONDERBERGH (Thunder hill), because it thundered there frightfully at the time the first explorers of the river passed it; SWADEL RACK (Swath reach), a short strait between high hills, where in sailing through they encounter whirlwinds and squalls, and meet sometimes with accidents, which they usually call *swadelen* (swaths or mowing sweeps); DANSKAMER (Dancing chamber), a spot where a party of men and women arrived in a yacht in early times, and being stopped by the tide went ashore. Gay, and perhaps intoxicated, they began to jump and dance when the Indians who had observed them, fell upon them in the height of their merriment, and drove them away. In remembrance of this circumstance the place has since been called the Dancing chamber. It is on the west side of the river, just through the Highlands. BOTERBERG (Butter hill), and HOYBERG (Hay hill), the one, because it is like the rolls of butter which the farmers in Holland take to market, and the other, because it is like a haystack in Holland; 'T CLAVER RACK (Clover reach), from three bare places which appear on the land;[1] and KINDER HOECK (Children's point), NOTEN HOECK (Nut point), POTLEPELS EYLANT (Potladle island), KOCK ACHIE, &c.[2]

Above Fort Albany there are occasionally good flats on both sides of the river, at the foot of the hills, and also some fine islands up to the *Cahoos;* which is where the colony of Rentselaerwyck is planted. The river begins above Fort Albany to divide itself, first by islands, and then by the main land, into two arms or branches, one of which turns somewhat towards the west and afterwards

---

[1] A fancied resemblance to *trefoil* or three leaved clover (*claver*).

[2] Coxsackie; the true orthography of this name is probably *Koeksrackie* (the Cook's *little* reach) to distinguish it from the *Koeks rack* (the Cook's reach) below the Highlands, near New Amsterdam. See Nic. J. Visscher's map of New Netherland (*Novi Belgii Tabula*).

entirely west through *Schoonechten*, towards the country of the *Maquaas*, and this branch, on which the *Cahoos* lies, is called the *Maquaas* kil. The other preserves the course of the main river for the most part, or a little more easterly, and retains also the name of the North river. It runs far up into the country, and has its source in a lake 120 to 160 miles in length, out of which a stream probably empties into the St. Lawrence, a river of Canada; for not only do the Indians, but the French also, pass over here in canoes from Canada. We, ourselves, have conversed with persons who have thus come over, some by water, and others by land and on foot. Of the *Cahoos* we have already spoken, in relating our journey there. Those falls are a great and wonderful work of God; but, although they have so much water that the wind causes the spray and moisture to rise continually in the air, so that spectators, who stand two hundred feet or so, higher, are made wet, especially when there are any gusts of wind driving from one side, as happened to us, yet we regard the falls on the Northwest kil [the Passaic], as more curious, though smaller, and having less water. Even on the North river, there are several small creeks and falls more rare to see than the *Cahoos*. Beyond the *Cahoos*, the land is not so high above the water; and no fish pass from below, into the river above, in consequence of the interruption caused by the falls, nor can any boats be carried over the falls, up or down, which is a great inconvenience for those who live above the *Cahoos*, at Schenectady and other places, although when the country shall become more inhabited, and they shall have more occasion, they will take means to remedy this difficulty. Through the whole of that extensive country they have no fish, except some small kinds peculiar to the streams, such as trout, sunfish, roach, pike, &c.; and this is the case in all the creeks where there are falls.

The North river abounds with fish of all kinds, throughout from the sea to the falls, and in the branch which runs up to the lake. To relate a single instance; some persons near Albany, caught in a single haul of a common seine, between five and six hundred fine shad, bass, perch and other fish, and there were, I believe, over five hundred of one kind. It is not necessary for those who live in the city [of New York], and other places near the sea, to go to the sea to fish, but they can fish in the river and waters inside; or even to the Great bay, except such as live upon it, and they can by means of fuycks or seines not only obtain fish enough for their daily consumption, but also to salt, dry and smoke, for commerce, and to export by shiploads if they wish, all kinds of them, as the people of Boston do; but the people here have better land than they have there, where they, therefore, resort more for a living to the water.

There is much beautiful quarry stone of all kinds on this river, well adapted for building purposes and for burning lime; and as fine cedar wood as we have seen anywhere. Nevertheless, for suitableness of navigation, and for rich land on both sides, all the way up, the South river excels the North; but what gives the North river the preference, and crowns it over the South river is, its salubrious climate; though above Christina creek, the South river is healthy, and it is every day becoming more so, along the whole of that river. On the North river, however, one has not to wait and die before this improvement may take place.

As soon as we arrived in the city, we resolved upon going to Long Island, for the purpose of taking leave according to promise of the kind acquaintances we had living there; and, therefore, on the

9*th*, *Thursday*, we started about ten o'clock. In crossing the ferry we met Elbert [Elbertsen Stoothoff], the father-in-law of Jan Theunissen, who came over with us and professed so much friendship towards us. Elbert was going to the city and intended to return again soon; but we thought it would not be before evening, which would be too long to wait for him. We, therefore, proceeded on to his house at the bay, where we arrived at noon. We found there Gerrit, the wheelwright; and Jan Theunissen soon came in from the fields; but, as the father [in-law], was not home we had to tarry, although we had intended to go to *Najack*. While we were sitting there, *Domine Van Sucren*[1] came up, to whom the boors called out as uncivilly and rudely as if he had been a boy. He had a chatting time with all of them. As Jan Theunissen had said to us in the house, that if the domine only had a chance once to speak to us, Oh, how he would talk to us! that we avoided him, and, therefore, could not be very good people; now, as we were there, we sat near him, and the boors, and those with whom he was conversing. He spoke to us, but not a word of that fell from him. Indeed, he sat prating and gossiping with the boors, who talked foully and otherwise, not only without giving them a single word of reproof, but even without speaking a word about God, or spiritual matters. It was all about houses, and cattle, and swine, and grain; and then he went away.

10*th*, *Friday*. The morning was rainy, and we could not go out early; but the weather became better after breakfast, about nine o'clock, when we took our leave and left for *Najack*, where we arrived at eleven o'clock at Jaques's. He had been sick with a large ulcer on his neck, but that was now better. We were welcome. Among other mat-

---

[1] This was the Rev. Casparus Van Zuren who succeeded Rev. Theodorus Polhemus in the charge of the Dutch churches on Long Island in 1677. He continued in this pastoral service until 1685, when he received a call from his former church at Gouderak in Holland and returned to Fatherland. *Strong's History of Flatbush*, 79–80.

ters, he told us that he had heard the report about our Theunis, but he did not know what to believe or think of it. We told him the whole truth about it, as he was capable of believing it, for he was, at the best, a Socinian. Theunis had formerly lived in that neighborhood and Jaques at that time missed a cow which was pasturing in the woods with the other cattle, as they always do. They made a thorough search after her, but could not find her. Although Jaques had some suspicion of Theunis, he did not manifest it even to those who spoke to him about Theunis in connection with the subject. It happened that Theunis came to Jaques's house, when Jaques embraced the opportunity, and took him on the shore near his house. After talking of various matters, Jaques spoke to him about his cow, how she was carried off, and they never could hear any thing about her. He then began to push Theunis a little closer, who laughed at it heartily at first; but by hard pressing and proofs which Jaques gradually brought forward, and especially by appeals to his conscience, whether he had not the fear of God before his eyes, Theunis acknowledged he had done it, and, falling on his knees, prayed for forgiveness. He had stolen the cow, and killed her. Jaques, who is one of the justices, said, I forgive you from the bottom of my heart, but I do this, only to cause you to reflect and desist from your wickedness, and to show you that you do not know or fear God, and that you may fear him more. Whereupon Theunis was much affected, and went away entirely subdued, while Jaques was rejoiced that he had had the opportunity of relieving his mind about Theunis. Jaques, who had known him from his youth up, said he had been a very godless person, cursing and swearing, and, in a word, living in direct hostility to God. We told Jaques that better things were now to be expected from him, at which Jaques was pleased.

We dined with Jaques; and his little son came and presented us a humming bird he had shot. Jaques impressed us very much with his sincerity and cordiality in everything we had to do with him, or wherein he could be of any service to us. We left with him the little book which we had lent to him, and which he said he had found much pleasure in reading, *Les Pensees de M. Pascal.* We took our leave of him, and went directly through the fields to *Gouanes*, where we arrived at two o'clock. Simon and his wife were out upon some newly cleared land planting water melons; for water melons must always have new ground, or the worms will destroy them. They went into the house with us. They also spoke about Theunis, and we disabused them of several things. They showed us some pieces of ambergris, which their brother had brought from the Caribbean islands, and which we thought was good. We said to them what we deemed proper for them, and took our leave, reaching the city in good time.

De la Grange and his wife, arrived this evening from the South river by land, leaving their nephew behind, who had made arrangements to come over with Ephraim in eight days. Meanwhile, we made inquiries about going to Boston, and they informed us that a vessel had sailed during our absence, but we were not ready, and there would be another one going in eight or ten days.

11*th*, *Saturday.* We finished with our tailor, and paid him 77 guilders in zeewan, that is 25 guilders and 8 stuivers in Holland money [ten dollars and sixteen cents].

13*th*, *Monday.* We settled with our old hosts and paid them. We continued our inquiries for an opportunity to leave, but without success.

15*th*, *Wednesday.* As we were crossing the street, the lord governor passing by, saw us and called to us. We went to him, and he asked us what we thought of the lands around Albany. We answered, they were very good, but limited, being flats here and there, and that the woodland, in particular, was not worth much. But, he said, you have not been to *Wappings kil.* We replied, that we had not. That is, he rejoined, a beautiful place, about three-quarters of an hour inland, on a fine creek which you can navigate with yachts, and it lies just through the Highlands, directly opposite the *Dans kamer.* And with that he left us.

16*th*, *Thursday.* As there was still a portion of our small stock of goods remaining, we traded it with de la Grange, who expected his boat from the South river with peltries and other articles, with which he would pay us.

17*th*, *Friday.* The boat which they had said would sail to-morrow, was posted to sail next Wednesday; but we think it will be postponed still longer.

18*th*, *Saturday.* We prepared our letters for *patria.*

19*th*, *Sunday.* A ship arrived from the Barbadoes. One had also arrived last week from London, which had been six weeks and three days on the voyage; but we did not receive any letters, nor did de la Grange, and we could learn nothing certain.

Meanwhile we conversed with several persons who came to visit us, among others with a woman who had undergone several years ago, some remarkable experiences; of a light shining upon her while she was reading in the New Testament about the sufferings of the Lord Jesus, which frightened her very much. It did not continue long but soon passed off; yet it left, nevertheless, such a joy and testimony in her heart as she could not describe. She kept it to herself, without making it known to any one except only one woman. Some years afterwards, while lying abed in the morning, she heard a voice which said to her, she must make this glory known, which she did do to Domine Nieuwenhuise, who told her he did not know what to say. She had also mentioned it to others, and to one man who played the part of a wise man, but who was not a good man. He said to her, "you must not go any more to church, for you are wise enough, and will become still wiser. You must not go to the Lord's Supper, for the Lord has said, 'do that until I come,'" and many other such things, in order to frighten the poor woman. He once came to her house and asked her very harshly and roughly, why she continued to do so, and in whose hands she would rather fall, into the hands of God, or the hands of men? She said, poor woman, in the words of David, "Rather in God's hands." "And I not," said he; "I would rather fall in the hands of men," and then went away. This has so sorely disturbed this poor woman, that for a long time, she has not known what to do; for not to go to church, and to leave the Lord's Supper, she could not in her heart consent. We told her that as regards what had happened to her, many things had occurred to us, and further, what was serviceable therein, without, however, condemning them in her; but, that the person who had so spoken to her was a false teacher, and she must be cautious of him; that for herself in all these and the like matters, she must seek for true grace, for a new heart and power unto true repentance of life, and for true humility of soul and renunciation of herself and the world. And, thereupon, she left. Her name was *Marie*. She was a Frenchwoman; and her husband, a Frenchman, who had also been to us twice. He was the son of *Pierre Jardinier* of whom we have before spoken. He had a book with the title of *Le Grand Heraut*, &c., which he highly esteemed; but he was a real reformed, of France, as they said. The other person, who played the wise man, was also a Frenchman. His name was *Nicolas de la Pleyne*, a relation of her's and professed to be of the reformed. He had not, for a long time, been to the Lord's Supper, but had now gone to it again. He was a tobacco twister by trade.

We wrote up the river to Robert Sanders, of Albany, and to the poor sick man at the *Hysopus*, sending him a *vomitorium* by Meus Hoogboom. We also went to see the Boston skipper, but he had not obtained any freight.

22*th*, *Wednesday*. Mr. Reinderman arrived over land from the South river, leaving Ephraim still there. He started the same day that de la Grange left there, but was not able to overtake him. He had been all this time on the road, and had had a difficult journey, in consequence of there being so much water upon the land.

23*d*, *Thursday*. We went again to inquire after our boat, and found that the time was changed for the voyage, which made it a great inconvenience to us to be here so long, without being able to accomplish any thing. But some other Boston vessels had arrived, which, they said, would return the first opportunity.

24*th*, *Friday*. Ephraim arrived from the South river at noon to-day, with his wife, and her sister's mother, and other company, over land.

25*th*, *Saturday*. We went this forenoon to welcome him. He was still very much attached to us, and so was his wife, and both were persuaded and touched with the love which we had shown them, and the wife particularly, for the favor I had granted her, in sending her the translation of the *Verheffinge des Gestes*, in reading which, she had experienced great enjoyment, and had been sometimes tenderly affected. She thanked us for the little parcel of braided goods, we had sent her, which had been very agreeable to her. He promised, moreover, if it should please God to call us again into this country to live and to establish his beloved church, we need not be at a loss to find a place; that the land which belonged to him, namely, Bohemia in Maryland, where his father lived, and of which we have before spoken, should with his consent, be applied to no other purpose; that it should never go into English hands, hoping that God would give him this grace. He had brought with him a piece of spermaceti, a portion of which he presented to us. He told us of the disposition of the heart of the Heer Jan Moll, towards us, who showed us so much friendship, as we have before related, and will show us all possible kindness in the future; that he had taken well to heart what we had commended to him, and had even reformed several matters in his household, and otherwise; and how it grieved him that Domine Tessemaker had not grace or ability enough to accomplish any thing serious in the congregation there, of which he was the elder, as well as president of the king's court. His wife was so far gone in consumption, that they saw no hope of her recovery.

26th, Sunday. Domine Niewenhuyse being sick, there was no preaching yet to-day.

27th, Monday. We went to call upon Ephraim again, in order to speak to him particularly, but did not succeed in consequence of his being visited so much, the more so because his wife's sister was soon to be married.

28th, Tuesday. The supercargo of the last arrived Boston vessel, named *Padechal*, was at M. van Clief's, who spoke to him about our wishes, and he promised to give us every attention and accommodation, and that he would leave in the coming week. This inspired us with new hope of getting away finally after so much delay.

29th, Wednesday. The before mentioned Boston trader came to speak with us himself, at the house of M. van Cleif. We talked with him, and he promised us every thing fair. The fare from New York to Boston is twenty shillings, in English money for each person, which with the loss of exchange, is a pound sterling in the money of Old England, which certainly is dear enough.

30th, Thursday. It was now Ascension day, according to the old style, a day greatly observed by the English. It reminded us of the day we left home on our travels, which was Ascension day, old style. We wrote to-day to Robert Sanders at Albany, in order, as we were so long in New York contrary to our intentions, he might regulate himself in the matter of our poor Wouter, the Indian, who, according to our mutual understanding, was to go to Boston by land, with an address from Mr. Robert Sanders, to one *John Pisgeon*, merchant, of that city, so that we might find him, or he us, in order to go to Europe with us, which he so earnestly desired, and we endeavored with our whole heart to effect; and as this could not well be done by the way of York, on account of the governor and other hindrances, we had chosen that way, as it seemed to us the best.

M. de la Grange came with his wife to invite me to accompany them in their boat to the *Wale bocht*, a place situated on Long Island, almost an hour's distance below the city, directly opposite *Correlaers hoeck*, from whence I had several times observed the place, which appeared to me very pleasant, although I had never been there He had an old aunt and other friends living there. We set off accordingly in the boat, but the strong flood tide carried us beyond the *bocht* (bay), to a place called the Burnt Mill (*Verbrande Meulen*), where we could let the tide run out. Meanwhile, we fished a little, but we caught nothing except a small codfish. From there we landed on the Mahatans, a little north of the Burnt mill, on a beautiful farm, having two fine ponds of water before the door, where a mill was standing. These ponds were full of sunfish, and other fish, some of which we caught. The flood having run out at noon, we left there and arrived about two o'clock at the *Wale bocht*. This is a bay tolerably wide where the water rises and falls much, and at low water, is very shallow and much of it dry. Inside of the easterly point there was a ship aground, which had struck on the reef of rocks which put out from Corlaer's hook towards this bay, and had floated over here and sunk. She was a French privateer, which had taken some rich Dutch prizes in the bay of Campeachy and was going through here to New England, in order to dispose of the goods which would not bring money enough in New York. There were many goods still in the sunken ship, and they have tried several times to raise her, but to no purpose. We went ashore here, and observed several kinds of fish, which I had not seen before in this country, such as flounders, plaice, sole, &c. The aunt of de la Grange, is an old Walloon from Valenciennes, seventy-four years old. She is worldly-minded, living with her whole heart, as well as body, among her progeny, which now number 145, and will soon reach 150. Nevertheless, she lived alone by herself, a little apart from the others, having her little garden, and other conveniences, with which she helped herself.[1] The ebb tide left our boat aground, and we were compelled to wait for the flood to set her afloat. De la Grange having to train next week with all the rest of the people, at New York, bespoke here a man to go as his substitute. The flood tide having made, we arrived home by evening.

31*st*, *Friday*. We sold to the wife of Evert, the late mate of our ship, a small looking-glass, a steel thimble, a pound

---

[1] This woman, in some respects an historical personage, was Catalina Trico, one of five of her sex, who came over in 1623, in the first ship sent out to New Netherland by the West India Company. She married Joris Jansen de Rapalje, by whom she had ten children. She went first to live at Fort Orange, where she resided three years, and where her first child, Sarah, "the first born Christian daughter in New Netherland," was born, on the 9th of June, 1625. She afterwards settled at the Waleboght, where she died September 11, 1689, aged 84 years. Her depositions made the year before her death, to be found in the *Documentary History of New York*, III, 31–2 (4to, edition) 49–51, (8vo, edition), establish the time of her arrival in this country, and her first residence.

and a half of white darning yarn, and a half a pound of brown thread, for which she gave us a piece of eight.

JUNE 1*st*, *Saturday*. Nothing transpired to-day, except several persons came to converse with us, to each of whom we spoke according to his state.

2*d*, *Sunday*. There was no preaching in consequence of Domine Niewenhuise's continued sickness. Ephraim and his wife, among others, called upon us, and we had several conversations with them, and satisfied them in regard to our departure.

3*d*, *Monday*. We went to enquire whether our voyage would take place, as they said, on Wednesday. They now fixed the last of the week, which did not please us a great deal, because there was so much fine weather passing away without our being able to do any thing; and also because we discovered we could depend as little upon the word of the people of New England, as of others, although they wished to pass for more upright persons, which we have not been able to perceive.

4*th*, *Tuesday*. We were again visited by several persons, and also by Ephraim, and one *Pieter Beyaert*, a deacon of the Dutch Church, a very good sort of person whom God, the Lord, began to touch and enlighten, both in regard to the destruction of the world in general and of himself in particular. He had a good intention to perform, through

---

It will be observed, that the record, which styles her daughter, Sarah, "the first-born Christian *daughter* in New Netherland," (*Benson's Memoir in New York Historical Collection*, II, 94, second series), does not conflict with the statement of Jean Vigné (*ante*, p. 114), that he was the first *male* born here of European parents; although, Judge Benson, and others, from this record only, call her the first born *child*.

Some further particulars in regard to Catalina Trico, and her daughter Sarah, who married Hans Hansen Bergen, the ancestor of the Bergen family, in this country, may be found in the genealogy of *The Bergen Family*, 12, *et seq*.

the grace of God, whatever God convicted him the truth of; for, he said, he had for some time past felt that God had some purpose concerning him, and to incite him to serve God with more earnestness; but it was impossible to do so in the city, and in this city of traders, where he lived; and as he observed the hand and providence of God in this matter because there had fallen to him a good piece of land and farm, without any effort of his; and as he felt that a private life was better for him, and brought him nearer to God, he intended to abandon the city and commerce and go and live upon his farm, which is on the South river, a small distance below where Caspar Hermans lives. We said to him on this subject what we believed he was in need of, which he received kindly.

The large ship of Frederick Flipsen, of which Singleton was captain, besides being lank of herself, was also very badly stowed and laden. In attempting to run out to sea, she was compelled to put back to Staten Island, in order to be restowed, which delays his voyage for several weeks.

5th, Wednesday. We now learned that our voyage was postponed until Monday, and perhaps longer, so little calculation can be made upon voyages in these parts.

6th, Thursday. We visited Theunis, whom we found well, the Lord confirming and strengthening him in the grace he had manifested towards him, which comforted us, and we wished him the blessing of the Lord.

7th, Friday. We went to take our leave of the lord governor, who was very much engaged with the officers of the burghers, who were to train the next day, and also with the affair of the Lord Carteret, governor of New Jersey. After we had been waiting a long time, he observed us and called us. He asked us what we came to say, not with his accustomed kindness, but a little peevishly, as if he were tired of us and we annoyed him. We answered, we came to take our leave of him, as we intended to leave for Boston, and to thank him for the favor and kindness he had shown us. He enquired with whom we were going; and we named the person. He then asked, when; and we said on Monday. Well, said he, you will undoubtedly find there in the east a better opportunity than you have found here. We felt that he said this in irony; and replied, we did not think so, as we had seen several good situations within his government, and had been informed they were not so good at the east. He cut off the conversation by wishing us a happy voyage, for which we thanked him and left. We also went to take leave of Frederick Flipsen, whom we requested, in case any letters addressed to us came into his hands, he would be so kind as to direct them to us in the Fatherland, which order we afterwards changed, and gave to M. de la Grange, because we were apprehensive, as he and the governor were one, it might be that our letters, coming from the Fatherland, had been withheld from us by them, as some persons had absolutely declared, and others had half insinuated.[1]

8th, Saturday. There was a training and muster to-day, which had not taken place before in two years, because the small-pox had prevailed so much the last year. Some were on horseback, and six small companies were on foot. They were exercised in military tactics, but I have never seen anything worse of the kind. They comprised all the force of New York and the adjacent places. De la Grange, who supposed he could put in a substitute, had to appear on horseback himself, although some who were to come so, did substitute others in their places.

This day was the anniversary of our departure from home, and we would have now taken our departure from here, if it had not been postponed.

---

[1] See note at the end of this chapter in regard to Frederick Phillipse and his wife Margaret.

9*th*, *Sunday*. Pinxter (Whitsunday). Domine Niewenhuyse, having recovered from his sickness, we went to hear him preach, in order not to give any cause of offense at the last. His text was the usual one.

10*th*, *Monday*. The second day of Pinxter. We had several visitors whom we received with love and affection, each one according to his circumstances.

11*th*, *Tuesday*. We called upon Ephraim, from whom we received in charge some spermaceti, with orders to send him from Amsterdam a good new Bible. He presented us on behalf of his wife, who was not at home, two beautiful otter skins, which we dared not refuse, and accepted with thanks.

The governor, attended by his whole retinue of ladies and gentlemen, escorted Carteret, the governor of New Jersey, in great pomp, home to Achter kol. As we are now about to leave New York, and the affair of the Heer Carteret appears to be finished, which happening during our stay here, we would have noticed from time to time, only we thought it was not well to write then what we saw, for various reasons, we do not regard it improper now to state what we heard of it.

These two governors lived at first in friendship and concord. Carteret came often to New York, and generally to church, when he usually went to the governor's, in the fort. A difference afterwards arose between them, but the cause of it I have not heard, or whether it was personal or public. It is certain, however, that the governor of New York wished to bring Carteret and his government, to some extent, in subordination to him. Carteret claimed to be as perfectly governor of his province, as the other was of his, and to possess the same prerogatives as the governor of New York, and even more than he, in respect to trade and other privileges. The governor of New York disputed with him all right of navigation, declaring the North river was under his own jurisdiction, and, therefore, all persons who passed in or out of it, must acknowledge him, pay him duties, and even unlade there, and actually commenced seizing some vessels. Carteret thereupon complained to England, and the governor of New York sent Captain Dyer over there as a commissioner, which he disavowed with an oath, as it is said. This Dyer returned with skipper Jacob, or about that time, but with what instructions I do not know. There also arrived with him a collector for Boston, on behalf of the king, as they said, which was contrary to their privileges of liberties, and he was, therefore, never acknowledged as such by the merchants there.[1] From this time forth the governor of New York began to act more stringently towards Carteret, and also towards his own subjects. Carteret obtaining information of what had been done in England by Captain Dyer, called together all the principal men among his people, who represented under their signatures the circumstances of the case, and sent the paper to England. The governor of New York went to Staten Island, as to the jurisdiction over which they disagreed, and sent for Carteret to come there in order, as he said, to negotiate with him in peace and friendship. Carteret probably perceiving his purpose, refused to go, and requested of him if he had any thing necessary to communicate to come to him, as he was now not far from his residence, and as he, Carteret, had been so frequently at the fort in New York, he should come once to his house, where he might be assured he would be welcome. Hereupon the governor returned again to New York with his object unaccomplished, and shortly afterwards, by proclamation, declared the nullity of the government of Carteret; that at the most he was only the head of a colony, namely, New Jersey; and that he was guilty of misusing the king's

---

[1] This has reference undoubtedly to Edward Randolph.

name, power and authority. He sent boats several times to Achter kol to demand the submission of the place to his authority, which the people of Achter kol jeered at and disregarded, being ready to uphold the king and their own governor, whom they bound themselves by an oath to maintain. This occurred repeatedly, and Carteret said that so far from wishing himself to oppose it, he would, on the contrary, immediately submit, if the governor of New York would produce the least authority from the king for what he claimed or did. He, however, never brought forward any thing of the kind, but continued his proceedings; and, at night, and unseasonable hours, and by surprise, took from New Jersey all the staves of the constables out of their houses, which was as much as to deprive them of the power to act. Seeing he could accomplish nothing by force, he declared the inhabitants released from their oaths to the Heer Carteret; they answered they could not acknowledge any release from their oaths, unless by the same authority which had required it of them or the exhibition of a higher one, that of the king. At length he corrupted one of Carteret's domestics, for Carteret had no soldiers or fortifications, but resided in a country house only. He then equipped some yachts and a ketch with soldiers, arms, and ammunition, and despatched them to Achter kol in order to abduct Carteret in any manner it could be done. They entered his house, I know not how, at midnight, seized him naked, dragged him through the window, struck and kicked him terribly, and even injured him internally. They threw him, all naked as he was, into a canoe, without any cap or hat on his head, and carried him in that condition to New York where they furnished him clothes and shoes and stockings, and then conducted him to the fort and put him immediately in prison. When they seized him at Achter kol the armed boats had gone home, and the seizure was accomplished through treachery. Two of the head men of Carteret immediately took possession of his papers, such as were of importance to him and traveled, one to Maryland, and the other, crossing the upper part of the North river, to Boston over land, and both to England, in order to remonstrate. The governor sent immediately to Achter kol, took possession of the place, posted up orders, and caused inquiries to be made for the man who had set Carteret over the river, but without success.

While Carteret was in prison he was sick, very sick, they said, in regard to which there were various surmises. Meanwhile a court of assizes was convened, to which on every occasion the governor was conducted by three trumpeters in advance of him. Carteret was brought before the same court, after him. The governor had caused a seat to be erected in the court room high up above all the others, and higher than usual; on which he sat. Governor Carteret, as a criminal, was in the middle. The court being seated, the governor presented Carteret as guilty of misusing the king's name, power, and authority, and usurping the government of New Jersey; that he was only the head of a colony, &c. Whereupon, Carteret having the right to speak, said, it was far from his intention to seek to defend his case before that court; he did not acknowledge it as a court having power to decide his case, because, in the first place the question could not be determined in a court of assizes, as it did not concern a private right, but the right of the king; in the next place, if such a question could be disposed of in such a court, this, nevertheless, could not act, because he was not subject to its jurisdiction; and thirdly, because it was a court of one party, and he said this without wishing to offend any of the individual members of the court; yet, notwithstanding all this he was content that he and his case should be brought before them in order that they might be witnesses of what was done and to be done. As to what the governor of New York alleged, he said it was wonderful to him that he should be thus treated, and that they should dispute a matter which neither the governor of New York, nor his court, nor any one in the world had ever disputed, or with reason could dispute. The governor said he had never acknowledged him as governor of New Jersey. It is surprising, said Carteret, that at one time there can be disavowed before all the world, what has been assented to before all the world at another; and thereupon he took out of his pocket, several letters of the governor of New York all addressed to the governor of New Jersey. The governor did not know what to say to this except that he had so directed them, because Carteret was generally styled governor, and not because he was so in fact; "for," said he, "although I have done that, can I, therefore, make you governor?" "No," replied Carteret, "but the king has made me governor, and you as well as all the world have acknowledged me as such." The acts of the king in relation to the governorship were then produced, and it was found that the one to Carteret was some time older than that to the governor of New York, and, therefore, said Carteret, it is to be preferred. The governor of New York replied, "mine is younger, and yours is therefore annulled by it."[1] "That is to be shown," re-

---

[1] Sir George Carteret, as already observed, derived his title to East Jersey from the Duke of York, first by deed to him and Lord Berkeley, jointly on 24th June, 1664, of the whole of New Jersey, and afterwards by confirmatory deed to himself alone on 29th July, 1674, of East Jersey, according to the partition between him and Lord Berkeley. On the day last mentioned the king had confirmed the grant to the Duke of York, of the whole territory between Connecticut river and Delaware bay. These confirmatory patents were deemed necessary in consequence of the intermediate reconquest of the country by the Dutch. But before they were made, king Charles issued his proclamation dated the 13th of June, 1674, acknowledging the title of Sir George Carteret to East Jersey and

joined Carteret. Although the governor of New York had employed a lawyer, he could not succeed. When at last the jury retired, in order to consult among themselves, Carteret exhibited letters from the king himself, in which he called him governor of New Jersey. The jury returned and declared Carteret not guilty of what was charged against him. The governor made them retire a second time, saying to them it would be well for them to consider what they did, as more depended upon the matter than they imagined. They came back a second time with the same verdict. Whereupon the governor became very angry, and caused them to go out again with threats that they should look to what they did as there was too much depended upon it, for themselves, their entire condition and welfare. Whereupon Carteret told them they had nothing to fear in committing themselves into the king's own hands who had given him authority. Again the jury returned and gave in the same verdict: that as Carteret was not under them and did not acknowledge them as his judges, they could not do otherwise in the case; but they advised Carteret to return to his house and business at Achter kol as a private individual until the case be decided by higher authority, which Carteret was willing to do, not because it was a sentence of theirs against him, or even their advice, but because he was compelled to do so and could not at that time do otherwise. And thus the affair stood at our departure, the governor taking him back to Achter kol with all the magnificence he could. Some think this was all a made up piece of work, and that the governor of New York only sought to possess the government and had no design against the person of

---

his right to *govern* the same. Andros was commissioned governor by the Duke of York, of his territories, on 1st July, 1674. *Leaming and Spicer*, 49, *et ante*. It is this state of the case undoubtedly that was exhibited in Governor Carteret's trial.

Carteret; and having obtained what he wanted, had no other or better means than to release him with some show. The principal persons who have assisted the governor herein, are Captain Dyer before mentioned, Captain Nicols, and some others. This matter transpired before all the world. The principal speeches which were made in court were related to us and as regards the other transactions we saw them. It is fortunate we were there when the affair terminated, as we were thus enabled to understand the nature of this government as well as of the governor.[1]

---

[1] A brief account of his trial written by Carteret himself, though not quite so circumstantial in all respects as that here given, is to be found in *Leaming and Spicer*, 683-4. "My imprisonment," he says, "was five weeks before they brought me to trial. When I came to my trial my intention at first was not to have entered a plea, and to have protested against the jurisdiction of the court; but finding the court over-ruled by him, I was forced to enter a plea and pleaded not guilty of what he alleged against me in my presentment, and was also ready to make out and justify my actings as governor of New Jersey to be legal and by virtue of power derived from the king, to which purpose recommended to the view of the court my commission with other instructions to manifest the same which was delivered with a charge to the jury, who after a perusal of the same were to make a return of their verdict concerning it, with their verdict in matter of fact, which was thus brought in by the jury: The prisoner at the bar not guilty. Upon which he asked them questions and demanded their reasons, which I pleaded was contrary to law for a jury to give reasons after their verdict given in. Nevertheless he sent them twice or thrice out, giving them new charges, which I pleaded as at first to be contrary to law, notwithstanding the last verdict of the jury being according to the first brought in by them, *The prisoner at the bar not guilty*, upon which I was acquitted accordingly." There seems to be no reasonable doubt that these proceedings of governor Andros were carried on under the sanction of the duke, that the visit of Captain Dyer, to England as explained by our journalist, was made for the purpose of obtaining instructions on this point, that he brought them verbally or in writing and they were kept secret. The right seems clearly to have been with Carteret. Upon the arrival of the report of the proceedings of Andros in England, the opinion of Sir William Jones was asked and obtained to the effect, that in the grant to Sir George Carteret, there was no reserva-

As to what the governor has done in regard to his own subjects: wherever they lived, they had the right to do whatever they considered best for a livelihood; but as this country yields in abundance every thing most essential for life, if the inhabitants so apply it, its shipping does not amount to much, for the reason that they have every thing at home, and have little occasion to borrow or buy from their neighbors; and as the exports or imports were not much, and produced few customs or duties in which his profit consists, there was little bought from the merchants of articles obtained from abroad. There was, therefore, no profit from that source to them or him — for he also is a merchant, and keeps a store publicly like the others, where you can buy half a penny's worth of pins. They usually make at least an hundred per cent profit. And here it is to be remarked, that as *Fredrick Flipsen* has the most shipping and does the largest trade, it is said he is in partnership with the governor, which is credible and inferable from the privileges which Frederick enjoys above the other merchants in regard to his goods and ships. Now one of the principal navigations of this place, is that with the Barbados, which formerly did not amount to much, for the people could obtain the productions of Barbados cheap enough from Boston, which had a great trade with that island, and where its productions are cheap in consequence of their exemptions from duties, for they paid scarcely any duty, customs, or other charges. As no French brandies can come into the English dominions, they can not be

---

tion of jurisdiction.—*Colonial History of New York*, III, 284. And a release was executed by the Duke to Sir George Carteret, heir of Sir George, the original grantee, who had died the preceding year. Andros was ordered home, apparently to answer for his conduct in this and other matters in which he evidently had acted under the duke's orders. He remained in favor and was appointed in 1686 by the Duke of York, then King James II, governor of New England, New York and New Jersey.

imported into New York, though they are free at Boston; and as New Netherland is a country overflowing with grain, much liquor was distilled there from grain, and, therefore, they had no necessity of going elsewhere to buy strong liquors. This brought no profit to the merchants, but on the contrary a loss, for in the first place, a large quantity of grain was consumed in distillation, by which means the grain continued too dear, according to the views of the merchants, who received it from the poor boors in payment of their debts, there being no money in circulation; in the second place, it prevented the importation of rum, a spirituous liquor made from sugar in Barbados, and consequently any duties; and thirdly, the merchants did not realize the double per centage of profit, namely, upon the meal they might send to Barbados, and upon the rum which they would sell here. The governor, therefore, prohibited the distilling of spirituous liquors, whereby not only were many persons ruined who supported themselves by that business, but the rum which had to be procured from the merchants, rose in price, and they sold it as high as they pleased; on the other hand the price of grain fell very much, because it could not be consumed, and the merchants gave no more for it than they chose. And thus the poor farmers soon had to work for nothing, all their sweat and labor going with usury into the pockets of the tradesmen. The trade to the Barbados now began to increase, and the merchants and the governor to make more gains. The common people, who could not trade to the Barbados, but could buy what they wanted at Boston as cheaply as they could order it from the Barbados, sent their flour to Boston, and obtained their goods much cheaper than their own merchants sold them. But as this was contributing too much to Boston, although the trade had always been free there, and was injuring the profits of the merchants of New York, the governor forbid any further trading to Boston; though the people of Boston should have the privilege to come and buy at New York on their own account. This took away almost all the trade with Boston, which had been very large, and straightened the farmers and common people still more, while the merchants became, if not worse, at least great usurers and cheats. The grain, by this means, fell still lower in price, and while we were there, the people could not obtain more than four or five guilders in zeewan for a schepel of fine wheat, that is, sixteen stuivers or one guilder of Holland money.[1] On the other hand, the merchants charged so dreadfully dear what the common man had to buy of them, that he could hardly ever pay them off, and remained like a child in their debt, and consequently their slave. It is considered at New York a great treasure and liberty, not to be indebted to the merchants, for any one who is, will never be able to pay them. The richest of the farmers and common people, however, in company, or singly, sent their goods to Barbados, on their own account, and ordered from there what they thought proper; and although they had to pay duties and freight to the merchants for the goods which were carried in their ships, they nevertheless, saved to themselves the profits on the goods. The governor at last has forbidden any flour to be bolted except in the city, or to be exported, unless [the exporters] come and reside in the city, and buy their burger or trader-right, which is five beaver skins, and has forbidden all persons whomsoever from carrying on trade, except those whom he licenses, and who know what they must pay him yearly, according to the amount of their sales. All goods sold outside of the city, in the country, must be bought in New York, and not imported on private account from abroad. Madame Rentselaer had even erected a new bolting mill before the last harvest by his advice, which was not

[1] Forty cents for one bushel and a fifth of a bushel.

yet in operation, when he prohibited bolting. Such was the situation of affairs when we left there. It is true that all goods imported into the South river from abroad, had to pay not only import, but also export duties, but those bought in New York, or from the merchants there on their own account, pay little or no export duty. And it would appear as if the whole of the proceedings with Carteret and him were founded in this, if they have no higher cause.

They say now, as he has accomplished these objects in regard to his own people and Carteret, he will turn his attention to the quakers on the South river, who claim they are not subject to his government, and also to the people on the Connecticut (*Versche rivier*), who claim to be members of the *republic* of Boston, and even to those of Boston; but whether all this is designed by him is doubtful.

The shoemakers, in consequence of the abundance of hides and bark in the country, have prepared their own leather; but as it was not necessary that every shoemaker should have his own tannery, some of them have put up several tanneries jointly, and others who were not so rich or had not so much to do, had their leather tanned by them, or tanned it themselves in those tanneries, satisfying the owners for the privilege. The proprietors of the tanneries began to exact too much from those who had their leather tanned, whereupon the poorer ones complained to the governor about it. He seized the opportunity to forbid all tanning whatsoever, and to order that the hides should be sent to Europe, and the leather ordered from there for the purpose of making shoes, or else ready made shoes imported. By this means the farmers and others would be compelled to come and sell their hides to the merchants, who would give for them what they chose, he would derive taxes and duties from them and the merchants, their freight and percentage of profit; leather which is dear in Europe would pay perhaps taxes once or twice there, and freight and taxes or duties again here; the merchants would have their profit, and then the shoemaker would get the leather for the purpose of making shoes. A pair of shoes now costs 16 or 20 guilders, that is, four guilders in Holland money [one dollar and sixty cents], what would they cost then? And as labor in Europe is cheaper than here, it is certain that shoes made there would be cheaper than the leather would cost here, and thus all the shoemakers here would be ruined, and all their means go to the governor and the merchants. This subject was under discussion, and had not yet gone into effect when we left. As they discovered that leather is contraband, I think the order is stopped for that reason. The intention, however, is evident.

He has taken away land from several country people, and given it to others who applied to him for it, because it was not inclosed, and he wishes, as he says, the land to be cultivated, and not remain waste. But it is impossible that all the land bought in the first instance for the purpose of being cultivated by the purchasers or their heirs, as they generally buy a large tract with that object, can be put in fence immediately and kept so, much less be cultivated. He has also curtailed all the farms in the free colony of Rentselaerswyck, as well as their privileges. Some persons being discouraged, and wishing to leave for the purpose of going to live under Carteret, he threatened to confiscate all their goods and effects. He said to others who came to him and complained they could not live under these prohibitions: "if they do not suit you, leave the country, and the sooner you do it the better."

A certain poor carman had the misfortune to run over a child which died. He fled, although the world pitied him, and excused him because he could not have avoided it. The court, according to some law of England, on account of his having seven sons, acquitted him, provided his wife with her seven sons would go and prostrate themselves before the governor, and ask pardon for their husband and father. The carman was restored by the court to his business, which he began again to exercise, when the governor meeting him on his cart in the street, asked him who had given him permission to ride again. The carman replied: "My Lord, it is by permission and order of the court." "Come down at once," the governor said, "and remember you do not attempt it again during your life." Thus he violated the order of the court, and the poor man had to seek some other employment to earn his bread.

A citizen of New York had a dog which was very useful to him. This dog, by accident, went into the fort, where madam, the governor's wife was standing, and looked steadily at her, in expectation, perhaps, of obtaining something from her, like a beggar. The lady was much discomposed and disturbed, and related the circumstance to her husband. The governor immediately caused inquiries to be made as to the ownership of the dog, summoned his master before him, spoke to him severely, and ordered him to kill the dog forthwith. The man was very sorry for the dog, and endeavored to save him till the anger of the governor was over. He placed him on board of a vessel sailing from and to the city, so as to prevent his coming on land. The governor being informed of this by some spy or informer, I know not whom, but of such there is no lack, summoned the man again before him, and asked him if he had killed his dog. The man answered he had not, but had done thus and so, whereupon the governor reprimanded him severely, imposed a heavy fine upon him, and required, I believe two of his sons to be security until he had killed the dog in the presence of witnesses whom he would send for that purpose.

This will be enough, I think, to enable such as have understanding, to comprehend him. As for us, we did not have much difficulty in interpreting him from the first. Grace and power have been given us to act, so that neither he nor any one else should have any hold upon us. For, as we were openly before the world, he had not much to do with us, the more so, as you could trust no one, because he has people everywhere to spy and listen to every thing, and carry what they hear to him; so every one endeavors to stand well with him. In a word he is very politic; being governor and, changeably, a trader, he appears friendly because he is both; severe because he is avaricious; and well in neither capacity because they are commingled. The Lord be praised who has delivered us safely, and the more, because we were in every one's eye and yet nobody knew what to make of us; we were an enigma to all. Some declared we were French emissaries going through the land to spy it out; others, that we were Jesuits traveling over the country for the same purpose; some that we were Recollets, designating the places where we had held mass and confession; others that we were sent out by the Prince of Orange or the states of Holland, and as the country was so easily conquered, to see what kind of a place it was, and whether it was worth the trouble to endeavor to recover it, and how many soldiers it would require to hold it; others again that we had been sent out as the principals to establish a new colony, and were, therefore, desirous of seeing and examining every thing. And thus each one drifted along according to his wishes. The papists believed we were priests and we could not get rid of them; they would have us confess them, baptize their children, and perform mass; and they continued in this opinion. The quakers said we were quakers, because we were not expensively dressed, and did not curse and swear, that we were not willing to avow ourselves as such; but they were jealous because we had not associated with them. Some said we were Mennonists;

others that we were Brownists, and others again that we were David Jorists.[1] Every one had his own opinion, and no one the truth. Some accused us of holding conventicles or meetings, and even at the magistrate's or burgomaster's, and named the place where and the persons who attended them, some of whom were required to purge themselves of the charge, and others were spoken to in a different way. It was all finally found to be false, and that they were mistaken, though few of them were cured of their opinion. The ministers caused us to be suspected; the world and the godless hated and shunned us; the hypocrites envied and slandered us; but the simple and upright listened to us and loved us; and God counseled and directed us. May he be praised and glorified by all his children to all eternity, for all that he is, and all that he does, for all that he is doing for them, and all that he may do for them, to all eternity.

12*th*, *Wednesday*. Theunis came to our house and took leave of us with great tenderness and with many tears, he committing us, and we him, to God and his grace, recommending himself to our prayers and the prayers of God's children,—his beloved brothers and sisters, he said, to whom, although he had never seen them, he requested us to make his salutations.[2] In the evening Ephraim also came to take leave, intending to go south in order to leave his wife there during her confinement. We said to each of them what we deemed necessary.

13*th*, *Thursday*. It was first announced we were to leave

---

[1] David Joris, or George, the founder of the sect called David Jorists or David Georgians, was a native of Delft in South Holland. He proclaimed himself the son of God; and denied the existence of good and evil, of heaven and hell, and future punishment. "He reduced religion to contemplation, silence and a certain frame or habit of soul, which it is equally difficult to define and to understand."—*Mosheim*, XVI, 3, 24.

[2] The community of Wiewerd.

on Wednesday, then the following Saturday, afterwards on Tuesday, and again on Thursday without fail. Finally we spoke to the skipper or supercargo, *Paddechal*, who told us he could not leave before the governor returned, who had some letters of importance to send by him. This evening *Annetje Sluys*, of whom we have spoken, came to see us. She had some ambergris which she wanted us to take, but we did not know what to do in regard to the terms. Among others, we made three different propositions; namely, we would fix the price at eight pieces of eight the ounce here, and would endeavor to sell it in Holland as high as we could, and would take one-half of what it brought over that valuation for our trouble, provided we could take our portion of the profit out in ambergris at the current price; or, we would take it all ourselves at eight pieces of eight the ounce to be paid for in Holland; or, she should give us one ounce for our trouble and we would sell the rest of it for her and send back the proceeds to her in goods. The second proposition seemed to be the most profitable, if we had a correct knowledge of the ambergris, but we had none at all; and if it were not good it would be a great loss. The first proposition might, or might not, yield us a profit, but it seemed to us too tradesmanlike. It therefore remained with the last one. There were twelve ounces of it good, or what we considered good, and four ounces bad. One ounce was weighed off for us, and the rest was taken upon that condition. My comrade gave her a receipt, acknowledging it was received from her on such conditions, and she gave a memorandum of the goods which she wanted for the proceeds.

[Here occurs a break in the journal, embracing a period of five days, that is, from June 13th, to June 19th, and filling twenty-four pages of the manuscript, equal to thirty printed pages. The missing part probably contained a general description of the city of New York, according to the practice of the journalist on taking final departure from a place, and as promised in regard to that city, under date of 8th of May.]

NOTE TO PAGE 345.

Frederick Philipse, and Margaret, his wife, who was the acknowledged owner and supercargo of the Charles, and was, with her daughter, Annetje, a fellow passenger of our travelers in that ship on their voyage to New York, have figured largely in these pages, and seem, therefore, before we part from them, to require some particular notice, especially as he and some other members of the family were conspicuous in the early history of the colony of New York; and more particularly because the public records, colonial and ecclesiastical, prove that the statements hitherto published in regard to them are exceedingly erroneous.

Frederick Philipse, whose name is thus anglicised from the Dutch, namely, Flipsen, or as he himself spelt it, Flypsen, that is, the son of Flip or Philip, was born in the year 1626, at Bolsward, in Friesland, the little town near Wiewerd, where our travelers, it will be recollected, entered the canal boat on the morning they set out for Amsterdam, to take ship for New York. In what year he left Friesland, does not appear; but it was not in 1658, as the accounts referred to state, for he was in New Amsterdam in 1653, when we find him named as an appraiser of a house and lot of Augustine Heermans in that city. If he came over with Governor Stuyvesant, as it is asserted and as is not impossible, then he arrived here in May, 1647. But he came in no lordly capacity, nor for the purpose of taking possession of landed estates, which it is pretended, he had acquired here. He was a carpenter by trade, and worked as such at first for Governor Stuyvesant.

Margaret, his first wife, was the daughter of Adolph Hardenbrook, who came from Ervervelt, in Holland, and settled at Bergen, opposite New Amsterdam. She married Peter Rudolphus De Vries, a merchant trader of New Amsterdam, in 1659, and had by him one child, a daughter, baptized October 3, 1660. Rudolphus died in 1661, leaving a considerable estate, which, by law, devolved upon his widow and child with a community of interest.

In October, 1662, bans of marriage between Frederick Philipse and Margaret Hardenbrook were published, when the Court of Orphan Masters of New Amsterdam summoned her before them, to render an inventory of her child's paternal inheritance. This she declared she was unable to do, probably in consequence of the commercial character of the assets;

whereupon the court received the ante-nuptial contract between her and Frederick Philipse in lieu of the inventory, in consequence of its embodying an agreement on his part to adopt the child of Rudolphus as his own, and to bequeath her one-half of his estate, unless he had children born to himself, and in that case to give her a share equally with them. Adoption was permitted by the laws, and also the limitation of successory estates by marriage contracts, and the child thus in legal intendment, became the child of Frederick Philipse upon the consummation of the marriage in December following. In the baptismal record, the name of this child is written Maria. This may have been, and probably was, an error of the registrar; certain it is, that Frederick Philipse, by his will, made provision for a child, which he calls his oldest daughter, named Eva, who was not his child by marriage, as it seems; and he makes no provision for Maria, as he was bound to do by his marriage contract, unless it be that for Eva. The conclusion, therefore, seems irresistible, that Eva and Maria were one and the same person.

By his marriage with Margaret Hardenbrook, Frederick Philipse became entitled to a community of property with her. She did not, however, relinquish to him the sole management of the estate which she possessed, but on the contrary, continued the business of her former husband, a practice not uncommon in the colony, and became a woman-trader, a character which does not appear to have always been a very amiable one, judging from our journalist's description of her, and of the mistress of Illetie the Indian at Albany. She went repeatedly to Holland in her own ships, as supercargo, and bought and traded in her own name. By her fortune, thrift, and enterprise, however, as well as by his own exertions, Philipse soon came to be the richest man in the colony. His property was valued in 1674 by commissioners appointed by Governor Colve, at 80,000 guilders; an amount large in those days, and yet small compared with his subsequent wealth. On her death, his commercial operations became more extensive. It is not certain when Margaret died, though it was not in 1662, as strangely stated by some, for that was the year of her marriage with Frederick Philipse. She was alive, and a passenger in the ship with our travelers in 1679, but she must have died before 1692, when Frederick Philipse espoused Catharine van Cortlandt, widow of John Derval and daughter of Oloff Stevensz van Cortlandt, for his second wife. He became the largest trader with the Five Indian Nations at Albany, sent ships to both the East and West Indies, imported slaves from Africa, and engaged, as it was with good reason alleged, in trade with the pirates at Madagascar. His gains and profits were much enhanced, it was believed, by his connection with the government, and his intimacy with the governors, by which he obtained immunities not granted to others. He was a member of the council under all the governors, from Andros to Bellomont, embracing an uninterrupted period of twenty years, with the exception of the brief usurpation of Leisler. When the latter event occurred, he was in conjunction with Stephen van Cortlandt, left in charge of the government by

Lieutenant Governor Nicholson. After resisting for a few days the proceedings of Leisler, as became his position, he wisely, when the public sentiment pronounced itself in favor of them, submitted to them as the acts of the government *de facto*, much to the chagrin of Bayard and his associates. He was subsequently clothed by Governor Sloughter with similar powers, in conjunction with Nicholas Bayard, during the absence of that governor at Albany. He had the ear of Fletcher, who bestowed upon him and his son Adolphus, extravagant grants of land. When the Leisler party came into power under Bellomont, in 1698, he resigned his seat in council, in consequence, as he alleged, of his advanced age, which was then seventy-two, though in reality, it would seem, to avoid, if possible, the blow which was already given in an order for his removal by the home government, on account of his practices with the pirates, an order which arrived a few weeks after his resignation.

In 1680, he acquired a piece of land from the Indians, the title to which was confirmed by patent in the same year from Governor Andros, situated on the Pocanteco or Mill river, in the county of Westchester, running along Sleepy Hollow, the region since made famous in our legendary lore. This acquisition was the nucleus of the large tract in that county extending from Yonkers to the Croton river, which, with a small piece on the opposite side of the Hudson, near Tappaan, and the bridge across the Spytenduyvel, called Kingsbridge, were purchased or patented by him, and erected by Governor Fletcher in 1693, into a manor, with the customary privileges of a lordship, of holding court leet and court baron, and exercising advowson and right of patronage of all churches to be erected within its limits, to be held by him, his heirs and assigns, by the name of the manor of Philipsborough. This property remained in the family until the American revolution, when, by reason of the adherence to the British crown of the proprietor, Colonel Frederick Philipse, great grandson of the founder of the estate, it was confiscated by the state of New York.

Frederick Philipse was, as we have seen, twice married. He had no children by Catharine van Cortlandt, his second wife. By Margaret Hardenbrook, he had four: I. Philip, baptized March 18, 1664. II. Adolphus, baptized November 15, 1665. III. Annetje, baptized November 27, 1667, and IV. Rombout, baptized January 9, 1670. The genealogy in *Burke's Dictionary of the Landed Gentry of Great Britain and Ireland*, says he had two children, Frederick, born in 1656, and Eva, and makes Philip and Adolphus to be sons of this Frederick by Margaret Hardenbrook; while that in *Bolton's History of Westchester County*, gives him one child, Frederick, born in 1656, *at Bolsward*, and makes Margaret Hardenbrook to be the wife of this Frederick, and Philip, Adolphus, Eva and Annetje to be his children. The errors of these statements are so palpable on the face of them, as hardly to require being pointed out. Margaret Hardenbrook married Frederick Philipse, as the record shows, in December, 1662; surely then, her husband could not have been born in 1656, only six years before. Frederick Philipse was in this country as early as 1653, remained here and married his first wife in 1662. He could not have had a son born to him in Friesland in 1656. All this confusion arises from the mistake of these writers in supposing that there was a son Frederick born to the first Frederick, and attributing to two Fredericks what pertains to one.

Frederick Philipse, the first of the name in this country, and the subject of this sketch, died in 1702, in the seventy-seventh year of his age. He left a will, by which he devised to Frederick Philipse, his *grandson*, the son of Philip, his *oldest son*, the Yonker's plantation and other lands; to Eva, his *oldest* daughter, who married Jacobus van Cortlandt, May 7, 1691, a house and ground in New York, and a mortgage of Domine Selyns; to his son Adolphus, the land at the upper mills in Westchester county; and to his daughter Annetje, wife of Philip French, a house and ground in New York, and an estate in Bergen. Rombout is not mentioned in the will, having probably died in infancy; nor is there any mention of any son Frederick, or of the children of such a son. Eva, his oldest daughter, was, as we have concluded, such by adoption, and not by birth. This is to be inferred from the absence of her name in the baptismal record, and by the times of the birth of his other children as given by the same record.

Adolphus Philipse was, for several years, speaker of the colonial assembly. Mary, daughter of Frederick Philipse, named in the will of the first Frederick, and sister of Colonel Frederick Philipse, in whose hands the manorial estate was confiscated, won, it is said, the affections of Washington, but the demands of his country called him away, and she became the wife of Colonel Morris, who embraced the cause of the king.

As this sketch of Frederick Philipse differs materially from the accounts heretofore published, we adduce here the authorities for all the essential facts presented. *O'Callaghan's Calendar of Dutch Manuscripts*, 56, 210, 218. *Valentine's History of New York*, 144. *New York Colonial Manuscripts*, X, 281. *Calendar of English Manuscripts*, 26, 118, 158, 206, 270. *New Netherland Register*, 100. *Valentine's New York Manual for* 1862, 617, 623; *for* 1863, 801-807. *Record of Court of Orphan Masters*, city clerk's office, New York, sub dato December 18, 1662. *New York Colonial History*, II, 699; III, IV, *passim*. *Records of Wills*, in surrogate's office, New York, Book VII, 101. *Burke's Dictionary of the Landed Gentry of Great Britain and Ireland for* 1851, I, 890; II, 1361. *Bolton's History of Westchester County*, I, 320, 323, and pedigree; II, 418, 466, 467. *Blake's History of Putnam County*, 80-3.

JOURNAL

OF OUR

VOYAGE FROM NEW NETHERLAND

UNTIL

OUR ARRIVAL AT WIEWERD, IN FRIESLAND.

BOSTON, AND THE VOYAGE HOME.

1680, JUNE 19*th*, *Wednesday*. We embarked at noon in the yacht of Mr. *Padechal*, supercargo and captain, residing in Boston. The anchor was weighed at last; but as we had to wait a long time for the governor's yacht, the tide was nearly all spent. The wind was from the northwest. The crew consisted of three men and a boy, besides the captain; but there was another sailor on board who was a passenger. Many persons came to escort the captain, and also a woman, who was going with us; and as soon as they had gone we hastened to leave. The wind being ahead, we tacked and towed, until we anchored at Hellgate, almost at flood tide, at four o'clock in the afternoon. The woman who was going over with us, was born at Rhode Island, in New England, and was the wife of the captain of the Margaret, one of Frederick Flipsen's ships. I have never in my whole life, witnessed a worse, more foul, profane or abandoned creature. She is the third individual we have met with from New England, and we remarked to each other, if the rest of the people there, are to be judged by them, we might, perhaps, do them great injustice; for the first one from Boston whom we saw was a sailor, or he passed for one, on board the ship in which we sailed from the Fatherland. They called him the doctor, and if he were not, or had not been a charlatan, he resembled one; the second, was our skipper, Padechal, who had told us so many lies; and now, this infamous woman. They all belong to this people who, it is said, pretend to special devoutness; but we found them, the sailor, and the rest, like all other Englishmen, who, if they are not more detestable than the Hollanders, are at least no better.

20*th*, *Thursday*. It was about ten o'clock in the forenoon before the flood began to make. The wind was southwest, but light. We weighed anchor and towed through Hellgate, when the wind and tide served us until we passed Whitestone (*de witte klip*), as far as which the tide, from the direction of New York, usually reaches. We sailed bravely by and obtained the ebb tide in our favor which carried us this evening beyond Milford.

21*st*, *Friday*. We had shot ahead very well during the night, with the wind west and south southwest, on a course due east, so that by morning we reached the end of Long Island. The governor's yacht which had to stop at Fisher's island, a little to the leeward of us, which is subject to New England, but which the governor is now endeavoring to bring under his authority, and for that purpose had sent his yacht there with letters, left us this morning with a salute. We observed a vessel ahead of us under sail, running before the wind, and we came up to her about nine o'clock. She was a small flute from Milford, laden with horses and bound for Barbadoes. We hailed her, and as her captain was an acquaintance of our captain and an independent, our captain went on board of her where he staid two hours. When he returned we kept our course, and she sailed to the south in order to get to sea. As soon as we reached the end of Long Island, they began to throw their fish lines, and continued to catch mackerel all day long. I think the European mackerel are better and fatter. We came to an island called *Maertens Wingaert* (Martha's Vineyard), about four o'clock in the afternoon, having the Elizabeth islands on the larboard and sailing between the two, with our course easterly and a lighter wind. Our captain had prayers every evening, performed in this way. The people were called together, and then, without any thing being spoken previously, he read a chapter, then a psalm or part of one was sung, after that they all turned their backs to each other, half kneeling, when a common formulary of prayer was said which was long enough, but irreverently enough delivered. It was not done mornings. From what I have experienced the Hollanders perform it better, are more strict mornings and evenings, and more devout.

There was no moon, and the weather was cloudy. We continued sailing onward until two o'clock after midnight, when the captain going aloft, cried out, "Strike the sails! strike the sails! let them run! let them run! we are on the rocks, let the anchor fall!" This startled me so that I cannot tell how I reached the deck, and ran forward. I saw we were indeed close upon a reef of rocks directly before us, and that we were under considerable headway. We did our best to lower the sails, and throw the anchor over. The headway was checked some, but the anchor would not hold. We found that the spritsail had caught in the anchor stock in consequence of the hurry in lowering the sail and throwing anchor, but it was some time before we could discover what was the matter and get the anchor loose; it then held fast in three fathoms of water at a musket shot's distance from the reef and about as far from the shore. We lay there until daylight on a lee shore, but fortunately it did not blow hard.

22d, Saturday. As soon as the day broke, and we saw where we were, we got under sail again with the wind, the same as before. In sailing between the land, namely *Maertens Wyngaert* and the reef, the course is to the point of the island, running east southeast in three and two and a half fathoms till you have this point on the side, and then you have passed the reef. We continued on until we reached the westerly point of the island of *Nantocket*, along which we sailed to the easterly point, and thence due north until noon; but the flood tide running in strong, and the vessel not being well steered, we were carried to the west among the shoals. The weather was rather rough and the atmosphere hazy, so that we could not see far. The shoals were ahead of us, and we had only two fathoms, and even less, of water. The captain and helmsman, were confused, and hardly knew where they were. This happened two or three times. In order to avoid the shoals, we had to keep to the east. We were fearful we would strike upon them, and it was, therefore, best to look out and keep free of them. About three o'clock we caught sight of the main land of Cape Cod, to which we sailed northerly. We arrived inside the cape about six o'clock, with a tolerable breeze from the west, and at the same time saw vessels to the leeward of us which had an east wind, from which circumstance we supposed we were in a whirlwind. These two contrary winds striking against each other, the sky became dark, and they whirled by each other, sometimes the one, and sometimes the other being strongest, compelling us to lower the sails several times. I have never seen such a twisting and turning round in the air, as at this time, the clouds being driven against each other, and close to the earth. At last it became calm and began to rain very hard, and to thunder and lighten heavily. We drifted along the whole night in a calm, advancing only twelve or sixteen miles.

23*d*, *Sunday*. A breeze blew up from the northeast. It was fortunate for us, that we arrived inside of Cape Cod yesterday evening, before this unfavorable weather, as we would otherwise have been compelled to put back to Rhode Island. We could now still proceed; and we laid our course northwest to Boston. We arrived at the entrance of the harbor at noon, where we found a considerable rolling sea caused by the ebb tide and wind being against each other. There are about thirty islands here, not large ones, through which we sailed, and reached Boston at four o'clock in the afternoon, our captain running with his yacht quite up to his house in the Milk-ditch (*Melk-sloot*).

The Lord be praised who has continued in such a fatherly manner to conduct us, and given us so many proofs of his care over us; words are wanting to express ourselves properly, more than occasions for them, which we have had abundantly.

We permitted those most in haste to go ashore before us, and then went ourselves. The skipper received us politely at his house, and so did his wife; but as it was Sunday, which it seems is somewhat strictly observed by these people, there was not much for us to do to-day. Our captain, however, took us to his sister's where we were welcome, and from there to his father's, an old corpulent man, where there was a repetition of the worship, which took place in the kitchen while they were turning the spit, and busy preparing a good supper. We arrived while they were engaged in the service, but he did not once look up. When he had finished, they turned round their backs, and kneeled on chairs or benches. The prayer was said loud enough to be heard three houses off, and also long enough, if that made it good. This done, he wished us and his son welcome, and insisted on our supping with him, which we did. There were nine or ten persons at the table. It being in the evening, and we strangers, Mr. Padechal requested us to lodge with him this night, as we did, intending in the morning to look out for accommodations. We were taken to a fine large chamber, but we were hardly in bed before we were shockingly bitten. I did not know the cause, but not being able to sleep, I became aware it was bed bugs, in such great numbers as was inconceivable. My comrade who was very sleepy, fell asleep at first. He tumbled about very much; but I did not sleep any the whole night. In the morning we saw how it was, and were astonished we should find such a room with such a lady.

But before we part from the East river, we must briefly describe it. We have already remarked that it is incorrect to call this stream a river, as both ends of it run into the sea. It is nothing but salt water, an arm of the sea, embracing Long Island. It begins at the Little bay of the North river, before the city of New York, pouring its waters with those of the North river, into the sea, between Sandy hook and Coney island. In its mouth before the city, and between the city and Red hook, on Long Island, lies Noten island opposite the fort, *the first place the Hollanders ever occupied in this bay*. It is now only a farm with a house and a place upon it where the governor keeps a parcel of sheep. From the city, or from this island, the river runs easterly to *Correlaers hoeck*, and the *Wale bocht*, where it is so narrow they can readily hear one another calling across it. A little west of *Correlaers hoeck*, a reef of rocks stretches out towards the *Wale bocht*, half way over, on which, at low tide, there is only three or four feet of water, more or less. The river then runs up northerly to Hellgate, where there is an island, in front of which on the south side are two rocks, covered at high water, and close to the island, besides others which can be easily seen. Hellgate is nothing more than a bend of the river, which coming up north, turns thence straight to the east. It is narrow here, and in the middle of the bend or elbow, lie several large rocks. On either side it is wider, consequently the current is much stronger in the narrow part; and as it is a bend the water is checked, and made to eddy, and then, striking these rocks, it must make its way to one side or the other, or to both; but it cannot make its way to both, because it is a crooked bay, and therefore, it pursues its course until it is stopped on the opposite side of the bay, to which it is driven, so much the more because it encounters these rocks on the way. Now, between the rocks, there is no current, and behind them it is still; and as the current for the most part is forced from one side, it finds liberty behind these rocks, where it makes a whirlpool. You must, therefore, be careful not to approach this whirlpool, especially with small vessels, as you will be in danger of being drawn under. It makes such a whirlpit and whistling that you can hear it for a quarter of an hour's distance, but this is when the tide is ebbing, and only, and mostly, when it is running the strongest. The river continues from thence easterly, forming several islands, generally on the left hand side, although there are some in a large bay on the right. When you have passed the large bay of Flushing, which is about eight miles from Hellgate, or rather, as soon as you get round the point, and begin to see an opening, you must keep well to the northeast, in order to sail clear of a long ledge of rocks, some of which stick out of the water like the lizard in the channel near Falmouth. After you have passed this you sail easterly along the shore without any thing in the way. There are islands here and there, near the land, but they are not large. The end of Long Island, which is one hundred and forty-four miles long, runs off low and sandy. Continuing east you pass Plum island, which is about four miles in length. Behind the bay of Long Island called the *Cromme Gouwe* (Crooked bay)[1] there are several small islands, Gardiner's island, and others. At the east point of Plum island, there is a reef, or some small rocks, but keeping on to the eastward, you sail far enough from them. From Plum island to

[1] Peconic bay is meant.

Adriaen Blocx island, the course is east a distance of twenty or twenty-two miles. This island is eight miles long. Thence to *Maertens Wingaert* the distance is fifty-two to fifty-six miles further east, and *Blockx* island is hardly out of sight when you see *Maertens Wingaert.* Between Plum island and *Blockx* island, you leave Fisher's island to the north, nearest Plum island; and between *Blockx* island and *Maertens Wingaert* you leave on the coast Rhode Island, which does not lie within the coast, as the chart indicates, but outside, and lies nearest *Maertens Wingaert.* With *Maertens Wingaert* begins the Elizabeth islands, which consist of six or seven islands lying in a row, close to each other, towards the coast. The width between *Maertens Wingaert* and the Elizabeth islands is eight miles. There is a fine sound or strait for sailing between them, although *Maertens Wingaert* is somewhat longer. This island is about twenty-eight miles in length towards the east. A little within the east point of it a reef of rocks stretches out three miles from the shore, so that it is best to keep nearest the Elizabeth islands, although there is room enough between *Maertens Wingaert* and the reef to sail through with large ships, as there is three and two and a half fathoms of water at low tide. At the westerly point of the Elizabeth islands there are several rocks, one large and several small ones, called after their fashion, the *Sow and Pigs.* There is a beautiful bay, and anchorage ground [Holmes's hole] on the east end of *Maertens Wingaert.* From this point of *Maertens Wingaert* the course is east southeast about twenty miles, to *Nantocket* upon the west point of which there is a good bay with anchorage ground. The land is low and sandy; it is fourteen or sixteen miles long. There are several shoals outside in the sea, and also inside between the island and the main land, but they do not run out beyond the east point. When you have the east point to the west southwest of you, steer straight north to Cape Cod, about twenty-eight miles; but you must here time the tides, which run strong east and west; the flood to the west, and the ebb to the east. The flood tide pulls to the shoals, and the ebb tide on the contrary sets eastwardly to the sea. Cape Cod is a clean coast, where there are no islands, rocks or banks, and, therefore, all such laid down on the charts of the great reef of Malebarre and otherwise is false. Indeed, within four, eight and twelve miles, there is sixty to sixty-five fathoms of water. This cape or coast is about twenty-eight miles long due north; and from thence to Cape Ann it is also due north, but to Boston it is northwest. There are many small islands before Boston well on to fifty, I believe, between which you sail on to the city. A high one, or the highest, is the first that you meet. It is twelve miles from the city, and has a light-house upon it which you can see from a great distance, for it is in other respects naked and bare. In sailing by this island, you keep it on the west side; on the other side there is an island with many rocks upon and around it, and when you pass by it you must be careful, as a shoal pushes out from it, which you must sail round. You have then an island in front, in the shape of a battery which also you leave on the larboard, and then you come in sight of the island upon which the fort stands, and where the flag is flown when ships are entering. That, too, lies to the larboard, and you pass close enough to it for them to hail the ship, what you are, from whence you came, and where you are bound, &c. When you are there you see the city lying directly before you; and so you sail into the bay before the town, and cast anchor. There is a high hill in the city, also with a light-house upon it, by which you can hold your course in entering.

24*th*, *Monday*. We walked with our captain into the town, for his house stood a little one side of it, and the first house he took us to was a tavern. From there, he conducted us to the governor, who dwelt in only a common house, and that not the most costly.[1] He is an old man, quiet and grave. He was dressed in black silk, but not sumptuously. *Paddechal* explained the reasons of our visit. The governor inquired who we were, and where from, and where we going. Paddechal told him we were Hollanders, and had come on with him from New York, in order to depart from here, for England. He asked further our names, which we wrote down for him. He then presented us a small cup of wine, and with that we finished. We went then to the house of one John Taylor, to whom William Van Cleif had recommended us; but we did not find him. We wanted to obtain a place where we could be at home, and especially to ascertain if there were no Dutchmen. They told us of a silversmith, who was a Dutchman, and at whose house the Dutch usually went to lodge. We went in search of him, but he was not at home. At noon we found Mr. Taylor, who appeared to be a good sort of a person. He spoke tolerably good French, and informed us there was a ship up for England immediately, and another in about three weeks. The first was too soon for us, and we therefore, thought it best to wait for the other. We also found the silversmith, who bade us welcome. His name was William Ross, from Wesel. He had married an Englishwoman, and carried on his business here. He told us we might come and lodge with him, if we wished, which we determined to do; for to lie again in our last night's nest was not agreeable to us. We exchanged some of our money, and obtained six shillings and six-pence each for our ducatoons, and ten shillings each for the ducats. We

[1] Simon Bradstreet was then the governor of the colony of Massachusetts, having at the age of seventy-seven been elected the preceding year to succeed governor Leverett. He died in 1697, at the age of 94. He was the husband of Anne Bradstreet, the poetess.

went accordingly to lodge at the goldsmith's, whom my comrade knew well, though he did not recollect my comrade. We were better off at his house, for although his wife was an Englishwoman, she was quite a good housekeeper.

25*th*, *Tuesday*. We went in search of Mr. Paddechal this morning and paid him for our passage here, twenty shillings New England currency, for each of us. We wanted to obtain our goods, but they were all too busy then, and promised they would send them to us in the city the next day. We inquired after Mr. John Pigeon, to whom Mr. Robert Sanders, of Albany, promised to send Wouter, the Indian, with a letter, but he had received neither the letter nor the Indian; so that we must offer up our poor Indian to the pleasure of the Lord. We also went to look after the ship, in which we were going to leave for London. We understood the name of the captain was John Foy. The ship was called the Dolphin, and mounted sixteen guns. Several passengers were engaged. There was a surgeon in the service of the ship from Rotterdam, named Johan Ovins, who had been to Surinam and afterwards to the island of Fayal, from whence he had come here, and now wished to go home. There was also a sailor on board the ship who spoke Dutch, or was a Dutchman. The carpenter was a Norman who lived at Flushing.

26*th*, *Wednesday*. We strove hard to get our goods home, for we were fearful, inasmuch as our trunk was on deck, and it had rained, and a sea now and then had washed over it, that it might be wet and ruined; but we did not succeed, and Paddechal in this, exhibited again his inconsiderateness and little regard for his promise. We resolved to take it out the next day, go as it would.

27*th*, *Thursday*. We went to the Exchange in order to find Mr. Taylor, and also the skipper, which we did. We agreed for our passage at the usual price of six pounds sterling for each person, with the choice of paying here or in England; but as we would have less loss on our money here, we determined to pay here. After 'change was over there was preaching, to which we had intended to go; but as we had got our goods home, after much trouble, and found several articles wet and liable to be spoiled, we had to stay and dry them.

28th, Friday. One of the best ministers in the place being very sick, a day of fasting and prayer was observed in a church near by our house. We went into the church where, in the first place, a minister made a prayer in the pulpit, of full two hours in length; after which an old minister delivered a sermon an hour long, and after that a prayer was made, and some verses sung out of the psalms. In the afternoon, three or four hours were consumed with nothing except prayers, three ministers relieving each other alternately; when one was tired, another went up into the pulpit. There was no more devotion than in other churches, and even less than at New York; no respect, no reverence; in a word, nothing but the name of independents; and that was all.

29th, Saturday. To-day a captain arrived from New York, named Lucas, who had sailed from there last Friday. He said no ships had arrived there from Europe, and that matters remained as we left them. There was a report that another governor was coming to New York, and it was said he was a man, who was much liked in Boston; that many complaints had been made against the other one, such as oppressing the people, imposing high duties when his instructions provided they should not be more than two per cent, I believe; rendering a false account, in which he had charged a dock as having been made at a cost of twenty-eight pounds sterling which had not cost a cent, as the citizens had constructed it themselves,

&c.[1] This will, perhaps, cause some change in these parts and relieve the people. Lucas brought with him the sister and brother-in-law of Ephraim's wife, recently married, but we had never spoken to them.

30*th*, *Sunday*. We went to church, but there was only one minister in the pulpit, who made a prayer an hour long, and preached the same length of time, when some verses were sung. We expected something particular in the afternoon, but there was nothing more than usual.

JULY 1*st*, *Monday*. We wrote to de la Grange, at New York, concerning our letters from Europe, and also to Robert Sanders, at Albany, in relation to Wouter.

2*d*, *Tuesday*. We had a conversation with the captain at the Exchange. He intended to sail round Ireland, which suited us very well, for although it was said the Hollanders were at peace with the Turks, there were many English vessels taken by them daily, and under such circumstances we ran some danger of being plundered, fighting with them, and perhaps being carried into Barbary. It was, therefore, better to go around, although it would be late. We went on board the ship, with the captain, in order to look through her. She pleased us very much, as she was larger than the Charles, in which we came over. We bespoke a berth in the gunner's room, on the starboard side. The ship was said to be a good sailer, and the captain to be one of the most discreet navigators of this country. All that was agreeable to us. In the evening Ephraim's wife's sister and her husband called upon us, but they were not much in a state to be spoken to, in regard to what was most necessary for them, nor was there much opportunity.

---

[1] These charges against Andros were subsequently to this time officially inquired into. See Lewin's report and Andros's answer in *N. Y. Col. Hist.*, III, 302, 308.

3*d*, *Wednesday*. Our captain said he would leave a week from to-day. Nothing further occurred.

4*th*, *Thursday*. Nothing transpired.

5*th*, *Friday*. In the afternoon Thomas De Key and his wife, half sister of Elizabeth Roodenberg, came to visit us, but we conversed little about religious matters, following the providence of the Lord.

6*th*, *Saturday*. Nothing occurred.

7*th*, *Sunday*. We heard preaching in three churches, by persons who seemed to possess zeal, but no just knowledge of Christianity. The auditors were very worldly and inattentive. The best of the ministers whom we have yet heard, is a very old man, named John Eliot, who has charge of the instruction of the Indians in the Christian religion. He has translated the Bible into their language. We had already made inquiries of the booksellers for a copy of it, but it was not to be obtained in Boston. They told us if one was to be had, it would be from Mr. Eliot. We determined to go on Monday to the village where he resided, and was the minister, called Roxbury. Our landlord had promised to take us, but was not able to do so, in consequence of his having too much business. We, therefore, thought we would go alone and do what we wanted.

8*th*, *Monday*. We went accordingly, about eight o'clock in the morning, to Roxbury, which is three-quarters of an hour from the city, in order that we might get home early, inasmuch as our captain had informed us, he would come in the afternoon for our money, and in order that Mr. Eliot might not be gone from home. On arriving at his house, he was not there, and we, therefore, went to look around the village, and the vicinity. We found it justly called *Rocksbury*, for it was very rocky, and had hills entirely of rocks. Returning to his house we spoke to him, and he received us politely. Although he could speak neither Dutch nor French, and we spoke but little English, and were unable to express ourselves in it always, we managed, by means of Latin and English, to understand each other. He was seventy-seven years old, and had been forty-eight years in these parts. He had learned very well the language of the Indians, who lived about there. We asked him for an Indian Bible. He said in the late Indian war, all the Bibles and Testaments were carried away, and burnt or destroyed, so that he had not been able to save any for himself; but a new edition was in press, which he hoped would be much better than the first one, though that was not to be despised. We inquired whether any part of the old or new edition could be obtained by purchase, and whether there was any grammar of that language in English. Thereupon he went and brought us the Old Testament, and also the New Testament, made up with some sheets of the new edition, so that we had the Old and New Testaments complete. He also brought us two or three small specimens of the grammar. We asked him what we should pay him for them; but he desired nothing. We presented him our *Declaration* in Latin,[1] and informed him about the persons and conditions of the church, whose declaration it was, and about Madam Schurman and others, with which he was delighted, and could not restrain himself from praising God, the Lord, that had raised up men, and reformers, and begun the reformation in Holland. He deplored the decline of the church in New England, and especially in Boston, so that he did not know what would be the final result. We inquired how it stood with the Indians, and whether any good fruit had followed his work. Yes, much, he

---

[1] The justification of his separation from the Walloon church by de Labadie, was published in French, in a small tract which was subsequently enlarged and printed in Dutch, German and Latin, and in the latter language, under the title of, *Veritas sui vindex, seu solennis fidei declaratio. Joh. de Labadie, Petri Yvon et Petri du Lignon, pastorum, &c.*, Hervor, 1672; and afterwards, further enlarged, at Altona.

said, if we meant true conversion of the heart; for they had in various countries, instances of conversion, as they called it, and had seen it amounted to nothing at all; that they must not endeavor, like scribes and pharisees, to make Jewish proselytes, but true Christians. He could thank God, he continued, and God be praised for it, there were Indians, whom he knew, who were truly converted of heart to God, and whose profession was sincere. It seemed as if he were disposed to know us further, and we, therefore, said to him, if he had any desire to write to our people, he could use the names which stood on the title page of the Declaration, and that we hoped to come and converse with him again. He accompanied us as far as the jurisdiction of Roxbury extended, where we parted from him.

9th, Tuesday. We started out to go to Cambridge, lying to the northeast of Boston, in order to see their college, and printing office. We left about six o'clock in the morning, and were set across the river at Charlestown. We followed a road which we supposed was the right one, but went full half an hour out of the way, and would have gone still further, had not a negro who met us, and of whom we inquired, disabused us of our mistake. We went back to the right road, which is a very pleasant one. We reached Cambridge, about eight o'clock. It is not a large village, and the houses stand very much apart. The college building is the most conspicuous among them. We went to it, expecting to see something curious, as it is the only college, or would-be academy of the Protestants in all America, but we found ourselves mistaken. In approaching the house, we neither heard nor saw any thing mentionable; but, going to the other side of the building, we heard noise enough in an upper room, to lead my comrade to suppose they were engaged in disputation. We entered, and went up stairs, when a person met us, and requested us to walk in, which we did. We found there, eight or ten young fellows, sitting around, smoking tobacco, with the smoke of which the room was so full, that you could hardly see; and the whole house smelt so strong of it, that when I was going up stairs, I said, this is certainly a tavern. We excused ourselves, that we could speak English only a little, but understood Dutch or French, which they did not. However, we spoke as well as we could. We inquired how many professors there were, and they replied not one, that there was no money to support one. We asked how many students there were. They said at first, thirty, and then came down to twenty; I afterwards understood there are probably not ten. They could hardly speak a word of Latin, so that my comrade could not converse with them. They took us to the library where there was nothing particular. We looked over it a little. They presented us with a glass of wine. This is all we ascertained there. The minister of the place goes there morning and evening to make prayer, and has charge over them. The students have tutors or masters.[1] Our visit was soon over, and we left them to go and look at the land about there. We found the place beautifully situated on a large plain, more than eight miles square, with a fine stream in the middle of it, capable of bearing heavily laden vessels. As regards the fertility of the soil, we consider the poorest in New York, superior to the best here. As we were tired, we took a mouthful to eat, and left. We passed by the

---

[1] This was the true condition of Harvard college at that time. There was no president. The Rev. Urian Oakes was elected in 1675, but declined then to accept the position. He was reelected in February, 1679, but was not installed until August, 1680. He was the minister of Cambridge, and acted as superintendent of the college before he became president. The number of graduates in 1680 was five, and did not average that number for the ten preceding years.— *Quincy's History of Harvard University*, I, 472.

printing office, but there was nobody in it; the paper sash however being broken, we looked in; and saw two presses with six or eight cases of type. There is not much work done there. Our printing office is well worth two of it, and even more. We went back to Charlestown, where, after waiting a little, we crossed over about three o'clock. We found our skipper, John Foy, at the house, and gave him our names, and the money for our passage, six pounds each. He wished to give us a bill of it, but we told him it was unnecessary, as we were people of good confidence. I spoke to my comrade, and we went out with him, and presented him with a glass of wine. His mate came to him there, who looked more like a merchant than a seaman, a young man and no sailor. We inquired how long our departure would be delayed, and, as we understood him, it would be the last of the coming week. That was annoying to us. Indeed, we have found the English the same everywhere, doing nothing but lying and cheating, when it serves their interest. Going in the house again, Ephraim's brother-in-law, Mr. De Key, and his wife made us a visit.

10*th*, *Wednesday*. We heard that our captain expected to be ready the first of the week.

11*th*, *Thursday*. Nothing occurred.

12*th*, *Friday*. We went in the afternoon to Mr. John Taylor's, to ascertain whether he had any good wine, and to purchase some for our voyage, and also some brandy. On arriving at his house, we found him a little cool; indeed, not as he was formerly. We inquired for what we wanted, and he said he had good Madeira wine, but he believed he had no brandy, though he thought he could assist us in procuring it. We also inquired how we could obtain the history and laws of this place. At last it came out. He said we must be pleased to excuse him if he did not give us admission to his house; he durst not do it, in consequence of there being a certain evil report in the city concerning us; they had been to warn him not to have too much communication with us, if he wished to avoid censure; they said we certainly were Jesuits, who had come here for no good, for we were quiet and modest, and an entirely different sort of people from themselves; that we could speak several languages, were cunning and subtle of mind and judgment, had come there without carrying on any traffic or any other business, except only to see the place and country; that this seemed fabulous as it was unusual in these parts; certainly it could be for no good purpose. As regards the voyage to Europe, we could have made it as well from New York as from Boston, as opportunities were offered there. This suspicion seemed to have gained more strength because the fire at Boston over a year ago was caused by a Frenchman. Although he had been arrested, they could not prove it against him; but in the course of the investigation, they discovered he had been counterfeiting coin and had profited thereby, which was a crime as infamous as the other. He had no trade or profession; he was condemned; both of his ears were cut off; and he was ordered to leave the country.[1] Mr. Taylor feared the more for himself, particularly because most all strangers were addressed to him, as we were, in consequence of his speaking several languages, French, some Dutch, Spanish, Portuguese,

---

[1] On the 8th of August, 1679, a great fire occurred in Boston, in which, says Hutchinson, "eighty odd dwelling houses, and seventy odd warehouses with several vessels, and their lading were consumed to ashes. The whole loss was computed to be two hundred thousand pounds."—*History of Massachusetts*, I, 349. Mr. Drake adds, that by a manuscript record, it appears that at the court of assistants, held on the 2d September following, one Peter Lorphelin, a Frenchman, accused of uttering rash and insulting speeches in the time of the late conflagration, thereby rendering himself justly *suspicious* of having a hand therein, was seized and committed to the jails in Boston. His chest and writings were ex-

Italian, &c., and could aid them. There had also, some time ago, a Jesuit arrived here from Canada, who came to him disguised, in relation to which there was much murmuring, and they wished to punish this Jesuit, not because he was a Jesuit, but because he came in disguise, which is generally bad and especially for such as are the pests of the world, and are justly feared, which just hate we very unjustly, but as the ordinary lot of God's children, had to share. We were compelled to speak French, because we could not speak English, and these people did not understand Dutch. There were some persons in New York, who could speak nothing but French, and very little English. The French was common enough in these parts, but it seemed that we were different from them. Of all this, we disabused Mr. Taylor, assuring him we were as great enemies of that brood, as any persons could be, and were, on the contrary, good protestants or reformed, born and educated in that faith; that we spoke only Dutch and French, except my companion, who could also speak Latin, and had not come here to trade, but to examine the country, and perhaps some morning or evening the opportunity might arrive for us to come over with our families, when affairs in Europe, and especially in Holland, might be settled, as the times there had been bad enough; that if they would be pleased to listen to Mr. Eliot, the minister at Roxbury, he could give them other testimony

---

amined. In his chest were found two or three crucibles, a melting pan, a strong pair of shears to clip money, and several clippings of the Massachusetts currency, and some other instruments. He denied ever having made any use of these things, but said they were given him by a privateer. But on being remanded to jail, he made up another story by which he hoped to clear himself. All, however, to no purpose. He was sentenced to stand two hours in the pillory, have both ears cut off, give bonds of £500 with two sureties, pay charges of prosecution, fees of court, and stand committed till the sentence be performed.— *History of Boston*, 437, note.

concerning us, as we had particularly conversed with him. This seemed in some measure to satisfy him. I think this bad report was caused by some persons who came from New York, truly worldly men, whom we had not sought when we were there, nor they us, and who, although they knew better, or at least ought to have known better, yet out of hatred to the truth, and love of sin, said of us what they conceived, and their corruption inclined them to say. But the Lord who alone knows us rightly will forgive them, and make himself known to them if it pleases him, and then they will know us.

13*th*, *Saturday*. As we had promised Mr. Eliot, to call upon him again, we went to Roxbury this morning. We found him at home, but he excused himself that he had not much time, and had a great deal to do. He called his son, who was there, and who also appeared to be a minister, to speak with us; but we excused ourselves, and said we would not hinder him and would rather leave. However, several questions and reasons passed between us in relation to the Confession which we had given him, and which he praised highly, and in relation to the professors of it, both pastors and people, in regard to which we satisfied him; but the son who was neither as good nor as learned as his father, had more disposition or inclination to ridicule and dispute, than to edify and be edified. We told him what was good for him, and we regretted we could not talk more particularly to him. But the father remarked that if the professors were truly what they declared in the Confession, he could not sufficiently thank God for what he had done. We assured him it was so, and took our leave. He requested us to stop and dine with him, but we excused ourselves.

14*th*, *Sunday*. We went to church, but heard a most miserable sermon by a young person, a candidate.

15*th*, *Monday*. The burgesses drilled and exercised in

the presence of the governor. There were eight companies on foot, and one on horseback, all which divided themselves into two troops or squadrons, and operated against each other in a sham battle, which was well performed. It took place on a large plain on the side of the city. It did not, however, terminate so well, but that a commander on horseback was wounded on the side of his face near the eye, by the shot of a fusil, as it is usually the case that some accident happens on such occasions. It was so in New York at the last parade, when two young men on horseback coming towards each other as hard as they could, to discharge their pistols, dashed against each other, and fell instantly with their horses. It was supposed they were both killed, and also their horses, for there were no signs of life in them; but they were bled immediately, and after two or three hours they began to recover, and in two days were able to go out again. One of the horses died. We went to see John Taylor, and paid him for the wine and brandy. He seemed to have more confidence in us. We gave him to read as further proofs, the letters which Mr. Ephraim Hermans and Mr. John Moll had written to us from the South river, both of whom he knew. He told us the reformed of Rochelle had sent some deputies to the colony of Boston and the independent church there to request the liberty to come over and live in a place near them, or among them, and in their country, which was granted them; and that they returned home three months ago.[1]

16*th*, *Tuesday*. We packed our goods in readiness to leave.

---

[1] We find no allusion to this deputation of the Huguenots of Rochelle, in any of the writers or annalists of New England. In regard to the settlement by the French protestants five or six years later at Oxford, in Massachusetts, see *Dr. Holmes's Memoir in Collections of the Massachusetts Historical Society*, 3d Series, II, 1–83.

17*th*, *Wednesday*. We placed our goods on board ship.

18*th*, *Thursday*. We took leave of Mr. Taylor, thanking him for his attention and kindness, and presented him with a copy of our *Cantiques Sacreés*, for which he was thankful. We would cheerfully have given him the *Maximes*[1] also, but our goods were packed on board the ship, and we could not get at them. He was now of a better mind and well satisfied, returning us our letters with thanks. While we were sitting at table this noon, it thundered very hard, whereupon one of the daughters of the woman of the house where we were staying, commenced to scream and cry. We asked her if she were afraid of the thunder, upon which her mother inquired of us, if we were not. We said no, but the word had scarcely escaped our lips before there came a frightful clap, which seemed to cleave the heart from the body, and entirely changed our ideas. My comrade, Mr. Vorsman, turned as pale as a white sheet, and could hardly speak. I was fearful he had met with some mishap, but he recovered himself. It was said there had scarcely ever been heard there such thunder. One man was killed, and two others not far from being so. These three persons were running in a field, and two of them seeing and hearing the weather lay down flat on the ground under a tree; the third man played stout and brave, jeering at the others who called to him to come with them. Soon the lightning struck him dead to the earth, and separated the other two from each other. There was also a hard rock, not far from our lodgings, split through.

19*th*, *Friday and* 20*th*, *Saturday*. Nothing occurred.

21*st*, *Sunday*. Coming out of the church, Mr. Taylor

---

[1] This work was, an "*Abregé du veritable Christianisme on recœuil des Maximes Chretiennes. Par Jean de Labadie.*" A second edition in French was published at Amsterdam, in 1685.

spoke to us, and invited us to dine with him, but we thanked him.

22*d*, *Monday*. We took our leave, and went on board the ship, which was all ready to sail, except they were waiting for the captain.

23*d*, *Thursday*. After some delay the captain came on board with the rest of the passengers, accompanied by many of their friends. Weighed anchor at three o'clock in the afternoon it being most low water, and set sail with a southwest and south southwest wind. In passing the fort we fired the *salvo*, which it answered; the pilot and the company then left us and we put to sea. But before going further to sea we must give a brief description of New England, and the city of Boston in particular.

When New Netherland was first discovered by the Hollanders, the evidence is that New England was not known; because the Dutch East India Company then sought a passage by the west, through which to sail to Japan and China; and if New England had been then discovered, they would not have sought a passage there, knowing it to be the main land; just as when New Netherland and New England did become known, such a passage was sought no longer through them, but further to the north through Davis and Hudson straits. The Hollanders when they discovered New Netherland, embraced under that name and title, all the coast from Virginia or Cape *Hinloopen*, eastwardly to Cape Cod, as it was then and there discovered by them and designated by Dutch names, as sufficiently appears by the charts. The English afterwards discovered New England and settled there. They increased so in consequence of the great liberties and favorable privileges which the king granted to the Independents, that they went to live not only west of Cape Cod and Rhode Island, but also on Long Island and other places, and even took possession of the whole of the Fresh river [the Connecticut], which the Hollanders there were not able to prevent, in consequence of their small force in New Netherland, and the scanty population. The English went more readily to the west, because the land was much better there, and more accessible to vessels, and the climate was milder; and also because they could trade more conveniently with the Hollanders, and be supplied by them with provisions. New England is now described as extending from the Fresh river to Cape Cod and thence to Kennebec, comprising three provinces or colonies, Fresh river or Connecticut; Rhode Island and the other islands to Cape Cod; and Boston, which stretches from thence north. They are subject to no one, but acknowledge the king of England for their *honor* (*eer*[1]), and therefore no ships enter unless they have English passports or commissions. They have free trade with all countries; but the return cargoes from there to Europe, go to England, except those which go *under the thumb* [secretly] to Holland. There is no toll or duty paid upon merchandise exported or imported, nor is there any import or excise paid upon land. Each province chooses its own governor from the magistracy, and the magistrates are chosen from the principal inhabitants, merchants or planters. They are all *Independents* in matters of religion, if it can be called religion; many of them perhaps more for the purposes of enjoying the benefit of its privileges than for any regard to truth and godliness. I observed that while the English flag or color has a red ground with a small white field in the uppermost corner where there is a red cross, they have here dispensed with this cross in their colors, and preserved the rest. They baptize no children except those of the members of the congregation. All their religion consists in observing

[1] So in the original. Probably *heer* is intended, that is, lord.

Sunday, by not working or going into the taverns on that day; but the houses are worse than the taverns. No stranger or traveler can therefore be entertained on a Sunday, which begins at sunset on Saturday, and continues until the same time on Sunday. At these two hours you see all their countenances change. Saturday evening the constable goes round into all the taverns of the city for the purpose of stopping all noise and debauchery, which frequently causes him to stop his search, before his search causes the debauchery to stop. There is a penalty for cursing and swearing, such as they please to impose, the witnesses thereof being at liberty to insist upon it. Nevertheless, you discover little difference between this and other places. Drinking and fighting occur there not less than elsewhere; and as to truth and true godliness, you must not expect more of them than of others. When we were there, four ministers' sons were learning the silversmith's trade.

The soil is not as fertile as in the west. Many persons leave there to go to the Delaware and New Jersey. They manure their lands with heads of fish. They gain their living mostly, or very much by fish, which they salt and dry for selling; and by raising horses, oxen and cows, as well as hogs and sheep, which they sell alive, or slaughtered and salted, in the Caribbean islands and other places. They are not as good farmers as the Hollanders about New York.

As to Boston particularly, it lies in latitude 42° 20′ on a very fine bay. The city is quite large, constituting about twelve companies. It has three churches, or meeting houses, as they call them. All the houses are made of thin, small cedar shingles, nailed against frames, and then filled in with brick and other stuff; and so are their churches. For this reason these towns are so liable to fires, as have already happened several times; and the wonder to me is, that the whole city has not been burnt down, so light and dry are the materials. There is a large dock in front of it constructed of wooden piers, where the large ships go to be careened and rigged; the smaller vessels all come up to the city. On the left hand side across the river, lies Charlestown, a considerable place, where there is some shipping. Upon the point of the bay, on the left hand, there is a block-house, along which a piece of water runs, called the Milk ditch. The whole place has been an island, but it is now joined to the main land by a low road to Roxbury. In front of the town there are many small islands, between which you pass in sailing in and out. On one of the middlemost stands the fort where the ships show their passports. At low tide the water in the channel between the islands is three and a half and four fathoms deep, in its shallowest part. You sail from the city southeasterly to the fort, by passing Governor's island on the larboard, and having passed the fort, you keep close to the south, then southeast, and gradually more to the east to the sea. On reaching the sea we set our course due east, with the wind south southeast, and made good progress.

24*th*, *Wednesday*. The wind and our course continued the same; but it is to be observed, the compass here is a point and a half northwesting. We spoke an English ship bound to Virginia. We found our latitude 40′ north, and the distance we had sailed 96 miles.

25*th*, *Thursday*. The wind became more southerly, but we held our course the same as before, or east by south. Latitude 42° 68′. Distance reckoned to be 136 miles. The English ship which had remained in company until now, left us. It began to blow so hard in the evening, that we had to reef the topsails and take in the mainsail, and proceed with the mizzensail and foresail.

26*th*, *Friday*. The wind was due south, although it had

been a little more westerly during the night. We observed the latitude 42° 51′; reckoned the distance run 96 miles.

We had stipulated when we engaged our passage, to eat in the cabin, but when we got to sea, we did not do so. There were ten passengers besides us two, and among them two females. These ten had jointly bought a large quantity of provisions and groceries, and placed them in the cabin, they having such power over the captain. We were therefore compelled to remain outside, although we remonstrated. We saw afterwards that it was the Lord's doings, who would not that we should be in nearer communion with such wicked persons. We then arranged to eat with the mate and another passenger above on the half deck. We four brought together what provisions we had, and were well satisfied with each other. We had to-day a good topsail breeze and fine weather.

27*th*, *Saturday*. It was rainy during the night; and although our bunk was in the gunner's room, it leaked in there very much. At sunrise it cleared up a little. We could not obtain any observation, but supposed the latitude was 43°. The course was east southeast, the distance run 100 miles. As it was Saturday evening a hog was killed, there being seven or eight on board the ship.

28*th*, *Sunday*. The weather was fine, with a westerly wind, but not an entirely clear atmosphere.

Among the passengers in the cabin was a minister, an Independent, who had formerly been in the East Indies, at Bantam on the island of Java. He had been visiting his friends in New England, but undoubtedly could not obtain any situation among them, and was returning to England in order to sail if he could in the first ships back to the Indies. This poor minister, every morning and evening, made a prayer, read some chapters out of the Old and New Testaments, and sang a psalm, all after the manner of the Independents. On Sundays he preached both in the morning and afternoon, and we attended in order to avoid scandal and dissipate as much as possible the breath of calumny.

We could not obtain any altitude to-day, in consequence of the haze. Our course had been almost the whole night southeast by east and the course was therefore east by south; the distance was upwards of eighty miles. At noon it became calm, afterwards rainy, and in the evening the wind changed to the northwest, but continued still.

29*th*, *Monday*. We found the height of the pole at noon to-day 43° 29′, as to which another person and myself, who took the height, differed twenty minutes, and others ten. The distance run was forty miles; the course was about east. At noon a strong breeze sprung out of the northwest and we therefore went ahead again on a course east northeast. Gave a ham from our stores to be cooked.

30*th*, *Tuesday*. The wind northwest and our course east southeast. We had run only about eighty miles. Latitude 43° 43′. How unskillfully the steering was managed I cannot say. We supposed we had now passed the island of Sable, and held our course for the banks of Newfoundland. It was quite calm in the evening. We were daily amused at the swimming and tumbling of potshead whales, and the swiftness of the tunnies which are much more numerous here than about Europe; but we observed no other fish.

31*st*, *Wednesday*. The wind east and east by south, but light. Could not sail south southeast as we had done during the night, and at eight o'clock in the morning, we wore ship and were thus enabled to sail about northeast. We took the altitude of the pole above the horizon, and found it 43° 52′. Our whole progress was 32 miles to the northeast. We could afterwards sail east northeast, but made little progress. Towards evening it began to blow a little from the southeast, which caused us to go ahead more.

AUGUST 1*st*, *Thursday*. The beginning of this month brought to mind that we were in this region a year ago. We made good progress last night, east northeast. It was misty and rainy for which reason we could not take an observation. We reckoned we were in 45° 20′ and had sailed 96 miles, being about 100 miles northeast by north from Cape Race. The water was very clear which induced us to believe we were on a bank, not the great bank of Newfoundland, but the bank they call *Banc au vert*. After dinner the deep lead was thrown, as we had done for two or three days previously without sounding bottom. We now found thirty-eight fathoms of water and a bottom of white sand and small pebbles. Every thing was prepared in order to fish, most of the sails taken in, and the rest muzzled. We had at first three hooks and towards the last another, and in about three hours caught one hundred and fifty large codfish, which the captain salted down for the ship's provision. We had fresh fish for a day or two, but the English do not understand how to cook or dress fish. Catching such a large quantity of fish in such a short time, was very exciting; it seemed as if the entire bottom of the sea were covered with them, but you did not see them. Two hooks were constantly being pulled up while the others were being let down. Our hearts could not otherwise than ascend to God, admiring him as the source of such abundance, in the bosom of the wide ocean as well as upon the land, of creatures which he subjects as it were by force, to unworthy and sinful men, who instead of being drawn thereby to him to glorify him and sanctify themselves and these creatures, by their use, to God, are not only not affected at his plenitude and goodness, but misuse such good creatures to the scorn and dishonor of their Creator. I let my thoughts run as they come. I have found this reason for there being so many more fish at these places than at others. Although these banks are from 200 to 250 miles distant from Cape Race, the nearest land, there is, nevertheless, a great stream which can be easily discerned by the eye and is also found by observations in sailing. This current, or stream, coming across the entire sea, as we have shown, by the Caribbean islands, stopping and turning in the Gulf of Mexico, running thence through the channel of the Bahamas, along the coast of Florida, Virginia, New Netherland, New England, and Acadia to this latitude — this great stream, scouring all along the coast, carries with it whatever is found there, of food for fish, and also whatever is discharged into the sea, out of the numerous rivers it passes by, and brings the loose soil, pebbles, rubbish and food to these banks.

The reason why these are stopped here, and washed no further is, because a counter current comes behind Iceland, from Davis and Hudson straits, and from the great river St. Lawrence or Canada, and meet upon the point of Cape Race, and there make whirlpools with each other. In consequence of these whirlpools and choppings, all the stuff for the food of fish is collected together; and as this is constantly brought there by the stream so also are the fish. The codfish feed upon a species of crab or sea spider, and a small fish which lives in the sand, that we call smelt, in Zeeland, where many are taken from the sand on the shores. The bank upon which we caught them is designated on the sea chart by the name of *Banc au vert.*

The wind changed in the evening and blew harder. We therefore left off fishing, and set the sails again. The wind was easterly and we laid our course south, sailing southeasterly, but with short sails. The wind increased so that we had to take in the foresail, and lie by. It seemed as if we were compelled to pay for the pleasure of fishing and fish.

2d, *Friday.* It blew hard all night with a heavy beating of the sea in front. At the head of our bunk in the gunner's room, was a bunk crosswise, before the stem of the ship, and up almost against the deck. In this bunk there was a small window, which the passenger who slept there had forgotten to shut, and through which the water came occasionally upon him in consequence of the rolling of the sea. It came so strong at last that he became frightened, gasping for breath and screaming as if he had fallen into the sea. Indeed he not only thought he was in the sea, but that he alone was sinking. He awakened us all up, but we had to laugh at him.

We had drifted about eight miles north while we were fishing, as the wind was easterly. When the day broke, and after prayer, the mainsail was reefed so that it extended a little over the stem of the ship. Steering southeast with a course south by east or south southeast we reckoned our progress in all twenty-eight miles. At evening it was calmer.

3d, Saturday. Although it was more calm, we remained under short sails, with a frightful jolting and pitching of the ship, in consequence of the sea rolling in front of us, loosening and making every thing crack. In the forenoon the reefs were let out and topsail set, but we did not make much headway. We calculated we had made thirty-two miles, and the latitude was 44° 35′. At three o'clock in the afternoon we wore ship to the north, and laid our course northeast, that is, with the variation, northeast by north. The wind gradually veered to the south and increased some, but the sea was not entirely quiet.

4th, Sunday. Wind southwest, and course same as before. We could not obtain an observation, but reckoned the latitude 44° 6′ and the distance sixty miles. It was very foggy; nevertheless, saw six or eight vessels fishing, which we supposed were French, but we spoke none of them. I had several times suspected that our small stock of wine, which was lying behind our berth, had suffered an attack, for I thought I could perceive it had, as well as our bottle case of brandy; but to-day, after we came from prayer, wishing to tap a little of it, we found it had been touched, and a fourth part of it gone. We were, therefore, compelled to remove both wine and brandy from there and place them in the hut. It seems, while we sat at prayer, they went out in order to play this trick, and had performed it several times. And, therefore, although it was Sunday, we removed them in order that they might be protected from such birds of prey.

5*th*, *Monday*. The course at one time was east by south, and afterwards east. The distance was east sixty-six miles. The wind west northwest and northwest. We could take no observation, and we reckoned the latitude 45° 15′. We had thrown the lead early, and found thirty-eight fathoms of water. The sails were taken in, and we began to fish, but caught nothing. We drifted without any wind, and made little or no progress. In the afternoon we caught a fine codfish, whereupon the sails which had been set, were taken in, in order to fish again, but it was in vain. Several whales came to-day to amuse us by their swimming and tumbling, as a recompense for our catching no fish.

6*th*, *Tuesday*. Fourteen days at sea. We had made little progress during the night, but with the day came a fresh breeze from the south and southwest. We set all our sails and made good headway. It being misty at noon, we were prevented from taking an observation, but calculated the latitude 45°, 50′, and the distance upwards of forty miles. The course was east northeast, that is, northeast by east. The captain supposed we were still on the *Banc au vert*, and had not yet reached the great bank. We threw the lead at evening, although the water was black, but we run out more than 140 fathoms without finding bottom. The reason that our captain was fearful, was because on the land side of the great bank of Newfoundland there are twenty large rocks about sixty miles from Cape Race, lying southeast and northwest, which he last year came very near to, and was in great danger. We were compelled this evening to eat in the cabin, where those wretches laughed at our going upon deck, which we were obliged to do in order not to give them any umbrage, and on the other hand to take care lest we might be like them in any thing.

7*th*, *Wednesday*. The wind and course as before; atmosphere misty, and we therefore could not obtain the altitude. We calculated we were in 47° 10′, and that the distance sailed was 128 miles. In the afternoon, the wind was more westerly, and even northwesterly. We went along tolerably well the whole night.

8*th*, *Thursday*. The ship ran 160 to 168 miles in the twenty-four hours. It blew a storm in the first part of the night from the northwest; but after midnight it subsided, though the sea hove so, that not only was the progress stopped, but the ship tossed and pitched exceedingly.

9*th*, *Friday*. The wind was less at daylight, and the pitching of the ship gradually lessened. Reckoned the latitude 49° 30′, and the distance 140 miles. About midnight the wind shifted to the southwest, and afterwards south southwest, with heavy rain. The course was a little northeast by east, and afterwards in order to keep the ship straight before the wind, northeast by north.

10*th*, *Saturday*. The wind began with the day to subside gradually. The course was laid northeast. We reckoned the distance 120 miles.

11*th*, *Sunday*. It was quite good weather, but cloudy. The captain took an observation as well as he could, which gave 52° 23′. The distance was reckoned 100 miles. The captain and mate took an observation of the north star.

12*th*, *Monday*. The wind west northwest, a light topsail

breeze. Obtained a good observation; and found the latitude 53° 46′, the distance sailed 136 miles, the course held northeast. We were now about 640 miles from Ireland.

13*th*, *Tuesday*. The wind northwest, and north northwest, with a cloudy sky. Course northeast by east. The distance sailed 118 miles.

14*th*, *Wednesday*. Last evening the wind was northeast and north northeast, and we had, therefore, to sail on several courses, but the course held was east by south, and the distance made 60 miles. Although it began to be cold we could endure it the more cheerfully because we were approaching home.

15*th*, *Thursday*. It became quite calm. We obtained an observation at noon, and found the latitude 54° 49′. The distance was 56 miles, and the course held east by south, a little more easterly, but by noon it began to blow so that the topsails had to be reefed. Our passengers, who sat every night, almost the whole night, playing cards, minister and all, had played and drank so this night, that they were at daylight assaulting each other pell mell. They frequently deprived us of sleep. We had to thank God, which we did in our hearts, that he had kept us from being in their company.

16*th*, *Friday*. The wind as before, and the progress good. The course northeast. We obtained a good observation of 56° 20′. The distance sailed was 132 miles. In the afternoon the wind was west and west southwest.

At the time the sea burst into the gunner's room, it ran into the powder room where there was a large quantity of dry fish. This began to rot, and for a long time caused a stench in the gunner's room, the cause of which we could not imagine. We could hardly stay there day or night. There was also lying in the crib a wounded Holsteiner, who had lain sick three years with his wound at Boston, and was now going to Europe. We gave this poor fellow all the blame of the stench, and not altogether unjustly, for he could not help himself much; but, nevertheless, we had done him wrong, for the powder room being opened, all the fish had to be brought up in order to be dried, and those which were spoiled thrown overboard. There was also a large chest of cloaks, all new, which had been taken to the Barbados for sale, and thence to Boston; but were now being carried from Boston to England, because they could not be sold. They were now wet with foul, salt and stinking water, and half spoiled. There was also a case of white braided gloves for women and children, which had to be washed in fresh water and dried, and a large parcel of beaver skins.

17*th*, *Saturday*. I slept very little last night in consequence of the noise. We had sailed during the night a little to the east, because our captain was afraid of falling on the island of *Bus*, as he was not much west of it, though according to our reckoning he was to the east of it. We found our latitude was 57° 30′, and therefore hoped to pass *Bus* and the rock *Rockol*. We sailed on several courses, but the one maintained was northeast by north. The distance sailed was 100 miles. I remained on deck myself, in order to keep a lookout for the great rock *Rockol*.

18*th*, *Sunday*. We took an observation. Latitude 58° 30′. It was very cold here and the days long. The wind continued northeast and north northeast, with hard weather, which caused us to take in our sails, and about ten o'clock in the evening to tack about.

19*th*, *Monday*. We obtained an observation at 57° 51′, and we still more believed we were before the rock *Rockol*, which lies in 57° 40′: but we put our hope and trust in God, committing ourselves into his hands.

20*th*, *Tuesday*. It became gradually more still, and at last we could sail east northeast, and northeast. We had sailed 72 miles. We could not take an observation.

21*st*, *Wednesday*. The wind was northwest, and our course east and east by north, with little headway. We found the latitude 58° 10′; the course held was east by north; the distance 40 miles. We, therefore, supposed we were between *Rockol* and *St. Kilda.* Towards evening the wind shot from the north northwest, so that we could sail east northeast, and afterwards northeast by east; but there was a rolling sea, and, therefore, we could not go ahead much because it came from the front. The wind, however, improved.

22*d*, *Thursday*. The wind was west northwest, and the course northeast by east, with the sea continuing to roll against us in front. We found ourselves at noon in 59° 5′ at which we rejoiced, because we had to enter the North sea between the 59th and 60th degree. The distance sailed was 88 miles upon several courses. At noon the course was set northeast by east in order to sail above the island of little *Barro.* There was a small purse made up by the passengers, each one contributing what he pleased, for the person who should first discover land. We gave two shillings each. The minister would not give any thing. It seems that meanness is a peculiarity of this class of people. This was done, in order that the sailors might look out more zealously for land, and so we might not fall upon land unexpectedly. The purse was nailed to the mast, só that being always in sight, it might be a constant incentive, and whoever might first see land might take it off. We were becalmed the whole night.

23*d*, *Friday*. It was calm, beautiful weather. They thought they saw land; so the sailors said; and that it was Barro; but I could observe nothing. We also had greener water, and, therefore, supposed we were on soundings. The deep lead was thrown, but at 200 fathoms it came short. The latitude was 79° 34′. The wind northeast, and we sailed east, for we were almost in the latitude of the south point of Shetland. We saw several times, quantities of spermaceti drifting, a yellowish fat, which lies in the water, all together, but solid like the green scum, which floats in ditches. We also saw rockweed floating; and a small land bird came on board the ship, from which we concluded we were approaching land. The wind was more free, and after running out and in, it remained north northeast. It blew so hard that the topsails had to be reefed at first, and then taken in. We sailed sometimes east, then east by north and east by south, and again east.

24*th*, *Saturday*. It blew very hard from the north northeast accompanied by rain, and we, therefore, could not ascertain the latitude but reckoned we were in 59° 20′. The course was held half way between east and south, which brought us near the before mentioned rocks. It became calm at night.

25*th*, *Sunday*. It continued calm until noon. We obtained the altitude, 59° 30′. Our progress was 40 miles, and the course a little more north than east. At noon the wind was south and south southeast, with a fresh breeze. We saw this morning a flock of land birds, like finches; also pigeons and small gulls, which keep themselves on the shore. Towards evening it was very foggy. We sailed during the night east southeast.

26*th*, *Monday*. It was tolerably good weather, but it soon came up thick and rainy with a strong wind. We continued sailing east by south. Calculated the distance 56 miles. We kept a good look out, for my reckoning upon the one chart was out and differed from the other only 32 miles. The Lord protects us from disaster, and will guide us further, as we fully trust in him.

27*th*, *Tuesday*. We had not had during the whole voyage such hard weather as during this night. The wind was southeast and south southeast, with a thick mist and rain, which at last made us lie by, with only the mizzen sail, in a hard short sea which tossed and pitched us. We saw all day many land and sea birds which caused us to look out carefully for land. The distance made was 84 miles. At evening the wind was south southwest, whereby we sailed or drifted east by south and south southeast until day.

28th, Wednesday. It was better weather, and we again began to sail. The wind was southwest. The lower sails were well reefed, but we shipped several heavy seas. The sea rolled the whole day. It was lucky for a sailor that the Lord preserved him from being washed overboard by an over-breaking sea; it was a narrow escape, but in floating off he caught a rope or something, to which he clung and was saved. We saw much sea weed, and whole flocks of rock and land birds, and also a species of ducks and geese, besides another kind of bird. Fish lines were made ready, but we could catch nothing. The latitude was 59° 51′, which was a good height and encouraged us. We sailed still east southeast on a maintained east course.

29th, Thursday. While we were at prayer this morning, "Land! Land!" was called out; and although these prayers were so drowsy and miserable, especially for us, who were opposed to their doctrines, I had to restrain and mortify myself by not going up on deck, as several did, and almost all wished to do. It was the gunner who first discovered land, and took from the mast the little purse in which he found 28 shillings and 6 pence sterling, that is, fifteen guilders and fourteen stuivers, a good day's wages. The land we saw was the Orkney islands, 28 to 32 miles south southeast of us which we sketched as well as we could. About two hours afterwards we saw very high land in front of us to the leeward, which we supposed at first was Fairhill, but we soon saw other land in front on the starboard, and we now discovered that the land to the larboard was the rock Falo, and that on the starboard was

Fairhill.[1] I sat on the main yard to observe how the land rose up, and while there, saw a vessel or a sail, which soon caused great consternation on board of our ship, and still more when I said there were two of them. They were afraid they were Turks; and so much did this idea blind them, that eyes, understanding and reason had no office to perform. These small vessels were certainly large ships and Turks. Every thing was put out of the way; many did not know what they were doing from fear, which increased greatly, when they saw one of the vessels coming towards us before the wind. It was all hurly-burly and every one was ordered immediately to quarters. I was very busy, our place being on the quarter-deck where there were four guns, which I pushed into the port holes. These were loaded and we were soon ready for fight. In the meanwhile, the vessel coming nearer, the minister, who should have encouraged the others, ran below into the powder room, all trembling and shaking. He inquired if that was far enough below water, and if he could be shot there. Another person from the East Indies was with him. The surgeon had all things ready for the battle, but unfortunately I looked out and saw it was a Dutch smack with a small topsail, flying the Prince's flag. But they silenced me; Turk it was, and Turk it should remain, and I must go back to my quarters. At last she came along side, and they hailed her, but could not understand what was replied. I was then called upon to speak to them, and I went on the stern and saw it was as I had said. I inquired where they were from, and what they were doing there. They answered, they were from Amsterdam; were cruising in search of two East Indiamen which the chamber of Amsterdam had missed, and they

---

[1] A small island between the Orkneys and the Shetland islands. Several shore line views of it accompany the journal.

wanted to know whether we had seen any thing of them. We informed them we had seen no ships since we were on the banks of Newfoundland, and we were from New England, bound to London. We asked if there were any danger from the Turks. None at all, they said, which gave courage to our captain and others, as well as the minister, who had emerged from the powder room, where he had hidden himself. We also inquired how affairs stood with England, Holland and France. They answered well, as far as they knew. Having obtained this information, I told our captain such good news was worth a salute, and he fired a six-pounder shotted. The Dutch captain asked for a little tobacco in exchange for pickled herrings; but many excuses were offered, and he got none. He said the other vessel was a Hollander from Iceland, and we had nothing to fear; that almost all the ships which we might see in the North sea were ships from Holland; a remark which annoyed our captain and the others very much; and not being able to stand it, they tacked about ship and wore off, leaving the cruiser and passing outside, or between Fairhill and the Orkneys.

30*th*, *Friday*. We had lain over again at midnight, with a south southwest wind. At daybreak it was entirely calm. I was called out of my berth to go to the captain, in order to discriminate the land, distinguishing Fairhill and the Orkneys. He exhibited great ignorance and fear, for we had seen the land well the day before, and the cruiser had fully informed us; he knew well enough how we had sailed during the night, and with what progress, and that we all agreed with the foregoing height of the pole. We took several crayon sketches of Fairhill and the other lands, the more because they are not shown from that side in the *Zeespiegel of Lichtende-Colom.*[1] We found the

[1] *The Sea Mirror or Lightning Column*, a book of sea charts published by

latitude to-day to be 59° 40′. Many birds came round the ship, and some sparrow hawks and small blue hawks, which we caught with our hands. We stretched over again to the Orkneys, in order to be clear of Fairhill; the wind being southeast and southeast by east, we had foggy and misty weather.

31*st*, *Saturday*. We saw the Orkneys this morning, although we had shifted eight miles during the night. We stretched away from them again and discovered a strong current, which the nearer Scotland and the Orkneys it was the stronger it was. It runs mostly east and east southeast, and west and west northwest. The latitude obtained was 59° 26′. At evening we found ourselves about 28 or 32 miles from Fairhill north northeast. This is a beautiful round hill, as its name in English denotes. We held our course with several tacks, over and back, to reach the North sea. We saw several ships but could not get near enough to speak to them.

SEPTEMBER 1*st*, *Sunday*. The weather was misty; the wind as before, calm. Could not obtain the latitude, but we reckoned we had sailed about forty miles, east by south. We saw some herring-busses.

2*d*, *Monday*. The wind continued southeast and south southeast. The weather was good but calm and misty. We calculated the latitude 58° 40′. We kept beating from and to the shore.

3*d*, *Tuesday*. It was still drizzling and calm. We saw several vessels in which we would gladly have been, in order to see if there were no opportunity of going in them to Holland, whither they seemed to be sailing, or at least to obtain some refreshment of fish or something else; but

---

Peter Goos, of Amsterdam, both in Dutch and English. The edition before us is the English one, with the date of 1668.

the captain would not consent. At noon we turned towards the shore and sailed mostly south.

4*th*, *Wednesday*. The wind southeast and south southeast, with dead water as if we were sailing in a river. We had been near the shore all night, on various courses, of one, two and three points difference. We took a good observation, namely, 58° 8′; the distance sailed was sixty miles, the course held south southwest. At noon the water was greener, and we, therefore, supposed we were in deeper water. We saw this morning the four *ockers* [Dutch fishing boats], before mentioned behind us, but we were soon afterwards out of sight of them.

5*th*, *Thursday*. Our course was east by north and east northeast, now a little in, and then again out. The wind was mostly south southwest. We found the latitude 58° 34′, so much were we set north. We had not gone ahead far, as there was not much wind, and the sea rolled directly against us. We reckoned the distance to be at night forty miles. But it was entirely calm, and the wind subsided with mist and rain. We drifted thus all night. The deep lead was thrown at midnight, and eighty fathoms of water were found. We endeavored to catch some fish, but did not succeed. We caught several sparrow hawks and small blue hawks.

6*th*, *Friday*. We had made little progress. The wind was northwest. There was a thick mist with drizzling rain. Our course until noon was east southeast; the latitude was 79°; the distance 104 miles. We spoke an *ocker*, and inquired where we were. He said he was lying on the reef to fish, about 136 miles, he supposed, from New Castle, in Scotland, southwest of him, which agreed well with our calculation. Had 50 fathoms of water. This reef shoots out from the coast of Jutland and runs into the middle of the North sea, northwardly around the Shetland islands, and from thence almost to Rockol, but it lies nearer the Scottish coast than the coast of Norway, and a little more so than is represented on the chart. We caught many birds and also swallows.

7*th*, *Saturday*. It had been very calm through the night; but the wind shifted to the south, and we, therefore, had to change our course continually; at last it was south southeast, and we could not sail higher than west by north. We found the latitude 56° 24′, but could not judge well because the sun was obscured. The reckoning was 55° 55′; the course was south by west; the distance 56 miles. We here came into a whole school of tunnies which afforded us great amusement. We also saw several ships ahead of us, and heard much firing of guns.

8*th*, *Sunday*. Calm and rainy weather. We had made this whole night and from noon yesterday, not more than 28 or 32 miles progress. The course was south southeast sailing over against the wind, in order to come upon the Doggerbank. Saw several vessels, one of which ran before us, over to New Castle. Reckoned at noon to-day we were 40 miles from the Doggerbank.

9*th*, *Monday*. In the morning watch, threw the deep lead in 25 fathoms, sandy bottom, green, white and red. About ten o'clock we had 20 fathoms with the same ground. The atmosphere was thick and hazy. The latitude we supposed was 55° 19′. We were now certainly on the Doggerbank. We caught many young *spier hayties*, which the English call *dogs*, and because large numbers of these fish always keep there, the bank, which is very large and almost makes the figure of a fishing boat, is called the Doggerbank. At four o'clock we had 18 fathoms, and in the evening 17. The course still south southeast, and the wind northeast, breezy and calm, intermingled. In the night the deep lead was thrown several times, and we found 19, 18, 15 and 14 fathoms of water.

10*th*, *Tuesday*. The wind blew from most all points; at

ten o'clock it was northeast and east northeast, with 12, 11, 10, 9½ fathoms of water. The latitude was 54° 44′. We saw several large ships and heard heavy firing of guns which made our captain and others, very serious, for we heard 40 or 50 shots. Seeing a ship behind us, we let the sails run and waited for her. On her approaching us, we found she was a Dutch flute; and when we spoke her, they said they were from Muscovy, bound for Amsterdam. We wished with our whole hearts we were on board of her with our goods, for we would then sooner have been home. There was a rolling sea, so that there was no prospect of being put aboard of her; besides, the captain would not have been willing. They could not tell us much news. We asked where they reckoned they were, and they said not far from where we knew, that they were on the Doggerbank. In the evening we found the water deeper than 20 fathoms, and afterwards 25, at midnight 30, and in the day watch 45, with a bottom of fine sand.

11*th*, *Wednesday*. In the forenoon, found the water more shallow, 25, 23 and 20 fathoms, and we, therefore, believed we had passed from the Doggerbank to the *Welle*, another bank so called. We obtained a good observation, and the latitude was 54° net, the ship's altitude 5′ being deducted, left 43° 55′, which agreed very well with our chart, with the depth, and our reckoning. The distance was put at 40 miles. We saw many ships around us, but could speak none. It continued calm until evening, when we found 20 and afterwards 17 fathom water, over a coarse red and white sandy bottom, mixed with small stones. The course was south southeast.

12*th*, *Thursday*. The latitude 53° 45′, that is the height of our eyes above the water being deducted; the distance 24 miles; the course south southeast, a little southerly. We reckoned we were at the middle of the *Welle* bank. We longed for a good wind, and we were only sixty miles from Yarmouth and 100 or 104 from Harwich. We fished a little, but only caught two or three small codfish, and hauled up with the hook a great quantity of stone and sea weed. In the first watch the wind was north and northeast, with slack water in 15, 14, 17, 19 and 20 fathoms. The captain, therefore, sailed southeast and southeast by south, through fear of the *Lemenoirs* and other Yarmouth shoals.

13*th*, *Friday*. It blew a stiff topsail breeze. We had 17 and 18 fathoms of water, which looked quite white, and made me think we were near the White water, another bank so named, on which there is 17 and 16 fathoms. We sailed south southwest. We waited for a herring-bus coming towards us, and spoke to her. She was from Rotterdam, had been to sea a long time, and had seen no land. They told us they were between Wells and the White water, nearer the latter, and that South Foreland was south southwest of us. They could tell us nothing more. We wished we were in the bus, for then we might have been in the Maes that evening, as she had a good wind. The latitude was 52° 50′. We sailed southwest in 23 fathoms of water, with a bottom of fine sand a little reddish and mixed with black. In sailing towards the shore we had 18 fathoms; when about three, or half past three o'clock in the afternoon they cried out, land! and proceeding further on, we saw the grove near Yarmouth, and shortly afterwards Yarmouth steeple, southwest by west and west southwest from us. We sailed more southerly and discovered the whole coast. We came to anchor about seven o'clock in 16 fathoms.

14*th*, *Saturday*. It had been good weather through the night, and we had rested well. We saw when the sun rose, which shone against the coast and was entirely clear, how the coast ran. The land is not so high as it is west of the Thames to Land's End. There are many villages.

Yarmouth looked like a pleasant little place, as it lay north northwest of us. We saw many ships sailing one way and the other. Having waited for the ebb to run out we got under sail about eight o'clock. We sailed by *Sowls*,[1] and came to anchor again about three o'clock in the afternoon. The passengers had every thing ready to go ashore, and so over land to London. There was a signal made with the flag from our ship, and a shot fired for a pilot or some one else to come on board. Towards evening a small boat came with five men, but no pilot. The flood making about nine or ten o'clock in the evening, and running along the whole Scottish and English coast, from the Orkneys to the Thames, we sailed on again until we came to another village where our passengers went ashore. It was about midnight. The weather was fine and the moon shone bright; we fired five or six guns. The minister was sad and complained that it was Sunday, or Saturday evening, and he dared not go ashore, lest he should break the Sabbath; but finally he let his wishes override his scruples, and went off with the passengers. We obtained a pilot and some refreshments, and then sailed on till we came before Dunwich,[2] the oldest place in England, and once the mightiest in commerce. We came again to anchor in order to wait for the tide. The wind continued west southwest.

15*th*, *Sunday*. The wind mostly as before. We were under sail about ten o'clock, with the flood tide, and

---

[1] Southwold, a small seaport town on the east coast of England, 94 miles northwest of London. Southwold or Sole bay was the scene of the great naval battle between the Dutch, under De Ruyter, and the English and French, under the Duke of York and Marshal d'Estrees, in May, 1672.

[2] This town appears in old times to have been a great place of commerce in herring. In the year 1195, it was obliged to deliver 24,000 herrings to the king. Its importance has been entirely destroyed by incroachments of the sea upon its harbor.— *McCulloch.*

tacked along the land in seven fathoms of water to the point of Aldborough, to reach which we made five or six short tacks. Running close to the shore, we came among a fleet of, I think, full 200 coal ships, all beating up the river, which made it difficult to avoid each other. We passed through the King's channel. I have never seen so many sunken ships as there were in the mouth of the Thames, full eight or ten in different places, from various causes. The tide being spent we came to anchor before a village called St. Peter.

16*th*, *Monday*. The wind being mostly north, the weather was cold and piercing. The whole fleet was under sail, with the flood tide, and we along with them. They had talked loudly in Boston of the sailing qualities of our ship, but almost the whole coal fleet sailed ahead of us.

18*th*, *Wednesday*. The wind remained still, with mist. We saw it would be some days yet before the ship would reach the city, and, therefore, determined to go up in a wherry, that is, a row-boat, from Gravesend. As soon as one came along side we went aboard, and passed by Gravesend, and other villages. It was nine o'clock in the evening when we landed at St. Catharines, and went to a tavern called the Dutch Smack, but they would not receive us. We then went to the Inlander, the landlord of which was a Fleming, and a papist, but not the worst one. We paid for the boat three English shillings in all. We three, namely, *Vorsman*, Jan Ovins, the surgeon of our ship, a Rotterdammer, and myself, supped together; this was the first time we had slept in a bed in a long time.

19*th*, *Thursday*. We went through the city, the newly built portion, as well as the other, but we found it very different from what we had imagined. We went to the Exchange and conversed with our captain and the other passengers. We endeavored to find the first vessel going to Holland. They told us there were two smacks or galiots lying ready, and would leave on Monday, for which we prepared ourselves.

20th, Friday. We went to Whitehall, where the king resides, and where we supposed we would see something special in the buildings, but in this we were mistaken. There are better places in London; the best house there was the banqueting house, which does not surpass some merchants' houses in Amsterdam. We strolled into St. James's Park, which is nothing but a large inclosed meadow, with some canals and ditches dug through it, in one portion of which are ducks swimming, and willow trees planted. The guard on horseback coming ahead, we heard the king was in the park. We went in, but did not see him; but walking through we saw his curiosities of birds which he kept there in cages slightly enough closed, such as eagles, cranes, a very large owl, a toucan, birds which we call *hoontjen*, in Friesland, *virviteaus*, doves, starlings, and others of little importance. He had received from the Indies, by the last ships, two ostriches or cassowaries which were shut up and much prized, though they are very common in Holland. We came to his horse stable; there was only one horse in it, that was so lean it shamed every one, as also did the small size of the stable, which stood near that of the Duke of Monmouth, where there were six tolerable good Frisic horses, with a saddle horse or two. Our stables look more kingly than these. We were about leaving the place when we heard them cry out, "to arms! to arms!" to a troop of soldiers standing there, and looking around, we saw at a distance the king coming, accompanied by six or eight noblemen, from whom you could distinguish him only from his having his hat on his head, while they had theirs off. He saluted all who saluted him, as he passed along, which he also did us. I will not speak of his person as he has been sufficiently described by pen and *burin*.[1] Nor will I speak of the condition of London. The long and short of it is, that city is larger than Amsterdam, but does approach it, or any other city in Holland, either in neatness or in the regularity of the buildings, even those erected since the great fire. What are worthy of mention is a certain column, very high and well constructed, erected on the spot where the great fire broke out in 1666, and the tower, not prettily built, but very old, constructed by the Romans in the time of Julius Cæsar. Whitehall and Westminster, and all within them, are not worth going to see.

31*st*, *Saturday*. Our ship having arrived before the city yesterday, we went on board to bring away our goods, as also did the surgeon. We took leave of the captain, mate and carpenter, who was a young man and a Norman, stupid, but not the most evilly disposed. He had our love, and I had occasionally conversed with him when we were on the watch together at night, and sometimes made an impression upon him. He lived at Flushing, and wished, he said, he could go and live with me even for nothing. He desired me not to forget him. I must also say this of the captain, that he was well known in London, and in all Boston, as a pious, good and discreet man; but I was astonished when I saw and heard the following circumstance. A poor servant, who had served his time out in New England, came to him in Boston and asked if he could go over with him; he would do his best in working like any other sailor for his passage, as he well understood ship-work. The captain told him he might go with him. When we were at sea, this person was sick several days, and when he recovered did as well as he could, but, it is true, he did not do all that an experienced sailor could have done. When we arrived in the North sea the captain made

[1] Charles II.

a memorandum by which this poor fellow promised to pay half the passage money, that is, thirty guilders, when he arrived in London. He called him, and read it to him, and told him, because he could not work like a good sailor, he must sign that writing, and if he did not do so, he would sell him again when he reached London, which he assured him would be done. The man began to complain and cry, saying he had not so promised, but he would work like any other, and do as well as he could. But, notwithstanding his crying and objecting, he had to sign the paper, or be sold. In this, appeared the piety and sense of justice of our captain, though perhaps the other was not entirely without blame, though he had had blows enough. It seems he had some friends in London who paid the amount.

I must here mention another word about Boston, which is, that I have never been in a place where more was said about witchcraft and witches. From time to time persons had been put in prison, and executed; and a woman was in prison and condemned to die, when we left there.[1] Very strange things were told of her, but I will not repeat them here.

22*d*, *Sunday*. I went into the Dutch church where a young man, who was a Cocceian, preached. In the afternoon we went to the French church, and in going there, passed by a large gate, through which many people were entering into a great hall. We looked in, and when we saw they were quakers, walked quickly away, and went

---

[1] On the 20th May, 1680, Elizabeth Morse, the wife of William Morse, of Newbury, was indicted and tried in Boston, for practicing with craft upon her own husband. She was convicted and sentenced to be hung; and was in prison at Boston, at the time our journalist was there, awaiting her execution. It is, undoubtedly, her case to which he refers. She was, however, reprieved from time to time, and finally released altogether.—*Coffin's Newbury*, 122, 126, 134.

into the French church, whose congregation is much larger, and its church much smaller than the Dutch church — so small indeed, they could not all get in. When, therefore, the Lord's Supper was administered, they used the Dutch church, and the Dutch preached then in the French church, as they are not far apart. But as the French church was especially for the French, we went out, my comrade for the purpose of inquiring after Mr. Ovins, and I, to go to the Dutch church again, where another Cocceian preached well enough. I saw there the envoy from Holland, a Zeelander, whom I knew with his family; but he did not know me.

23*d*, *Monday*. It was said we were to leave to-day, but we saw it would not be the case. The captain, with whom we were to go, was one Douwe Hobbes of Makkum, who brings birds over from Friesland, every year for the king. There was a boat lying there ready to leave for Rotterdam, but it seems they intended to go in company.

24*th*, *Tuesday*. No departure to-day either. While we were at the Exchange, there was a great crowd of people in the street. We saw and heard two trumpeters, followed by a company of cavalry, dressed in red, then a chariot drawn by six horses, in which was the Duke of York. Then came some chariots of the nobility, and the Prince Palatine, with several chariots, and two trumpeters in the rear.

25*th*, *Wednesday*. Could not sail yet, but the Rotterdammer sailed with thirty passengers, with little or no freight. In going down she broke the bowsprit of our ship. Mr. Ovins left us in her, after we had taken leave of him.

26*th*, *Thursday*. Heard early this morning our ship was going down the river, for she lay opposite our room; we immediately hurried ourselves. It was very uncivil in the mate, for the captain was still in the city, and would go to

Gravesend. We took a wherry and went after her, as she had not gone far in consequence of the mist and lightness of the wind. We drifted to-day scarcely outside of the ships.

27*th*, *Friday*. It was misty and calm. We, therefore, did not go as far as the current would have carried us. We had to come to anchor, in consequence of the mist, in order not to drift against the ships, or upon the shoal.

28*th*, *Saturday*. We drifted and clawed along until we came to anchor, before Gravesend, as the Rotterdammer did an hour or two afterwards. Ovins, who was not very well accommodated, called out to us as we passed, and asked if we would not go ashore with him. We declined, for we could not have wished to have been better accommodated, as we two had a large, fine cabin to ourselves.

29*th*, *Sunday*. When we took our goods out of the ship at London, we let our trunks be examined, but there was nothing inspected. We gave the inspectors a penny and they were satisfied. Our skipper arrived now at Gravesend in the night, and had every thing made ready for the inspectors. We had ourselves ready for their arrival. They came on board about eight o'clock, but they looked once only in the hatches without asking any thing, and went away again. We went ashore in the forenoon and dined there. We had been to London, and the captain said we should eat the ship's ordinary fare, which seemed now to us, princely fare. However, as he was most of the time drunk when on shore, he had given it no consideration. We went through Gravesend to look at it, but it does not signify much — it is more foul and dirty, in name, than in fact. We also went out into the country a little, which pleased us best. I have never seen anywhere, so many blackberries, which were now ripe. The ebb tide having come, we got under sail yet before evening, the wind being good, but it did not continue so long. Opposite Gravesend, there is a strong castle well fortified, and another one of less importance, on the lower side. Whenever ships pass up or down; they must strike here in going between the two fortifications. We arrived at evening before the river of Chatham, where we anchored.

30*th*, *Monday*. The wind was easterly and light. We scratched along as far as to get in the King's channel, as also did the Rotterdammer, which sailed down with us.

OCTOBER 1*st*, *Tuesday*. The wind as before; we, therefore, tacked with the tide, before the Naze, intending to run into Harwich, both for the purpose of waiting for a good wind, and to buy a store of provision which the skipper, through his drunkenness had forgotten. The Rotterdammer, which had not kept along the shore with us, but had continued through the King's channel, finding no good harbor there, returned again to Chatham, in order, as the wind continued south southeast, to go out along the south shore, and thus we separated.

2*d*, *Wednesday*. The wind still easterly, we, therefore, made several tacks, and ran into Harwich; a miserably poor little fort stands on the east point of the bay, yet you must strike your flag as you sail by it. The bay is large and suitable to harbor a great number of ships. The town is on the west side, passing which, a small river runs up into the land. We anchored about ten o'clock in the morning. We went ashore and dined, and I then, in company with some others, walked out of town; but my comrade returned, having concluded to cross over in the packet boat, and went to inquire about it. When I returned he told me it would leave that evening, and would save much time. He spoke to our skipper, who was not willing to release us, without paying him the whole passage money, namely, two ducatoons a piece. Many words passed and hard enough they were on both sides, in which the skipper was very impertinent, yet not altogether in the wrong. We went aboard, and his passion having subsided, we satisfied him with two ducats, and took our goods to the packet boat. We went ashore to enter our names, according to the custom; *my comrade giving his acknowledged name, I was compelled to do the same.* We paid twelve shillings and six-pence each. We went into another room to take fresh leave of our captain and mate, when there came a scoundrel to take down our names, and examine our goods as he said, and we were compelled to give the same names again, in order they might agree with those given before; but he was a swindler and obtained from each of us another shilling, for he did not go on board to examine, although he could perhaps do so; we went quickly on board to look after our property. It was about nine o'clock at night when we started; but as it was so calm we came outside without casting anchor, having a full moon and delightful weather. A sand reef stretches out into the sea from the before mentioned little fort, inside of which the water is the deepest, being three and four fathoms at low water. It is shallowest in the middle, and level towards the west shore, having two fathoms of water or less. There are two lights in the town, which you bring in range, in order to sail in or out. The highest light stands most inside, and when that comes west of the lowest you are west of the gate or channel; and when it is east, you are east of the channel, and are on, or east of the reef.

3*d*, *Thursday*. The wind east southeast, and we, therefore, sailed along the shore past Orfordness into the sea. The course thence to the Maes, is east by south, but we sailed for the most part east, and sometimes east by north. I thought our Friesland smack was at sea before evening, for the wind was better for her than for us, as the course from Orfordness to the Texel, is east northeast, which was a due side wind. It was also better for the Rotterdammer.

4th, Friday. The wind east southeast and east by south, but still. We continued our course easterly, and sometimes a little more northerly. We threw the deep lead and had 18 fathoms of water. The latitude at noon was 52° 25′. I warned them that we were too low, and would come before *Schevelingh.* This packet was so full of fleas that it was impossible for me to sleep. Every passenger who desired a berth, had to pay five shillings for it, but we did not. There was such a hard rain in the night, accompanied by thunder and lightning, that we could not keep dry in the vessel below, for it leaked there as if it were open, or not much better. We had an English minister on board, who had been called to the English church at Rotterdam. He lay and prayed, and groaned, as hard and loud as if he would die of fear.[1] The wind shifting to the southwest we held it close.

5th, Saturday. When day came, and it had cleared up some, we saw at nine o'clock the tower of *Schevelingh,* directly east, or in front of us, and half an hour afterwards that of Gravesend to the leeward, whereupon, we were compelled to beat, in order to bring into the Maes, which we continued to do the whole day till midnight, before we reached Briel. Coming to the pier there, most of the passengers left for Maassluis, so as not to wait, but we could not do so on account of our goods.

6th, Sunday. As soon as it was day we put our goods on board the Rotterdam ferry-boat, which was to leave about nine o'clock. In the meanwhile, we went to look about the place, and in the church, where a Cocceian preaches. After breakfast we went on board, but it was ten o'clock before we got off. We had to beat as far as Schiedam,

[1] The Rev. John Spademan, of Swayton, in Lincolnshire, was called to the English Presbyterian church at Rotterdam, as successor to Mr. Maden, who died in June, 1680.

where some royal yachts were lying, which had sailed with us from Gravesend, and had brought over the Prince Palatine, who had gone on to the Hague. We were delayed somewhat here, in consequence of transferring some persons into another boat. We reached Rotterdam about two o'clock, and were informed that no boat carrying goods left for Amsterdam on Sundays; but that one left Delft at six o'clock, and we had time enough to go there. We left our goods on board the *treck-schuit*, for Delft, and started at three o'clock for that city, where we arrived at five, and learned we had been misinformed, and the boat from Delft to Amsterdam, left daily at four o'clock. We had to go and lodge in a tavern for twenty-four hours. We went to church.

7th, Monday. In order not to be all day at Delft, we walked on to the Hague, and passed by the house of my sister *d'Owerk.* I asked my comrade whether I should not inquire after our friends, and if perchance any of them were at the Hague; but he would not consent. We returned to Delft at two o'clock, and after dinner left at four for Amsterdam.

8th, Tuesday. Having passed through the night as best we could, we arrived at five o'clock in the morning before the gate of Amsterdam, which was opened at six, and we were admitted. We went close by the house of M. Bardewits,[1] where I was again inclined to go in, but my comrade not approving of it at the Hague, I abandoned the

[1] Of this person, we find the following mention by Jacobus Koelman. Before de Labadie left Amsterdam for Herford, "he persuaded a merchant at Amsterdam, who had heard him much, and had been his interpreter, to preach or lecture to three hundred, he said, in his own house, after the manner of the Christians in the church at Corinth, 1 Cor., xiv. This man having no mission or calling to the ministry, was nevertheless to proclaim the word in his house to those who might withdraw from the church but did not go away with Labadie. And so to this day, such meetings of the

idea. We put up at the inn where we lodged before our departure, and had our goods brought there, paying five shillings freight for our goods alone. We separated in order to do our business as speedily as possible. I went to deliver all the letters, and my comrade to sell the amber. We met on the Exchange at noon. When I had delivered my letters, I went to the boat for Sneek,[1] to inquire how it was at the house,[2] and when she would sail. They would leave on Thursday evening; and all went well at the house as far as they knew. My comrade who had also made inquiries, brought the same word. He told me also how he had succeeded with the amber; that it was all spurious, and was worth nothing. He, therefore, had determined to send it back again just as we had received it. We went in the afternoon to perform some errands for the woman with whom we had lodged at New York, delivering two beaver skins to her husband's daughter. And with this we consumed the day.

9th, Wednesday. This was a day of public prayer. We had nothing more to do except to buy a large Bible for Mr. Ephraim Hermans, according to our promise, with his spermaceti, which we did. It cost us twenty-eight guilders, because it was the last one of Ravesteyn's edition. There was a new edition in press at the Fish Market, at the place where we bought this one, upon the point of the gate as you go to the Post office. We put it on board of the ship of which *Jan Gorter* was captain and which would

---

separatists are held in the house of this merchant, named *Bardewits*, who not pretending to be a minister, nor daring to administer the sacraments of baptism and the Lord's supper, every Sunday morning and afternoon preaches after the manner of the public ministers, to a number of persons who seldom, or ever go to the public assemblies, as if he only had gifts and grace."—*Historisch Verhaal*, 96–7.

[1] In Friesland near Wiewerd.

[2] Thetinga-State, or Walta House, the residence of the community.

leave in a month's time, and addressed it to Mr. Arnout de la Grange, to whom we also sent the amber with directions what to do with them. My comrade wrote to Ephraim, and also to Annetie Versluis.

10*th*, *Thursday*. We had our goods in good time in the boat. My comrade had also a basket with distilling glasses (retorts) in it, which he had bought. I went to Joannis Van Ceulen, mathematician, who had made a new sea-atlas, a copy of which he had sent to the king of England, and also to the king of France. It is a beautiful work; but he was surprised, after having corrected it so much as he had, that I should point out to him several errors. I endeavored to obtain a chart of Maryland, from Augustine Herman's draught, but could not find it here; nor could I in England. At four o'clock we went on board of the boat. The wind was light and contrary, so we only drifted along. It was good weather. Our hearts gave thanks to God when we reflected through what ways he had conducted us, and how fatherly he had preserved us, and brought us here. There sprung up a breeze in the night, so that,

11*th*, *Friday*, in the morning, we passed by Urk,[1] and arrived at the Lemmer, where our goods were examined; but we had nothing to pay, and went on. It was so calm, with the wind contrary, that it was midnight before we arrived at Sneek. It was very dark and rainy, and we were fearful we could not find the way, else we would have gone to *The House* in the night.

12*th*, *Saturday*. Having given directions to our skipper, how he should send our goods after us, and having paid him, we went to speak to the boatman, who was to take the goods. It was about seven or half-past seven o'clock when we left Sneek on foot. After going some distance

[1] A small island in the Zuider zee, near the shore of Friesland.

on our way, we passed through Bosum; and about ten o'clock reached our house, where all arms and hearts were open to receive us, which they did with affection and tenderness, in the love of the Lord, who had been with those who had remained at home, and us who had traveled, all now brought together, and united by his mercy. To him be the power, and wisdom, and honor, and glory to all eternity. Amen.

FINIS.

INDEX.

LIST OF PLATES.

PLATE I.—FISHES, INDIAN WOMAN.

Translation of the memorandum at the top of this plate. "Although the Banks of Newfoundland are represented on the increasing degree chart, where the shoals are, yet it is probable they are larger, at least towards the south, as the water indicates even as far as 38° or 37°; and also that there are several smaller shoals which lie deeper and which are not represented on the chart."

The uppermost fish (mentioned p. 69, of the journal) is most probably the *Gempylus serpens*, first figured in *Sloanes's Jamaica*, plate 1, fig. 2, and to which the name of *Scomber serpens*, was given by Dr. Solander, who captured one three feet long in Sept., 1768, near the Canary islands. His description, still in manuscript, in the Banks Library, is quoted by Cuvier, *Histoire des Poissons*, vol. viii, p. 211, where another species is also described, from the Pacific. It is a rare fish, and it seems that no specimen of it is preserved in museums.

Another rare fish somewhat resembles this one, the *Alepidosaurus ferox*, first described and figured by the Rev. R. T. Lowe in the *Proceedings and Transactions of the Zoological Society of London*, in 1833, as from the Atlantic near Madeira. The first mentioned species has the finlets in advance of the tail, as represented in the figure, which this last has not. The faint indication of ventral fins in the figure would however make it an *Alepidosaurus*, but the long anal and the finlets are more like *Gempylus*.

The middle figure of this plate, marked *Dolphyn*, is the common dolphin of the Atlantic, the *Coryphaena hippurus*, of Linnæus. In the text, mention is made of these fish on pages 81, 82, 83, 85 and 86.

The lowest figure marked *Pici porck*, is the Pig fish or Trigger fish, the *Balistes vetula*, or perhaps the *Capriscus*, of Linnæus; a well known fish, about a foot long, found in the banks of floating sea weed, with a hard scaly skin, and with two spines on the back, a peculiarity in the articulation of which, gives the fish its name of Balistes. The longer forward spine, namely, A, cannot be depressed until the small hinder one B has been pushed down. This rigid defensive weapon, no doubt, prevents larger fish from swallowing it. This curious property of these spines is described on the plate as follows: "Caught in latitude 37°, 240 miles east of Maryland. The horns A and B can be laid flat on the back to C, where there is a hollow in the back in which the horns are placed; but they cannot be raised up more than is denoted in the figure. Whenever they stand up in that manner they cannot be pressed down at A, unless B be pushed down to C, when A falls as far as B is pressed down; like the lock of a gun or a fire-lock when it is shot off."

Several other fish are mentioned in the narrative. The one described as a *Sea cat*, page 63, was probably a small *Blennius;* the large *Sea pike*, page 71, was perhaps a Sword fish, the *Xiphias gladius* of Linnæus, and the one described as a Sea hedge hog, page 91, was either an *Antennarius*, or a *Malthea*, both of which have something like the limbs or paws of a quadruped. The other fish mentioned are too common to require further notice.

II.—VIEW OF THE ENTRANCE AT SANDY HOOK FROM FORT HAMILTON.

Mentioned on page 129 of the journal. The following is a translation of the note:

"Views of the land on the southerly and southwesterly sides of the great bay between the Neversincks and Long Island, 24 miles from New York.

"A. Coney island. B. The gate [or opening] to enter. C. Sandy hook. D. Rensselaer's hook, [now the Neversink highlands.] E. Some trees serving as a land mark, [probably on a line with Pigeon hill.]

"In order to sail in between the shoals, keep S. S. W. from them. [that is, close to the Hook.] D. E. F. The land called the Neversinckx. F. Kil van kol.

"All as it appears from Jacques [Cortelyou's] house at Najak [Fort Hamilton] on Long Island."

The bank drawn on the right is the West bank. Porpoises are still common in the bay, but whales, at that time frequently captured along our coast, are now rarely seen.

III.—VIEW OF NEW YORK FROM THE SOUTH-EAST.

This view, taken from Brooklyn heights, will prove exceedingly interesting to the local antiquarians of New York, from the number of details which are given of the city as it was in 1679. The draughtsman has tried to copy what he saw, with minute accuracy and without the least attempt to produce any effect. The city was at this time just beginning to creep beyond the palisades on Wall street, which for fifty years had bounded it on the north. It is unnecessary here to describe the different details represented, which, no doubt, will be studied and compared with other views and with plans and documents of the period. We merely draw attention to the accuracy of the view as proved by the fact that one block, the left hand one in the view, with thirteen houses, corresponds precisely with the plan given in *Valentine's Manual of the Corporation of New York*, which shows fourteen lots on the same block, fronting on Pearl street or the *Heere graft*. The middle house in the view occupies two of these lots, testing therefore the precision of the drawing. The fort with its church, the dock, the Stadthuys, the halfmoon forts, the guard house at the water gate, foot of Wall street, the ship yards, and the windmills on the hill near the corner of the present Fulton street and Broadway, are all to be seen in this curious sketch. From it an enlarged view of the Stadthuys, once the city tavern, has been made, and is given on plate VIII.

IV.—VIEW OF NEW YORK FROM THE EAST.

This, view looking along the shore of the East river, appears to have been taken from a point near the corner of the present Fulton and Water streets. It shows the north side of the dock, the water gate from the north, and the shipping. The church and Stadthuys are not distinctly seen, as the sketch was probably taken from near the water level. A portion of this sketch has been used in compiling the view on plate IX.

V.—VIEW OF NEW YORK FROM THE NORTH.

This was probably taken from two points, in order to show as much as possible of the south end of the island and of the North river. This has caused some confusion in the perspective and in the line of horizon, which is sought to be rectified in the compiled sketch on plate VII.

It appears to have been taken in part from near the head of the present John or perhaps Fulton street. The buildings near the Bowling green north of the fort, are hidden by the fall of the land there towards the Battery, and but little is seen of the main portion of the city along the East river from a similar reason, the slope towards the river. Broadway is a mere country road with fields open to the North river on the right, and but few houses on its east side.

One of the windmills was put up before 1664, and the other (the upper one), shortly after the transfer of the colony to the English.

The wagon appears to be turning down the Magdje Pad or Maiden Lane.

This is the only view of New York on the North river side at this early period, known to us, except that in Hartger and Vanderdonk.

VI.—MAP OF THE SOUTH OR DELAWARE RIVER FROM THE FALLS TO BURLINGTON.

From a plan accompanying the manuscript. It is mentioned at page 255 of the journal.

The preceding plates are in *fac simile* of the original drawings accompanying the manuscript. The following are new drawings, rectifying some portions of them; except the last, which is a view of the present appearance of the De Hart house at Gouanes, where the travelers were entertained and the Indians held their cantecoy. See pages 122, 264, 273 of the journal.

VII.—VIEW OF NEW YORK FROM THE NORTH.

Restored from the original sketch on plate V.

VIII.—THE STADTHUYS OF NEW YORK IN 1679.

Corner of Pearl St. and Coentys Slip.

This has been taken from the original sketch on plate III. It corrects in some points the appearance of this building, as given in *Valentine's Manual of the Corporation* and presents a life-like picture of the north-west portion of the city dock and its surroundings, all the material for which is to be found in the above mentioned sketch.

Erected as a city tavern in 1642, it was converted to the purposes of a City Hall in 1655, and was finally torn down in 1700. The small half moon fort in front of it once projected out into the river.

IX.—NORTH VIEW OF THE DOCK, NEW YORK, 1679.

Being a part of the original sketch No. IV.

X.—THE WATER GATE, FOOT OF WALL ST., NEW YORK, 1679.

Also from the original sketch, No. IV.

XI.—THE EAST RIVER SHORE NORTH OF THE WATER GATE, NEW YORK, 1679.

Taken from sketches Nos. III and IV.

XII.—THE DE HART HOUSE, ON GOUANES BAY.

As it appears in 1867.

VIEWS MENTIONED IN THE TEXT BUT NOT FOUND ACCOMPANYING THE MANUSCRIPT.

VIEWS OMITTED.

VOYAGE TO NEW YORK.

MEMOIRS

OF THE

Long Island Historical Society.

VOLUME I.

JOURNAL

OF A

VOYAGE TO NEW YORK IN 1679–80

BROOKLYN, N. Y.:
PUBLISHED BY THE SOCIETY.
1867

SANFORD PUBLICATION FUND.

COMMITTEE ON PUBLICATION.

RICHARD S. STORRS, JR., D.D.
ALDEN J. SPOONER,
J. CARSON BREVOORT,
THOMAS W. FIELD,
CHARLES E. WEST, LL.D.

EDITION.

1,000 COPIES, OCTAVO.
100 COPIES, ROYAL OCTAVO.

MUNSELL, PRINTER, ALBANY.

OFFICERS

OF THE

Long Island Historical Society.

1866 – 67.

President,	J. CARSON BREVOORT.
First Vice-President,	JOHN GREENWOOD.
Second Vice-President,	CHARLES E. WEST.
Foreign Corresponding Secretary,	HENRY C. MURPHY.
Home Corresponding Secretary,	JOHN WINSLOW.
Recording Secretary,	A. COOKE HULL.
Treasurer,	GEORGE S. STEPHENSON.
Librarian,	GEORGE HANNAH.

DIRECTORS.

J. CARSON BREVOORT,
R. S. STORRS, Jr., D.D.,
A. ABBOTT LOW,
CHARLES E. WEST, LL.D.,
JOSIAH O. LOW,
CHARLES CONGDON.
MILAN HULBERT,
THOMAS W. FIELD,
A. COOKE HULL, M.D.,
JOSHUA M. VAN COTT,
A. N. LITTLEJOHN, D.D.,
JAMES H. PRENTICE,
JOHN WINSLOW,
S. B CHITTENDEN,
HON. JOHN GREENWOOD,
GEORGE S. STEPHENSON,
HON. HENRY C. MURPHY,
WILLIAM POOLE,
HENRY SHELDON,
ETHELBERT S. MILLS,
W. I. BUDINGTON, D.D.,
ELIAS LEWIS, Jr.,
THEODORE L. MASON, M.D.,
HENRY E. PIERREPONT,
ALDEN J. SPOONER.

EXECUTIVE COMMITTEE.

R. S. STORRS, Jr., D.D., Chairman.
JOSHUA M. VAN COTT,
ALDEN J. SPOONER,
ETHELBERT S. MILLS,
JAMES H. PRENTICE,
HENRY SHELDON,
JOSIAH O. LOW,
GEORGE HANNAH, Secretary.

COUNSELLORS OF THE SOCIETY.

KINGS COUNTY:

HON. JOHN A. LOTT,
FRANCIS VINTON, D.D.,
HON. TEUNIS G. BFRGEN,
FREDERICK A. FARLEY, D.D.,
BENJAMIN D. SILLIMAN,
GEORGE W. PARSONS,

QUEENS COUNTY:

WILLIAM CULLEN BRYANT,
HON. JOHN A. KING,
HON. RICHARD C. McCORMICK,
JOHN HAROLD,
L. BRADFORD PRINCE,
SOLOMON D. TOWNSEND.

SUFFOLK COUNTY:

HON. SELAH B. STRONG,
JAMES H. TUTHILL,
HON. J. LAWRENCE SMITH,
REV. EPHER WHITAKER,
WILLIAM S. PELLETREAU,
HENRY P. HEDGES.

HONORARY AND CORRESPONDING MEMBERS.

HON. CHARLES GAYARRÉ, - - - - - - - *New Orleans.*
JOSEPH JACKSON HOWARD, LL.D., - - - - *Greenwich, England.*
HON. WILLIAM H. TUTHILL, - - - - - - - *Tipton, Iowa.*
HON. EMORY WASHBURN, LL.D., - - - - - - *Cambridge, Mass.*
REV. CALEB DAVIS BRADLEE, - - - - - - - - *Boston.*
CHARLES I. BUSHNELL, - - - - - - *New York.*
MISS FRANCES M. CAULKINS, - - - - - - *Norwich, Conn.*
PROF. JOSIAH P. COOKE, - - - - - - - *Harvard College.*
MAJOR-GEN. JOHN WATTS DE PEYSTER, - - - - *New York.*
SAMUEL G. DRAKE, - - - - - - - - - *Boston.*
THEODORE GILL, - - - - - - - - - *Washington.*
SAMUEL A. GREEN, M.D., - - - - - - - *Boston.*
FRANCIS S. HOFFMAN, - - - - - - - - *New York.*
JOHN A. McALLISTER, - - - - - - - - *Philadelphia.*
HENRY ONDERDONK, Jr., - - - - - - - *Jamaica, L. I.*
NATHANIEL PAINE, - - - - - - - - *Worcester, Mass.*
D. WILLIAMS PATTERSON, - - - - - *Newark Valley, N. Y.*
NICOLAS PIKE, - - - - - - - - - *U. S. Consul, Mauritius.*
JOHN G. SHEA, M.D., - - - - - - - *New York.*
HON. ANDREW D. WHITE, - - - - - - - - *Syracuse.*

THE LONG ISLAND HISTORICAL SOCIETY.

The Long Island Historical Society was incorporated in April, 1863, and has, therefore, nearly completed the fourth year of its existence.

It numbers at present 203 Life Members, and 802 Annual Members; with 20 Honorary and Corresponding Members, distinguished for their interest and success in historical studies.

Its Library contains nearly thirteen thousand volumes, with more than fifteen thousand pamphlets, exclusive, in both cases, of duplicates. Many of the volumes are rare and costly; and the pamphlets — especially the large number of them which concern the recent civil war — are becoming continually more important to students, and more difficult to be obtained. A considerable collection of valuable manuscripts, illustrating the early history of the state and of the country, has also been made by the Society.

The Museum contains many classified specimens, representing the Natural History of Long Island, together with a large number of medals, coins, and curiosities; and a Gallery of portraits, busts, bronzes, and historic memorials, which was commenced soon after the Society was organized, includes already many objects of interest, and is constantly being enriched with additional gifts.

Fifty-four papers on historical subjects have been presented at the regular or special meetings of the Society, besides twenty in the particular department of Natural History; and courses of popular historical lectures have twice been given — in the winters of 1864 and 1865 — under the auspices of the Society.

Through the generous and wise liberality of a number of its members, the institution now possesses permanent funds, amounting in the aggregate to more than sixty thousand dollars, for the maintenance and enlargement of its Library and Museum. These funds constitute an endowment, which is designed to be as enduring as the Society itself; but the income arising from it is to be annually expended, for the purposes specified, under the direction of the Board of Directors.

The Publication Fund, which is not included in the above, and by which the Society is enabled to print the volumes which it designs to issue, consists of two thousand dollars, given for this specific use by Mr. Edwards S. Sanford. This sum, or so much of it as shall be needed, will be expended in the preparation and publication of each volume in turn; and when, from the sale of such volume, the fund has been reimbursed, another in the series will follow.

The Directors congratulate themselves on being enabled to commence their work in this department with so unique and attractive a volume as that which they now have the pleasure of offering to the members of the Society; and they indulge the confident hope that through the successive annual publications, of which this is the first, the institution will do very much, not only for the gratification and the culture of those directly connected with it, but for the furtherance of historical studies, and for the extension of a just and lively interest in such studies, throughout the land.

BROOKLYN, N. Y., *February* 1, 1867.

VIEW OF THE ENTRANCE

Facsim. by G. Hayward & Co.

ARBOR FROM NAJAK,

)

NEW-YO

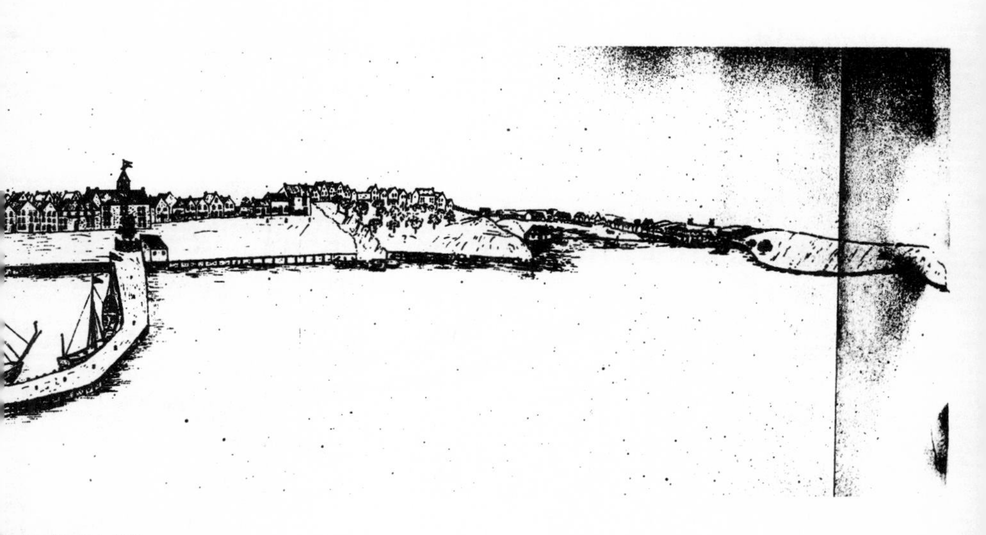

N HEIGHTS. 1679.

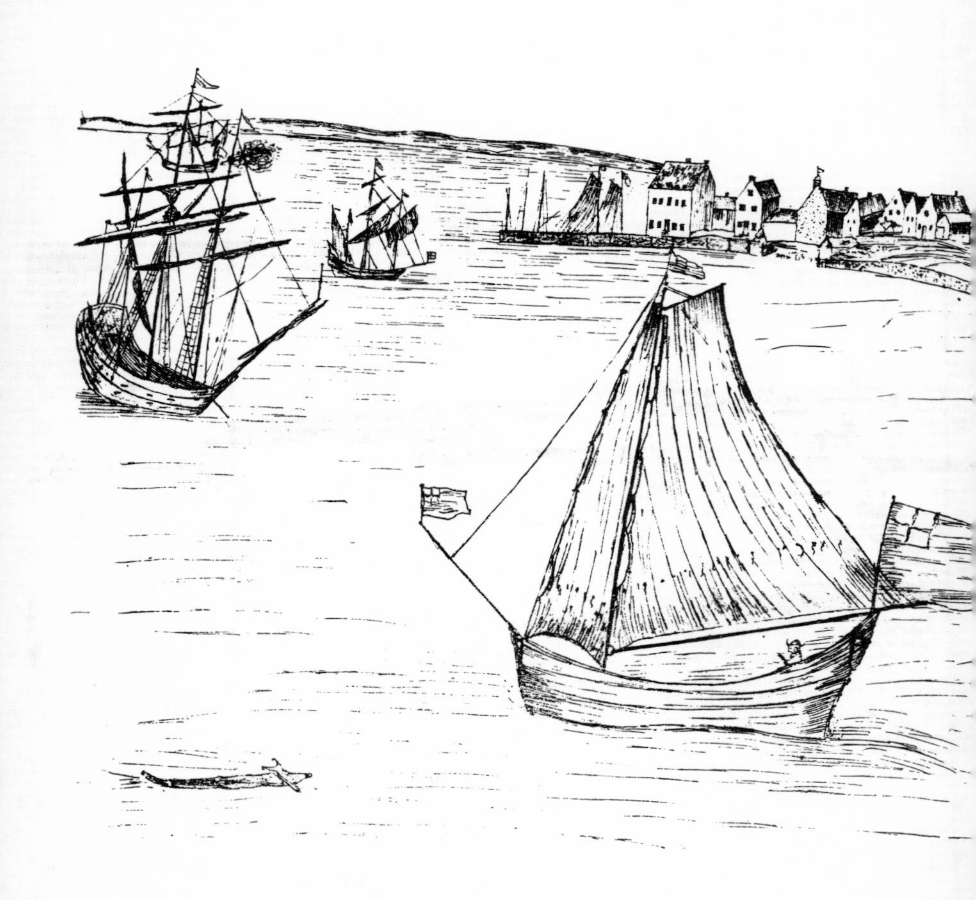

VIEW OF NEW-Y

Pl. IV.

york van ter syden
dat is van de oost kant

NORTH. 1679.

Facsimile by G. Hayward & Co 171 Pearl St. N.Y.

Nÿork van achte

noor

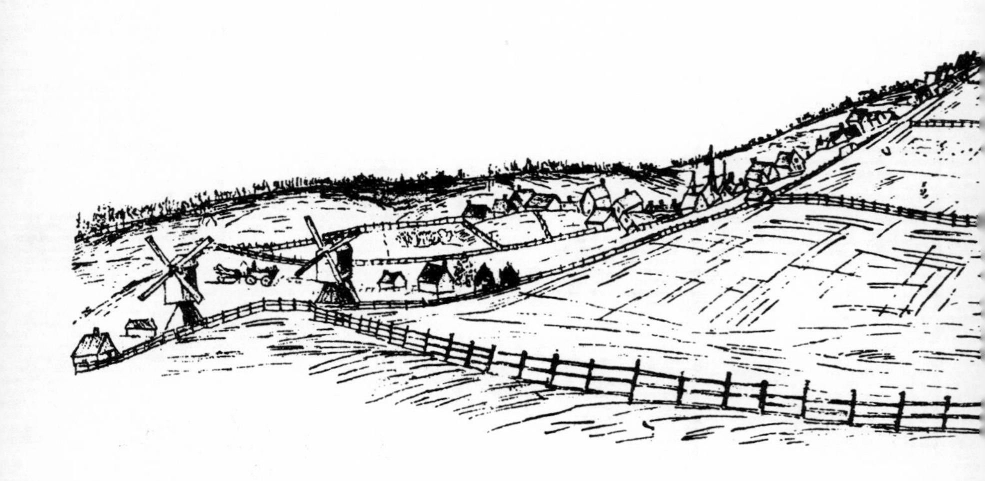

VIEW OF NEW

I THE NORTH.

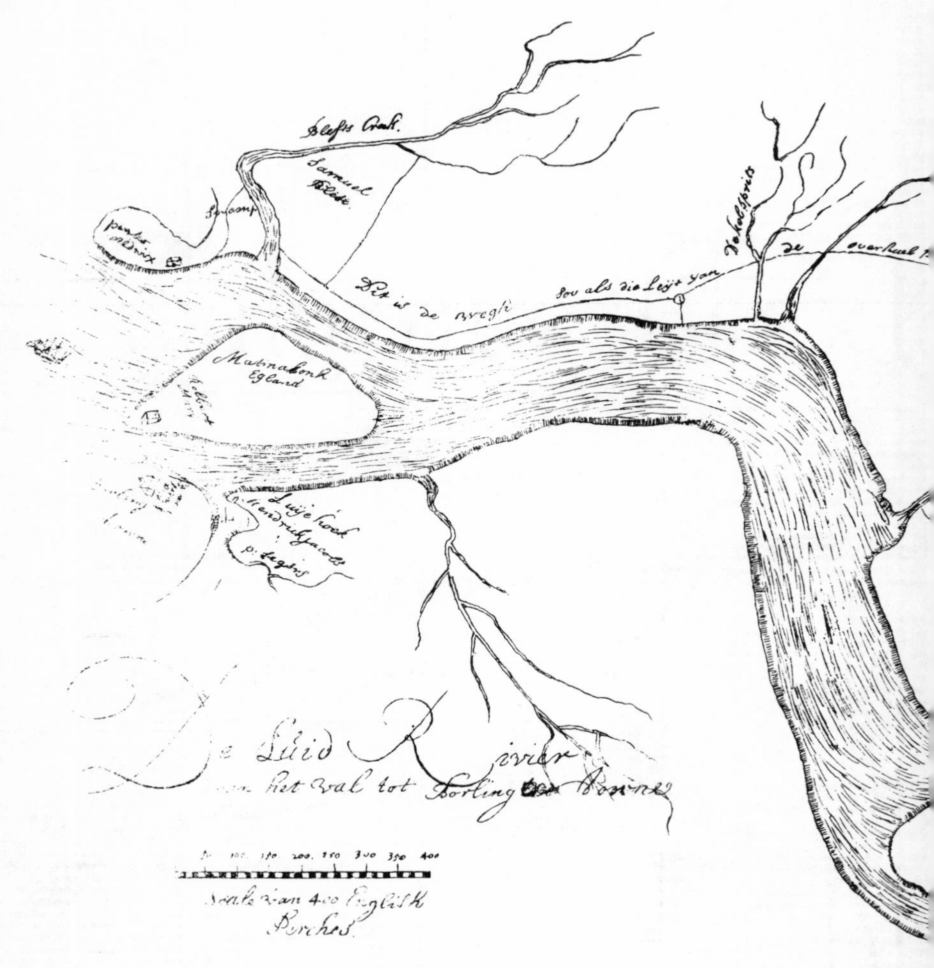

Facsimile by G. Hayward & Co. 171 Pearl S^t. N.Y.

THE DELAWARE RIVER FROM

Pl.VI.

S AT BURLINGTON. 1679.

THE STADTH

Corner of

G. Hayward & Co 171 Pearl St. N.Y.

NEW YORK IN 1679

nd Coentijs Slip.

NORTH VIEW OF THE

PL. IX.

K NEW YORK: 1679

Voyage to New Netherland

[illegible] hoe sij gestelt sijn in de wassende
[illegible] sij noch geen [illegible] ist affeeren
[illegible] der Suijden gelijck het water hier
[illegible] 33 gr: ook datter noch [illegible]
leggen [illegible] in de [illegible]

36: 14 — 334 gr. Lengte —

Dolphijn

Pico porck

gevangen op de poolshoogte
van 37½ [illegible]
[illegible] Lengte

deze hoorn A en B comende plat
op de rugge geleggen worden tot C
waer dat de pint in de rugge [illegible] daer
de hoorn [illegible] maer [illegible]
[illegible] waer inne dese staen
A naer voren en de B naer C [illegible]
[illegible] als het [illegible]
[illegible].

THE WATER GATE, FO

Pl. X.

[illegible] 171 Pearl St. N.Y

WALL ST. NEWYORK 1679.

VIEW OF THE EAST RIVER SHO

Pl. XI.

TH OF THE WATER GATE, N. Y.. 1679.

VIEW OF THE HOUSE
still standing

Pl. XII.

ON AERTSEN DE HART
nes Bay in 1867.